You are going the *wrong way!*

Manga is a *completely* different type of reading experience.

To start at the *BEGINNING,* go to the *END!*

That's right! Authentic manga is read the traditional Japanese way—from right to left, exactly the opposite of how American books are read. It's easy to follow: just go to the other end of the book, and read each page—and each panel—from the right side to the left side, starting at the top right. Now you're experiencing manga as it was meant to be.

A Kodansha Comics Trade Paperback Original
Attack on Titan: Before the Fall volume 15 copyright © 2018 Hajime Isayama/
Ryo Suzukaze/Satoshi Shiki
English translation copyright © 2018 Hajime Isayama/Ryo Suzukaze/Satoshi Shiki

Published in the United States by Kodansha Comics, an imprint of
Kodansha USA Publishing, LLC, New York.

Publication rights for this English edition arranged through
Kodansha Ltd, Tokyo.

First published in Japan in 2018 by Kodansha Ltd., Tokyo
as *Shingeki no kyojin Before the fall*, volume 15.

ISBN 978-1-63236-657-3

Character designs by Thores Shibamoto
Original cover design by Takashi Shimoyama and Kayo Hasegawa (Red Rooster)

Printed in the United States of America.

www.kodanshacomics.com

9 8 7 6 5 4 3 2 1
Translation: Stephen Paul
Lettering: Steve Wands
Editing: Lauren Scanlan
Kodansha Comics edition cover design by Phil Balsman

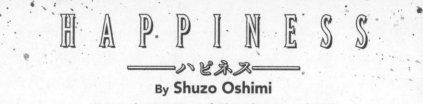

HAPPINESS

——ハピネス——

By Shuzo Oshimi

From the creator of *The Flowers of Evil*

Nothing interesting is happening in Makoto Ozaki's first year of high school. HIs life is a series of quiet humiliations: low-grade bullies, unreliable friends, and the constant frustration of his adolescent lust. But one night, a pale, thin girl knocks him to the ground in an alley and offers him a choice.

Now everything is different. Daylight is searingly bright. Food tastes awful. And worse than anything is the terrible, consuming thirst...

Praise for Shuzo Oshimi's *The Flowers of Evil*

"A shockingly readable story that vividly—one might even say queasily—evokes the fear and confusion of discovering one's own sexuality. Recommended." —The Manga Critic

"A page-turning tale of sordid middle school blackmail." —Otaku USA Magazine

"A stunning new horror manga." —Third Eye Comics

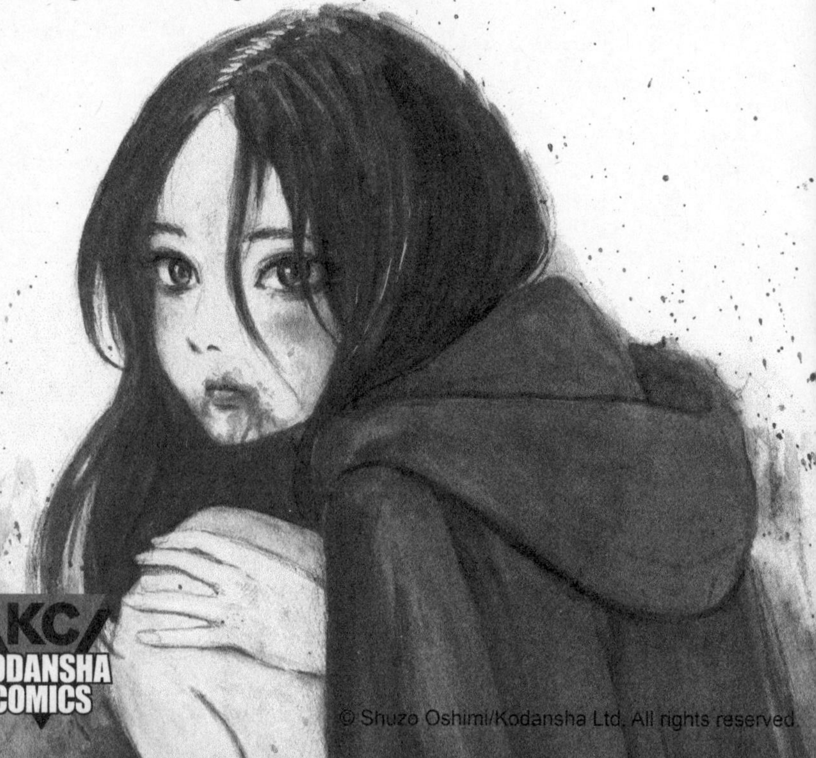

KC KODANSHA COMICS

KODANSHA COMICS

New action series from Hiroyuki Takei, creator of the classic shonen franchise Shaman King!

In medieval Japan, a bell hanging on the collar is a sign that a cat has a master. Norachiyo's bell hangs from his katana sheath, but he is nonetheless a stray — a ronin. This one-eyed cat samurai travels across a dishonest world, cutting through pretense and deception with his blade.

NEKOGAHARA

STRAY CAT SAMURAI

By
Hiroyuki Takei

Based on the critically acclaimed classic horror manga

The first new *Parasyte* manga in over 20 years!

NEO PARASYTE f

BY ASUMIKO NAKAMURA, EMA TOYAMA, MIKI RINNO, LALAKO KOJIMA, KAORI YUKI, BANKO KUZE, YUUKI OBATA, KASHIO, YUI KUROE, ASIA WATANABE, MIKIMAKI, HIKARU SURUGA, HAJIME SHINJO, RENJURO KINDAICHI, AND YURI NARUSHIMA

A collection of chilling new *Parasyte* stories from Japan's top shojo artists!

Parasites: shape-shifting aliens whose only purpose is to assimilate with and consume the human race... but do these monsters have a different side? A parasite becomes a prince to save his romance-obsessed female host from a dangerous stalker. Another hosts a cooking show, in which the real monsters are revealed. These and 13 more stories, from some of the greatest shojo manga artists alive today, together make up a chilling, funny, and entertaining tribute to one of manga's horror classics!

KC KODANSHA COMICS

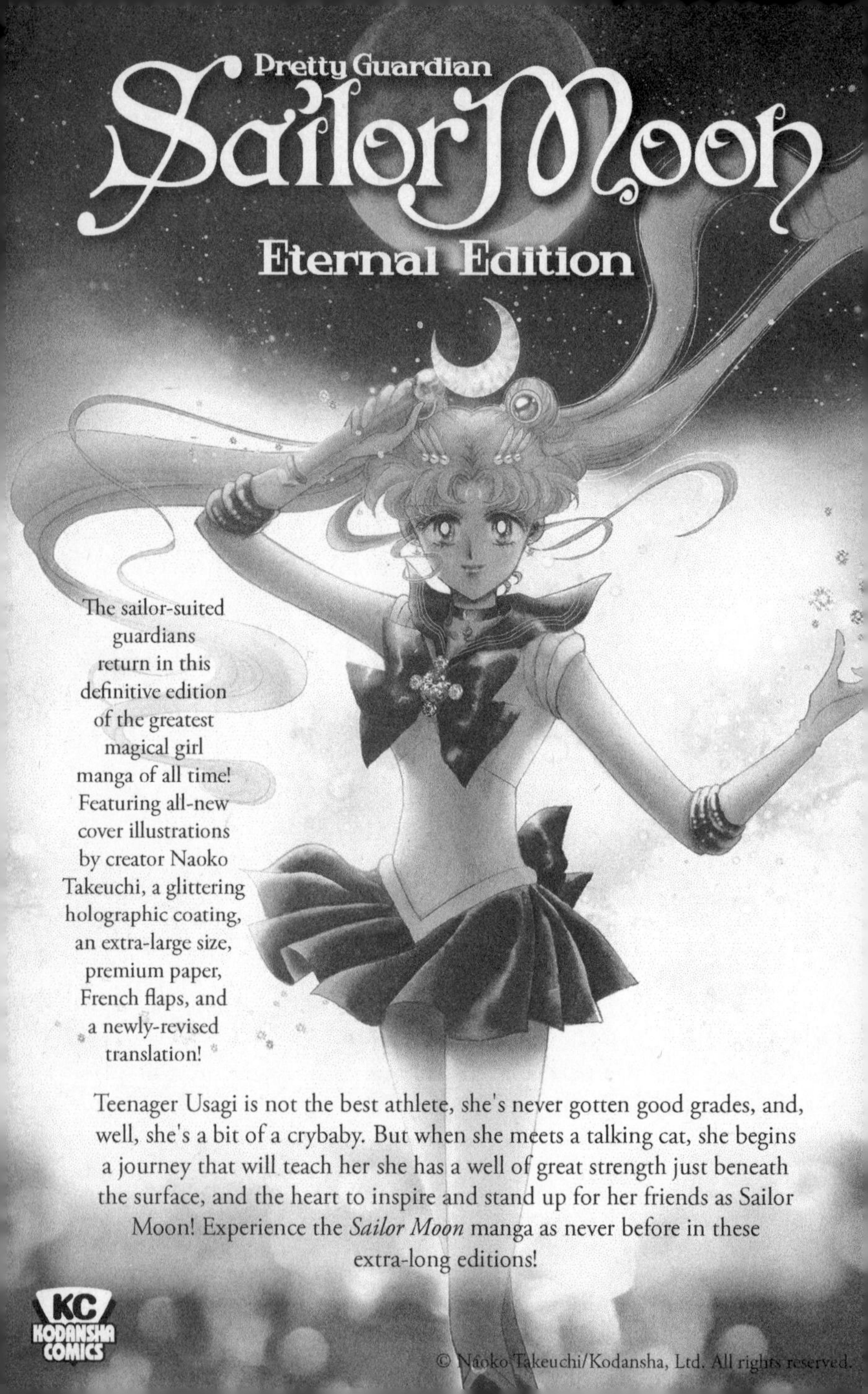
Pretty Guardian
Sailor Moon
Eternal Edition
The sailor-suited guardians return in this definitive edition of the greatest magical girl manga of all time! Featuring all-new cover illustrations by creator Naoko Takeuchi, a glittering holographic coating, an extra-large size, premium paper, French flaps, and a newly-revised translation!
Teenager Usagi is not the best athlete, she's never gotten good grades, and, well, she's a bit of a crybaby. But when she meets a talking cat, she begins a journey that will teach her she has a well of great strength just beneath the surface, and the heart to inspire and stand up for her friends as Sailor Moon! Experience the *Sailor Moon* manga as never before in these extra-long editions!
KC KODANSHA COMICS
© Naoko Takeuchi/Kodansha, Ltd. All rights reserved.

ANIME COMING OUT SUMMER 2018!

Mikami's middle age hasn't gone as he planned: He never found a girlfriend, he got stuck in a dead-end job, and he was abruptly stabbed to death in the street at 37. So when he wakes up in a new world straight out of a fantasy RPG, he's disappointed, but not exactly surprised to find that he's facing down a dragon, not as a knight or a wizard, but as a blind slime monster. But there are chances for even a slime to become a hero...

"A fun adventure that fantasy readers will relate to and enjoy."
—AiPT!

THAT TIME I GOT REINCARNATED AS A SLIME

Having lost his wife, high school teacher Kōhei Inuzuka is doing his best to raise his young daughter Tsumugi as a single father. He's pretty bad at cooking and doesn't have a huge appetite to begin with, but chance brings his little family together with one of his students, the lonely Kotori. The three of them are anything but comfortable in the kitchen, but the healing power of home cooking might just work on their grieving hearts.

"This season's number-one feel-good anime!" —Anime News Network

"A beautifully-drawn story about comfort food and family and grief. Recommended." —Otaku USA Magazine

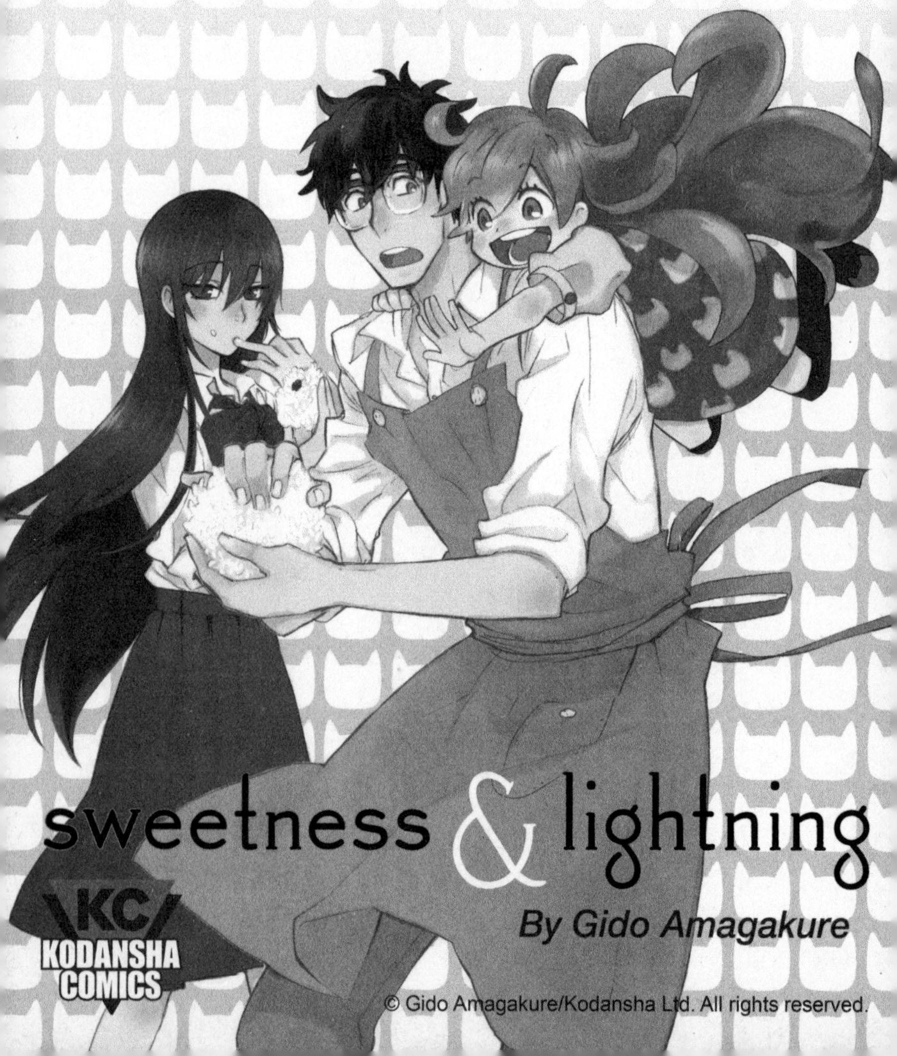
sweetness & lightning
By Gido Amagakure
KC
KODANSHA COMICS

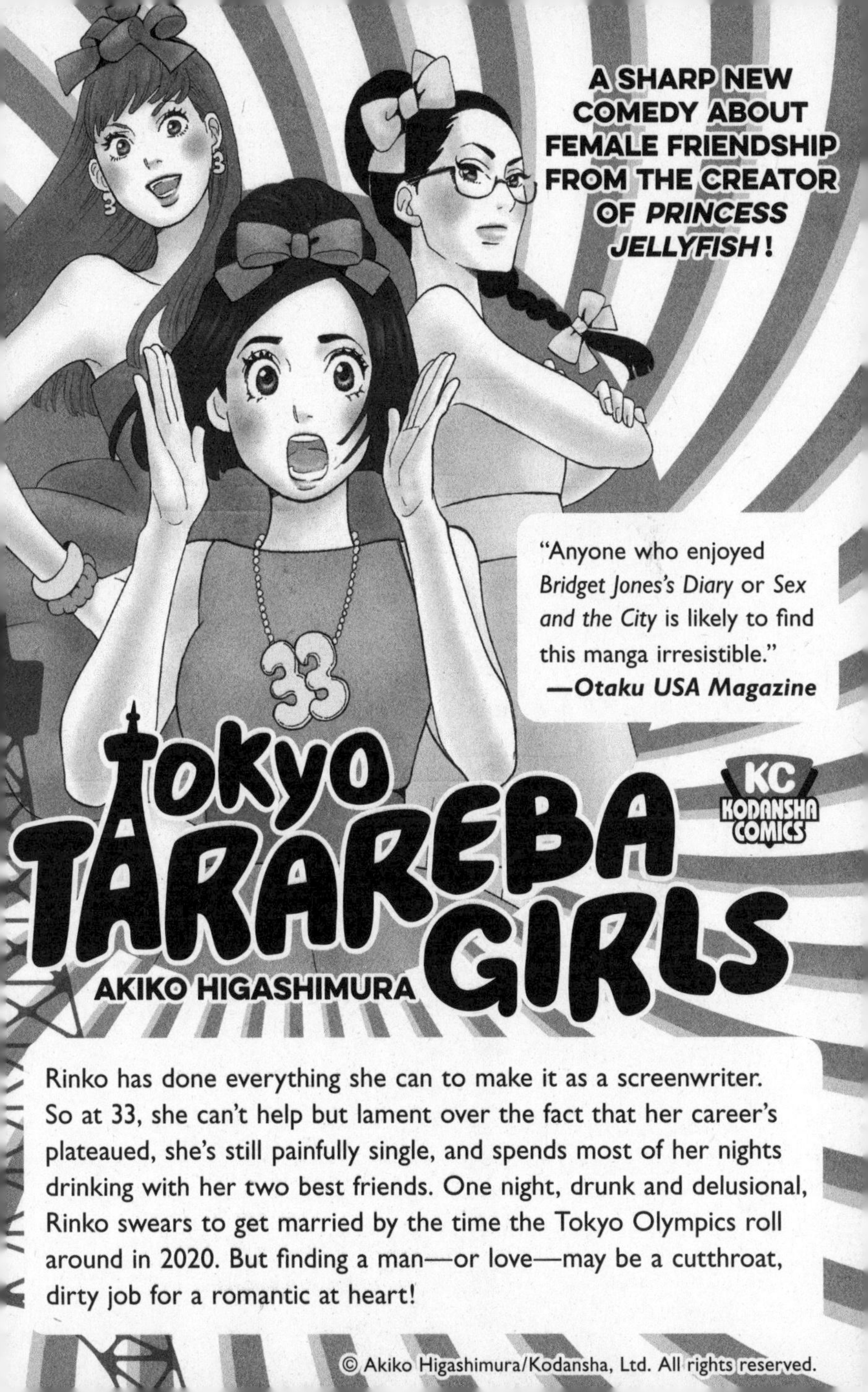
A SHARP NEW COMEDY ABOUT FEMALE FRIENDSHIP FROM THE CREATOR OF *PRINCESS JELLYFISH*!
"Anyone who enjoyed *Bridget Jones's Diary* or *Sex and the City* is likely to find this manga irresistible."
—*Otaku USA Magazine*
KC KODANSHA COMICS
TOKYO TARAREBA GIRLS
AKIKO HIGASHIMURA
Rinko has done everything she can to make it as a screenwriter. So at 33, she can't help but lament over the fact that her career's plateaued, she's still painfully single, and spends most of her nights drinking with her two best friends. One night, drunk and delusional, Rinko swears to get married by the time the Tokyo Olympics roll around in 2020. But finding a man—or love—may be a cutthroat, dirty job for a romantic at heart!
© Akiko Higashimura/Kodansha, Ltd. All rights reserved.

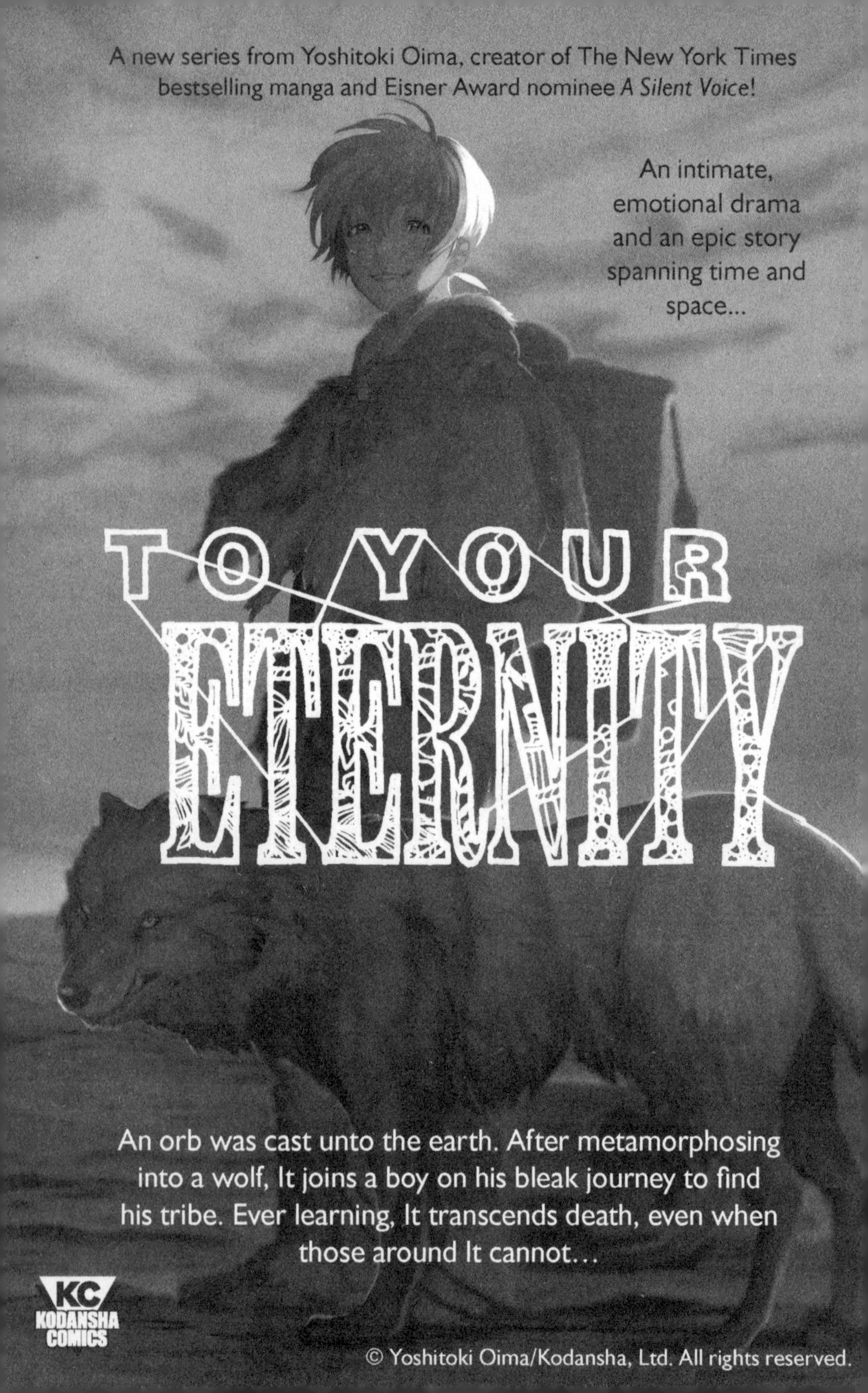
A new series from Yoshitoki Oima, creator of The New York Times bestselling manga and Eisner Award nominee *A Silent Voice*!
An intimate, emotional drama and an epic story spanning time and space...
TO YOUR ETERNITY
An orb was cast unto the earth. After metamorphosing into a wolf, It joins a boy on his bleak journey to find his tribe. Ever learning, It transcends death, even when those around It cannot...
KC KODANSHA COMICS
© Yoshitoki Oima/Kodansha, Ltd. All rights reserved.

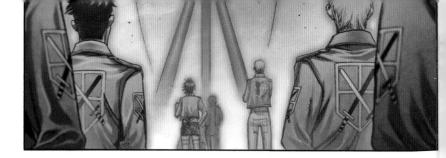

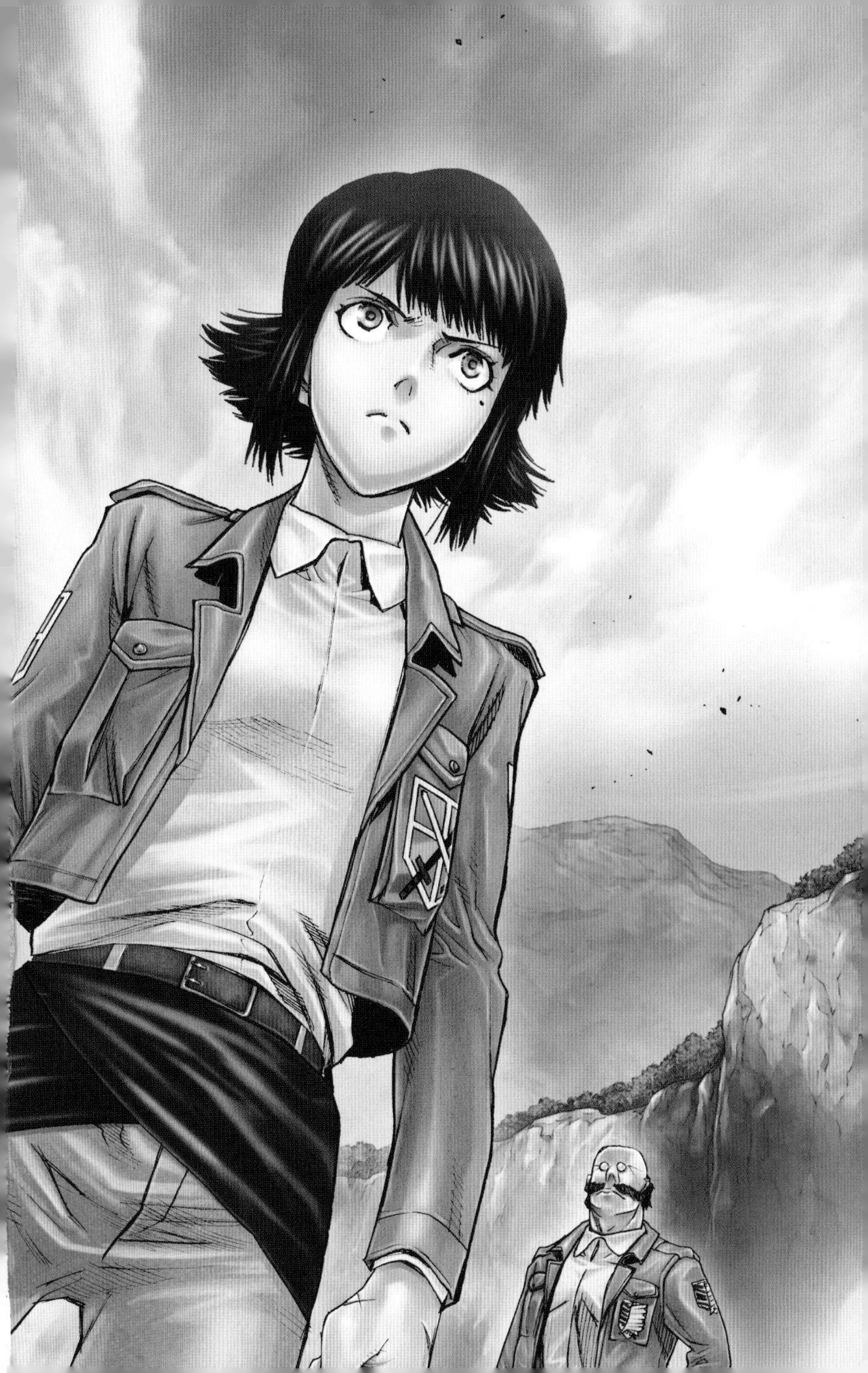

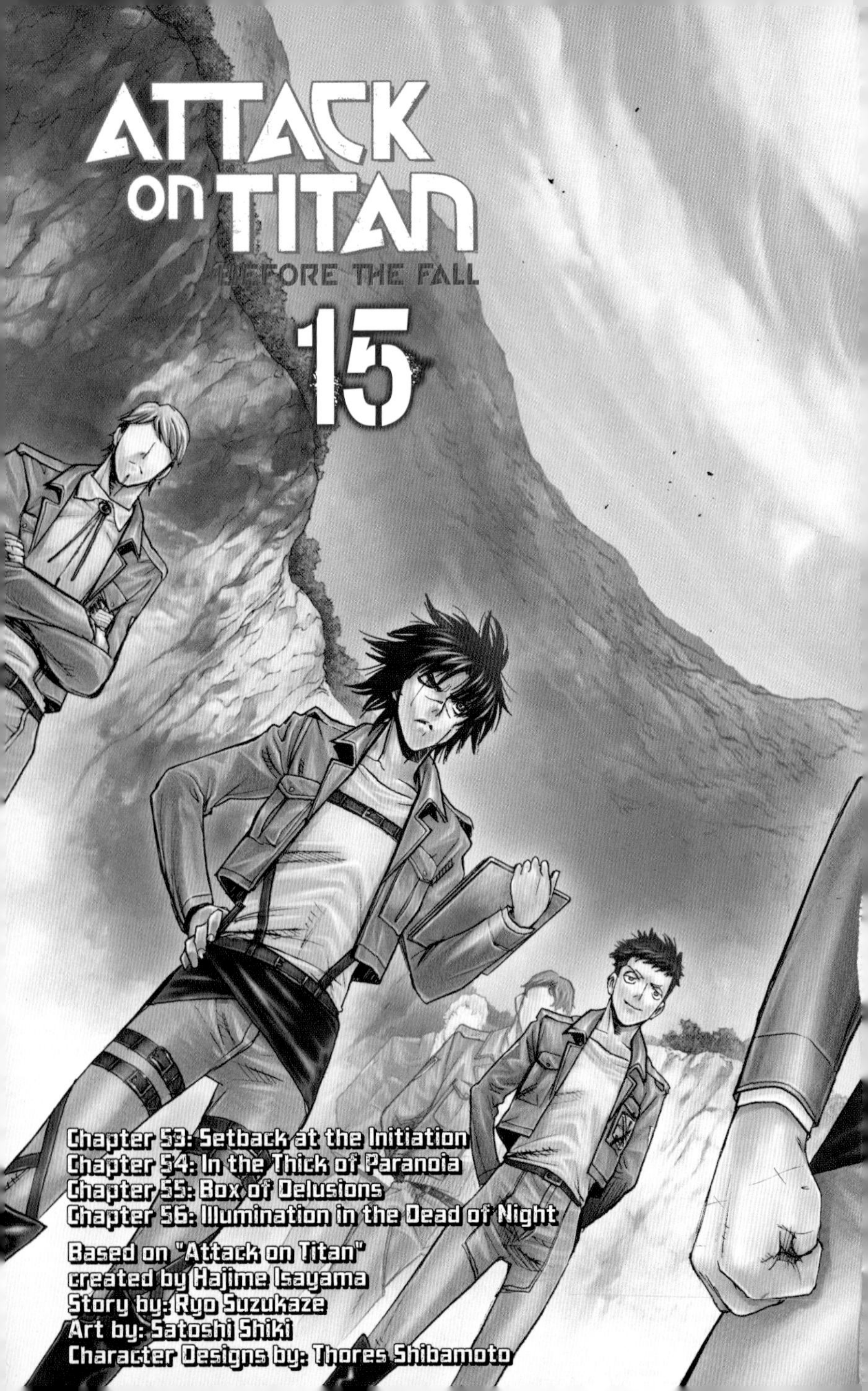
ATTACK ON TITAN
BEFORE THE FALL
15
Chapter 53: Setback at the Initiation
Chapter 54: In the Thick of Paranoia
Chapter 55: Box of Delusions
Chapter 56: Illumination in the Dead of Night
Based on "Attack on Titan"
created by Hajime Isayama
Story by: Ryo Suzukaze
Art by: Satoshi Shiki
Character Designs by: Thores Shibamoto

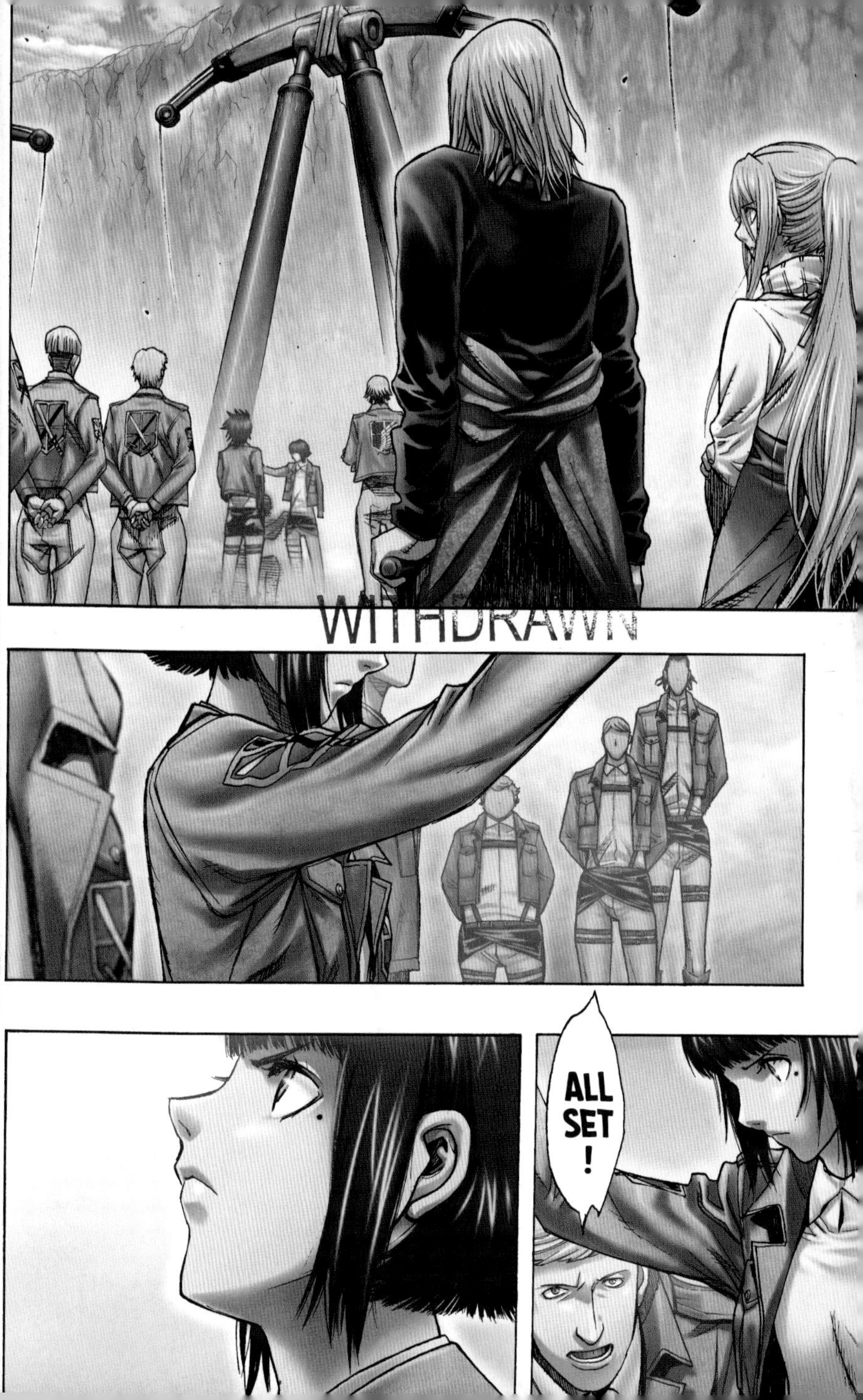
ALL SET !

Before the Fall — Character Profiles

Kuklo

A 15-year-old boy born from a dead body packed into the vomit of a Titan, which earned him the moniker, "Titan's Son." He is fascinated with the Device as a means to defeat the Titans. Xavi defeated him in battle and left him for dead, until Rosa's group found and rescued him.

Sharle Inocencio

First daughter of the Inocencios, a rich merchant family within Wall Sheena. When she realized that Kuklo was a human, she taught him to speak and learn. She escaped her family home and went into the underground ward in search of Angel, inventor of the Device.

Cardina Baumeister

Kuklo's first friend in the outside world, and his companion in developing the Device.

Carlo Pikale

Jorge's son and current captain of the Survey Corps. After they battled Titans together, he has great respect for Kuklo.

Jorge Pikale

Training Corps instructor. A former Survey Corps captain who was hailed as a hero for defeating a Titan.

Xavi Inocencio

Head of the Inocencio family and Sharle's brother. Member of the Military Police in Shiganshina District.

Rosa Carlstead

The daughter of Maria and Sorum, Angel's longtime friends. She's in training now, hoping to enter the Survey Corps.

Angel Aaltonen

A former inventor who developed a tool to fight the Titans 15 years ago, known simply as "The Device."

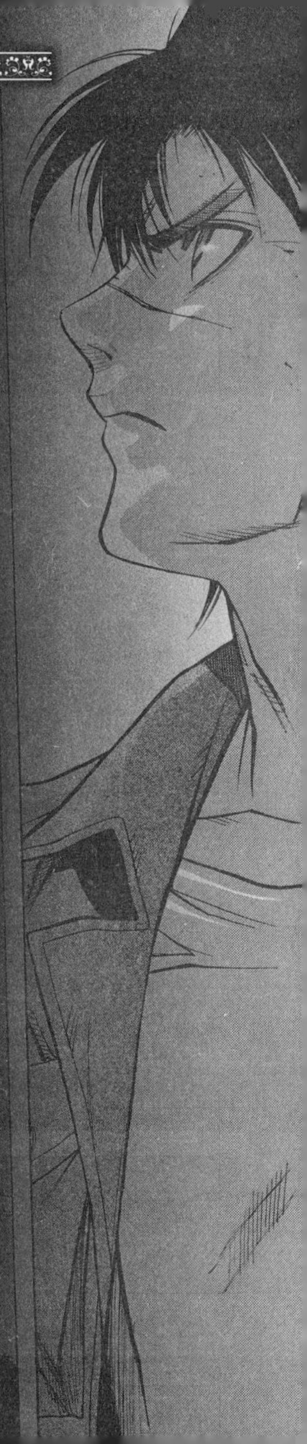

The Story So Far

When a Titan terrorized Shiganshina District and left behind a pile of vomit, a baby boy was miraculously born of a pregnant corpse. This boy was named Kuklo, the "Son of a Titan," and treated as a sideshow freak. Eventually the wealthy merchant Dario Inocencio bought Kuklo. Dario's daughter Sharle learned that he was human and not the son of a Titan, and decided to teach him the words and knowledge of humanity. Two years later, Kuklo escaped from the mansion along with Sharle, who was being forced into a marriage she did not desire.

In Shiganshina District, the Survey Corps was preparing for its first expedition outside of the wall in fifteen years. Kuklo snuck into the expedition's cargo wagon, but the Titan they ran across was far worse of a monster than he expected. He helped the Survey Corps survive, but inside the walls he was greeted by the Military Police, who wanted the "Titan's Son" on charges of murdering Dario. In prison, he met Cardina, a young man jailed over political squabbles. They hoped to escape to safety when exiled beyond the Wall, but found themselves surrounded by a pack of Titans. It was through the help of Jorge, former Survey Corps Captain, that the two boys escaped with their lives. The equipment that Jorge used was the very "Device" that was the key to defeating the Titan those fifteen years ago. Kuklo and Cardina escaped the notice of the MPs by hiding in the industrial city, where they found Sharle. It is there that the three youngsters learned the truth of the ill-fated Titan-capturing expedition fifteen years earlier, and swore to uphold the will of Angel, the inventor of the Device.

Next, Kuklo and Cardina headed back to Shiganshina to test out a new model of the Device developed by Xenophon, Angel's friend and rival, but while they were gone, a rebellion by anti-establishment dissidents broke out in the Industrial City. Kuklo was able to slip through the chaos to rescue Sharle from the dissidents, but then Sharle's brother Xavi arrived, now a member of the Military Police, and turned his sword on Kuklo. Xavi won the battle by inflicting a grievous blow on Kuklo, who fell into the river and only survived thanks to the help of Rosa, the daughter of Sorum, who lost his life on the fateful expedition fifteen years earlier.

After a month and a half of recovery, Kuklo accepted Jorge's offer of an assistant instructor position with the Survey Corps. Sharle escaped Xavi's grasp and visited Angel, inventor of the Device, who unveiled the finished version, the Vertical Maneuvering Equipment. But not all of their news was good: the Survey Corps would have to run an expedition in just two months' time, and bring back proof that the Vertical Maneuvering Equipment vanquished a Titan, or the Corps would be disbanded. Captain Carlo decided to split the trainees among an elite training class that would use what limited numbers of the equipment they could produce, and general trainees who would receive the typical Survey Corps regimen. Rosa wound up as a reserve member of the special training class, and overcame her fear of the Titans as witnessed from the top of Wall Maria, passing the secondary selection test.

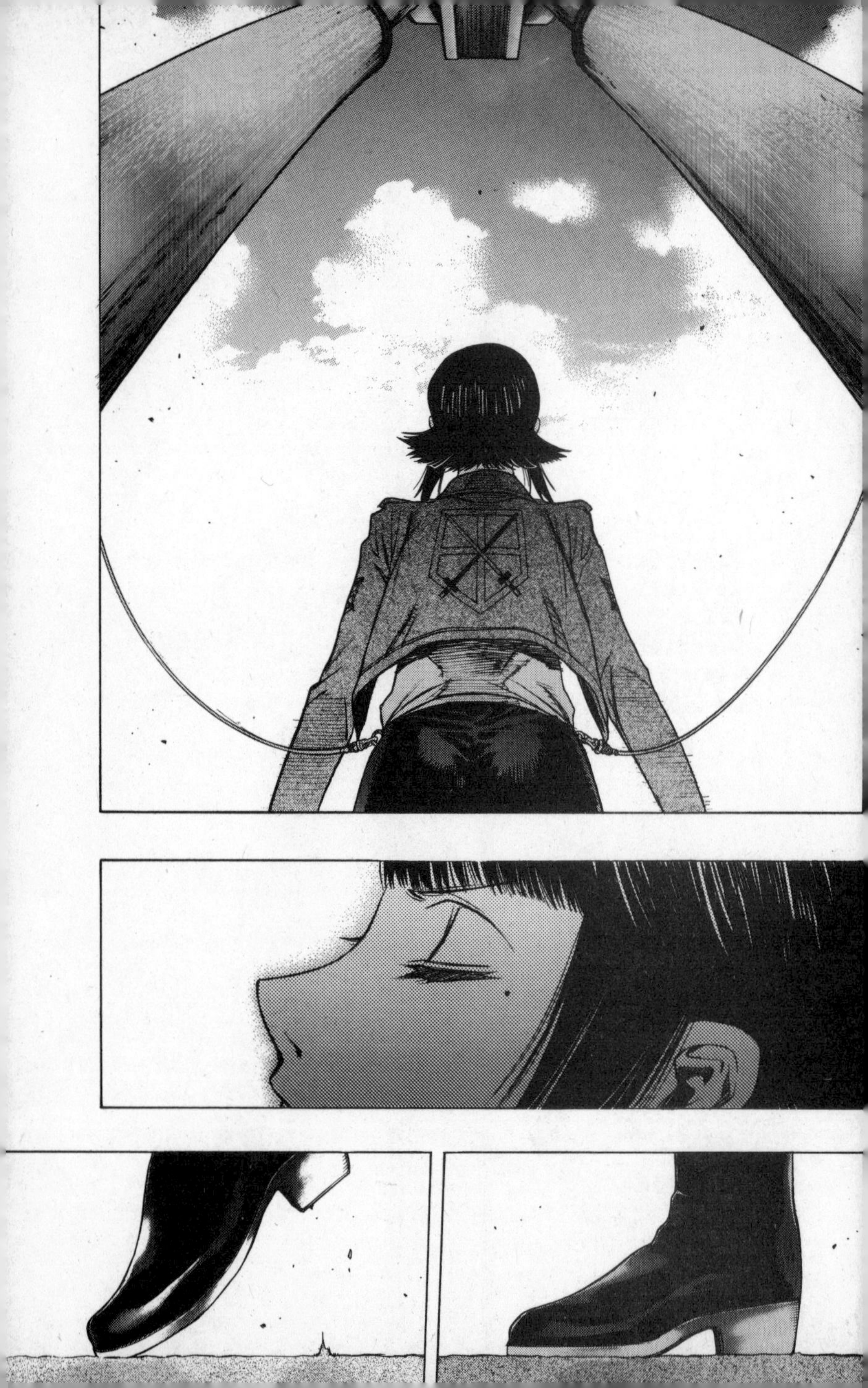

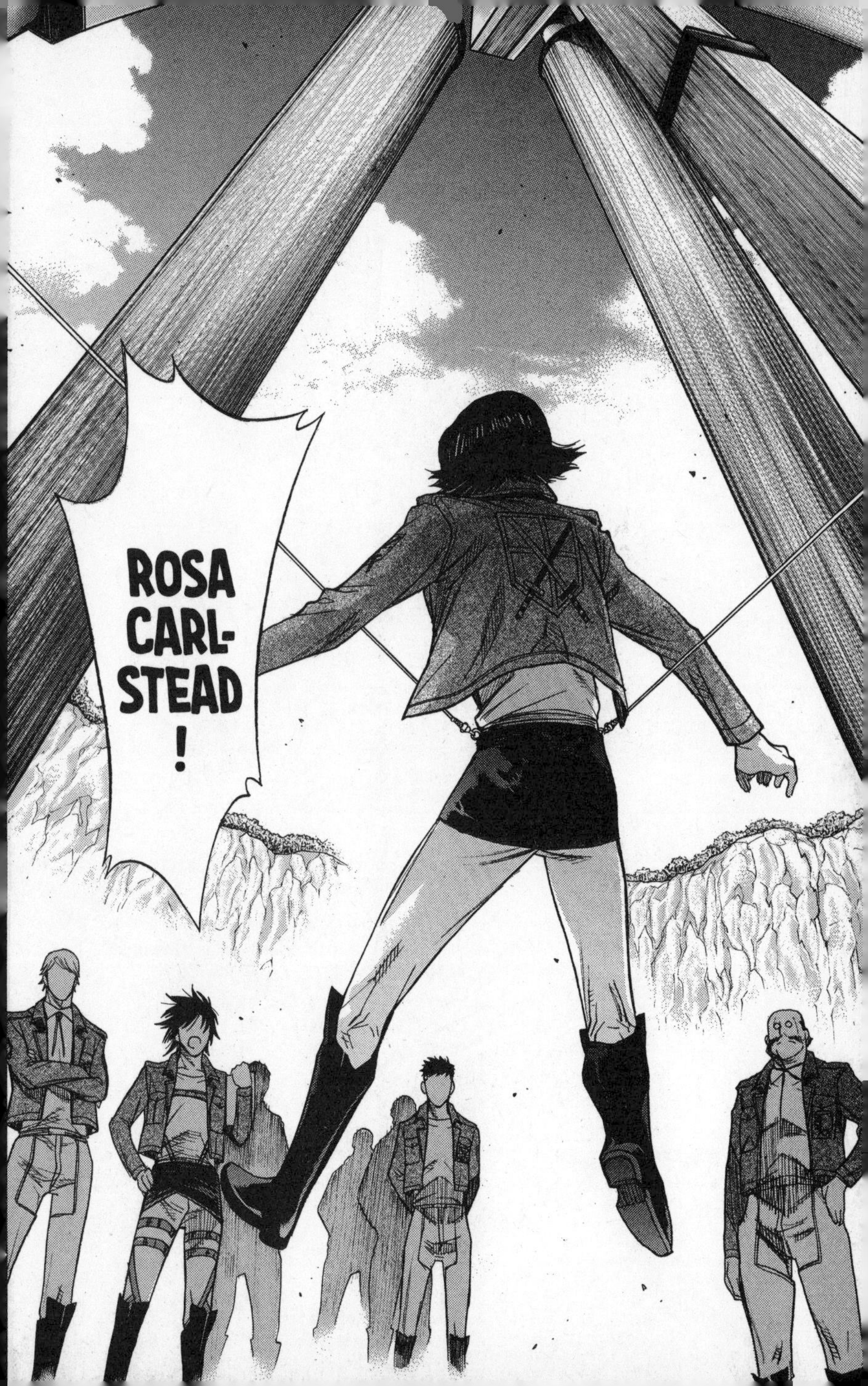
ROSA CARL-STEAD!

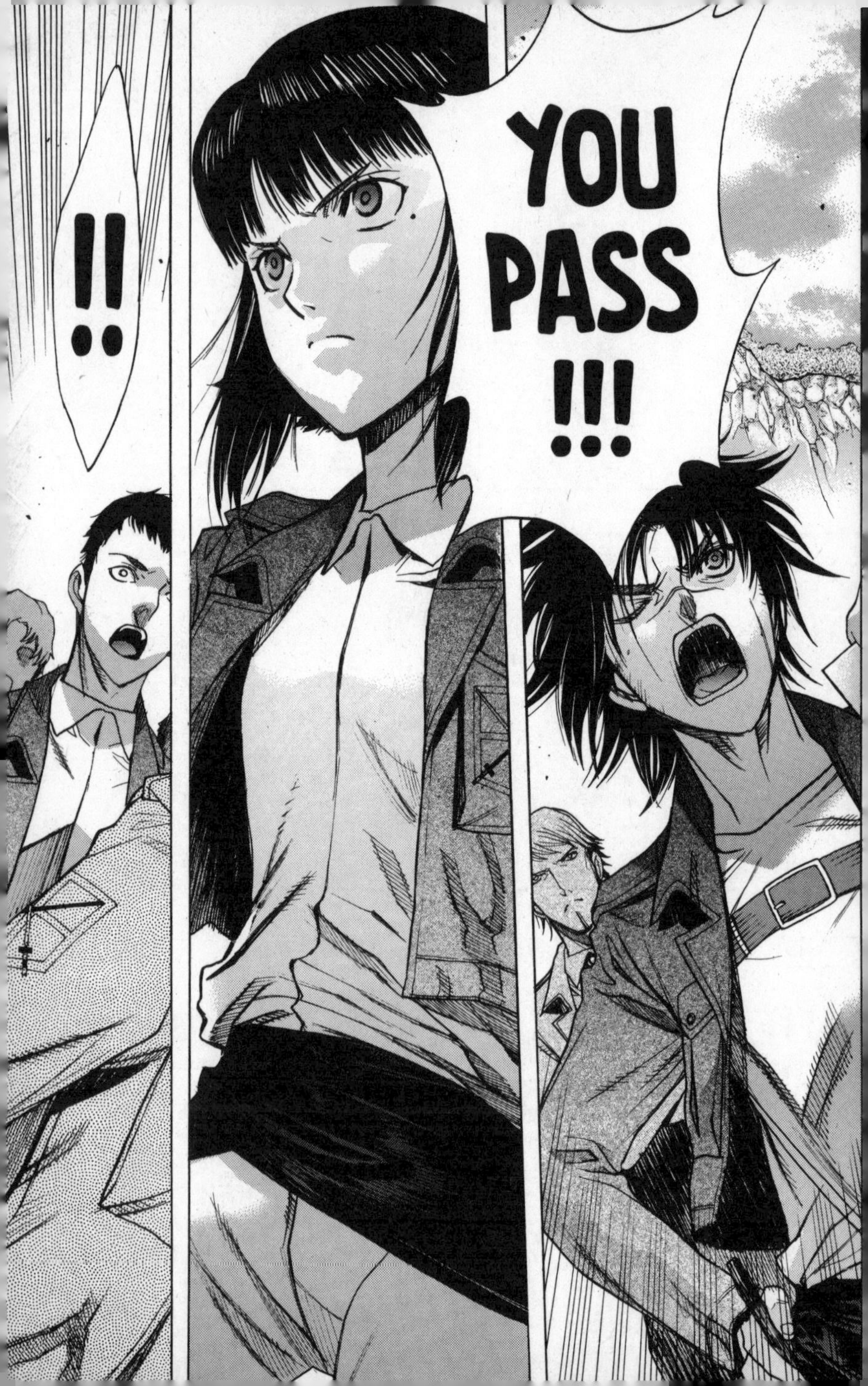
YOU PASS!!!
!!

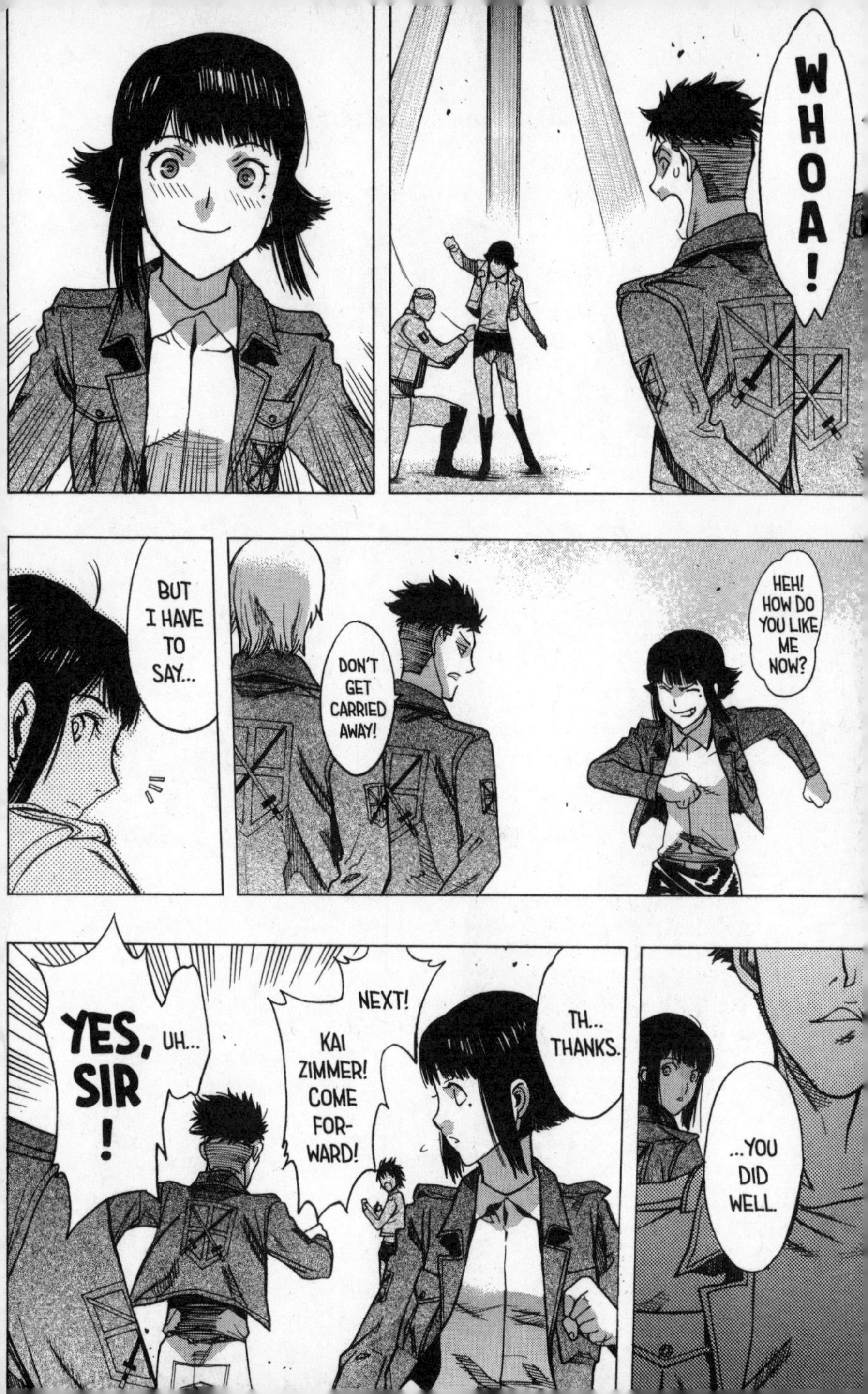
WHOA!
HEH! HOW DO YOU LIKE ME NOW?
DON'T GET CARRIED AWAY!
BUT I HAVE TO SAY...
...YOU DID WELL.
TH... THANKS.
NEXT!
KAI ZIMMER! COME FOR-WARD!
UH...
YES, SIR!

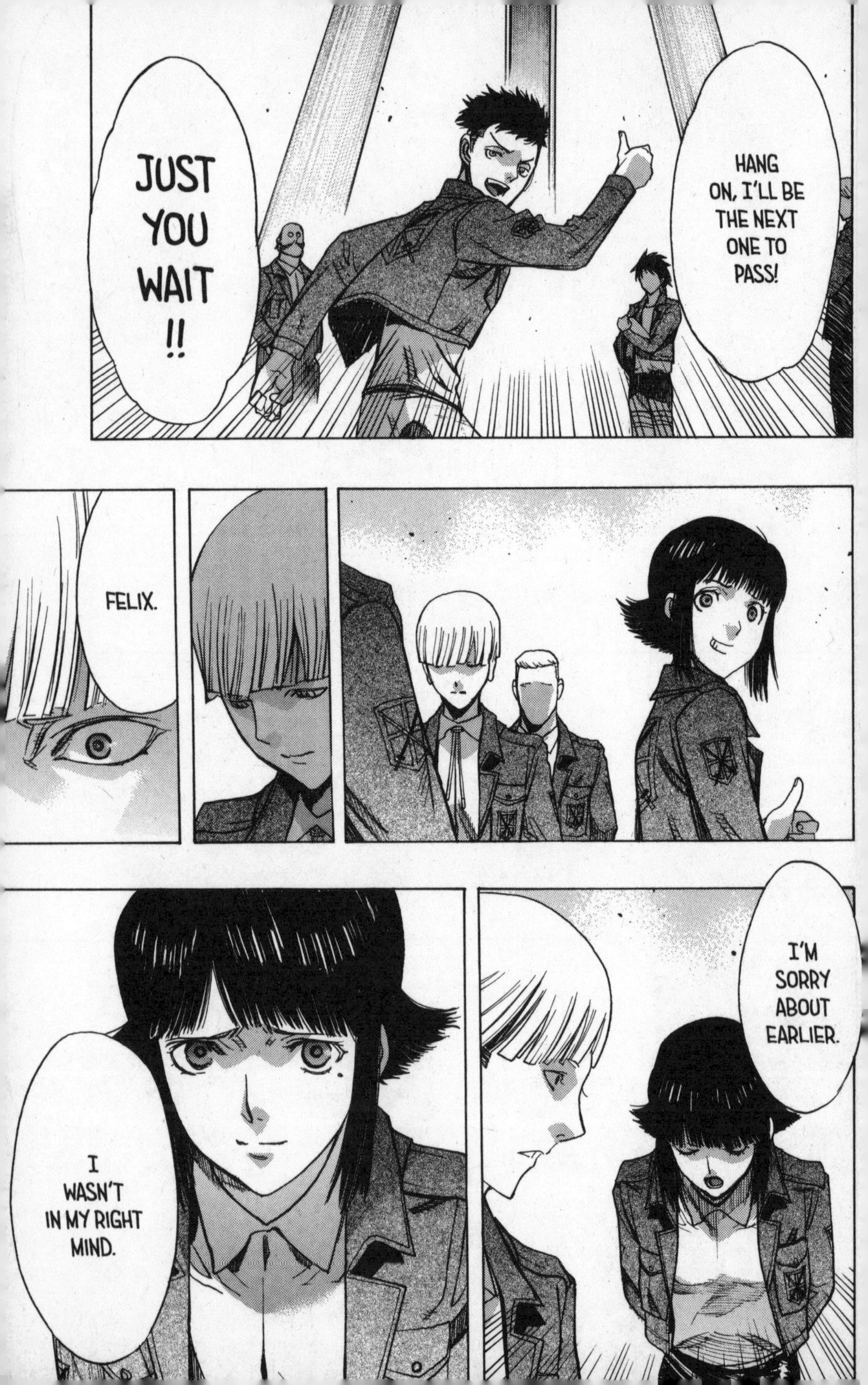
HANG ON, I'LL BE THE NEXT ONE TO PASS!
JUST YOU WAIT !!
FELIX.
I'M SORRY ABOUT EARLIER.
I WASN'T IN MY RIGHT MIND.

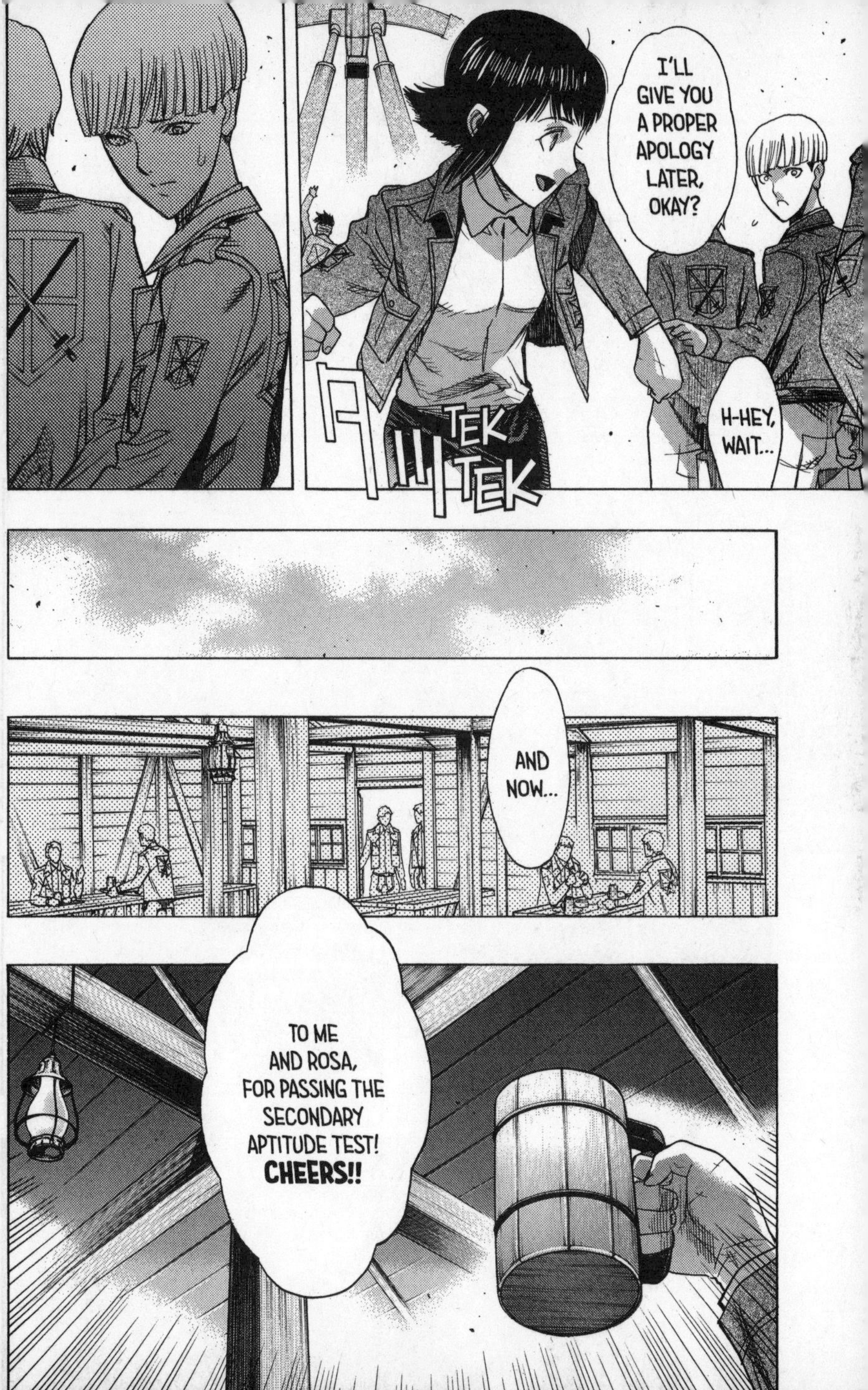
I'LL GIVE YOU A PROPER APOLOGY LATER, OKAY?
H-HEY, WAIT...
TEK TEK
AND NOW...
TO ME AND ROSA, FOR PASSING THE SECONDARY APTITUDE TEST! **CHEERS!!**

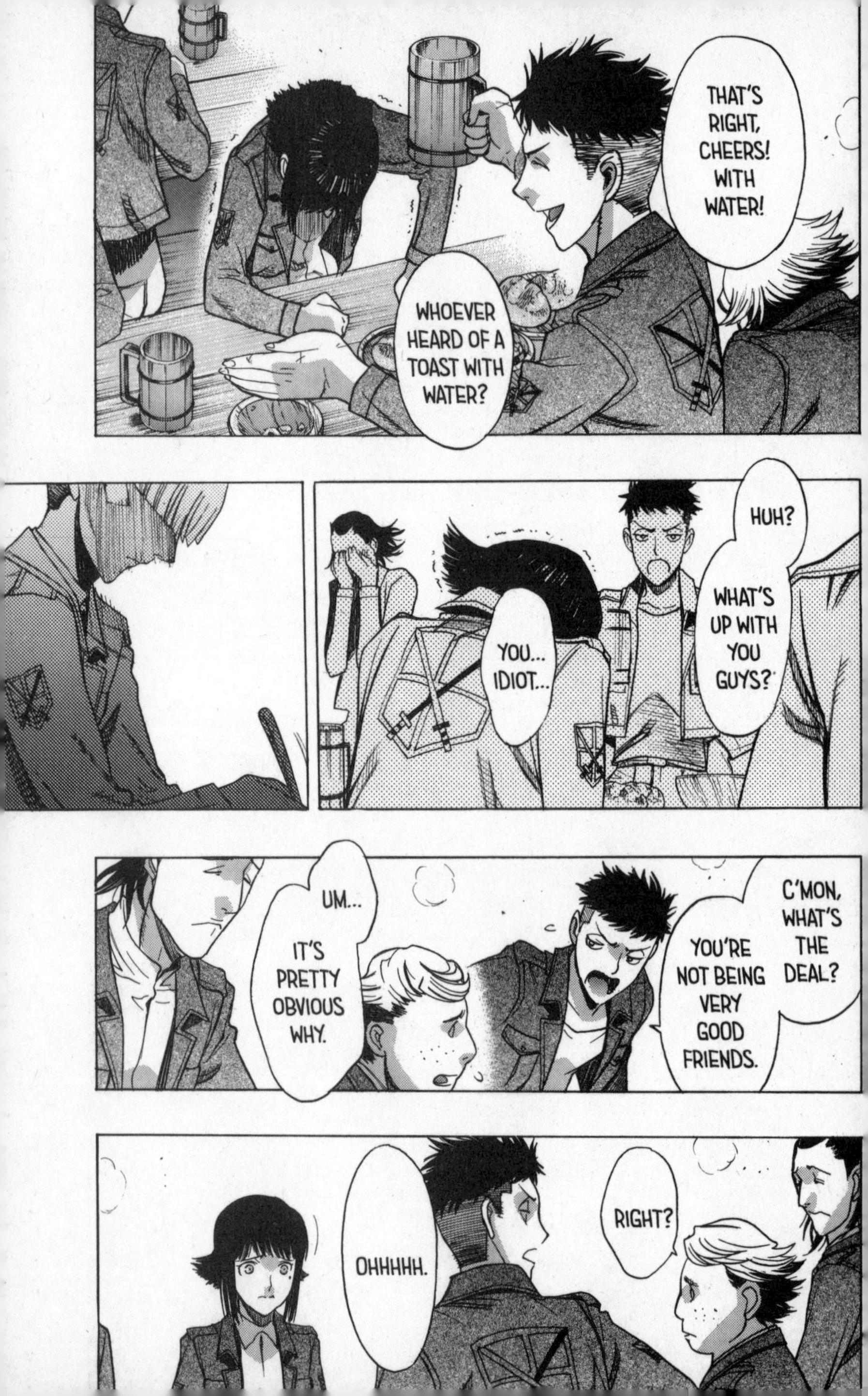
THAT'S RIGHT, CHEERS! WITH WATER!
WHOEVER HEARD OF A TOAST WITH WATER?
HUH?
WHAT'S UP WITH YOU GUYS?
YOU... IDIOT...
C'MON, WHAT'S THE DEAL?
YOU'RE NOT BEING VERY GOOD FRIENDS.
UM...
IT'S PRETTY OBVIOUS WHY.
RIGHT?
OHHHHH.

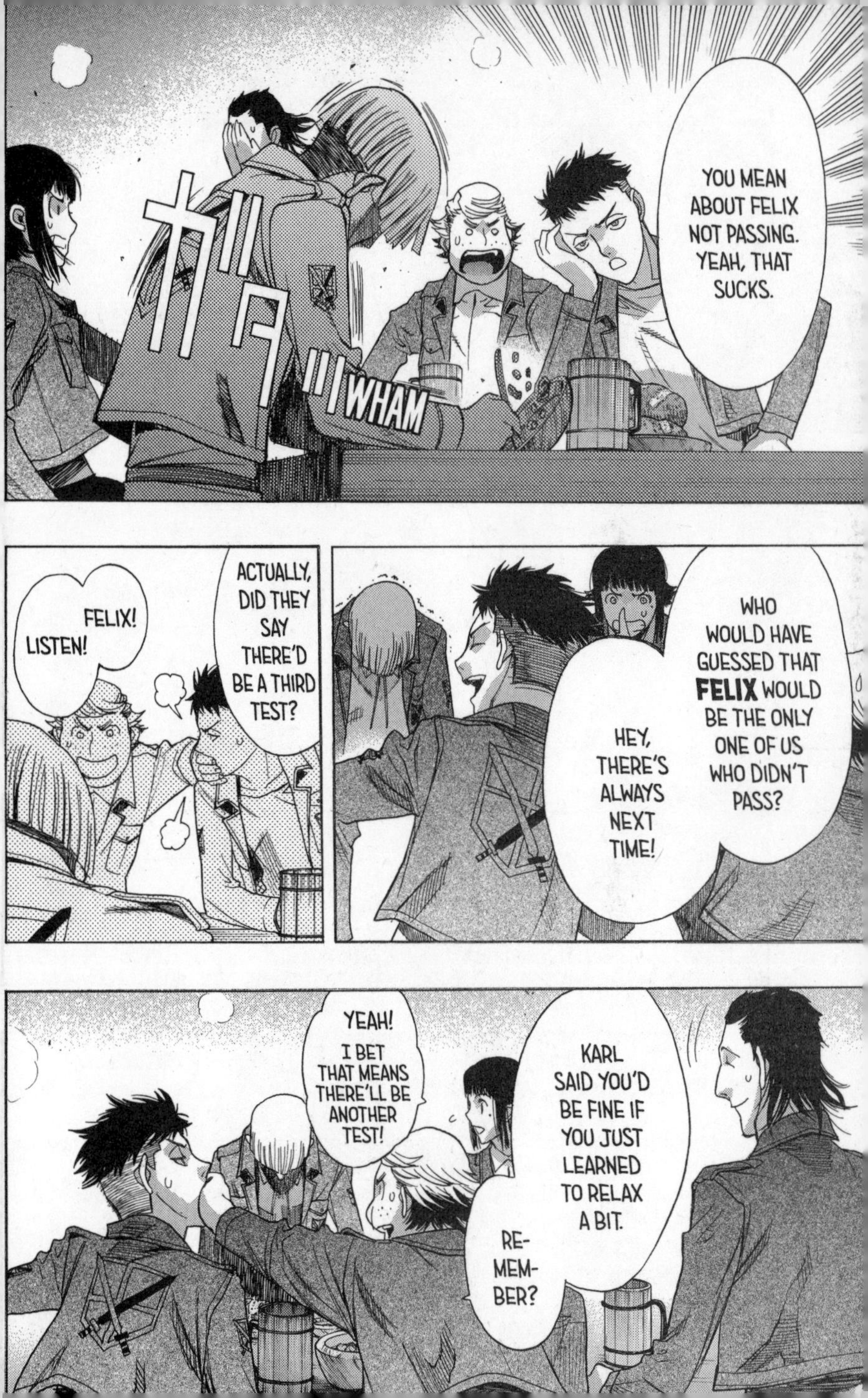
YOU MEAN ABOUT FELIX NOT PASSING. YEAH, THAT SUCKS.
WHAM
WHO WOULD HAVE GUESSED THAT **FELIX** WOULD BE THE ONLY ONE OF US WHO DIDN'T PASS?
HEY, THERE'S ALWAYS NEXT TIME!
ACTUALLY, DID THEY SAY THERE'D BE A THIRD TEST?
FELIX! LISTEN!
KARL SAID YOU'D BE FINE IF YOU JUST LEARNED TO RELAX A BIT.
RE- MEM- BER?
YEAH! I BET THAT MEANS THERE'LL BE ANOTHER TEST!

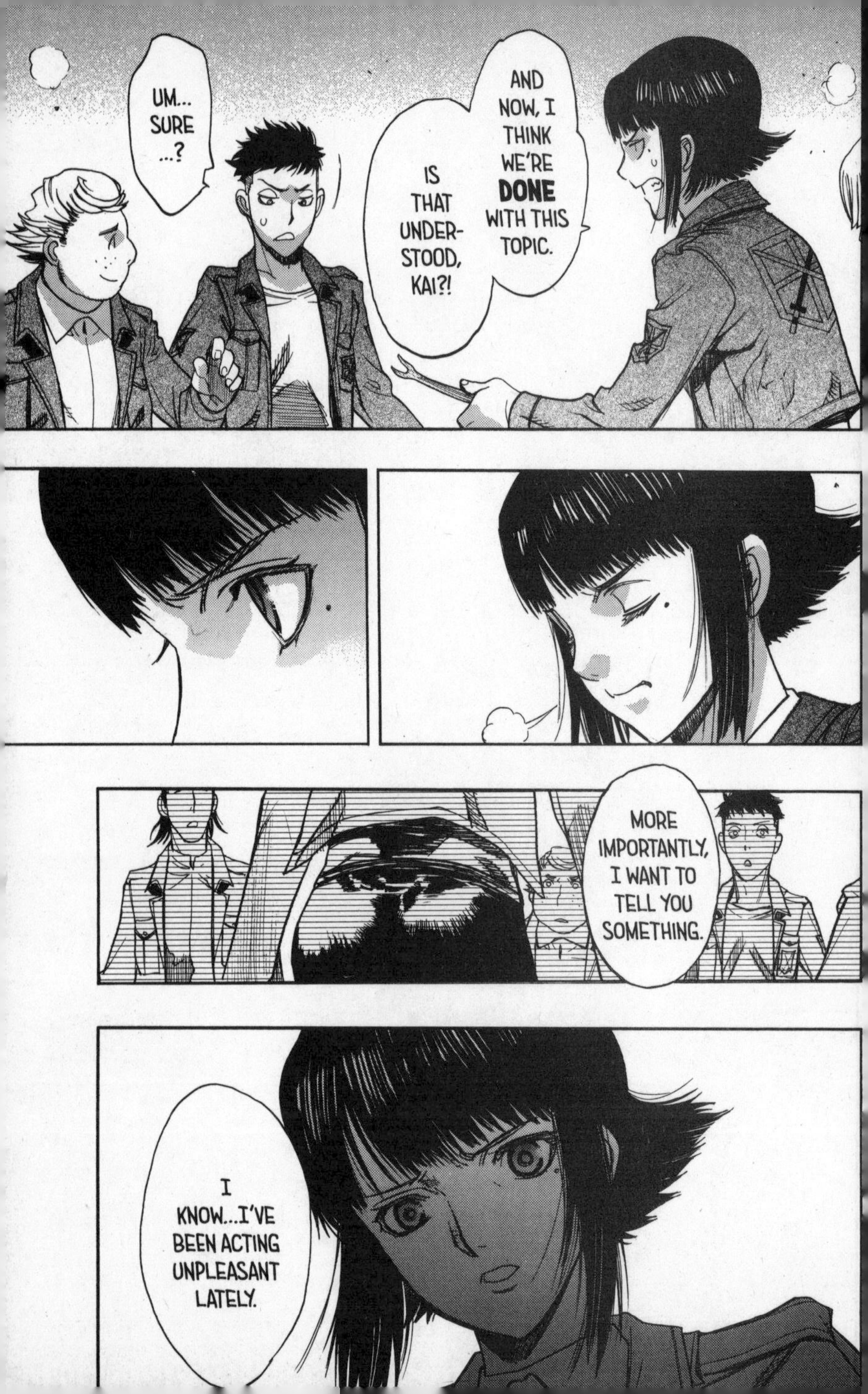
AND NOW, I THINK WE'RE **DONE** WITH THIS TOPIC.
IS THAT UNDER-STOOD, KAI?!
UM... SURE ...?
MORE IMPORTANTLY, I WANT TO TELL YOU SOMETHING.
I KNOW...I'VE BEEN ACTING UNPLEASANT LATELY.

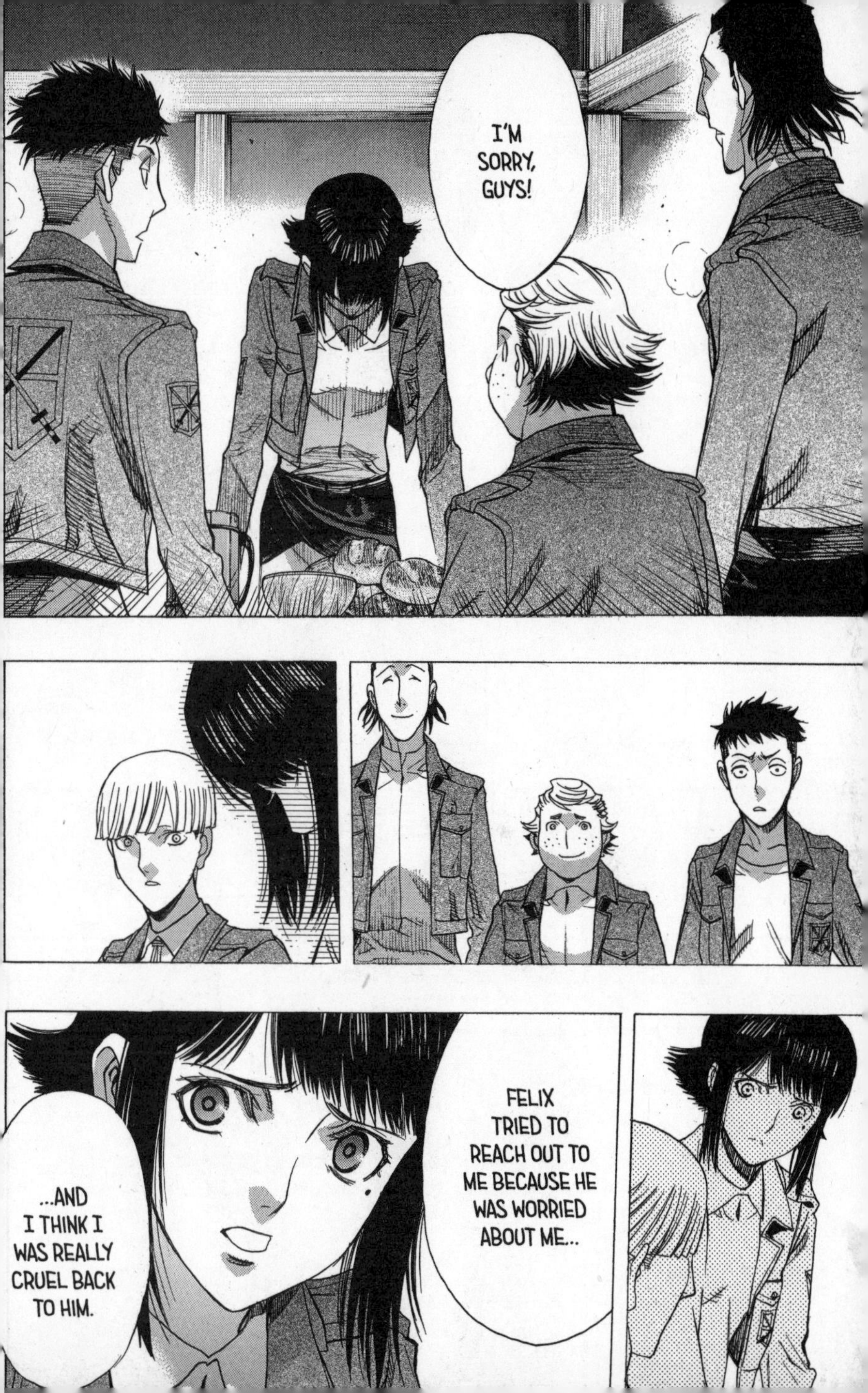
I'M SORRY, GUYS!
FELIX TRIED TO REACH OUT TO ME BECAUSE HE WAS WORRIED ABOUT ME...
...AND I THINK I WAS REALLY CRUEL BACK TO HIM.

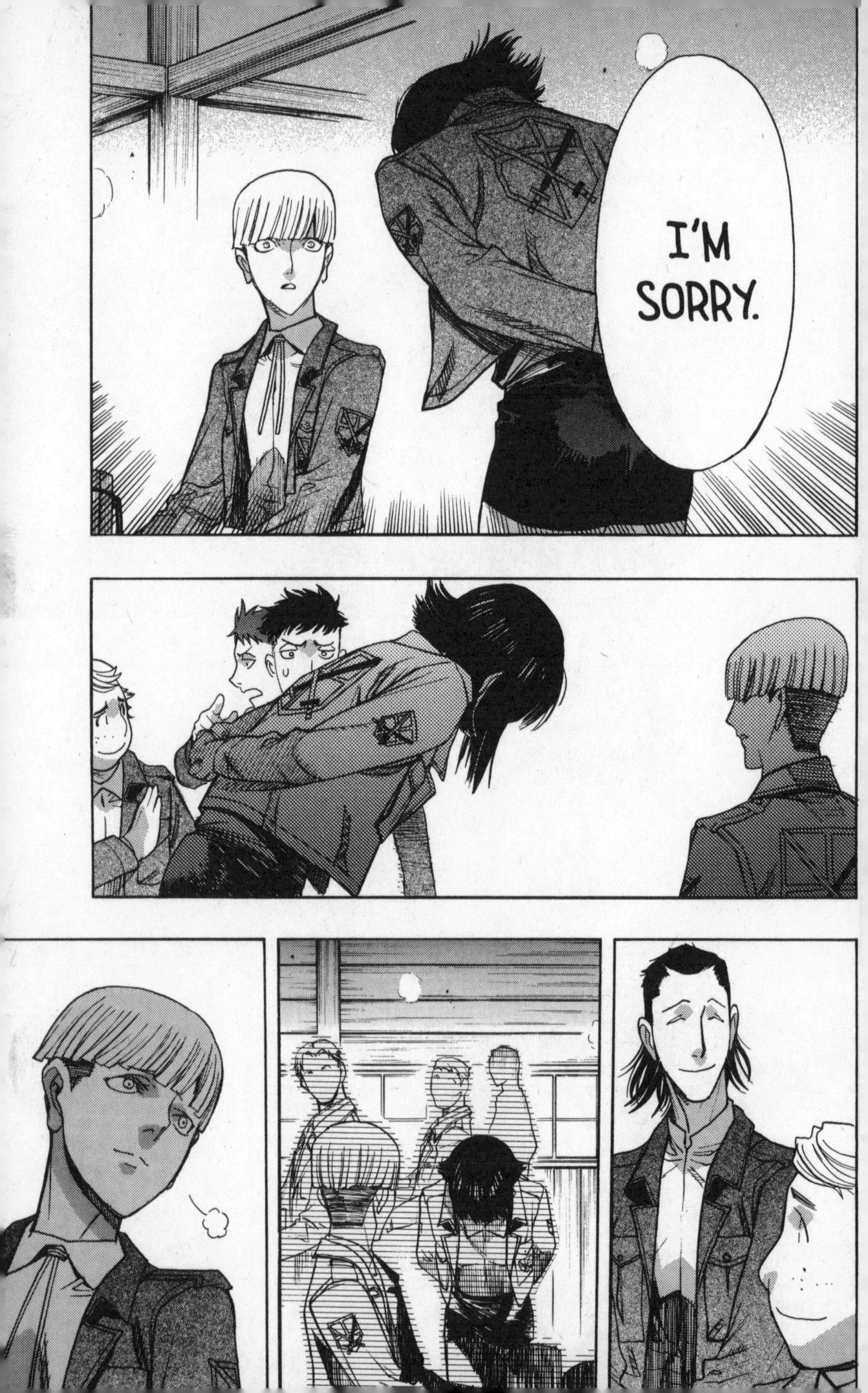
I'M SORRY.

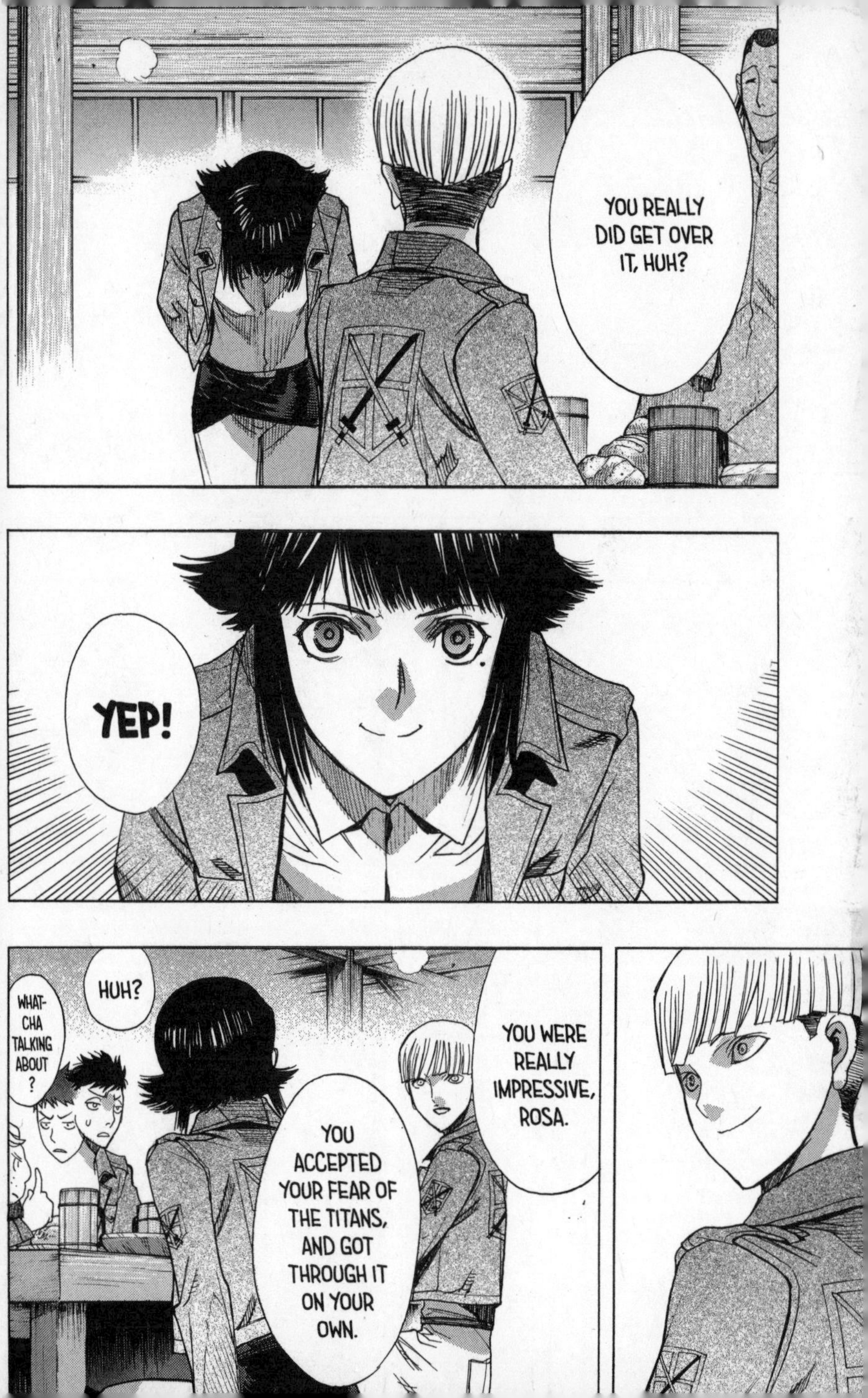
YOU REALLY DID GET OVER IT, HUH?
YEP!
YOU WERE REALLY IMPRESSIVE, ROSA.
YOU ACCEPTED YOUR FEAR OF THE TITANS, AND GOT THROUGH IT ON YOUR OWN.
HUH?
WHAT-CHA TALKING ABOUT?

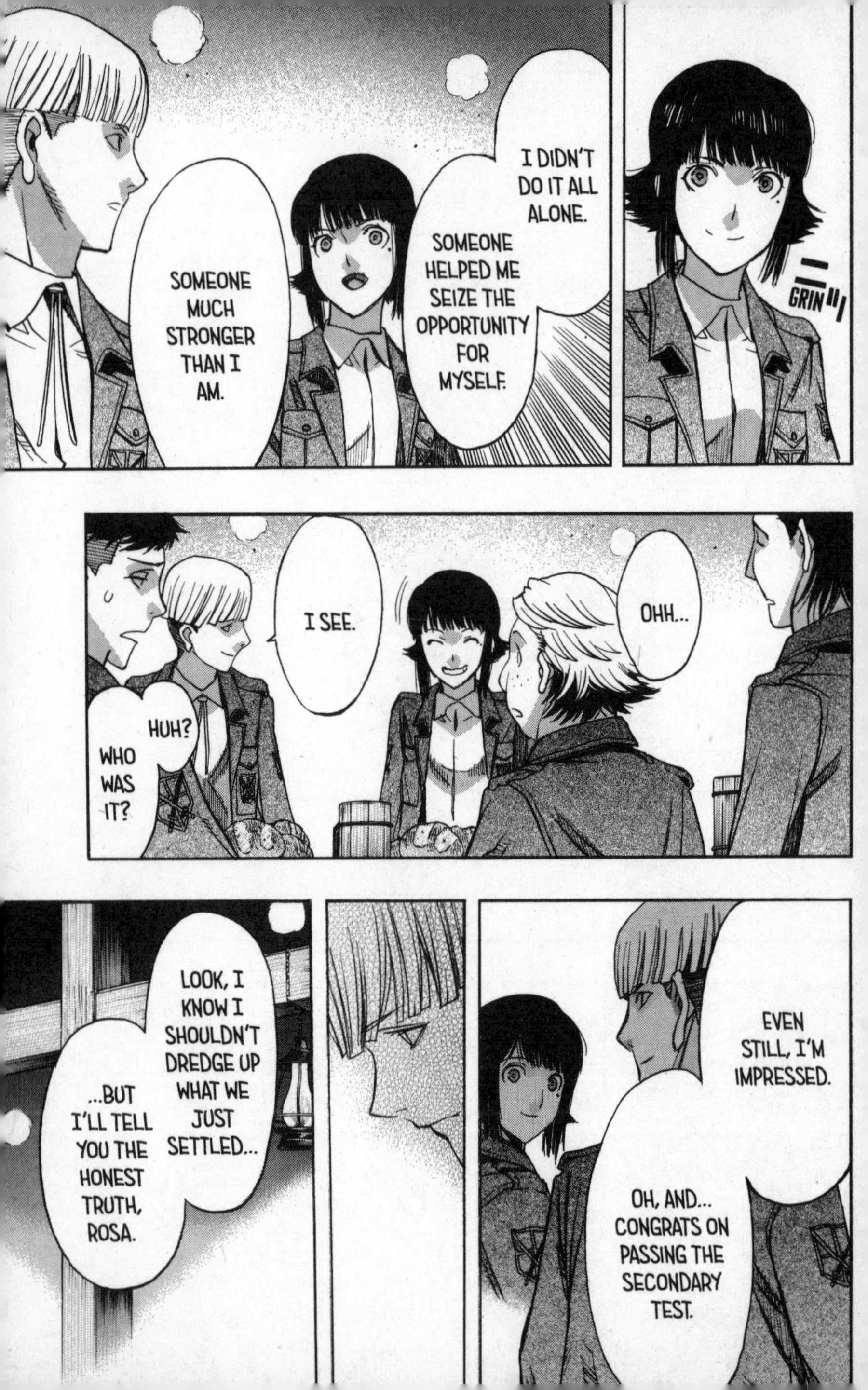
GRIN
I DIDN'T DO IT ALL ALONE.
SOMEONE HELPED ME SEIZE THE OPPORTUNITY FOR MYSELF.
SOMEONE MUCH STRONGER THAN I AM.
OHH...
I SEE.
HUH?
WHO WAS IT?
EVEN STILL, I'M IMPRESSED.
OH, AND... CONGRATS ON PASSING THE SECONDARY TEST.
LOOK, I KNOW I SHOULDN'T DREDGE UP WHAT WE JUST SETTLED...
...BUT I'LL TELL YOU THE HONEST TRUTH, ROSA.

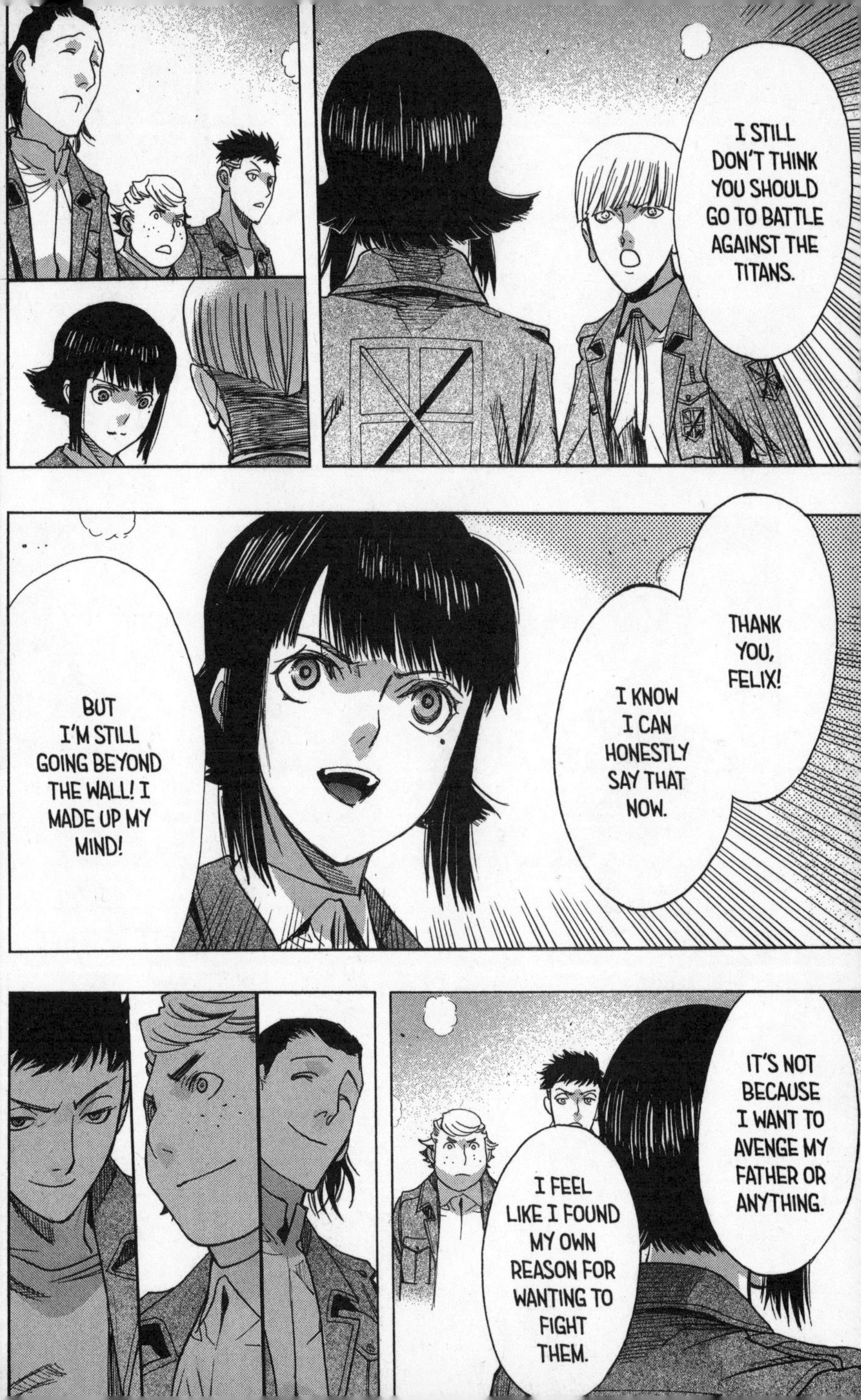
I STILL DON'T THINK YOU SHOULD GO TO BATTLE AGAINST THE TITANS.
THANK YOU, FELIX!
I KNOW I CAN HONESTLY SAY THAT NOW.
BUT I'M STILL GOING BEYOND THE WALL! I MADE UP MY MIND!
IT'S NOT BECAUSE I WANT TO AVENGE MY FATHER OR ANYTHING.
I FEEL LIKE I FOUND MY OWN REASON FOR WANTING TO FIGHT THEM.

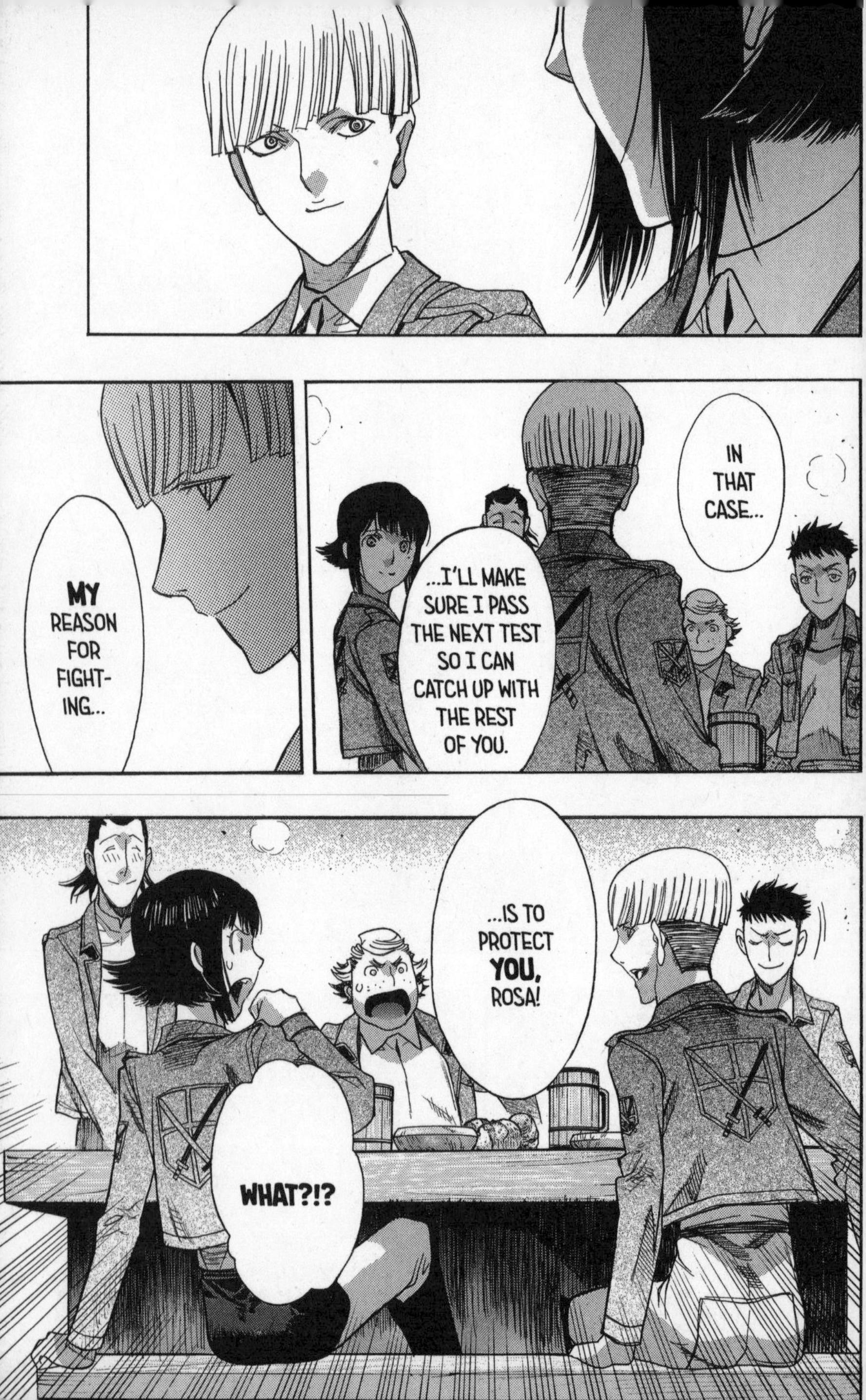
IN THAT CASE...
...I'LL MAKE SURE I PASS THE NEXT TEST SO I CAN CATCH UP WITH THE REST OF YOU.
MY REASON FOR FIGHT-ING...
...IS TO PROTECT YOU, ROSA!
WHAT?!?

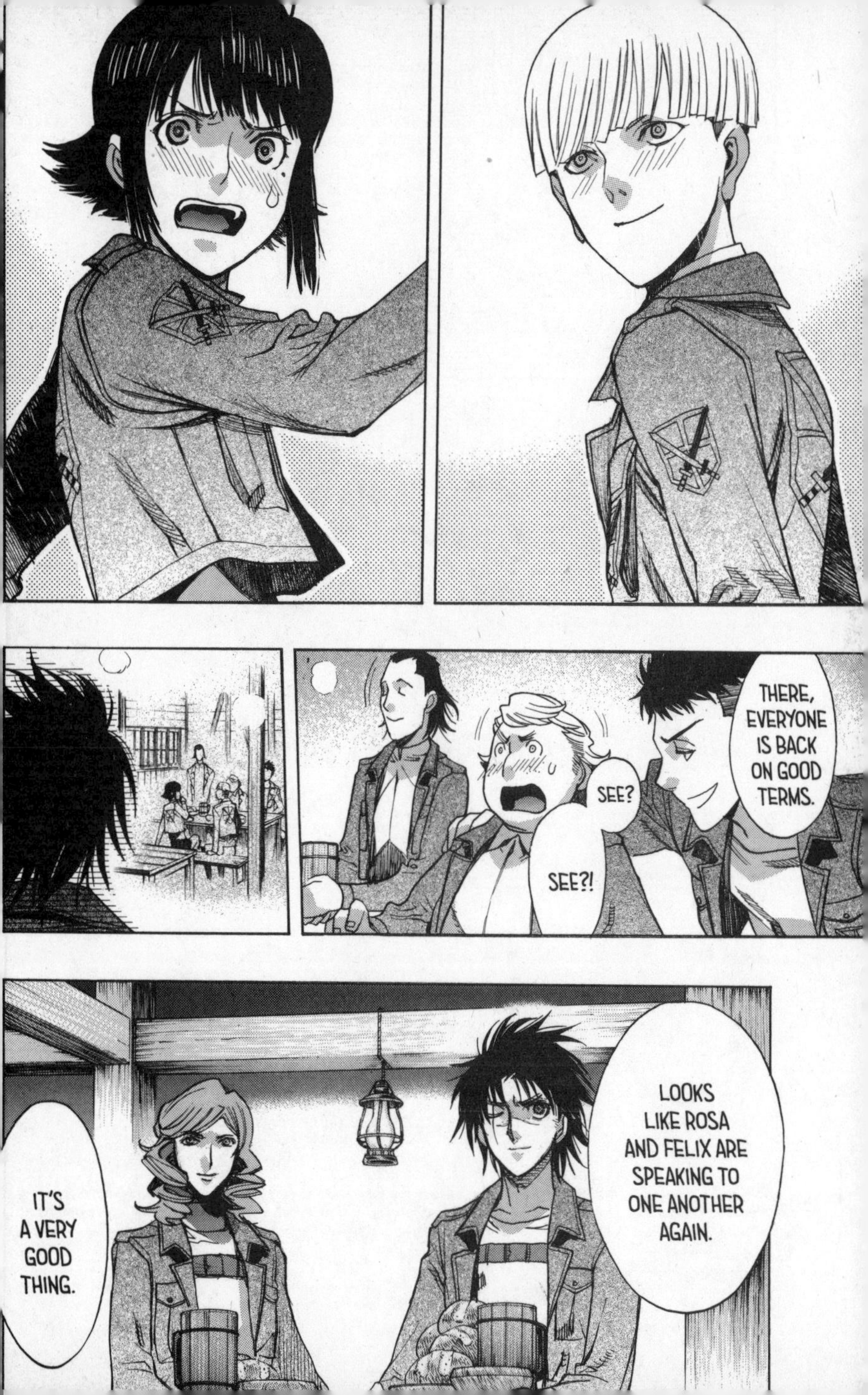
THERE, EVERYONE IS BACK ON GOOD TERMS.
SEE?
SEE?!
LOOKS LIKE ROSA AND FELIX ARE SPEAKING TO ONE ANOTHER AGAIN.
IT'S A VERY GOOD THING.

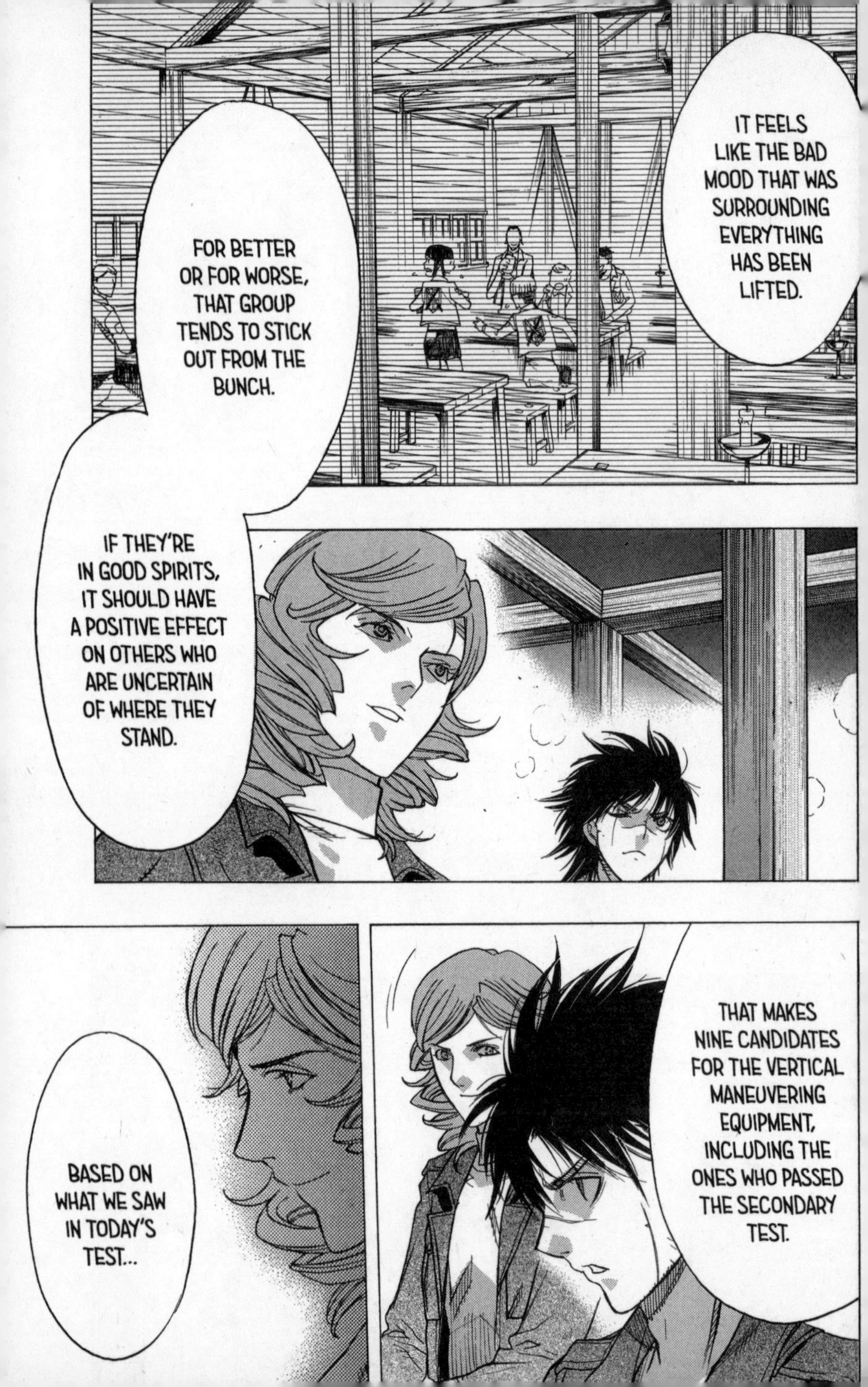
IT FEELS LIKE THE BAD MOOD THAT WAS SURROUNDING EVERYTHING HAS BEEN LIFTED.
FOR BETTER OR FOR WORSE, THAT GROUP TENDS TO STICK OUT FROM THE BUNCH.
IF THEY'RE IN GOOD SPIRITS, IT SHOULD HAVE A POSITIVE EFFECT ON OTHERS WHO ARE UNCERTAIN OF WHERE THEY STAND.
THAT MAKES NINE CANDIDATES FOR THE VERTICAL MANEUVERING EQUIPMENT, INCLUDING THE ONES WHO PASSED THE SECONDARY TEST.
BASED ON WHAT WE SAW IN TODAY'S TEST...

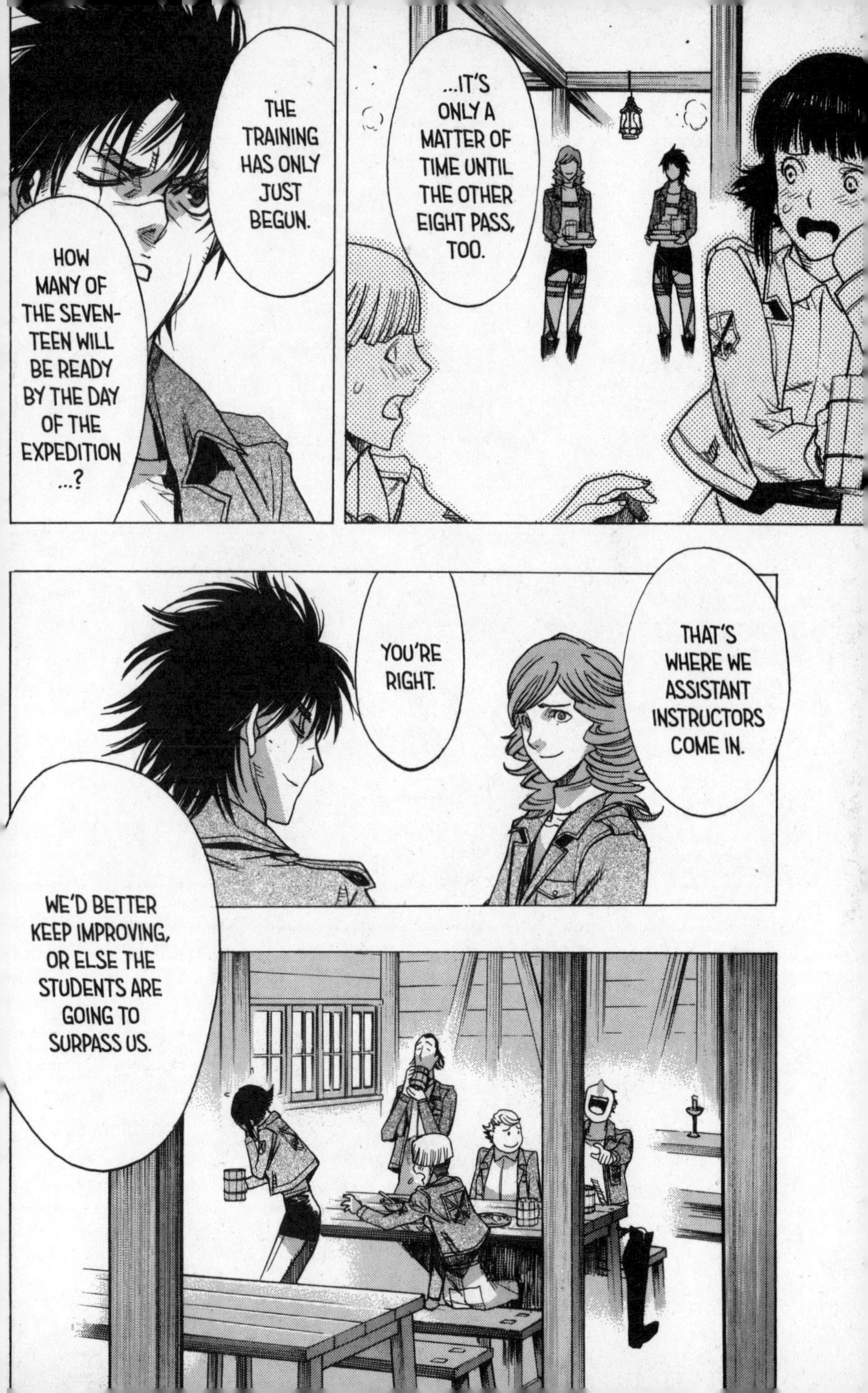
...IT'S ONLY A MATTER OF TIME UNTIL THE OTHER EIGHT PASS, TOO.
THE TRAINING HAS ONLY JUST BEGUN.
HOW MANY OF THE SEVEN-TEEN WILL BE READY BY THE DAY OF THE EXPEDITION ...?
THAT'S WHERE WE ASSISTANT INSTRUCTORS COME IN.
YOU'RE RIGHT.
WE'D BETTER KEEP IMPROVING, OR ELSE THE STUDENTS ARE GOING TO SURPASS US.

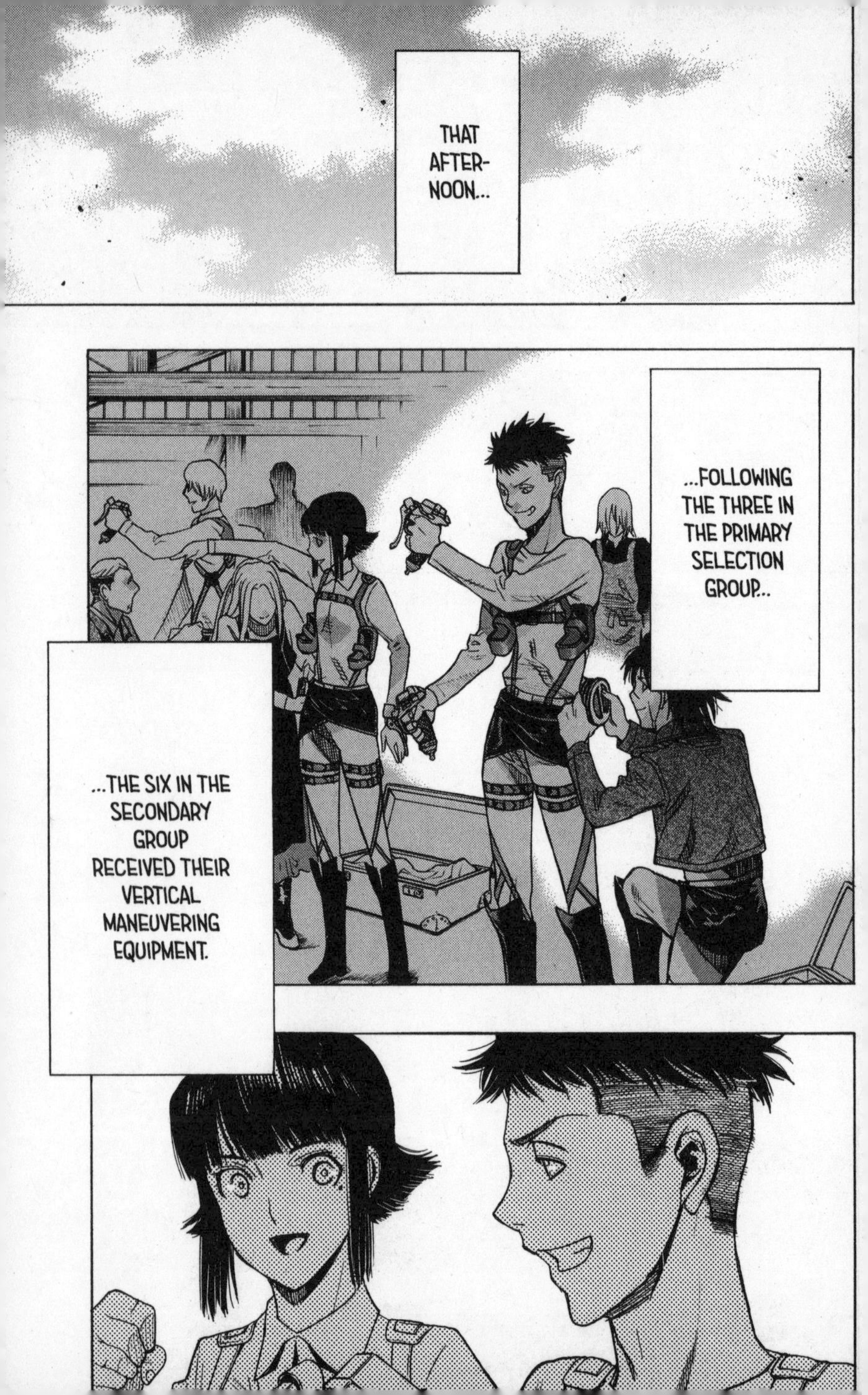
THAT AFTER-NOON...
...FOLLOWING THE THREE IN THE PRIMARY SELECTION GROUP...
...THE SIX IN THE SECONDARY GROUP RECEIVED THEIR VERTICAL MANEUVERING EQUIPMENT.

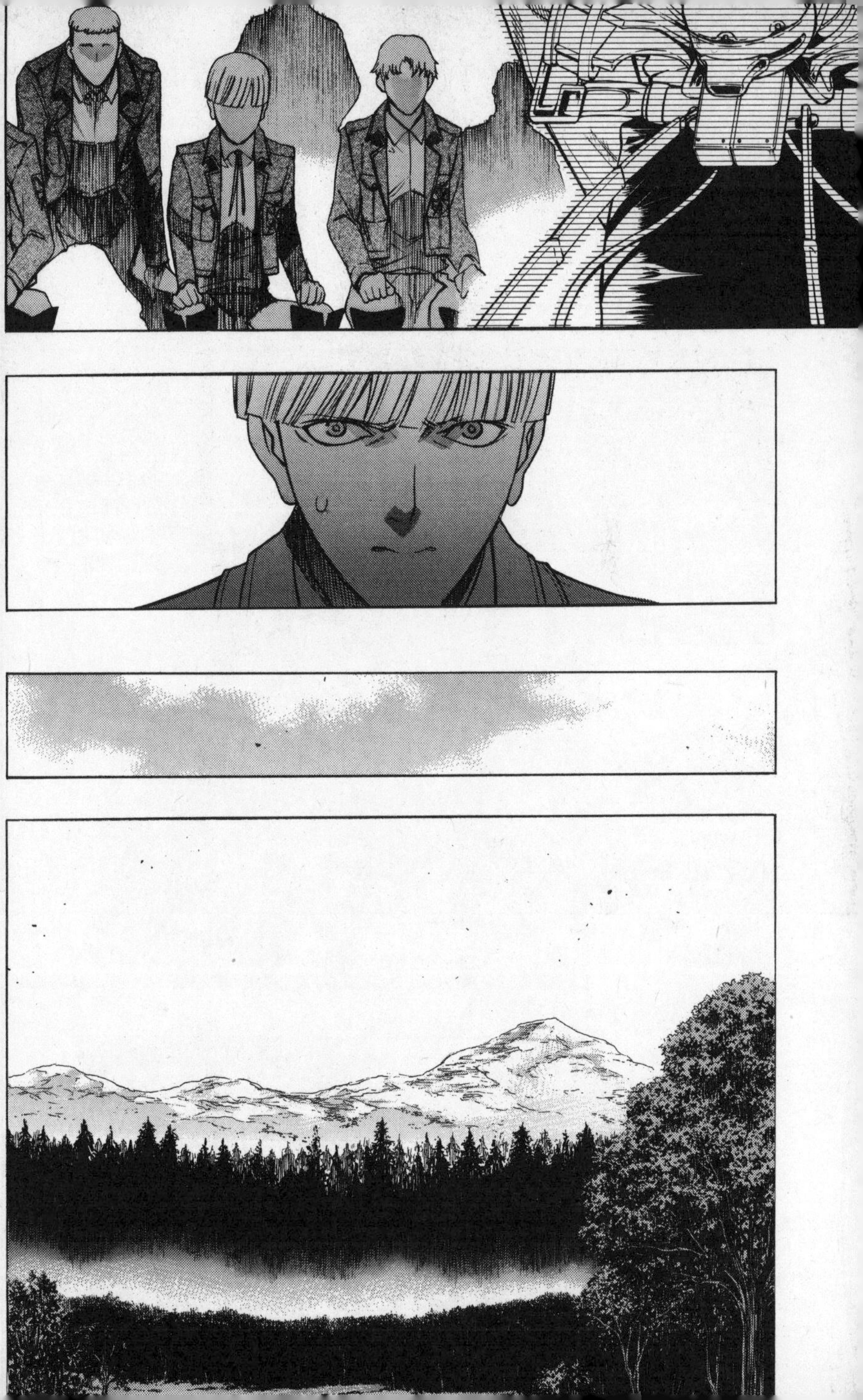

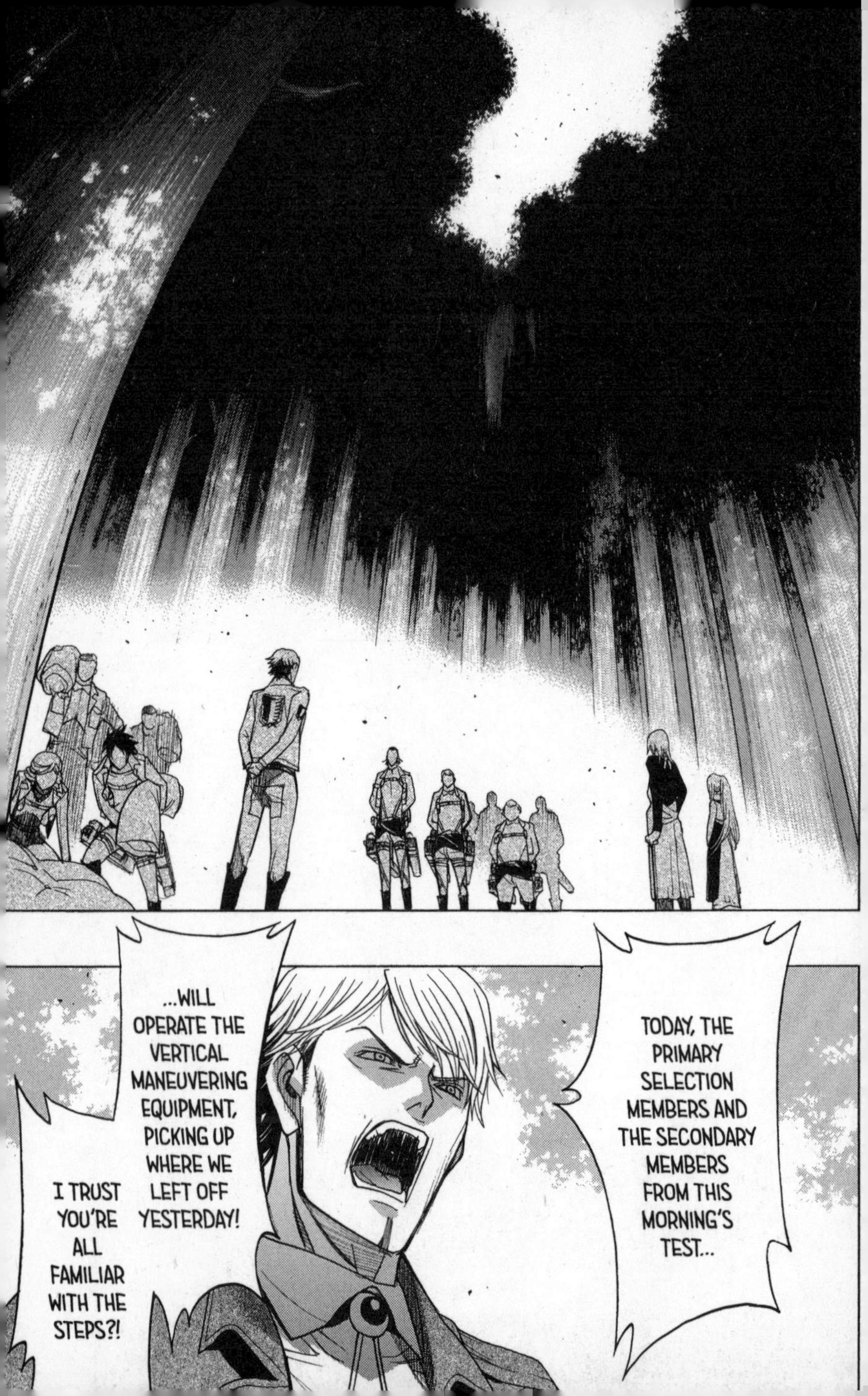
TODAY, THE PRIMARY SELECTION MEMBERS AND THE SECONDARY MEMBERS FROM THIS MORNING'S TEST...
...WILL OPERATE THE VERTICAL MANEUVERING EQUIPMENT, PICKING UP WHERE WE LEFT OFF YESTERDAY!
I TRUST YOU'RE ALL FAMILIAR WITH THE STEPS?!

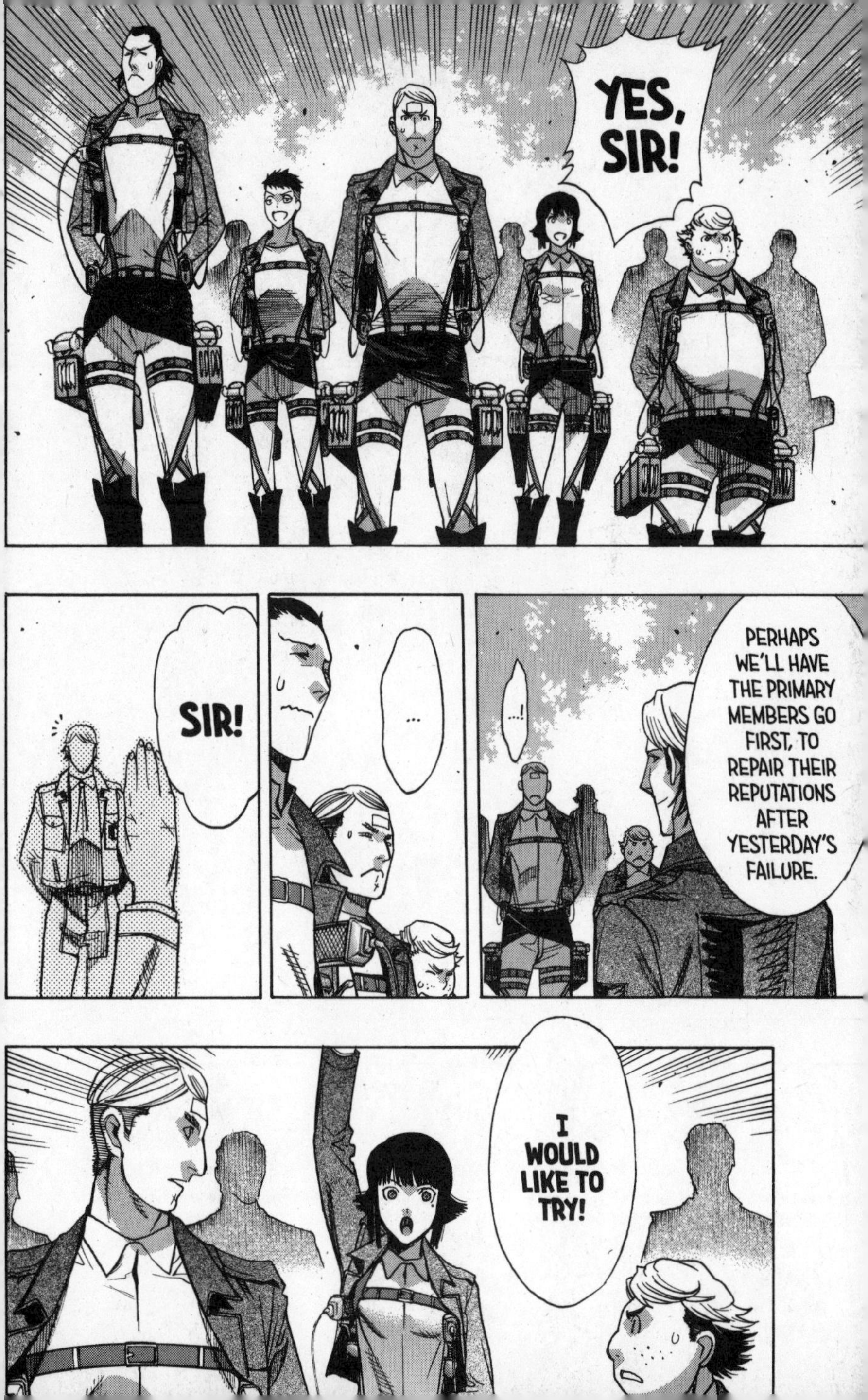
YES, SIR!
PERHAPS WE'LL HAVE THE PRIMARY MEMBERS GO FIRST, TO REPAIR THEIR REPUTATIONS AFTER YESTERDAY'S FAILURE.
...!
...
SIR!
I WOULD LIKE TO TRY!

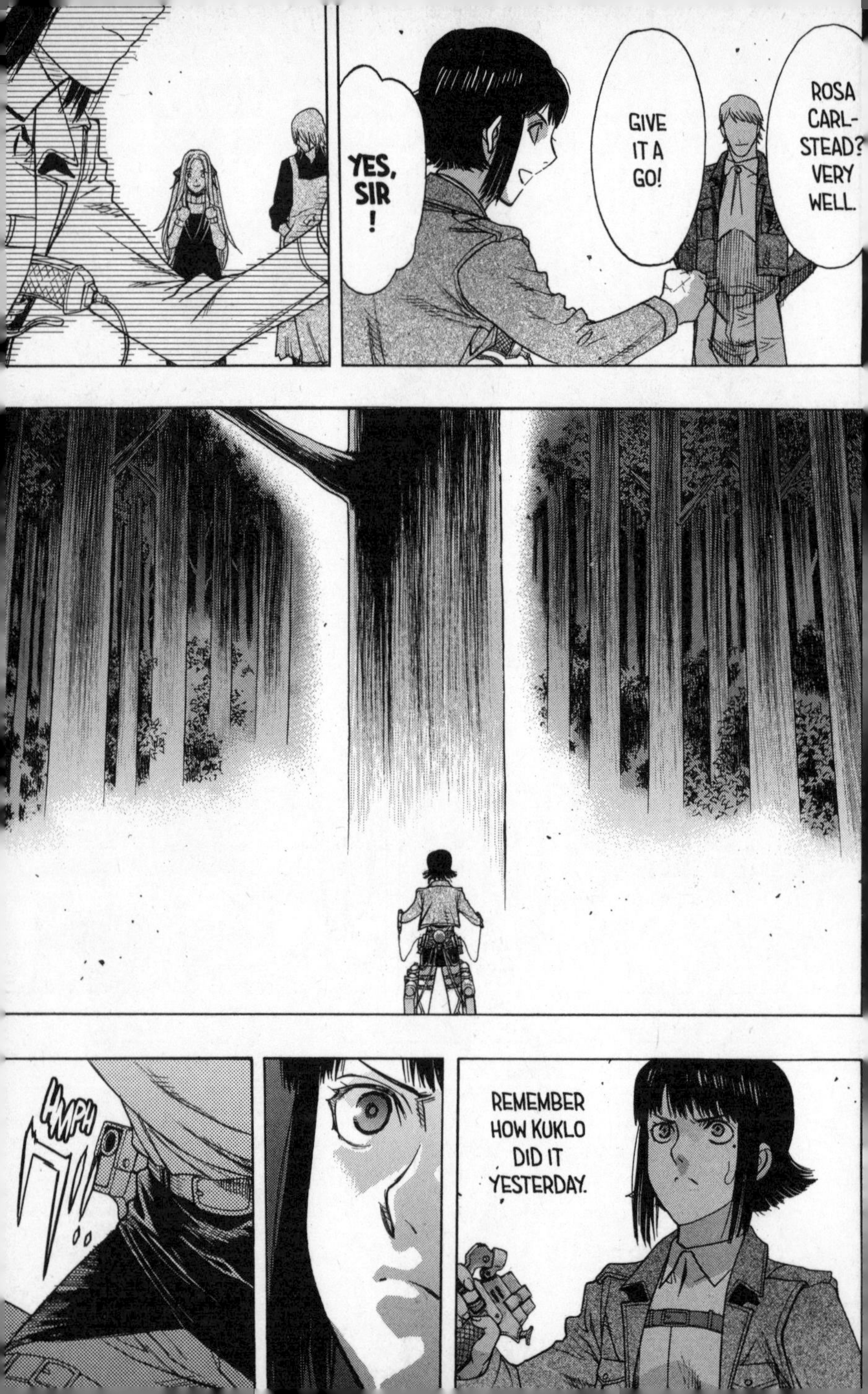
ROSA CARL-STEAD? VERY WELL.
GIVE IT A GO!
YES, SIR!
REMEMBER HOW KUKLO DID IT YESTERDAY.
HMPH

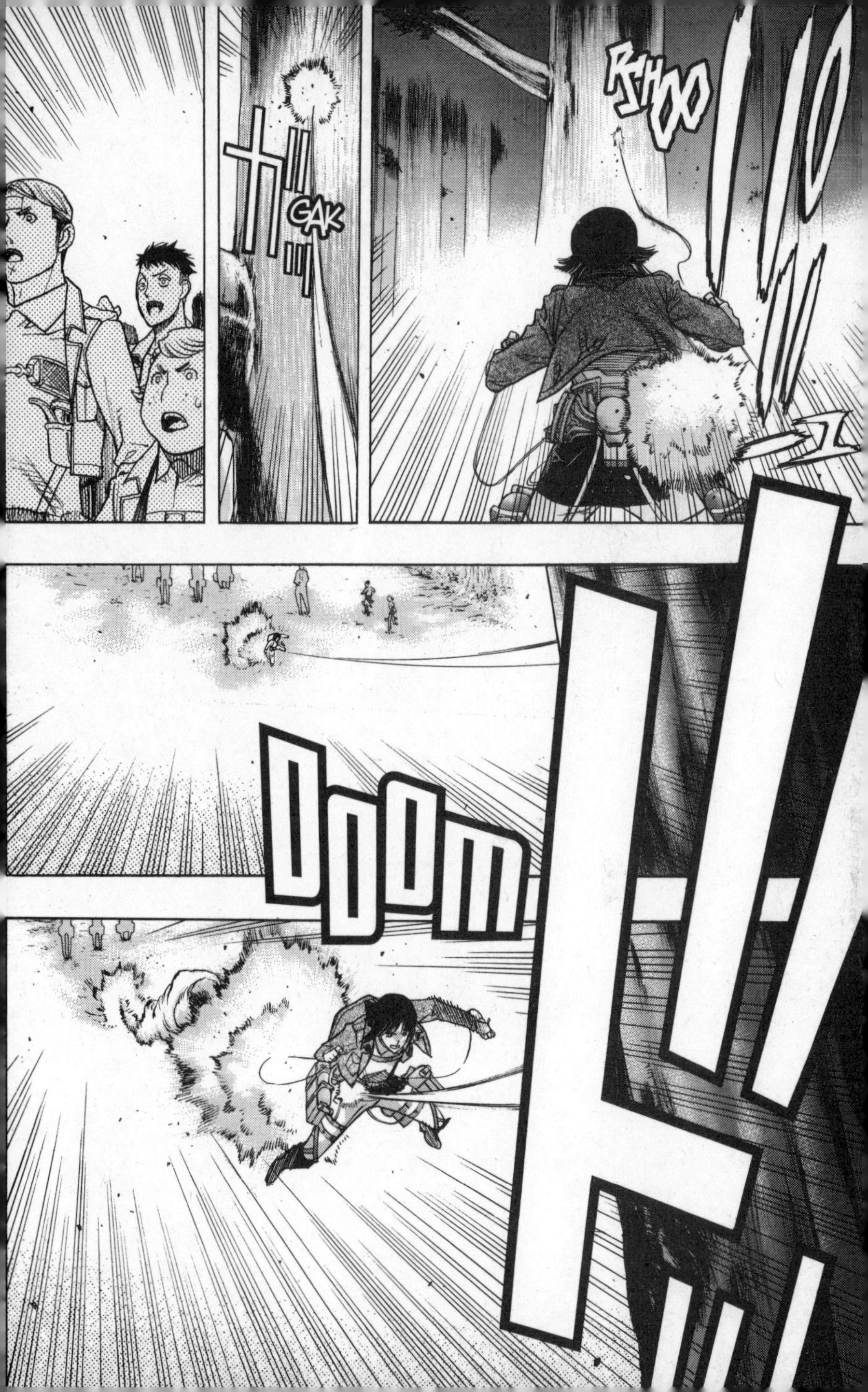
RSHOO
GAK
DOOM

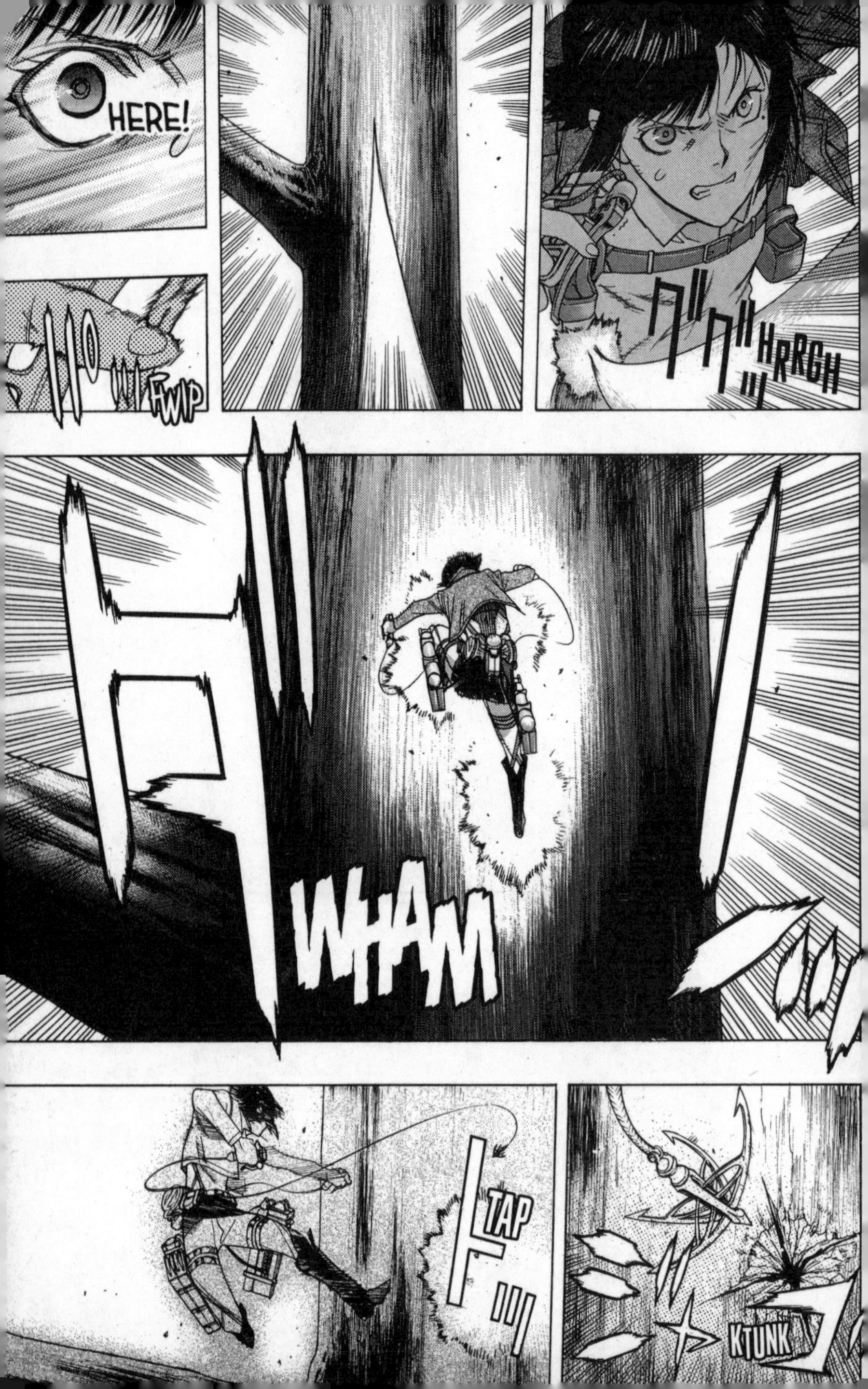
HRRGH
HERE!
FWIP
WHAM
KTUNK
TAP

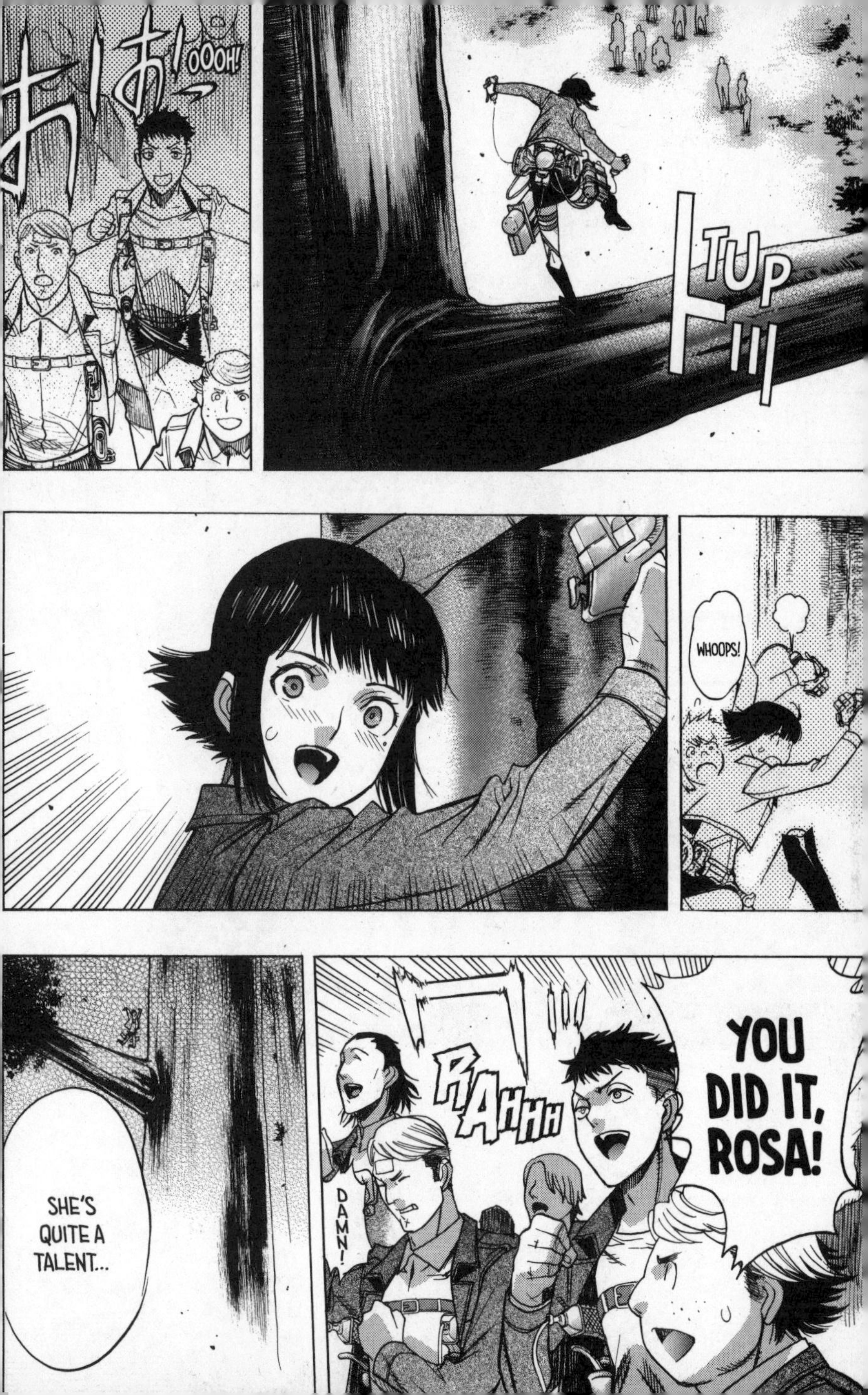
TUP
あ!あ! OOOH!
WHOOPS!
RAHHH
YOU DID IT, ROSA!
DAMN!
SHE'S QUITE A TALENT...

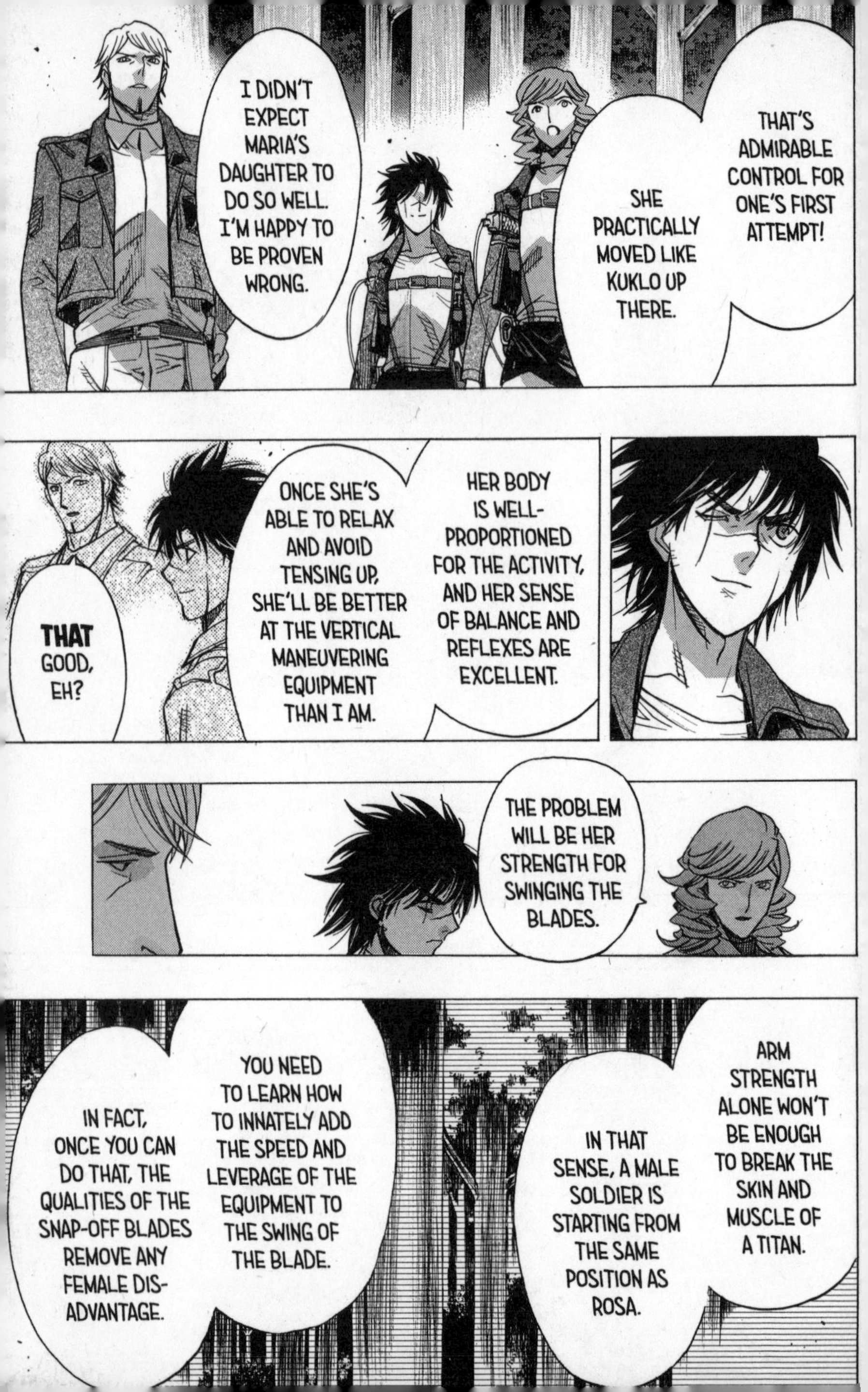
THAT'S ADMIRABLE CONTROL FOR ONE'S FIRST ATTEMPT!
SHE PRACTICALLY MOVED LIKE KUKLO UP THERE.
I DIDN'T EXPECT MARIA'S DAUGHTER TO DO SO WELL. I'M HAPPY TO BE PROVEN WRONG.
HER BODY IS WELL-PROPORTIONED FOR THE ACTIVITY, AND HER SENSE OF BALANCE AND REFLEXES ARE EXCELLENT.
ONCE SHE'S ABLE TO RELAX AND AVOID TENSING UP, SHE'LL BE BETTER AT THE VERTICAL MANEUVERING EQUIPMENT THAN I AM.
THAT GOOD, EH?
THE PROBLEM WILL BE HER STRENGTH FOR SWINGING THE BLADES.
ARM STRENGTH ALONE WON'T BE ENOUGH TO BREAK THE SKIN AND MUSCLE OF A TITAN.
IN THAT SENSE, A MALE SOLDIER IS STARTING FROM THE SAME POSITION AS ROSA.
YOU NEED TO LEARN HOW TO INNATELY ADD THE SPEED AND LEVERAGE OF THE EQUIPMENT TO THE SWING OF THE BLADE.
IN FACT, ONCE YOU CAN DO THAT, THE QUALITIES OF THE SNAP-OFF BLADES REMOVE ANY FEMALE DIS-ADVANTAGE.

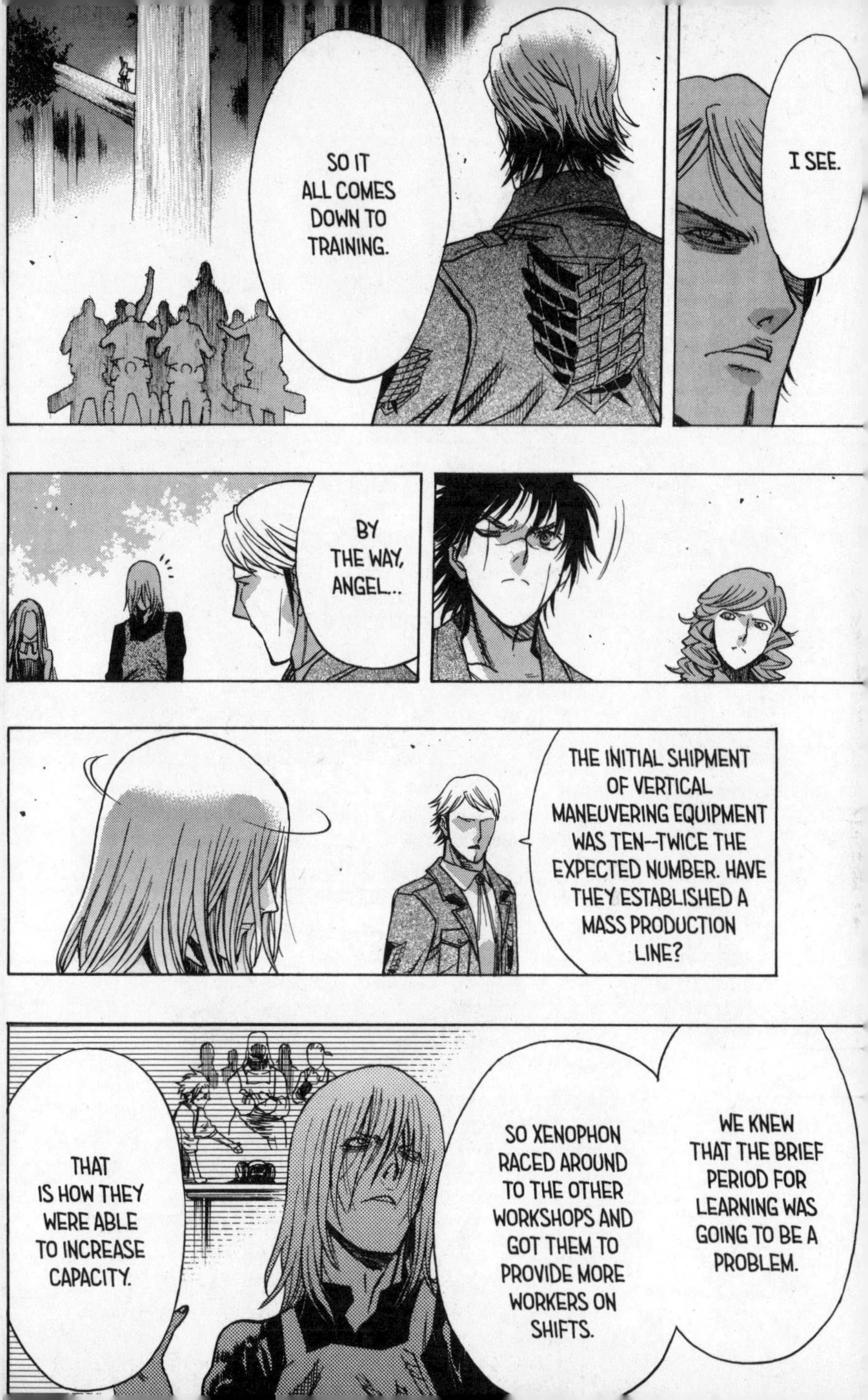
I SEE.
SO IT ALL COMES DOWN TO TRAINING.
BY THE WAY, ANGEL...
THE INITIAL SHIPMENT OF VERTICAL MANEUVERING EQUIPMENT WAS TEN--TWICE THE EXPECTED NUMBER. HAVE THEY ESTABLISHED A MASS PRODUCTION LINE?
WE KNEW THAT THE BRIEF PERIOD FOR LEARNING WAS GOING TO BE A PROBLEM.
SO XENOPHON RACED AROUND TO THE OTHER WORKSHOPS AND GOT THEM TO PROVIDE MORE WORKERS ON SHIFTS.
THAT IS HOW THEY WERE ABLE TO INCREASE CAPACITY.

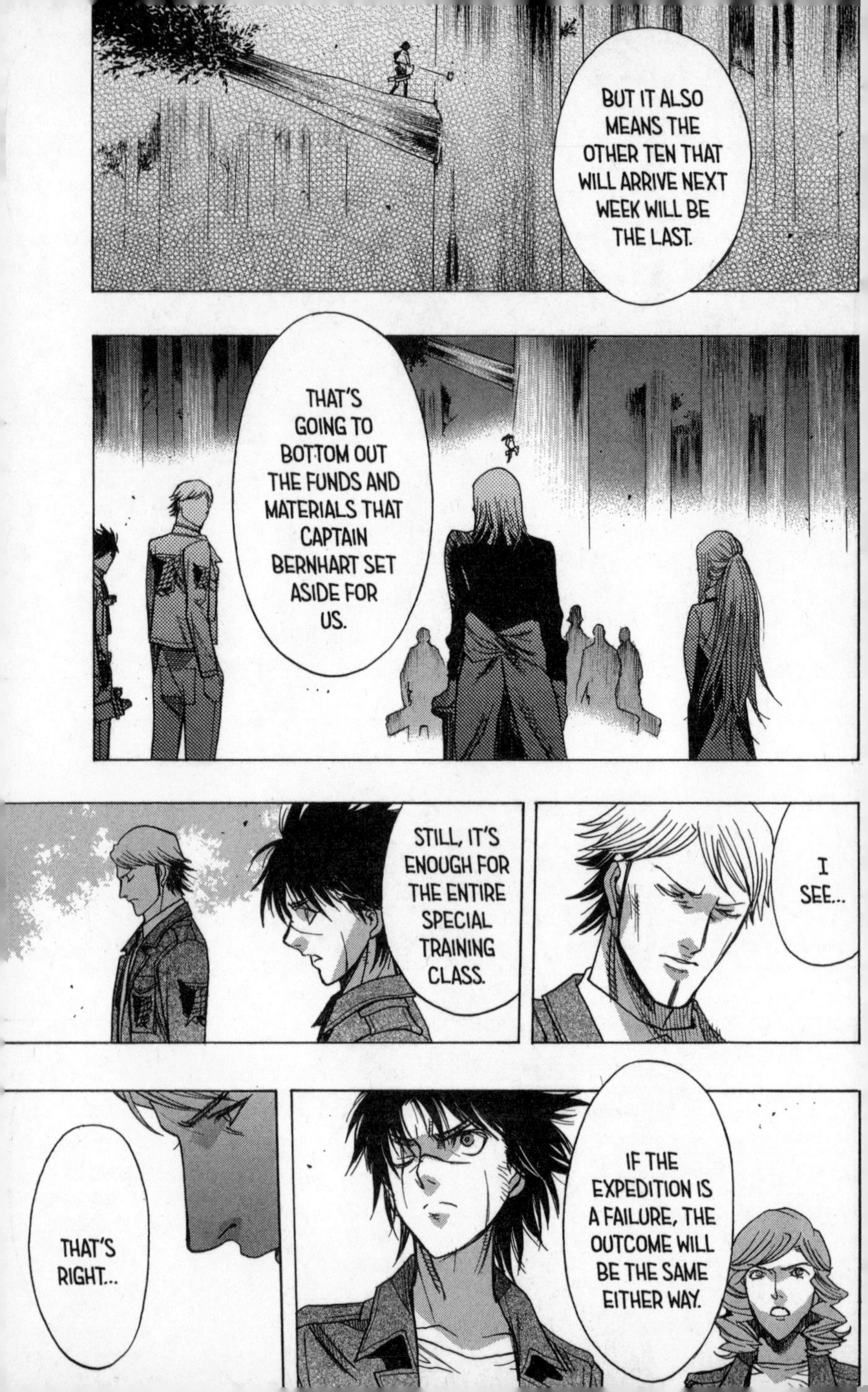
BUT IT ALSO MEANS THE OTHER TEN THAT WILL ARRIVE NEXT WEEK WILL BE THE LAST.
THAT'S GOING TO BOTTOM OUT THE FUNDS AND MATERIALS THAT CAPTAIN BERNHART SET ASIDE FOR US.
I SEE...
STILL, IT'S ENOUGH FOR THE ENTIRE SPECIAL TRAINING CLASS.
IF THE EXPEDITION IS A FAILURE, THE OUTCOME WILL BE THE SAME EITHER WAY.
THAT'S RIGHT...

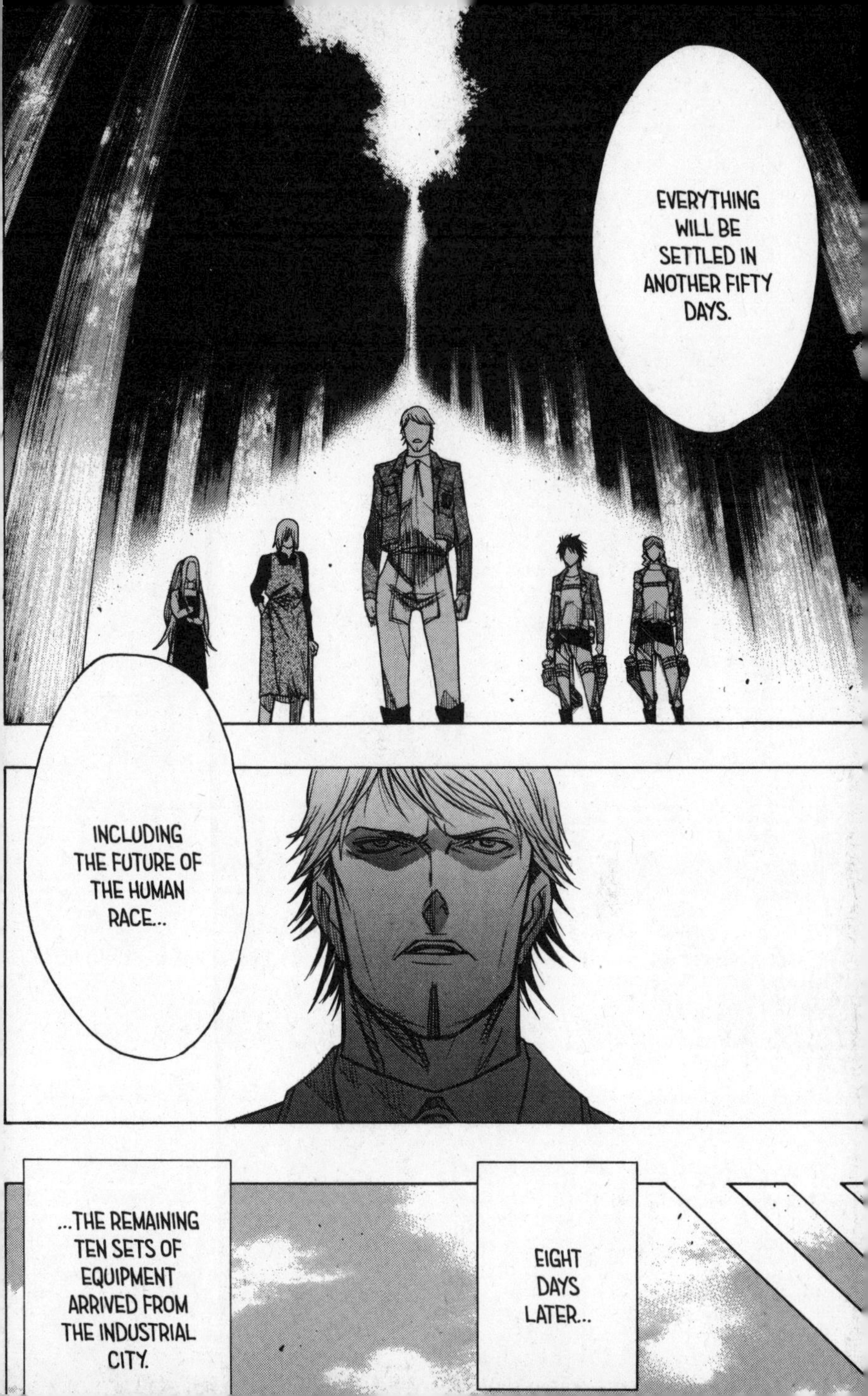
EVERYTHING WILL BE SETTLED IN ANOTHER FIFTY DAYS.
INCLUDING THE FUTURE OF THE HUMAN RACE...
EIGHT DAYS LATER...
...THE REMAINING TEN SETS OF EQUIPMENT ARRIVED FROM THE INDUSTRIAL CITY.

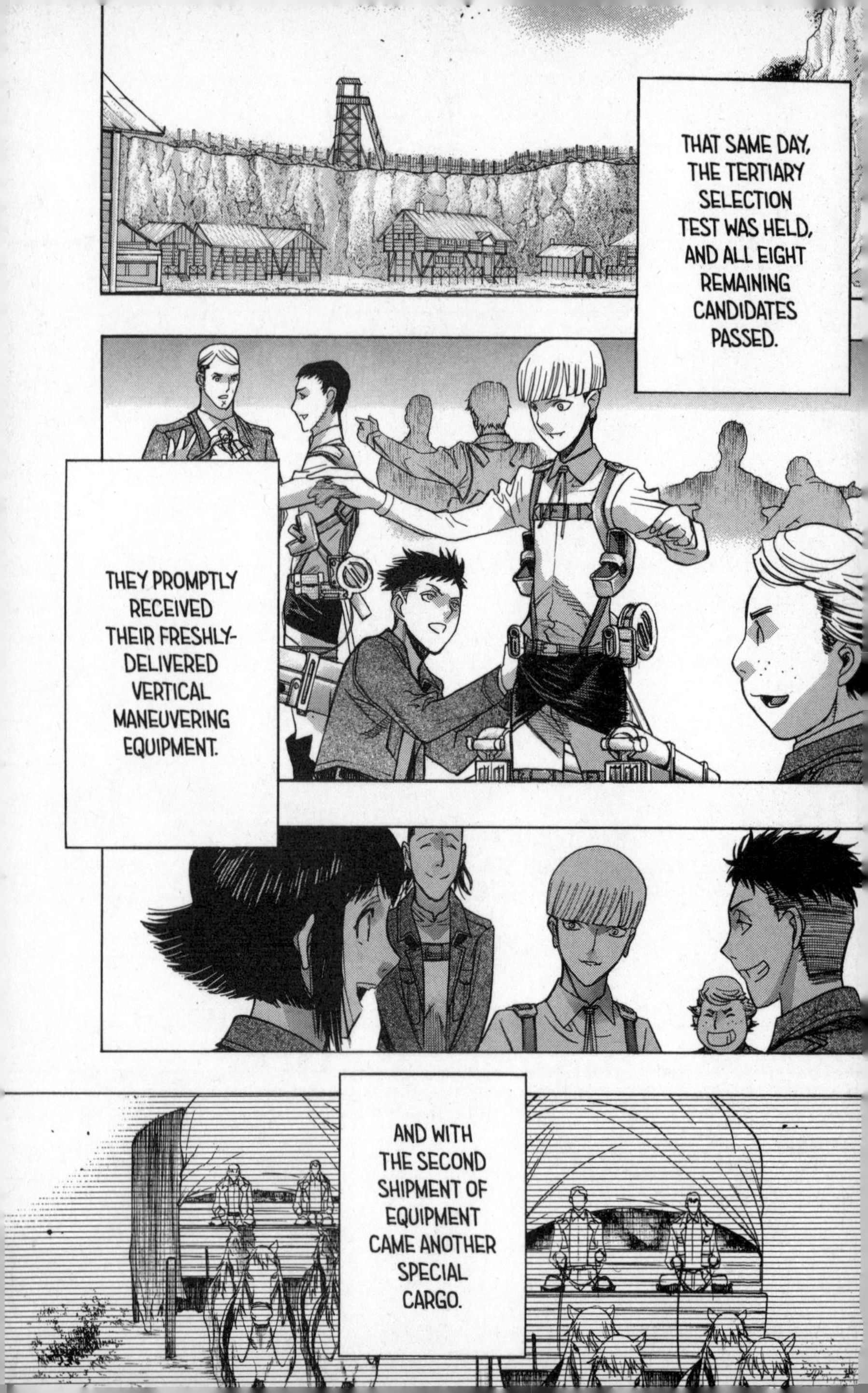
THAT SAME DAY, THE TERTIARY SELECTION TEST WAS HELD, AND ALL EIGHT REMAINING CANDIDATES PASSED.
THEY PROMPTLY RECEIVED THEIR FRESHLY-DELIVERED VERTICAL MANEUVERING EQUIPMENT.
AND WITH THE SECOND SHIPMENT OF EQUIPMENT CAME ANOTHER SPECIAL CARGO.

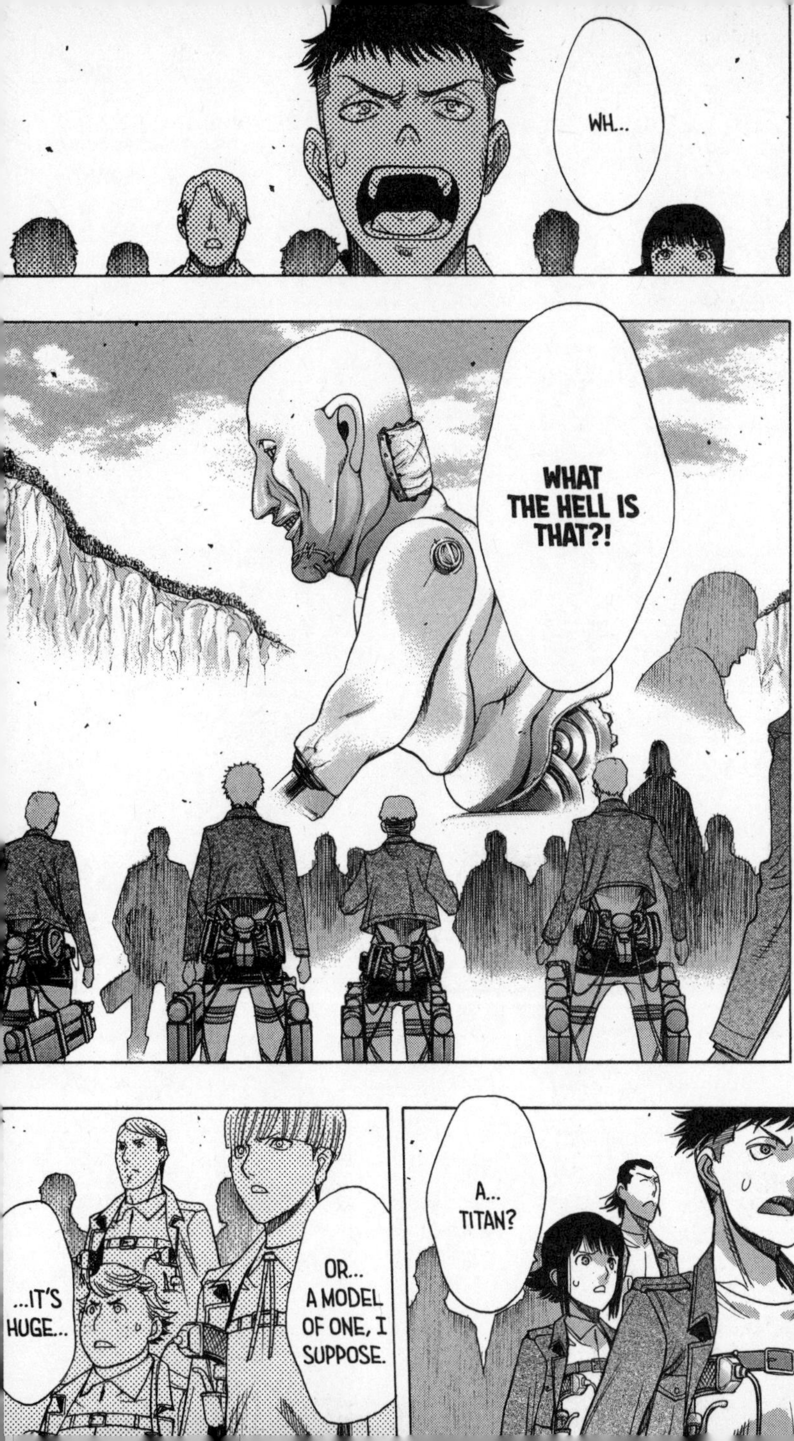
WH...
WHAT THE HELL IS THAT?!
A... TITAN?
OR... A MODEL OF ONE, I SUPPOSE.
...IT'S HUGE...

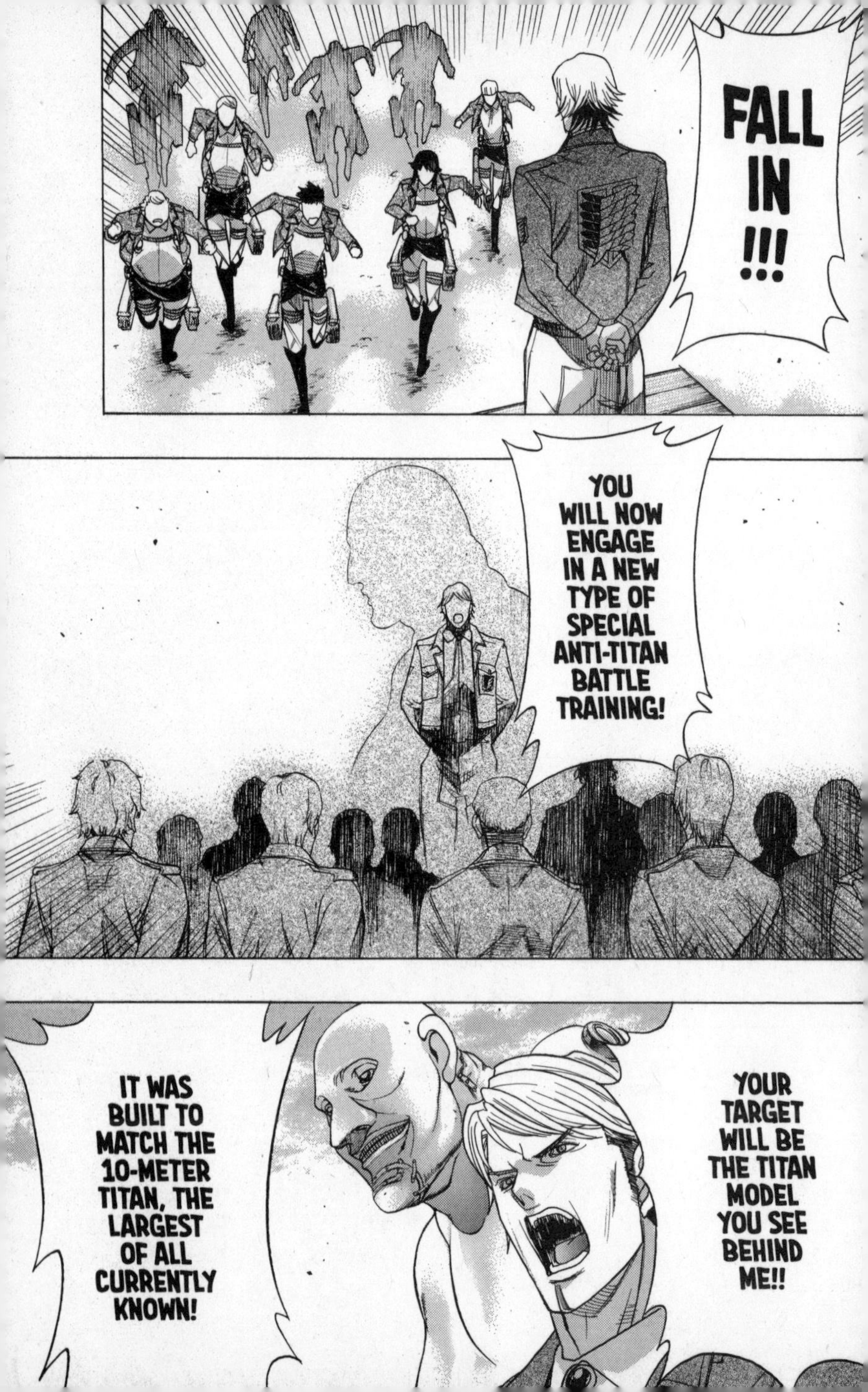
FALL IN!!!
YOU WILL NOW ENGAGE IN A NEW TYPE OF SPECIAL ANTI-TITAN BATTLE TRAINING!
YOUR TARGET WILL BE THE TITAN MODEL YOU SEE BEHIND ME!!
IT WAS BUILT TO MATCH THE 10-METER TITAN, THE LARGEST OF ALL CURRENTLY KNOWN!

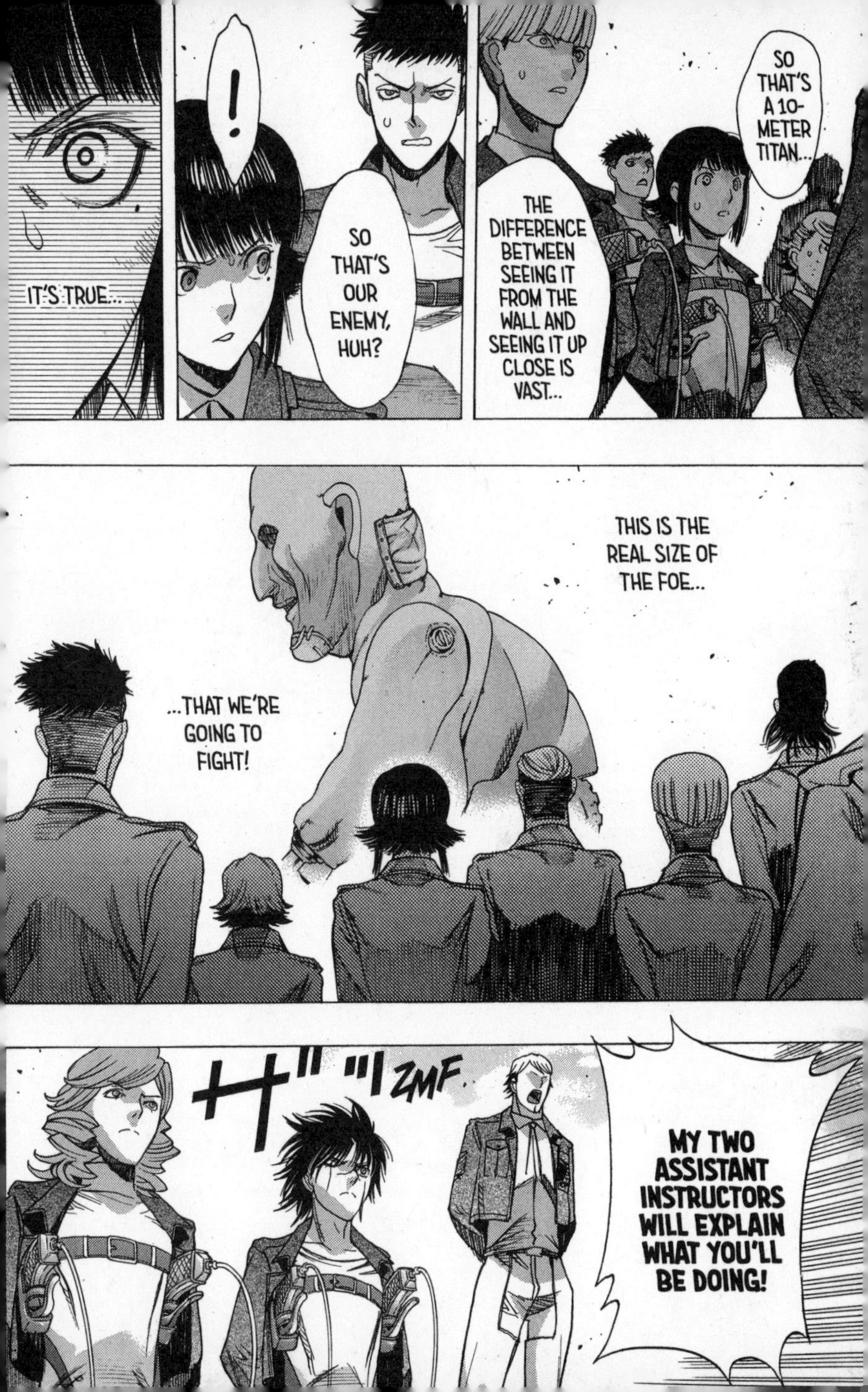
SO THAT'S A 10-METER TITAN...
THE DIFFERENCE BETWEEN SEEING IT FROM THE WALL AND SEEING IT UP CLOSE IS VAST...
!
SO THAT'S OUR ENEMY, HUH?
IT'S TRUE...
THIS IS THE REAL SIZE OF THE FOE...
...THAT WE'RE GOING TO FIGHT!
MY TWO ASSISTANT INSTRUCTORS WILL EXPLAIN WHAT YOU'LL BE DOING!
ZMF

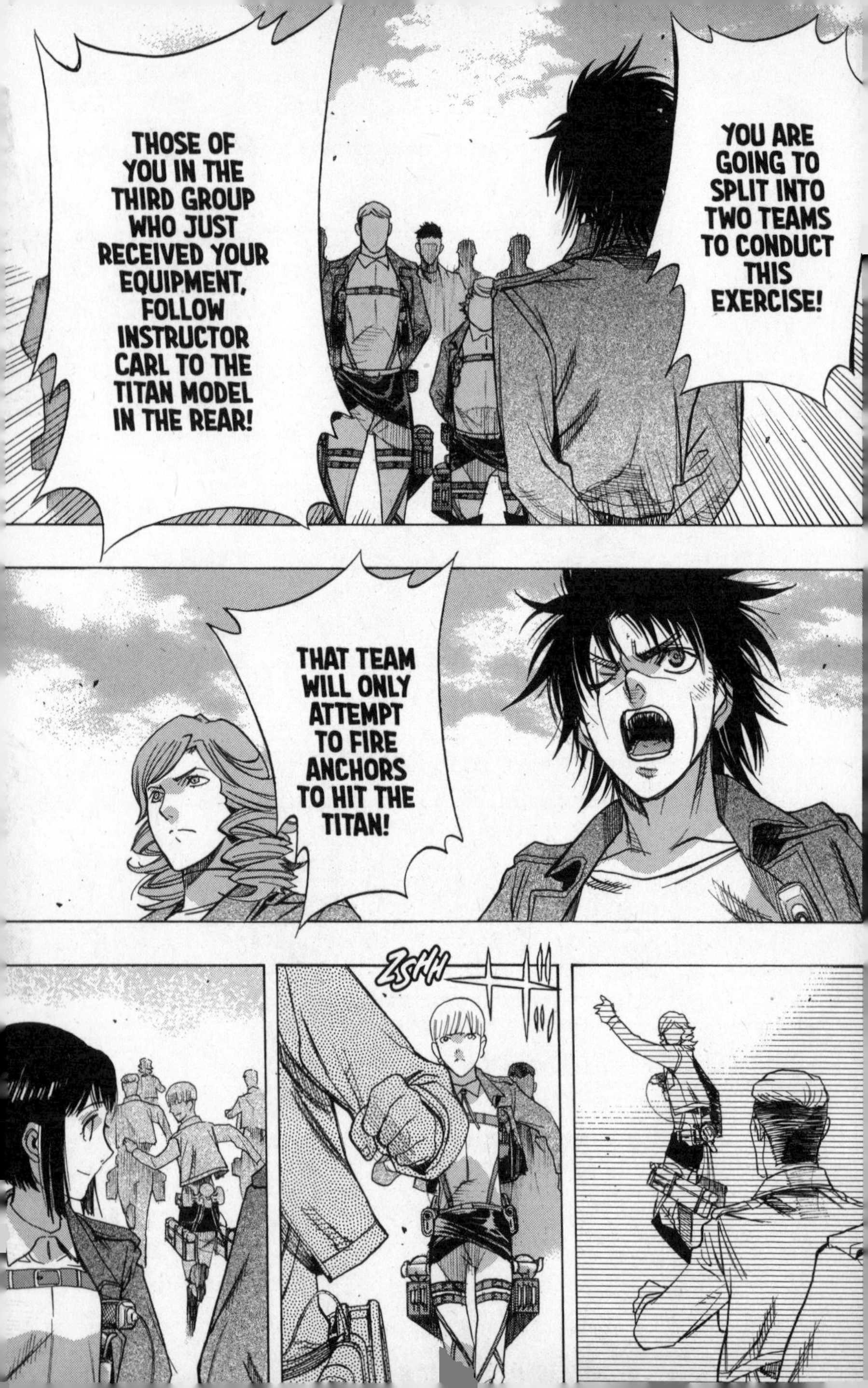
YOU ARE GOING TO SPLIT INTO TWO TEAMS TO CONDUCT THIS EXERCISE!
THOSE OF YOU IN THE THIRD GROUP WHO JUST RECEIVED YOUR EQUIPMENT, FOLLOW INSTRUCTOR CARL TO THE TITAN MODEL IN THE REAR!
THAT TEAM WILL ONLY ATTEMPT TO FIRE ANCHORS TO HIT THE TITAN!
ZSHH

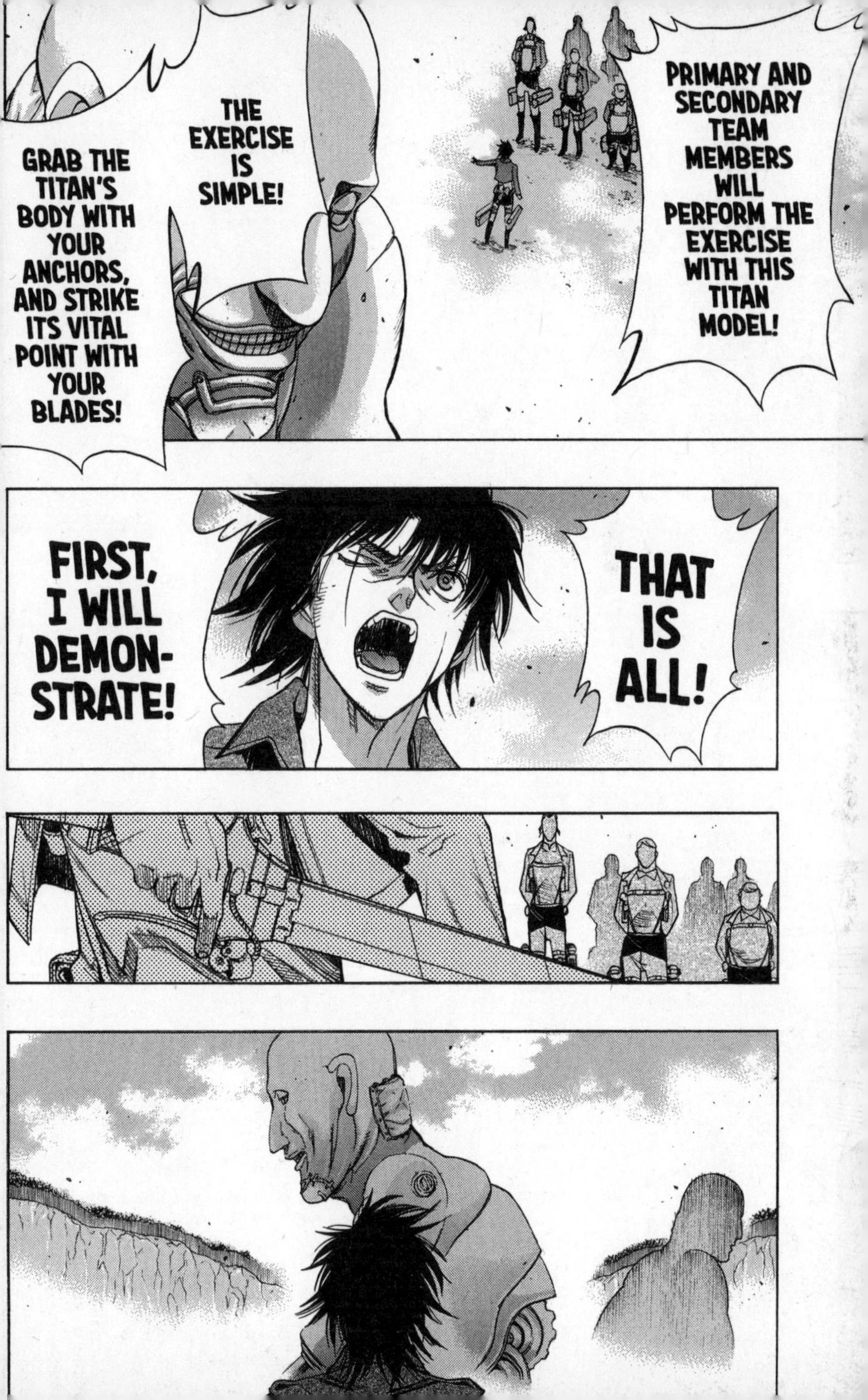
PRIMARY AND SECONDARY TEAM MEMBERS WILL PERFORM THE EXERCISE WITH THIS TITAN MODEL!
THE EXERCISE IS SIMPLE!
GRAB THE TITAN'S BODY WITH YOUR ANCHORS, AND STRIKE ITS VITAL POINT WITH YOUR BLADES!
THAT IS ALL!
FIRST, I WILL DEMON-STRATE!

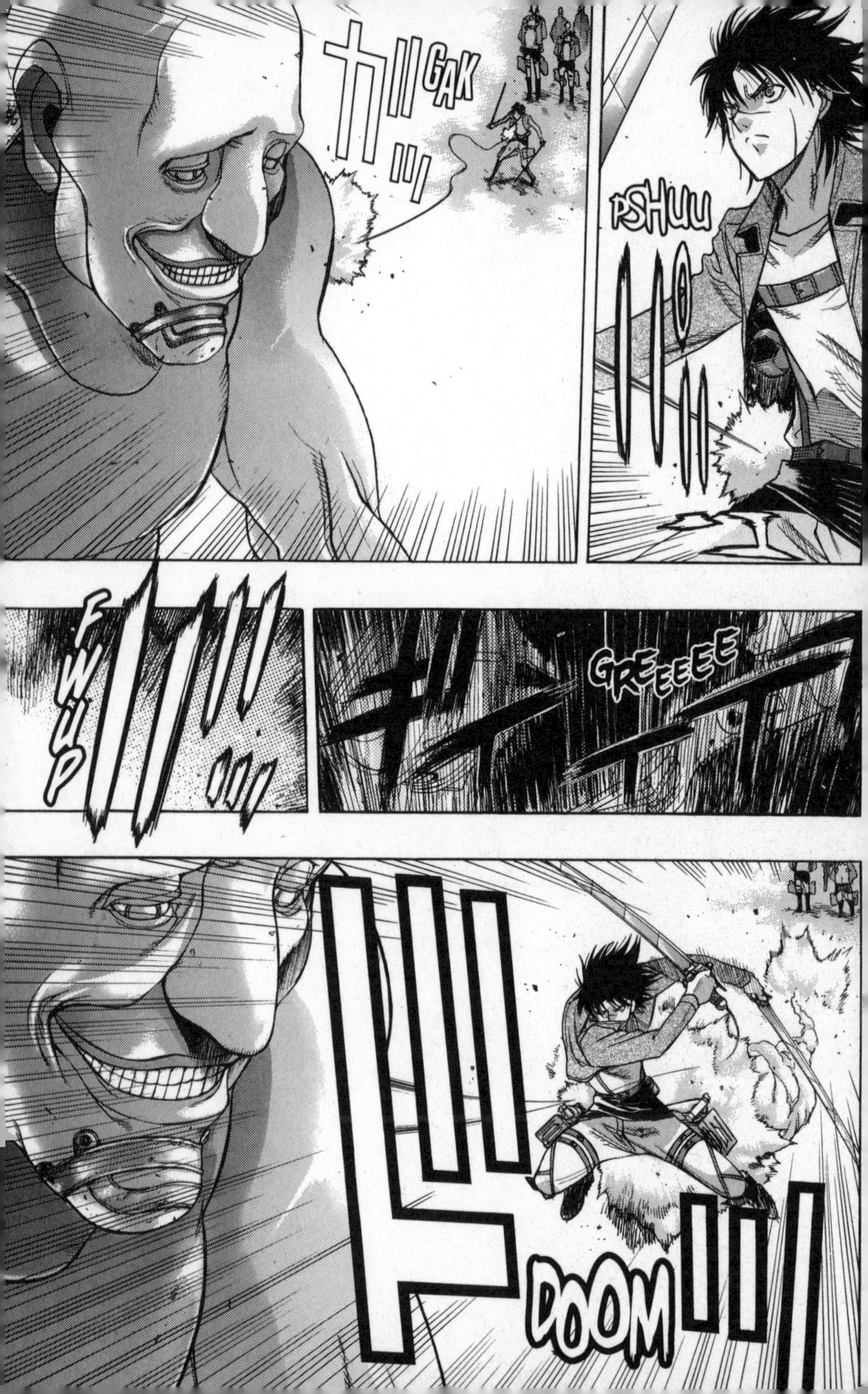
PSHUU
GAK
GREEEEE
FWUP
DOOM

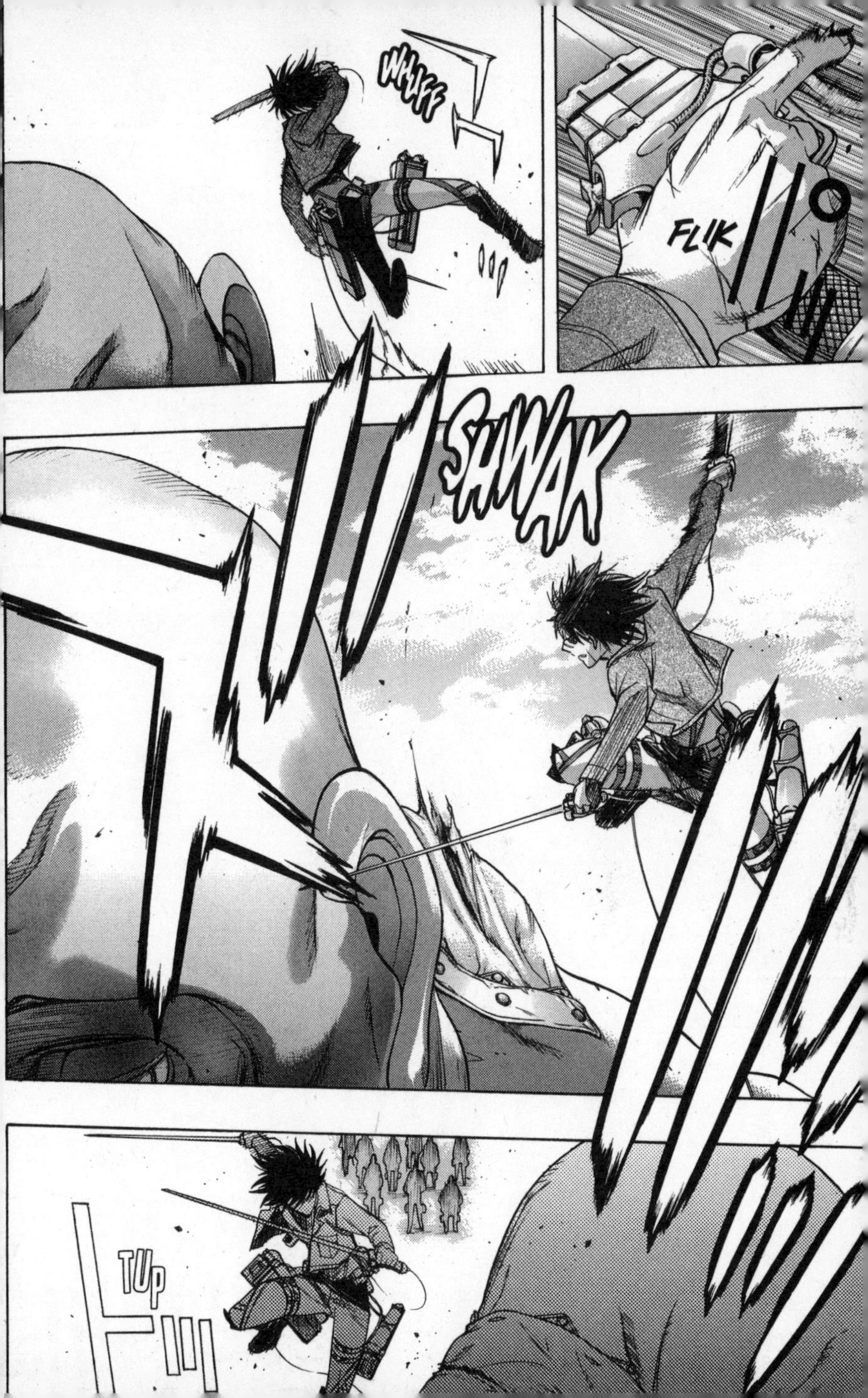
FLIK
WHIFF
SHWAK
TUP

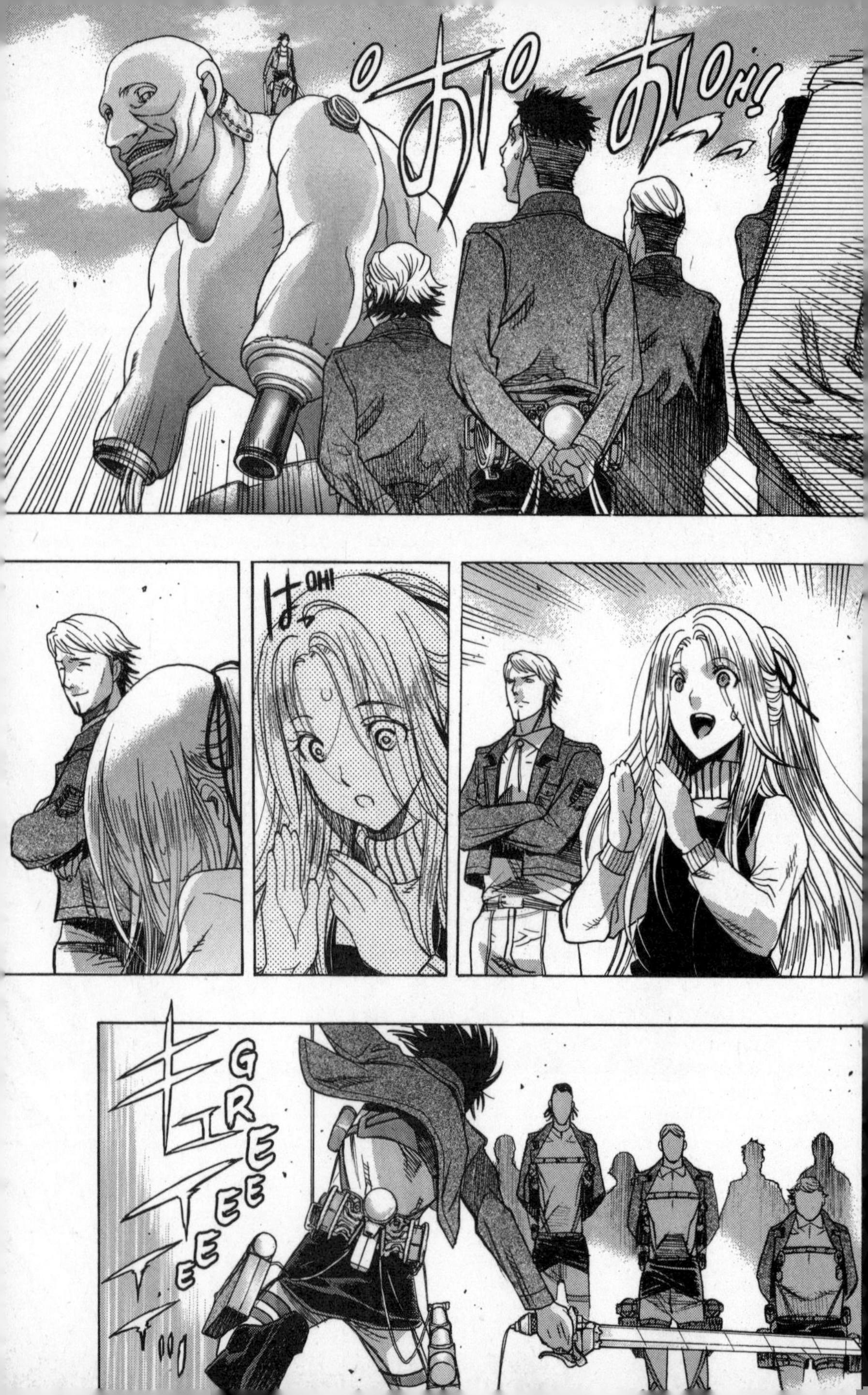

おお
OH!
は
OH!
キィーー
GREEEE

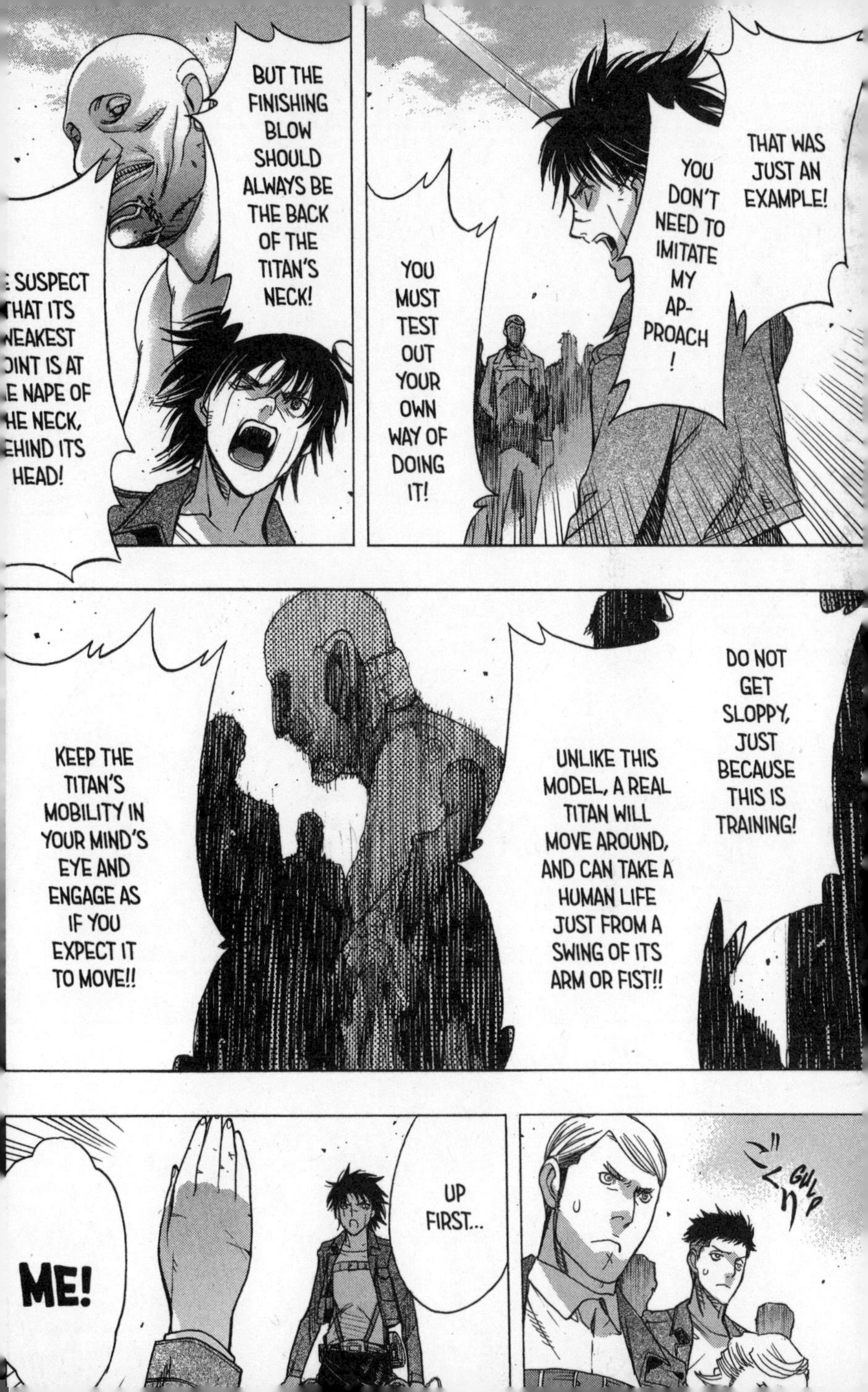
THAT WAS JUST AN EXAMPLE!
YOU DON'T NEED TO IMITATE MY AP- PROACH!
YOU MUST TEST OUT YOUR OWN WAY OF DOING IT!
BUT THE FINISHING BLOW SHOULD ALWAYS BE THE BACK OF THE TITAN'S NECK!
E SUSPECT THAT ITS EAKEST INT IS AT E NAPE OF HE NECK, EHIND ITS HEAD!
DO NOT GET SLOPPY, JUST BECAUSE THIS IS TRAINING!
UNLIKE THIS MODEL, A REAL TITAN WILL MOVE AROUND, AND CAN TAKE A HUMAN LIFE JUST FROM A SWING OF ITS ARM OR FIST!!
KEEP THE TITAN'S MOBILITY IN YOUR MIND'S EYE AND ENGAGE AS IF YOU EXPECT IT TO MOVE!!
ごくり GULP
UP FIRST...
ME!

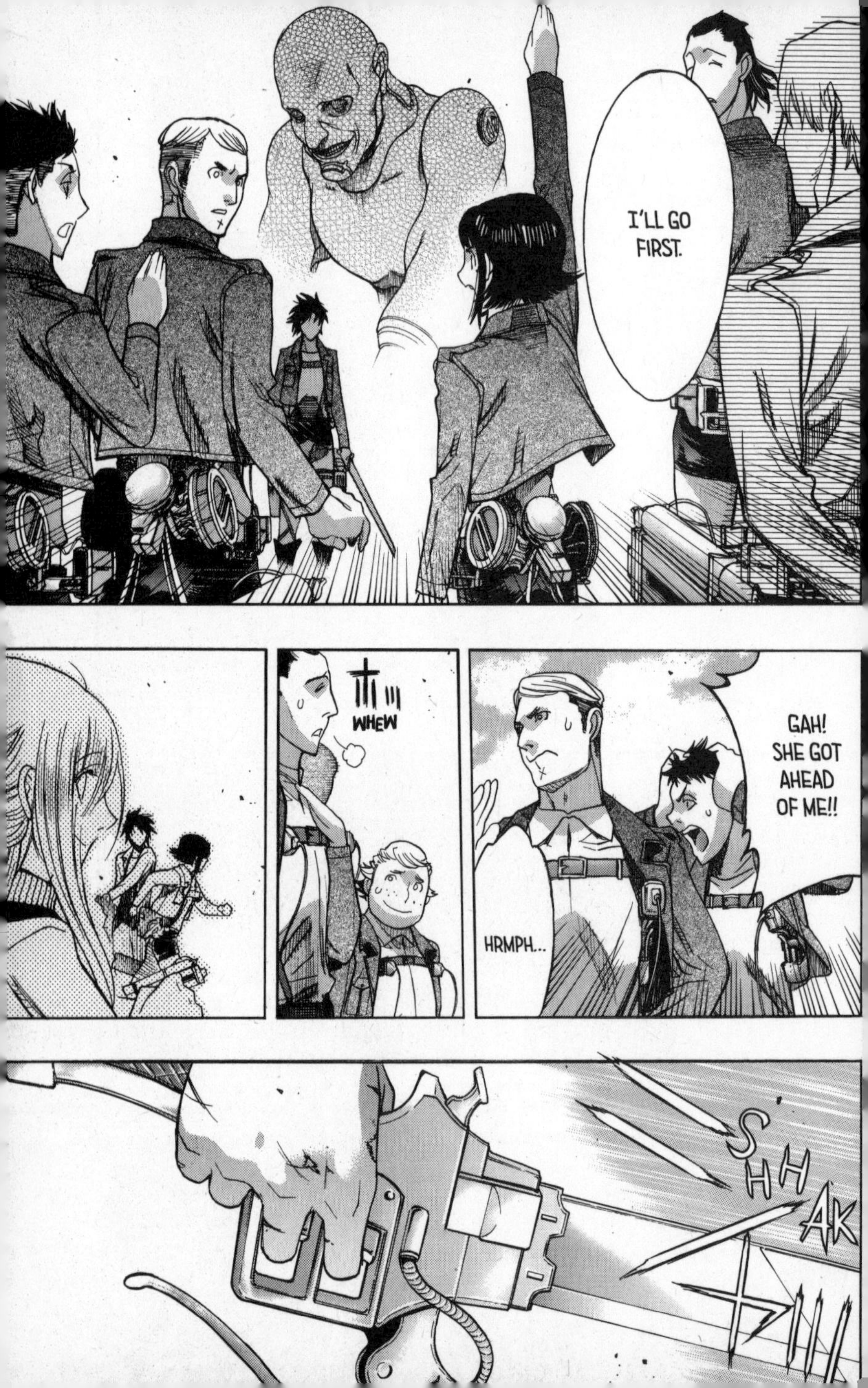
I'LL GO FIRST.
GAH! SHE GOT AHEAD OF ME!!
HRMPH...
WHEW
SHHAK

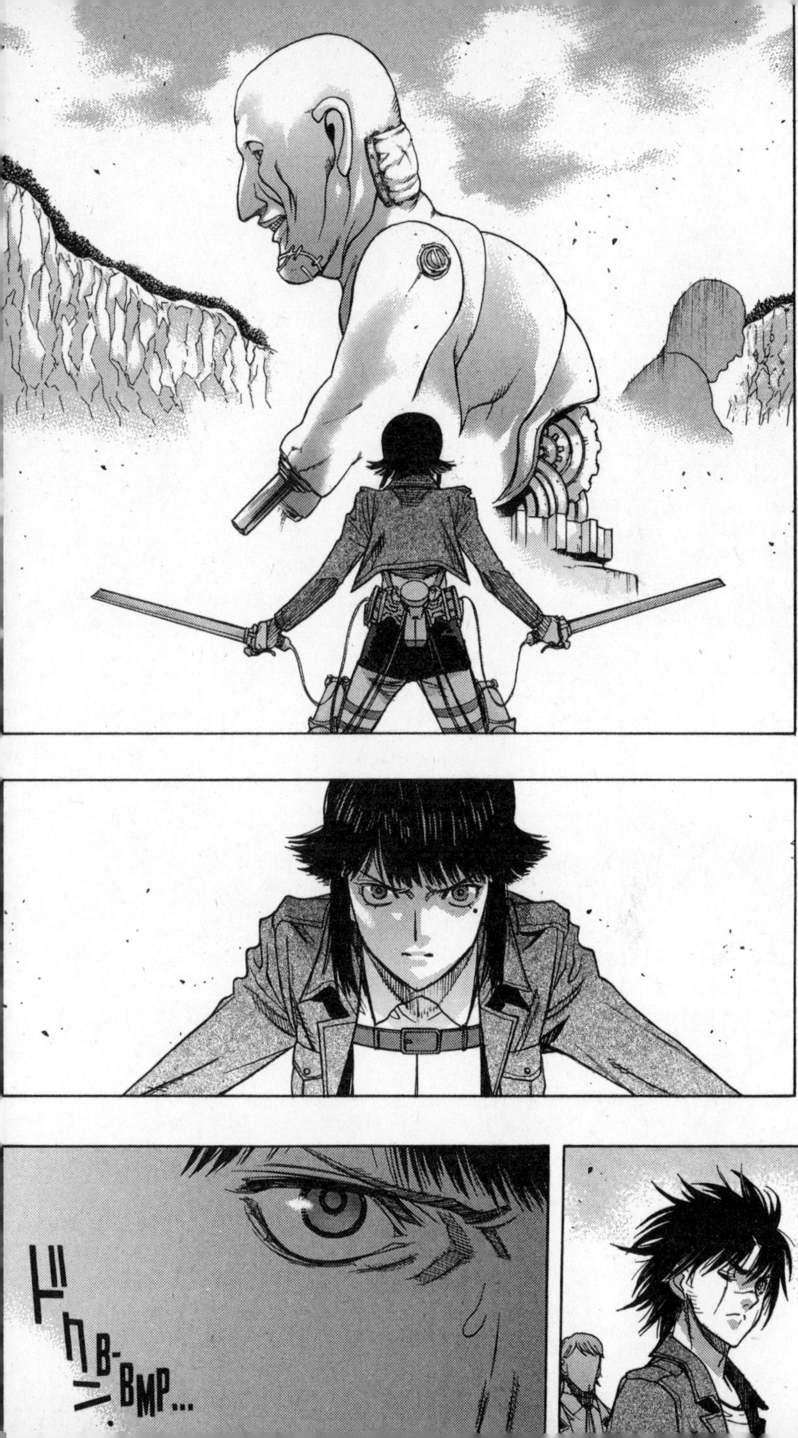

ドクン B-BMP...

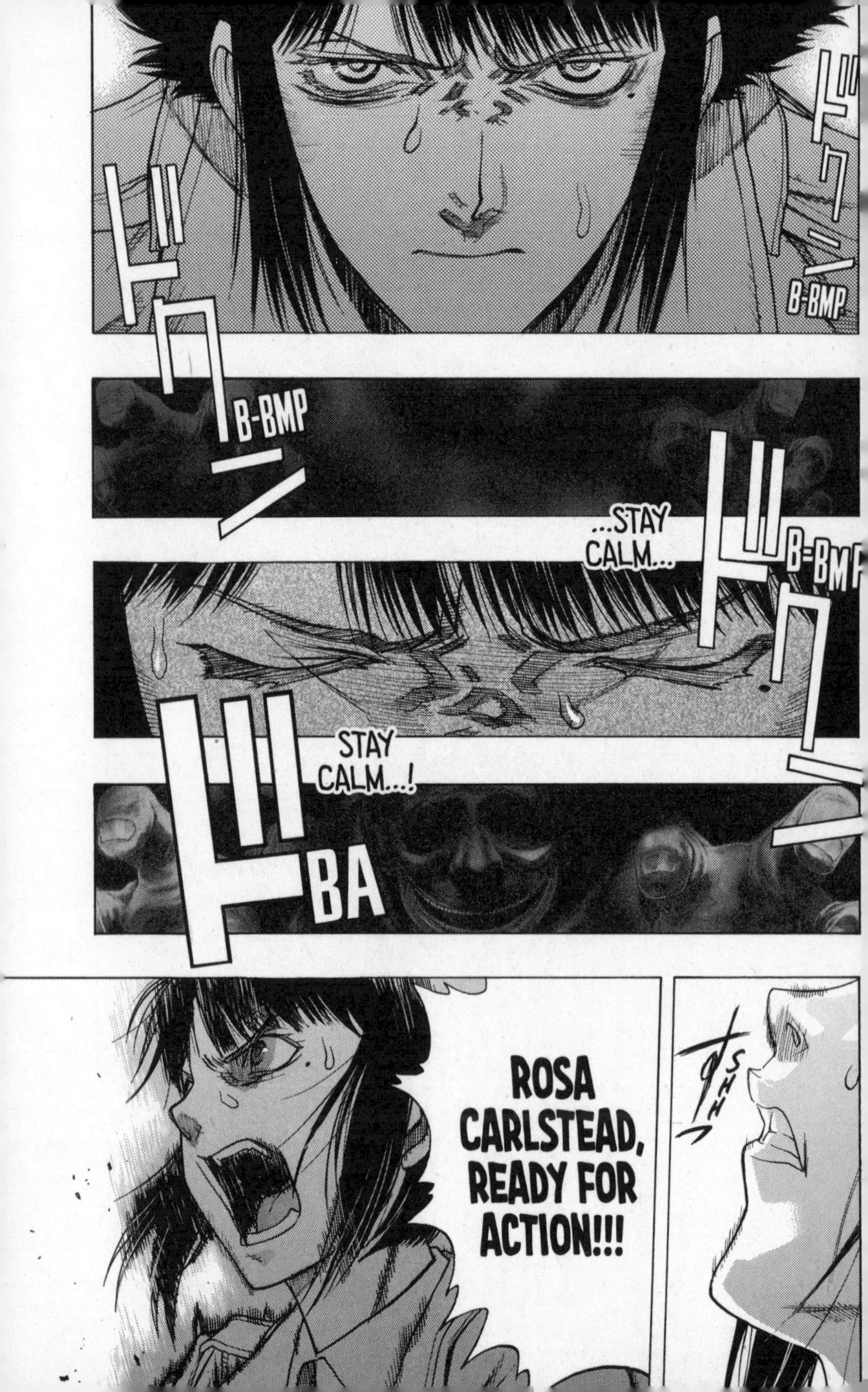
B-BMP
B-BMP
...STAY CALM...
B-BMP
STAY CALM...!
BA
SHH
ROSA CARLSTEAD, READY FOR ACTION!!!

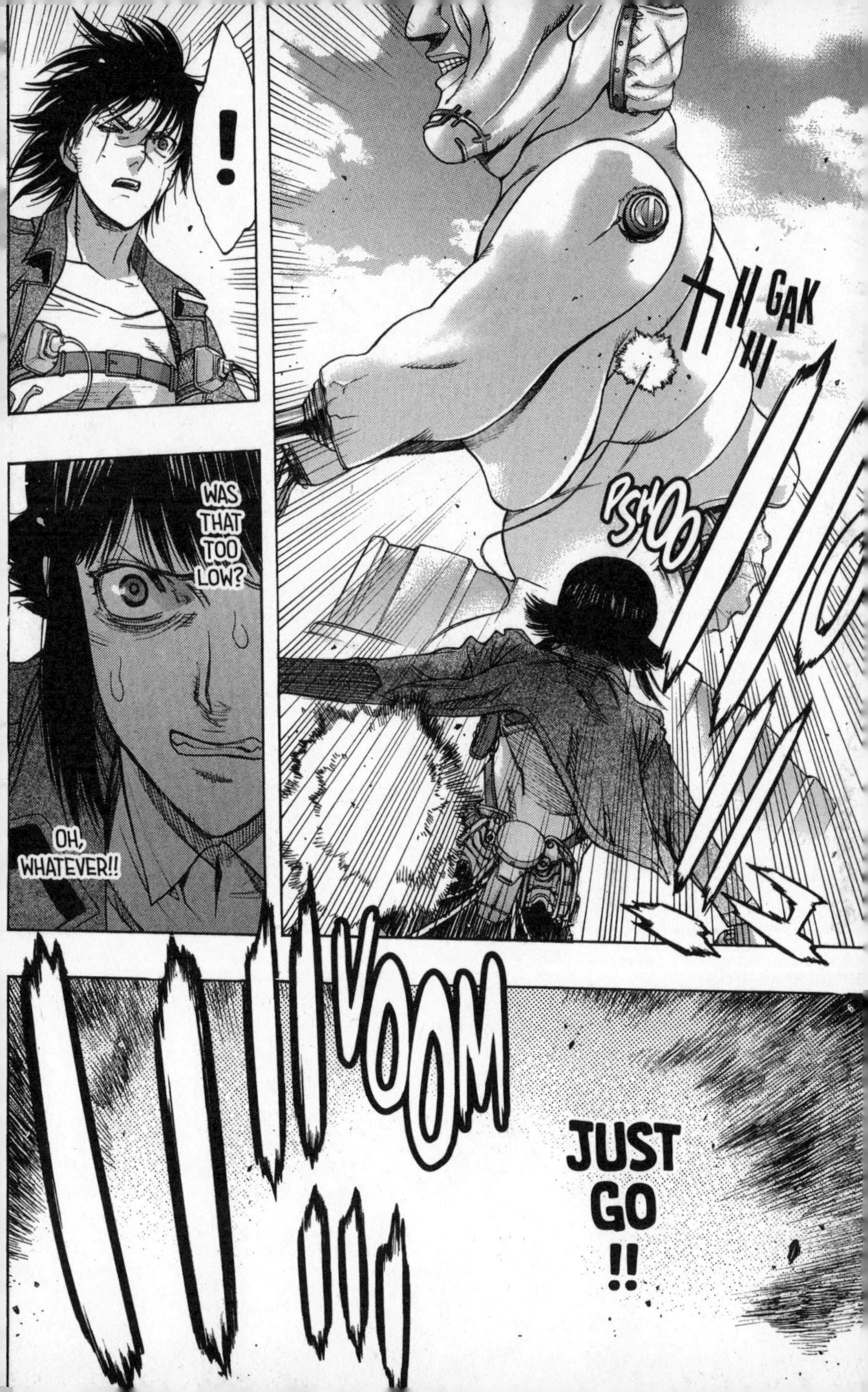
GAK
KI
PSHOO
!
WAS THAT TOO LOW?
OH, WHATEVER!!
VOOM
JUST GO!!

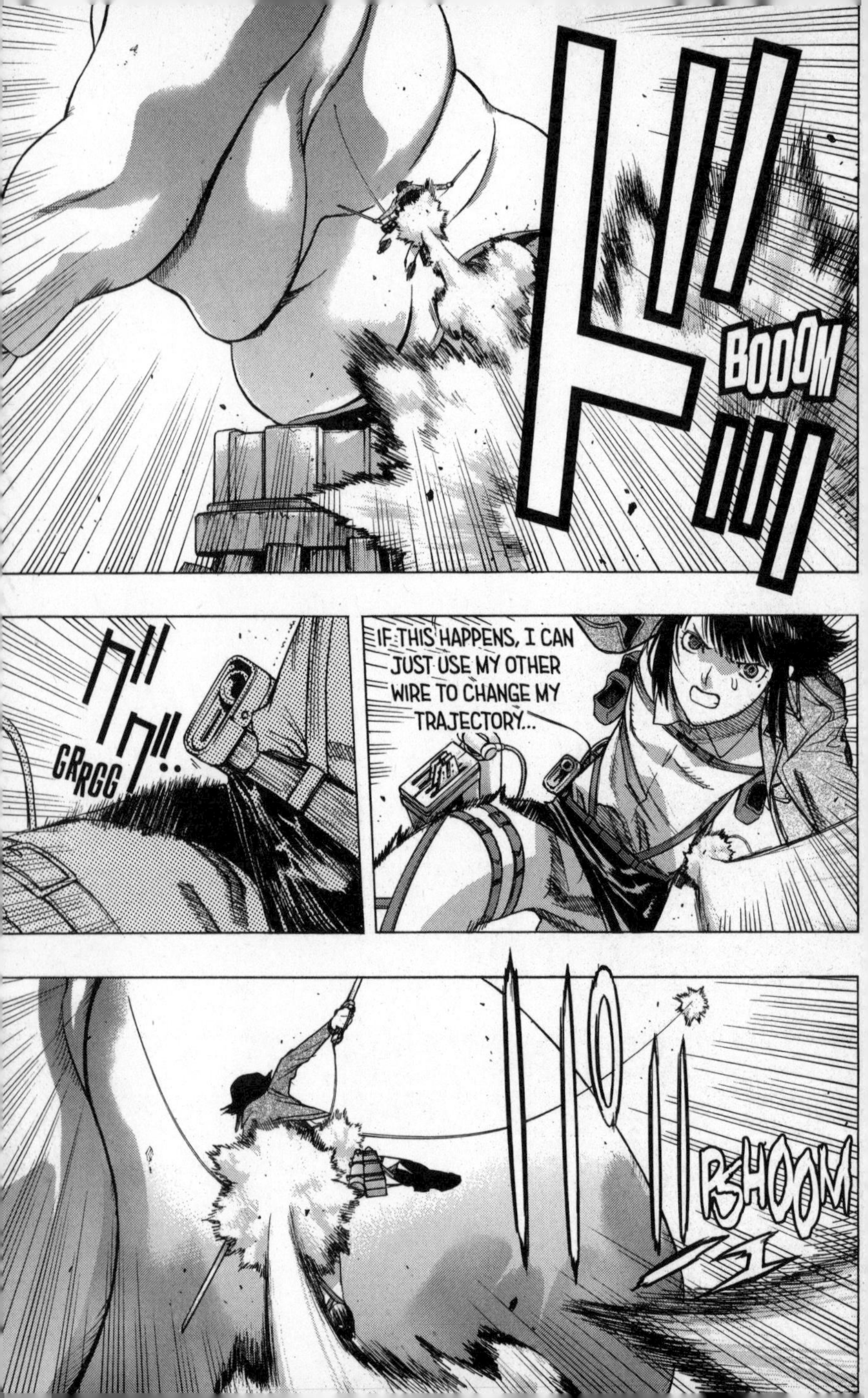
BOOOM
IF THIS HAPPENS, I CAN JUST USE MY OTHER WIRE TO CHANGE MY TRAJECTORY...
GRRGG
BHOOM

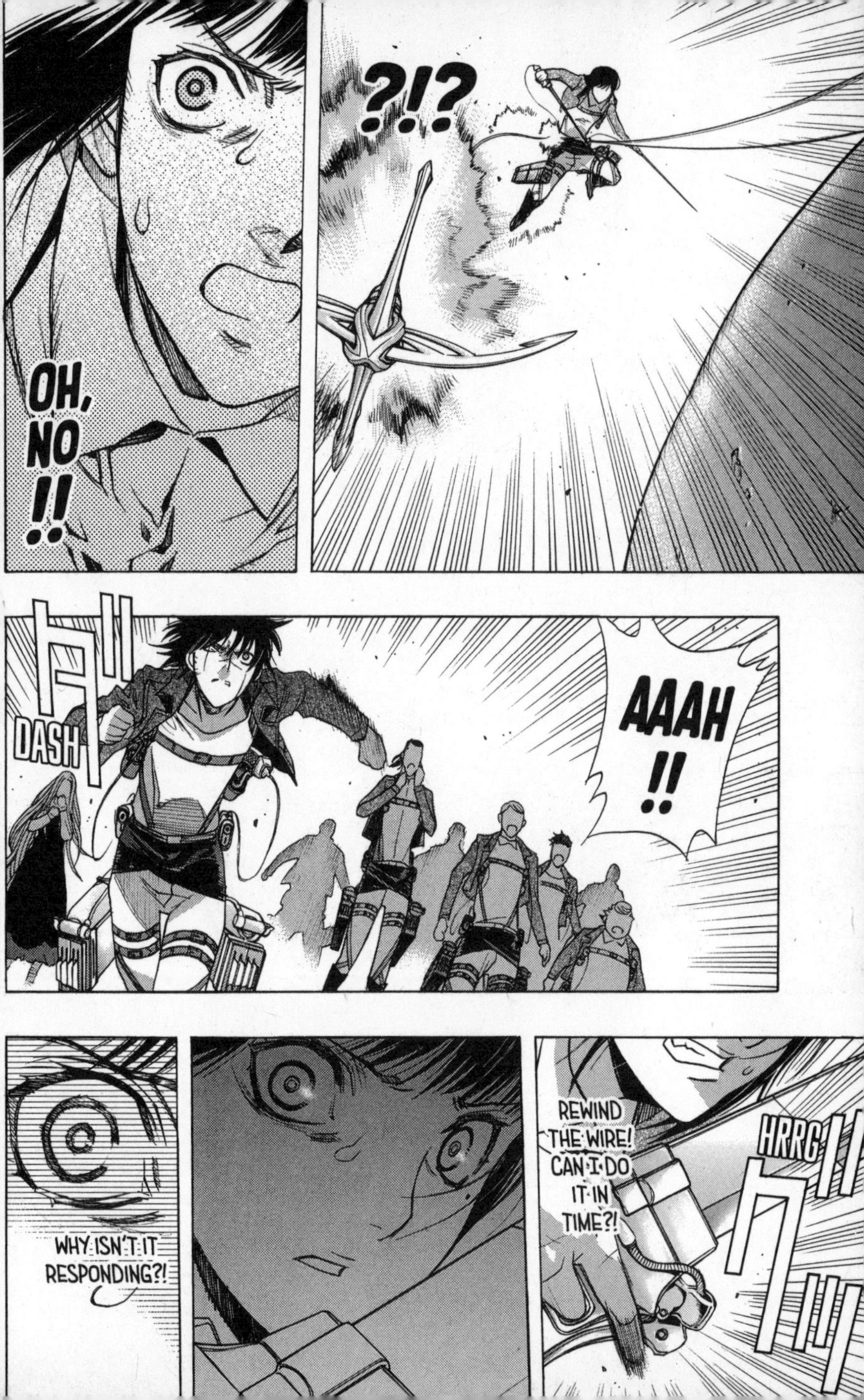
?!?
OH, NO!!
AAAH!!
DASH
REWIND THE WIRE! CAN I DO IT IN TIME?!
HRRG
WHY ISN'T IT RESPONDING?!

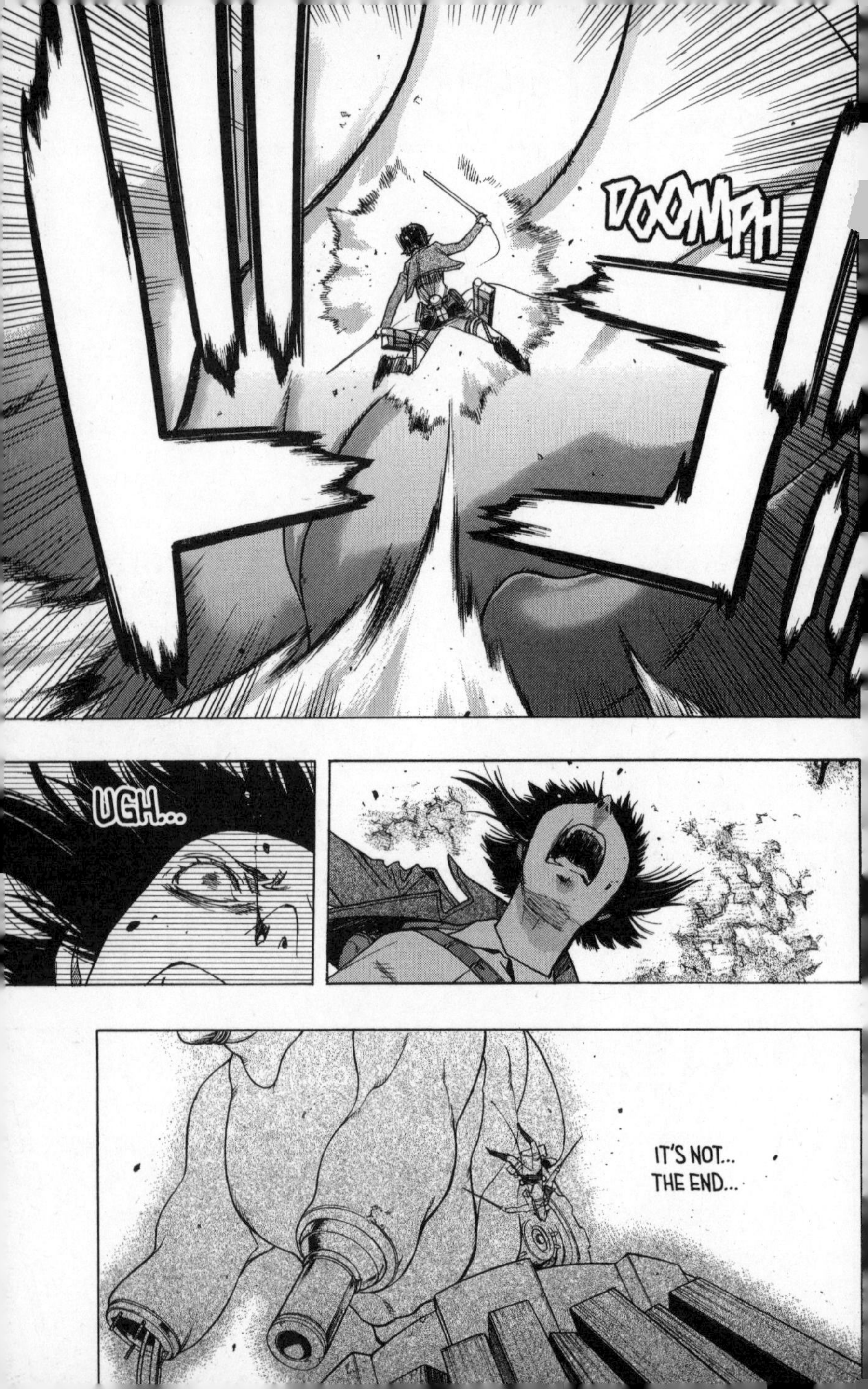
DOOMPH
UGH...
IT'S NOT... THE END...

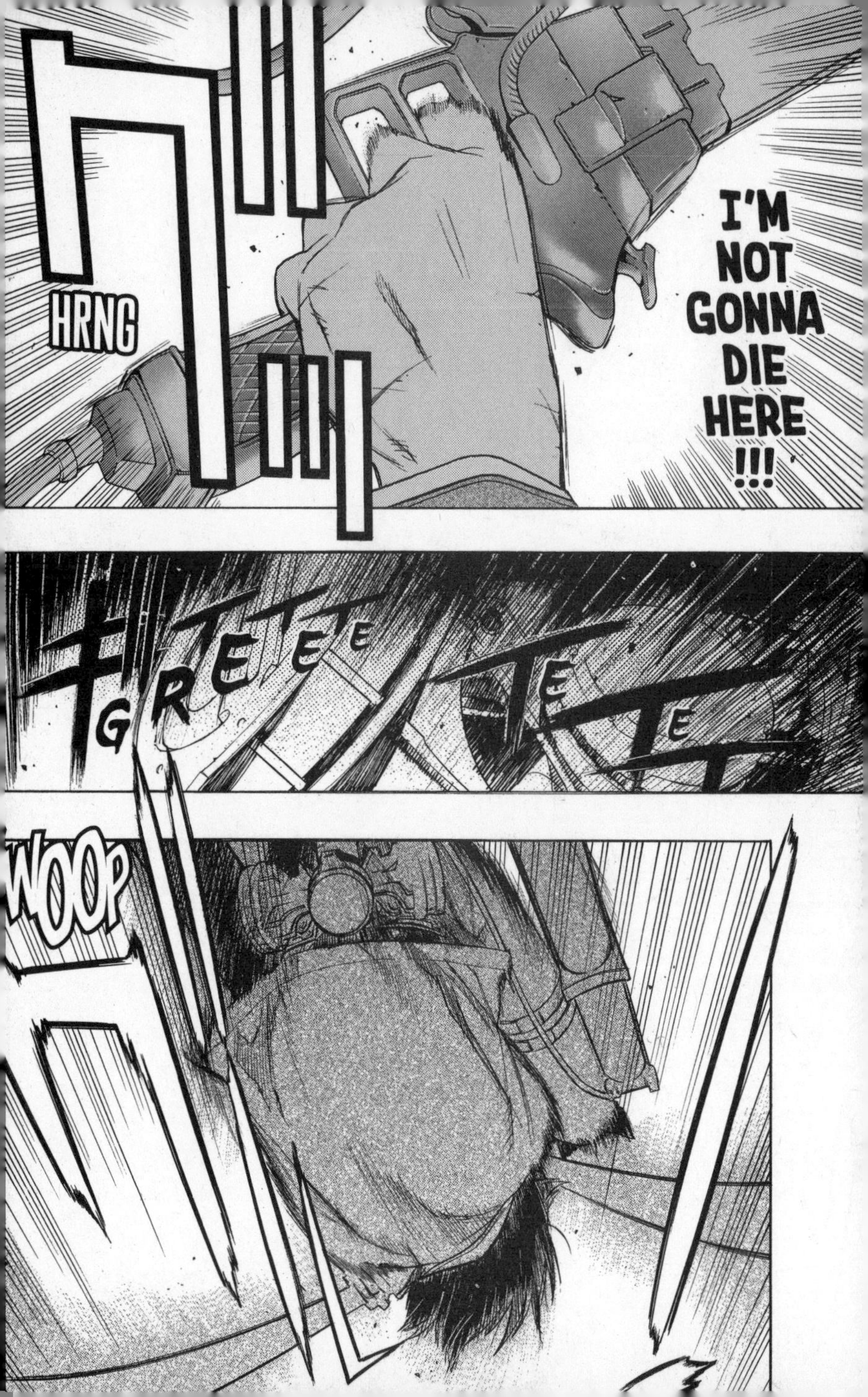

I'M NOT GONNA DIE HERE!!!
HRNG
GREEEE
WOOP

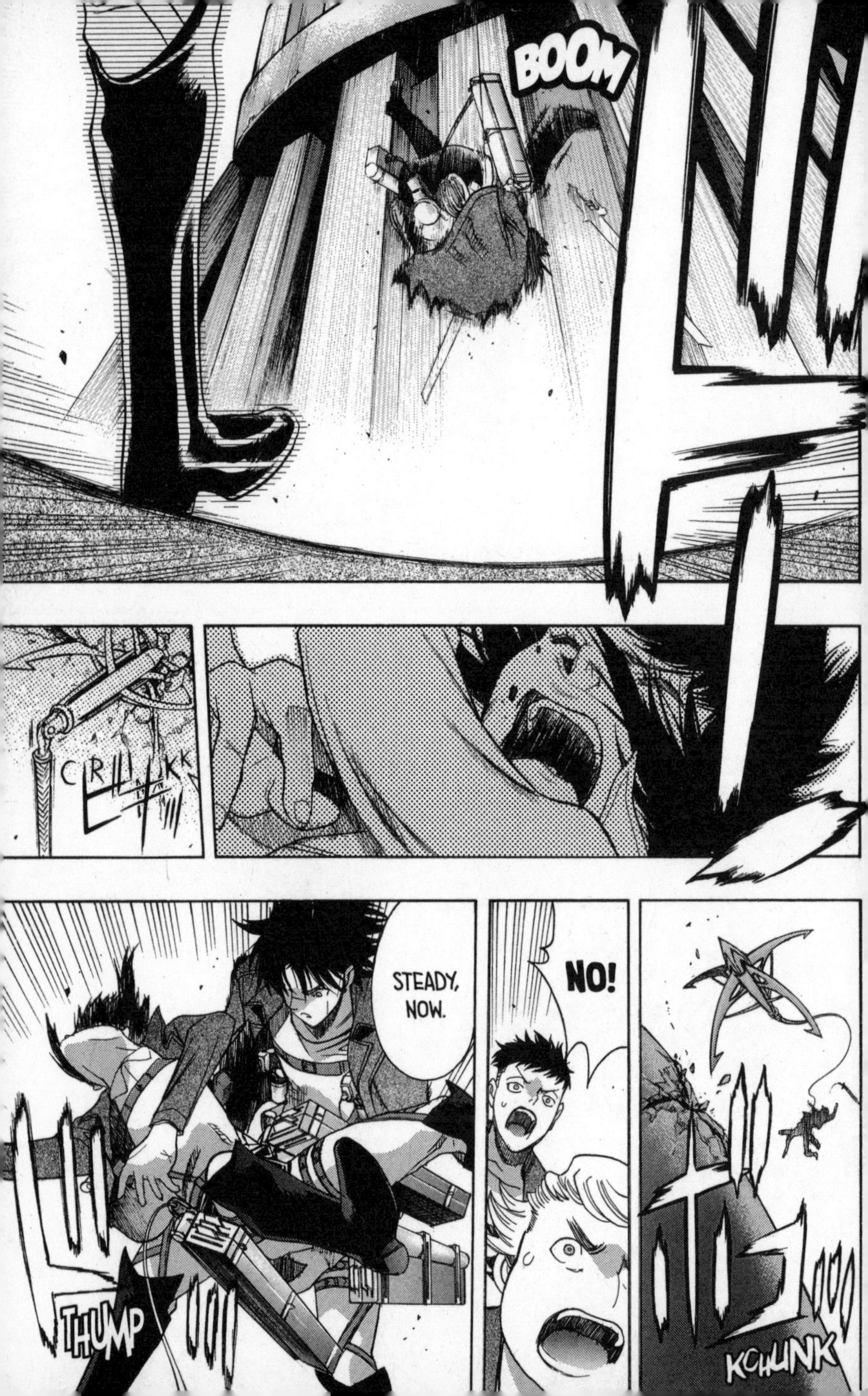
BOOM
CRIKK
KCHUNK
NO!
STEADY, NOW.
THUMP

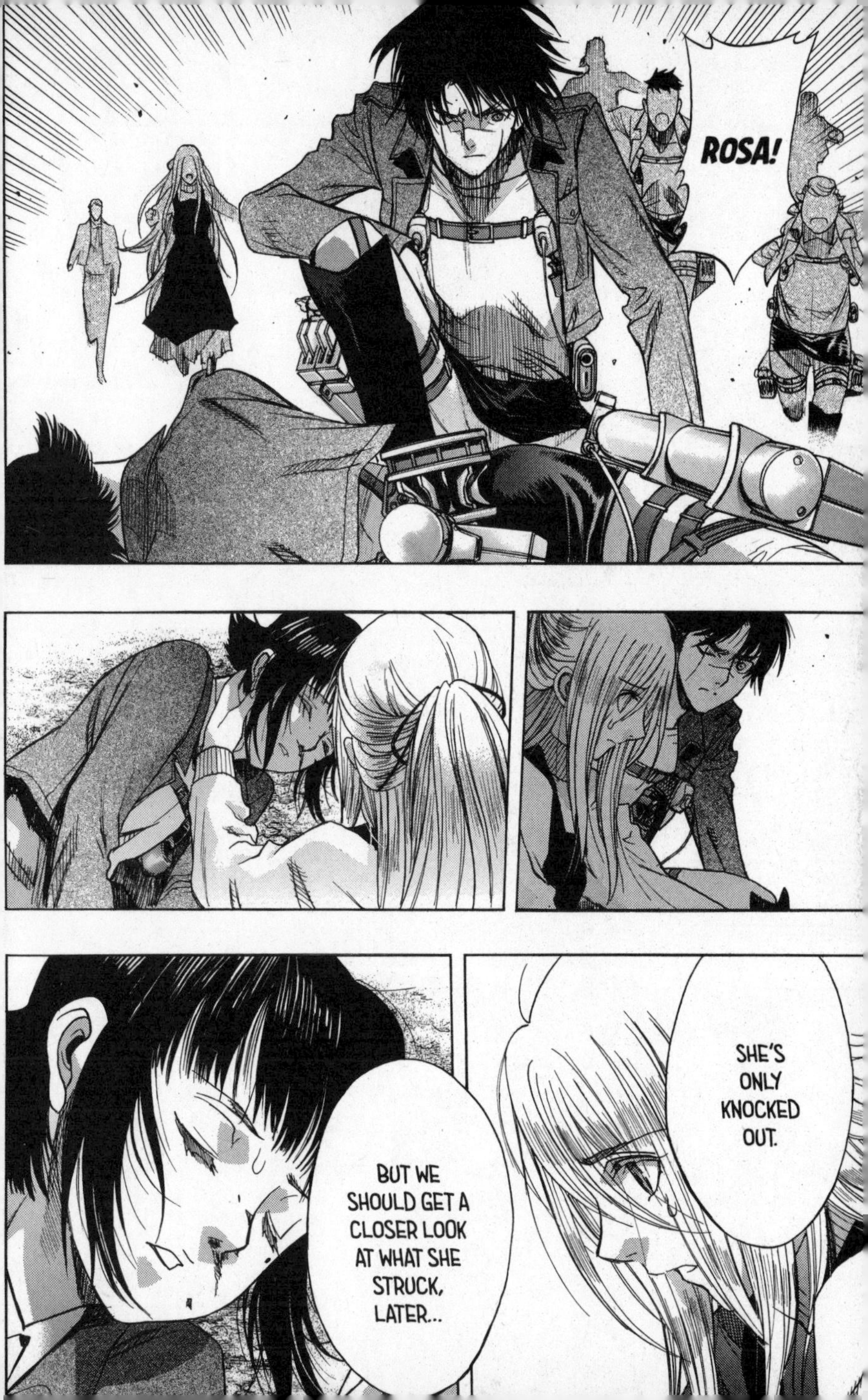
ROSA!
SHE'S ONLY KNOCKED OUT.
BUT WE SHOULD GET A CLOSER LOOK AT WHAT SHE STRUCK, LATER...

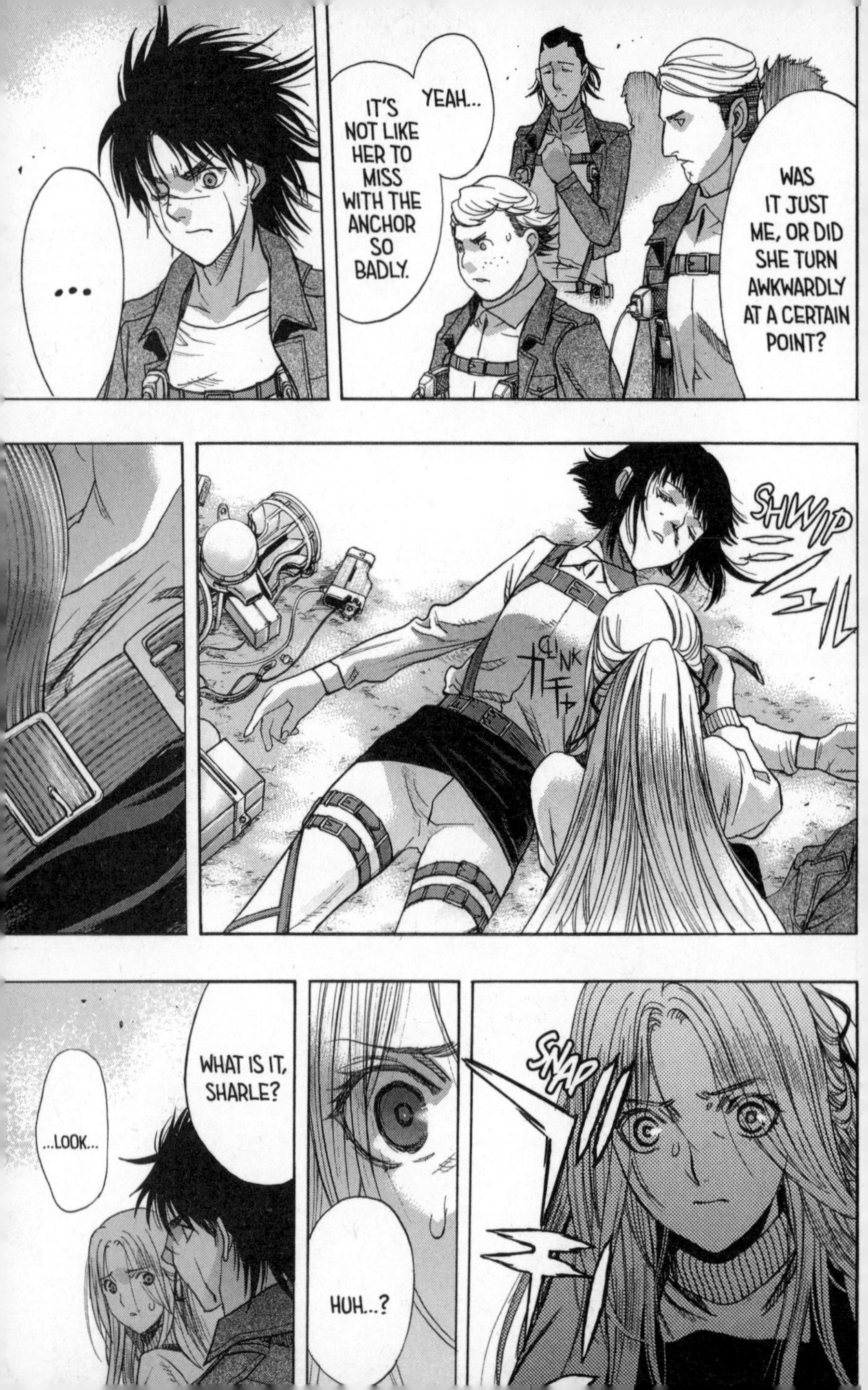
WAS IT JUST ME, OR DID SHE TURN AWKWARDLY AT A CERTAIN POINT?
YEAH...
IT'S NOT LIKE HER TO MISS WITH THE ANCHOR SO BADLY.
...
SHWIP
CLINK
SNAP
HUH...?
WHAT IS IT, SHARLE?
...LOOK...

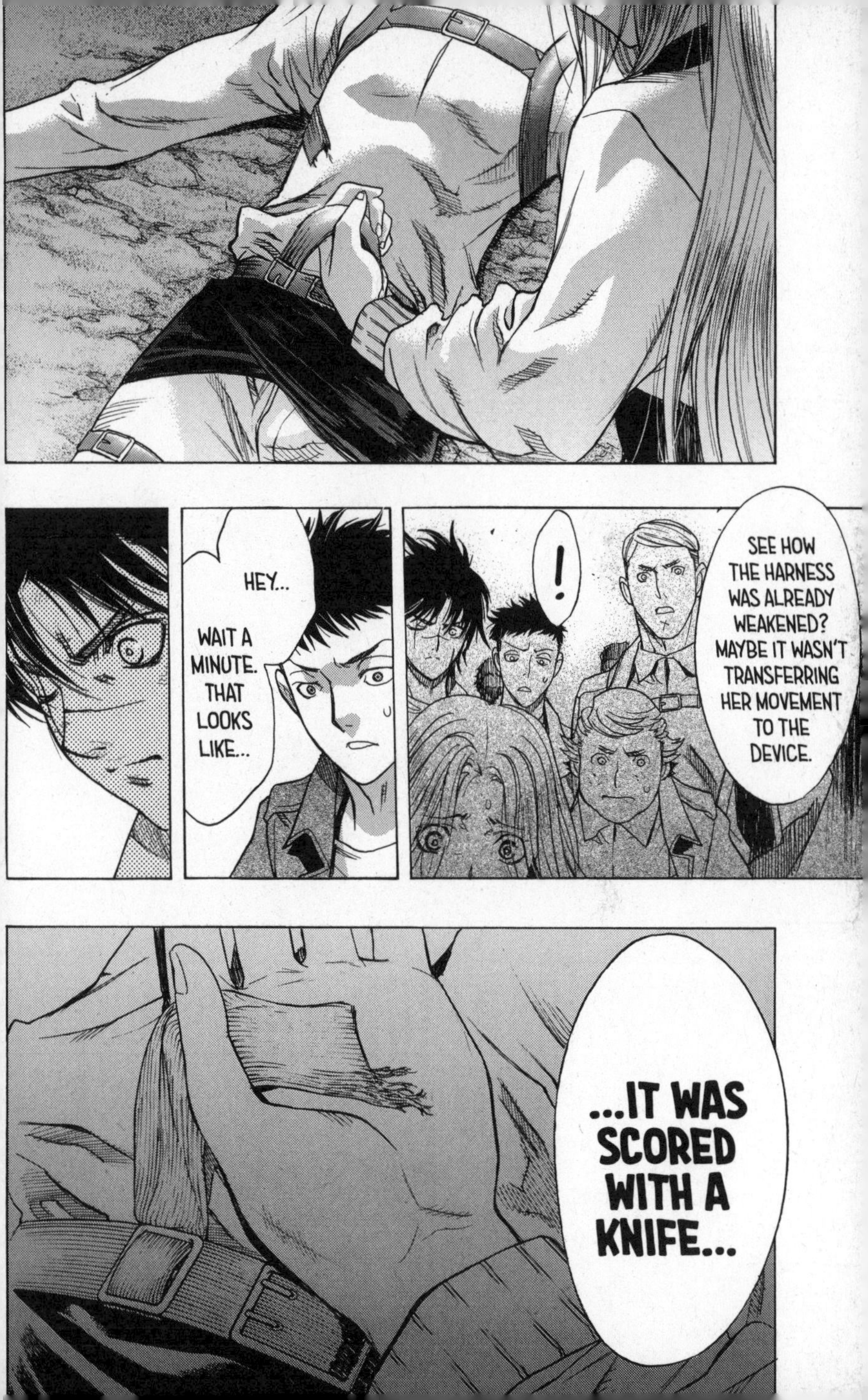
SEE HOW THE HARNESS WAS ALREADY WEAKENED? MAYBE IT WASN'T TRANSFERRING HER MOVEMENT TO THE DEVICE.
!
HEY...
WAIT A MINUTE. THAT LOOKS LIKE...
...IT WAS SCORED WITH A KNIFE...

Chapter 53: Setback at the Initiation · End

ATTACK on TITAN
BEFORE THE FALL

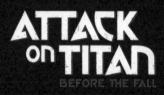

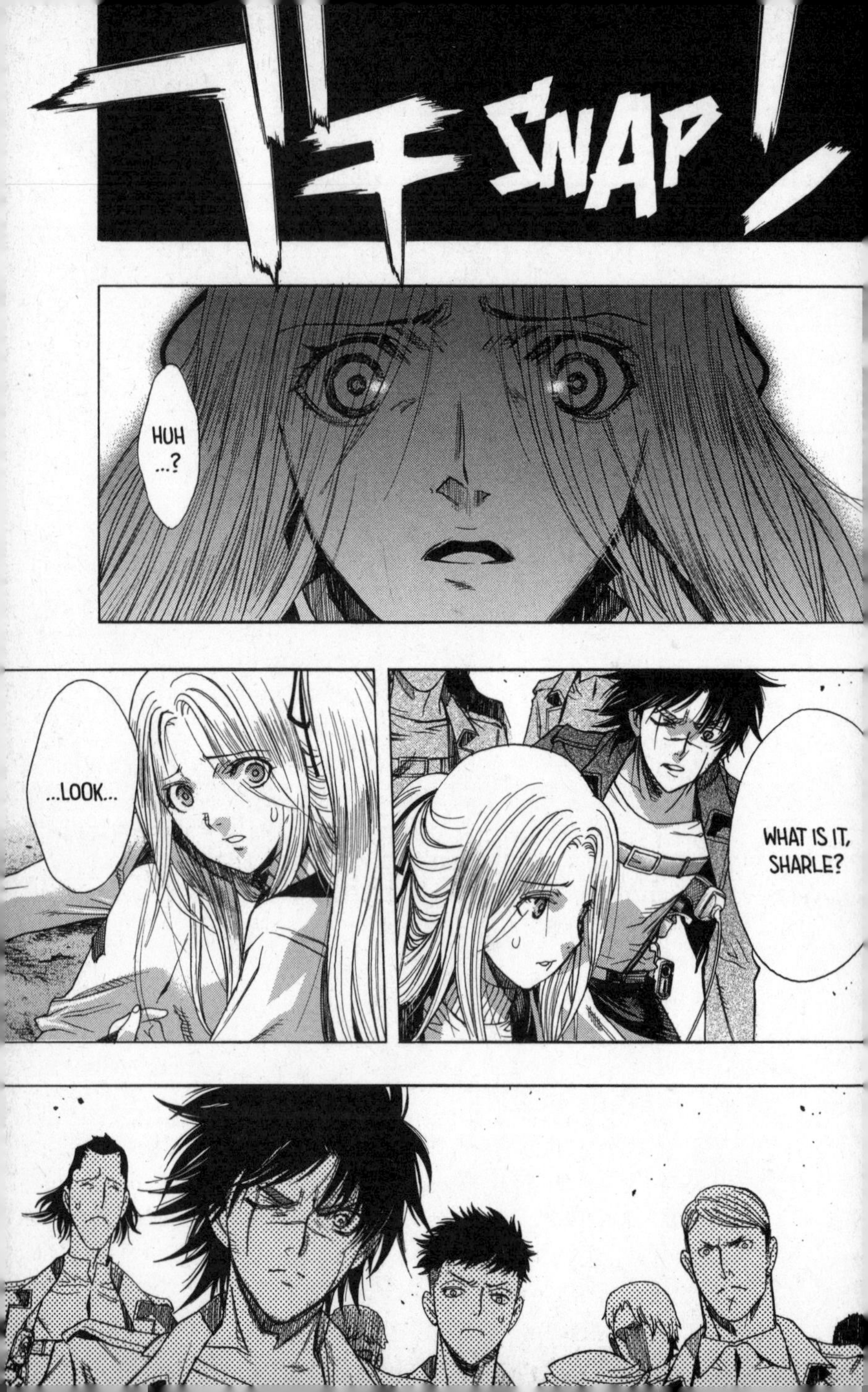
ブチ
SNAP
HUH ...?
WHAT IS IT, SHARLE?
...LOOK...

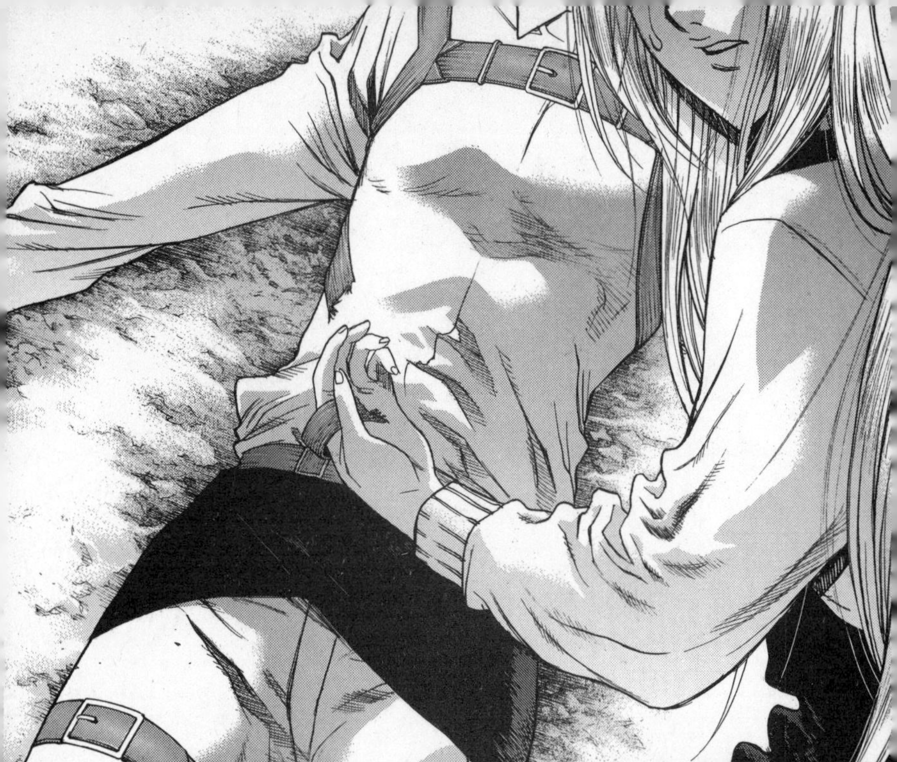
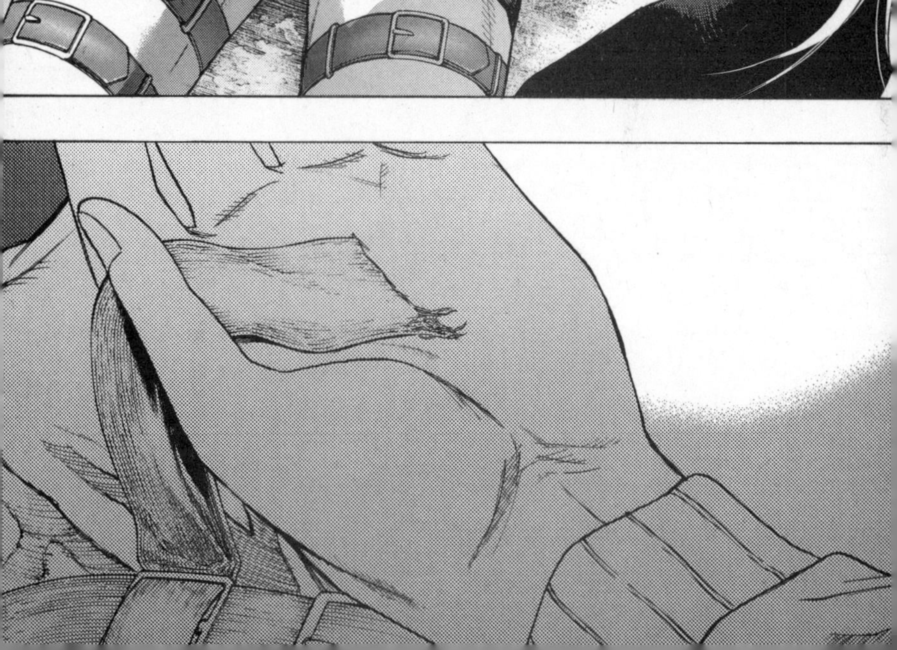

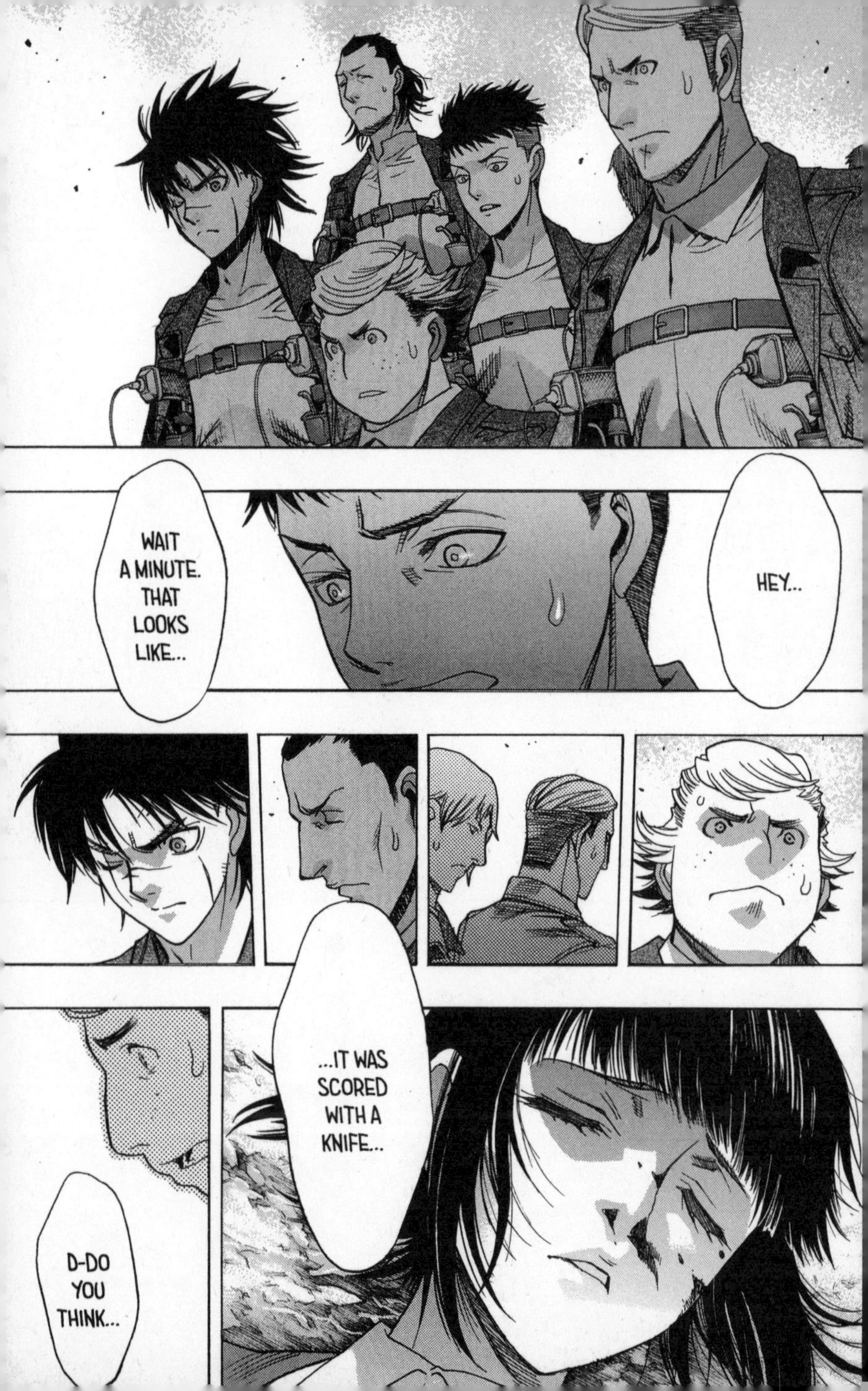
HEY...
WAIT A MINUTE. THAT LOOKS LIKE...
...IT WAS SCORED WITH A KNIFE...
D-DO YOU THINK...

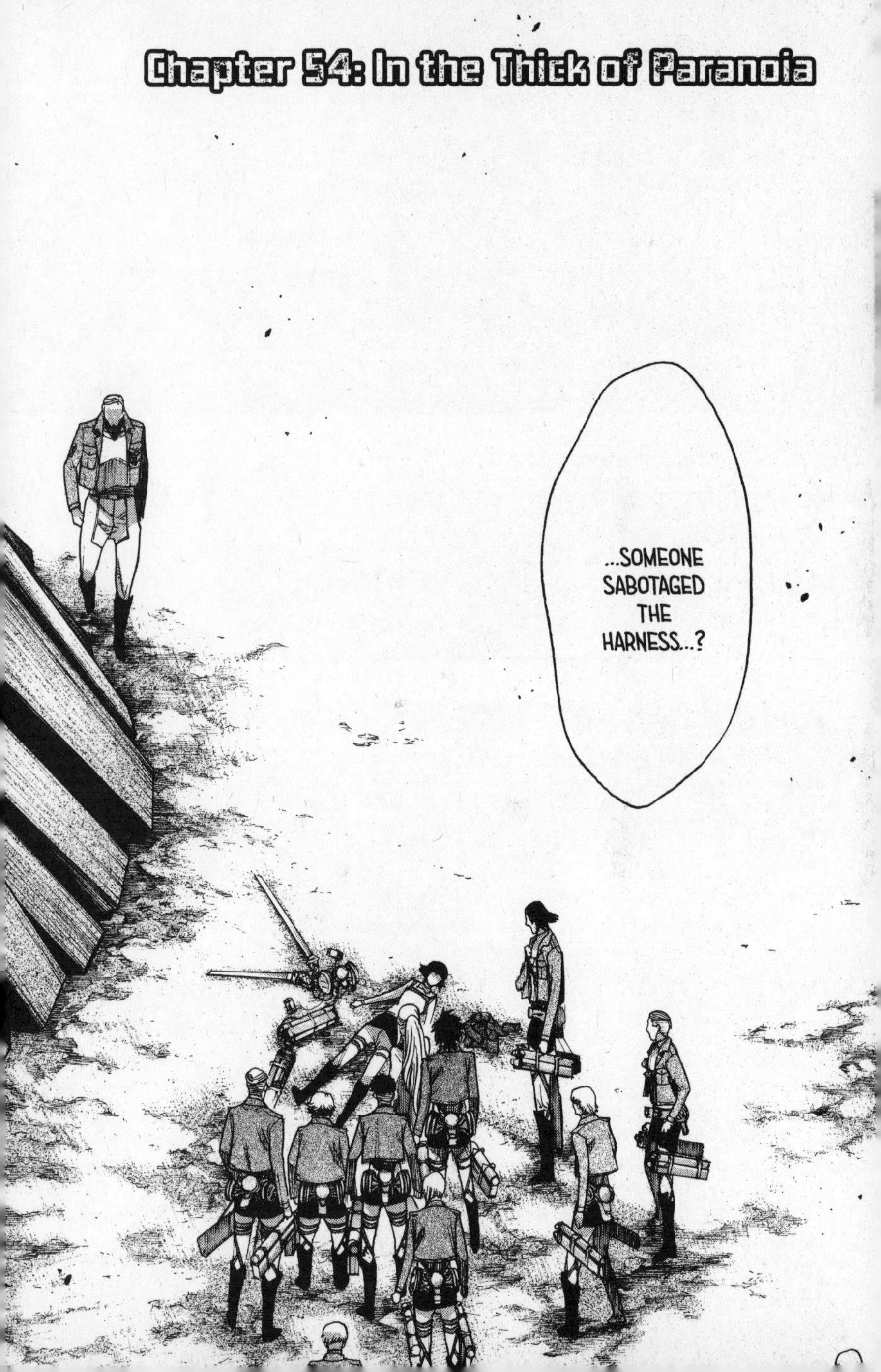
Chapter 54: In the Thick of Paranoia
...SOMEONE SABOTAGED THE HARNESS...?

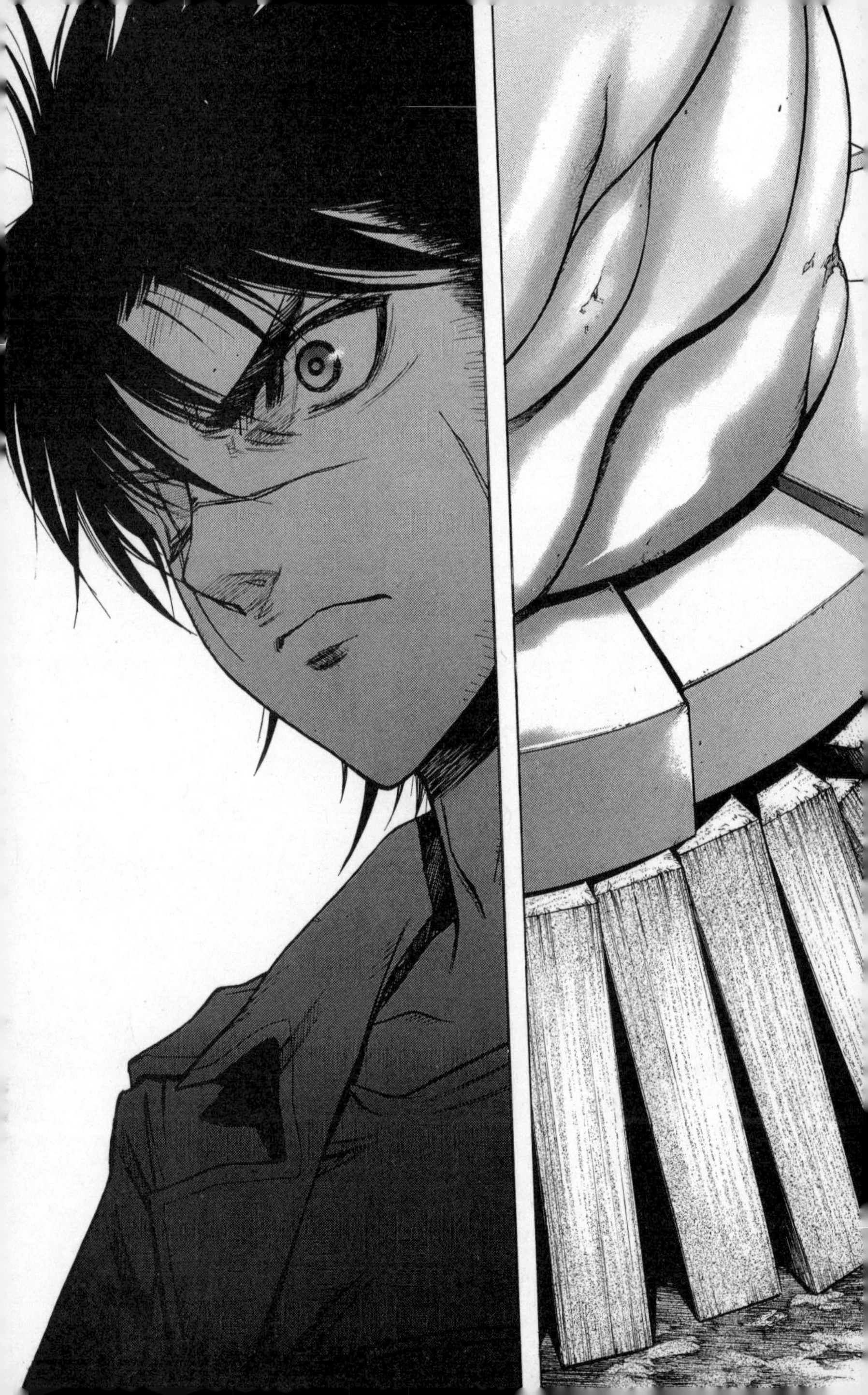

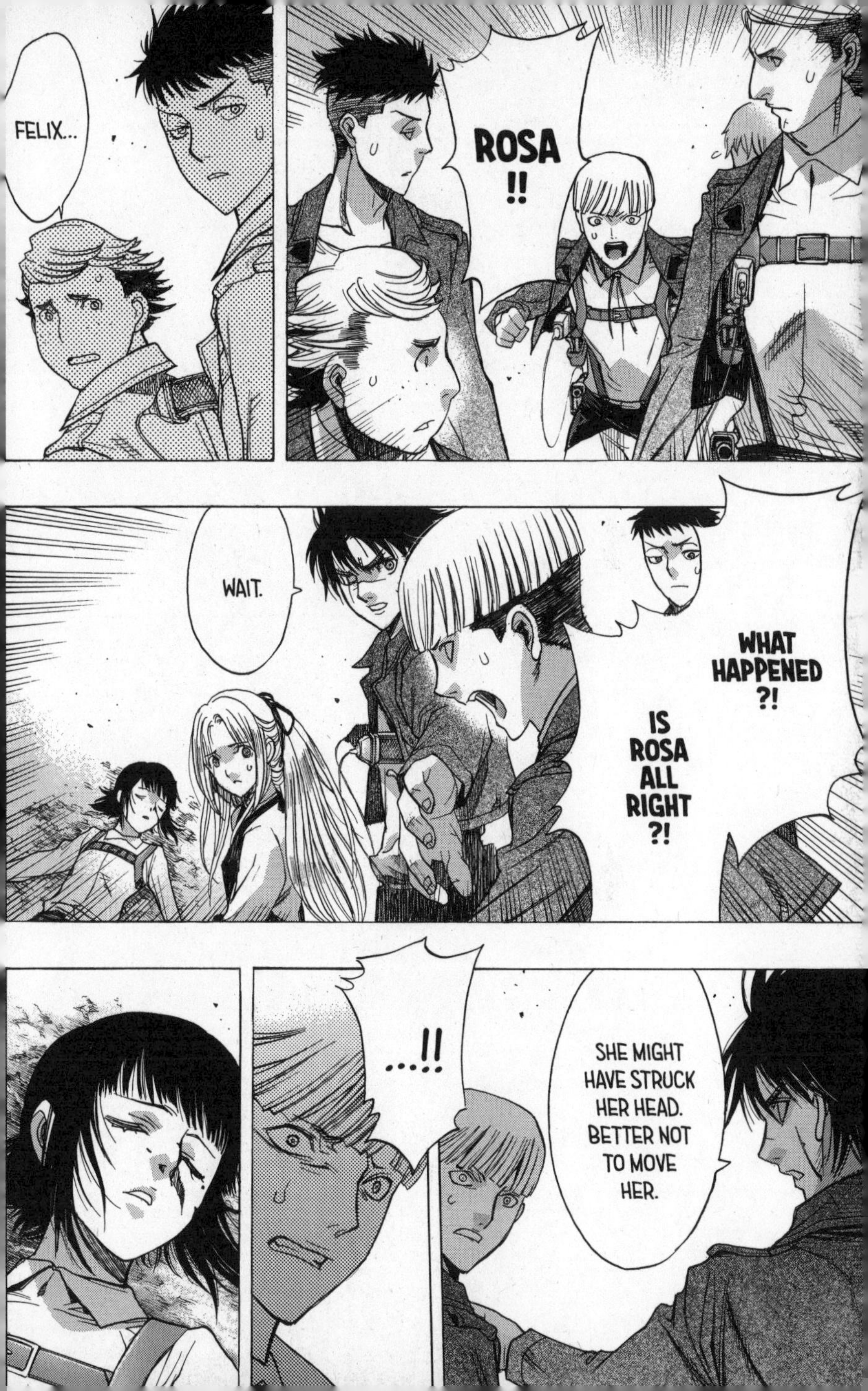
ROSA !!
FELIX...
WHAT HAPPENED ?!
IS ROSA ALL RIGHT ?!
WAIT.
SHE MIGHT HAVE STRUCK HER HEAD. BETTER NOT TO MOVE HER.
...!!

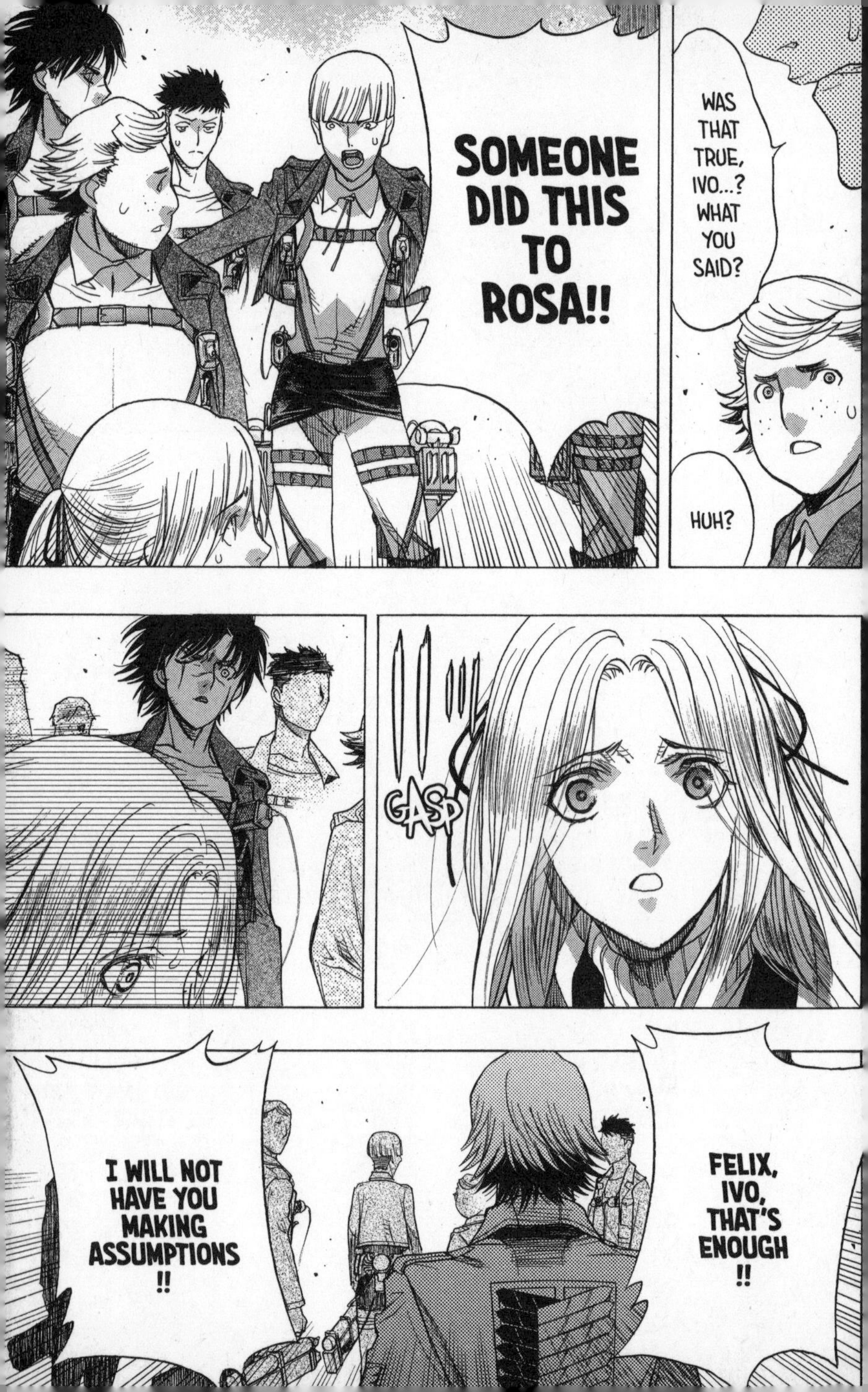
WAS THAT TRUE, IVO...? WHAT YOU SAID?
HUH?
SOMEONE DID THIS TO ROSA!!
GASP
FELIX, IVO, THAT'S ENOUGH!!
I WILL NOT HAVE YOU MAKING ASSUMPTIONS!!

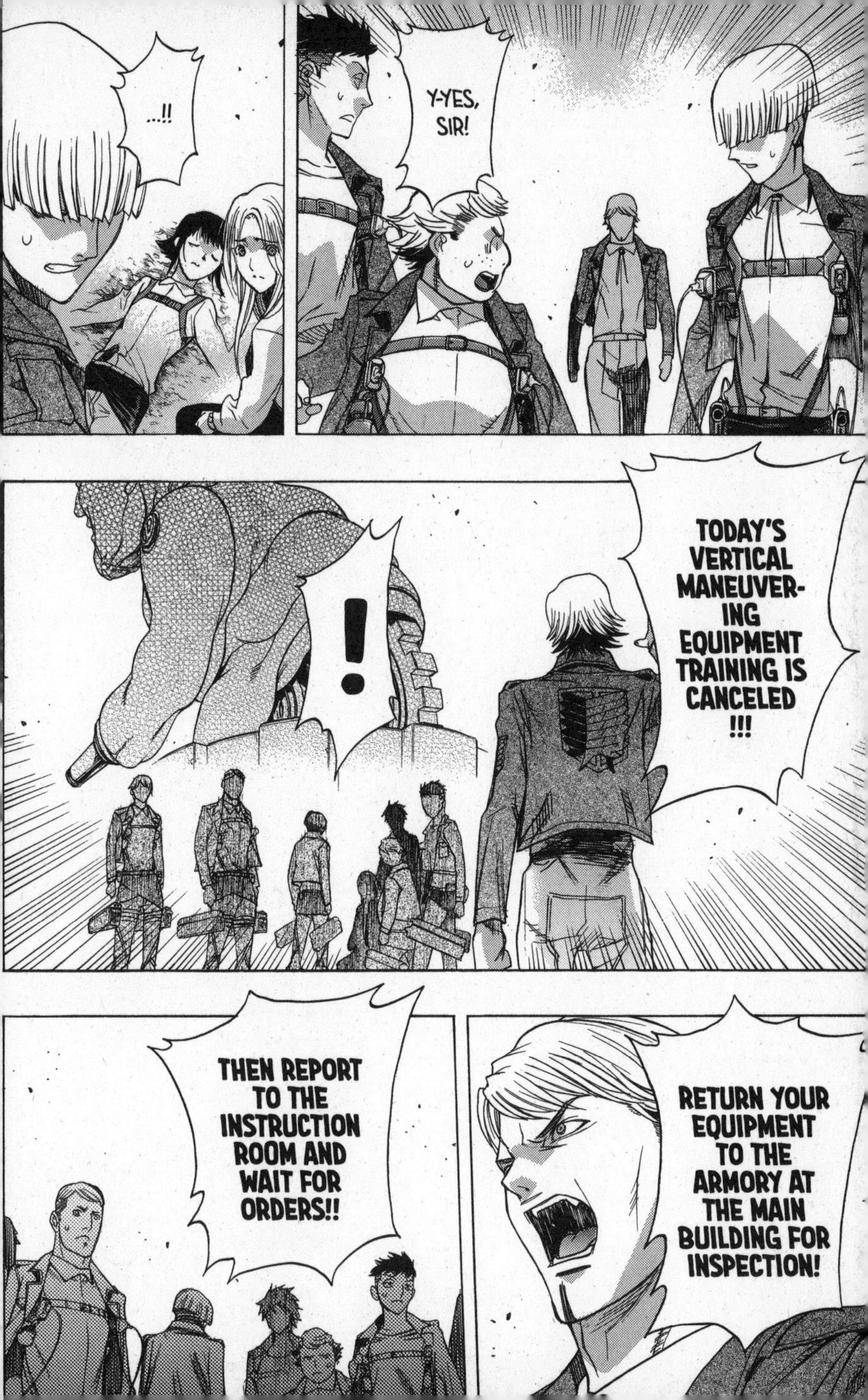
Y-YES, SIR!
...!!
TODAY'S VERTICAL MANEUVER-ING EQUIPMENT TRAINING IS CANCELED !!!
!
RETURN YOUR EQUIPMENT TO THE ARMORY AT THE MAIN BUILDING FOR INSPECTION!
THEN REPORT TO THE INSTRUCTION ROOM AND WAIT FOR ORDERS!!

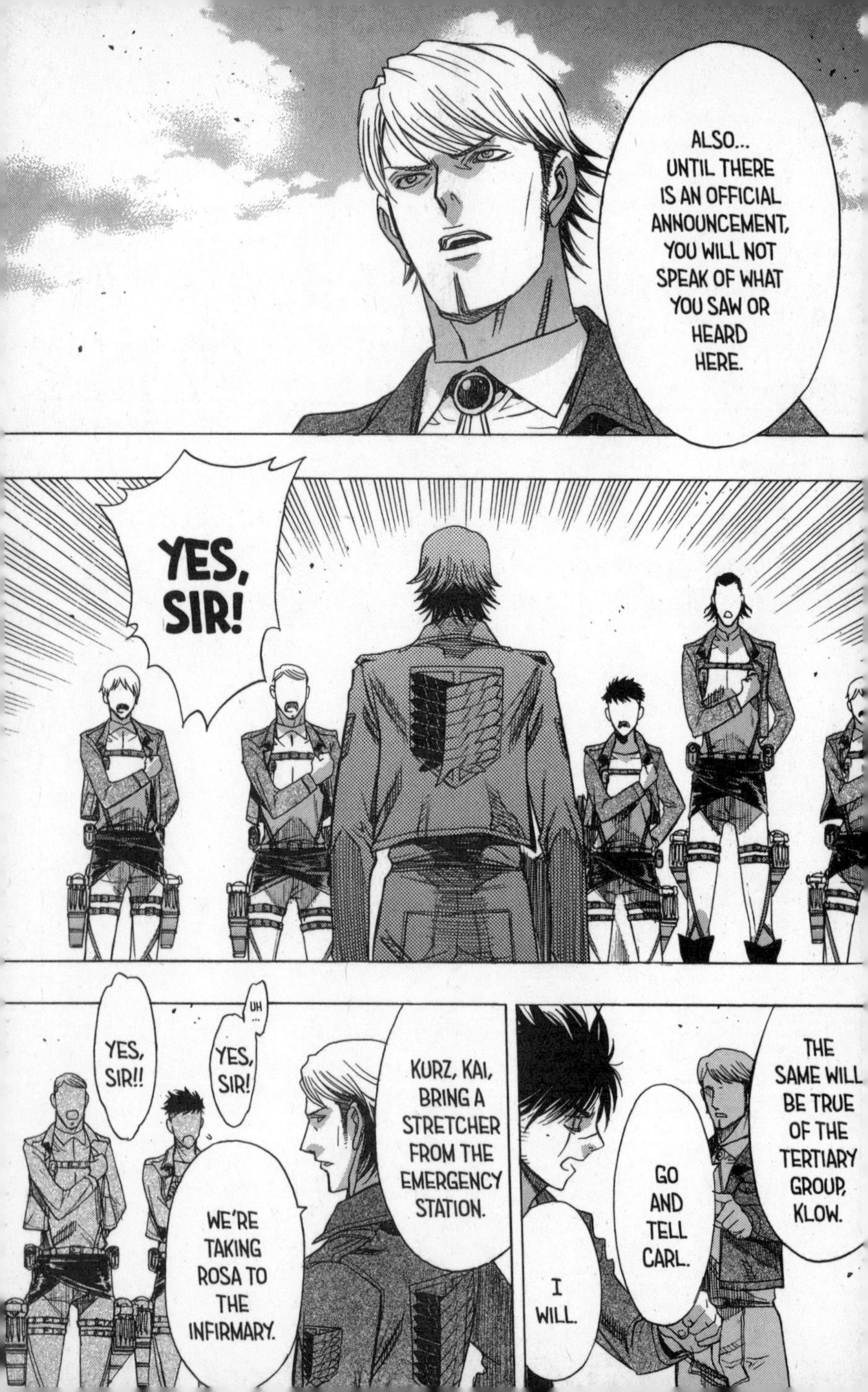
ALSO... UNTIL THERE IS AN OFFICIAL ANNOUNCEMENT, YOU WILL NOT SPEAK OF WHAT YOU SAW OR HEARD HERE.
YES, SIR!
THE SAME WILL BE TRUE OF THE TERTIARY GROUP, KLOW.
GO AND TELL CARL.
I WILL.
KURZ, KAI, BRING A STRETCHER FROM THE EMERGENCY STATION.
UH...
YES, SIR!
YES, SIR!!
WE'RE TAKING ROSA TO THE INFIRMARY.

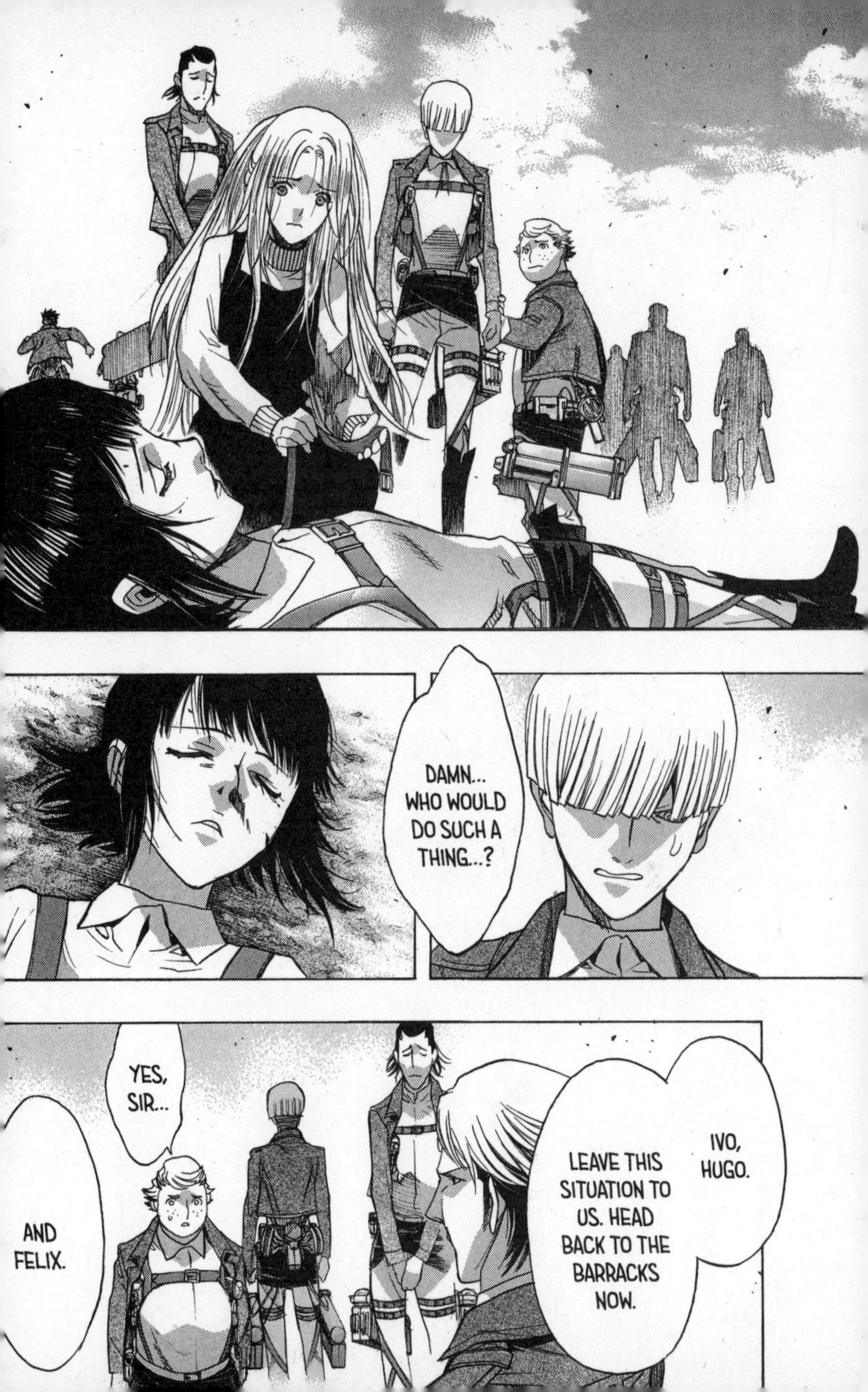
DAMN... WHO WOULD DO SUCH A THING...?
IVO, HUGO.
LEAVE THIS SITUATION TO US. HEAD BACK TO THE BARRACKS NOW.
YES, SIR...
AND FELIX.

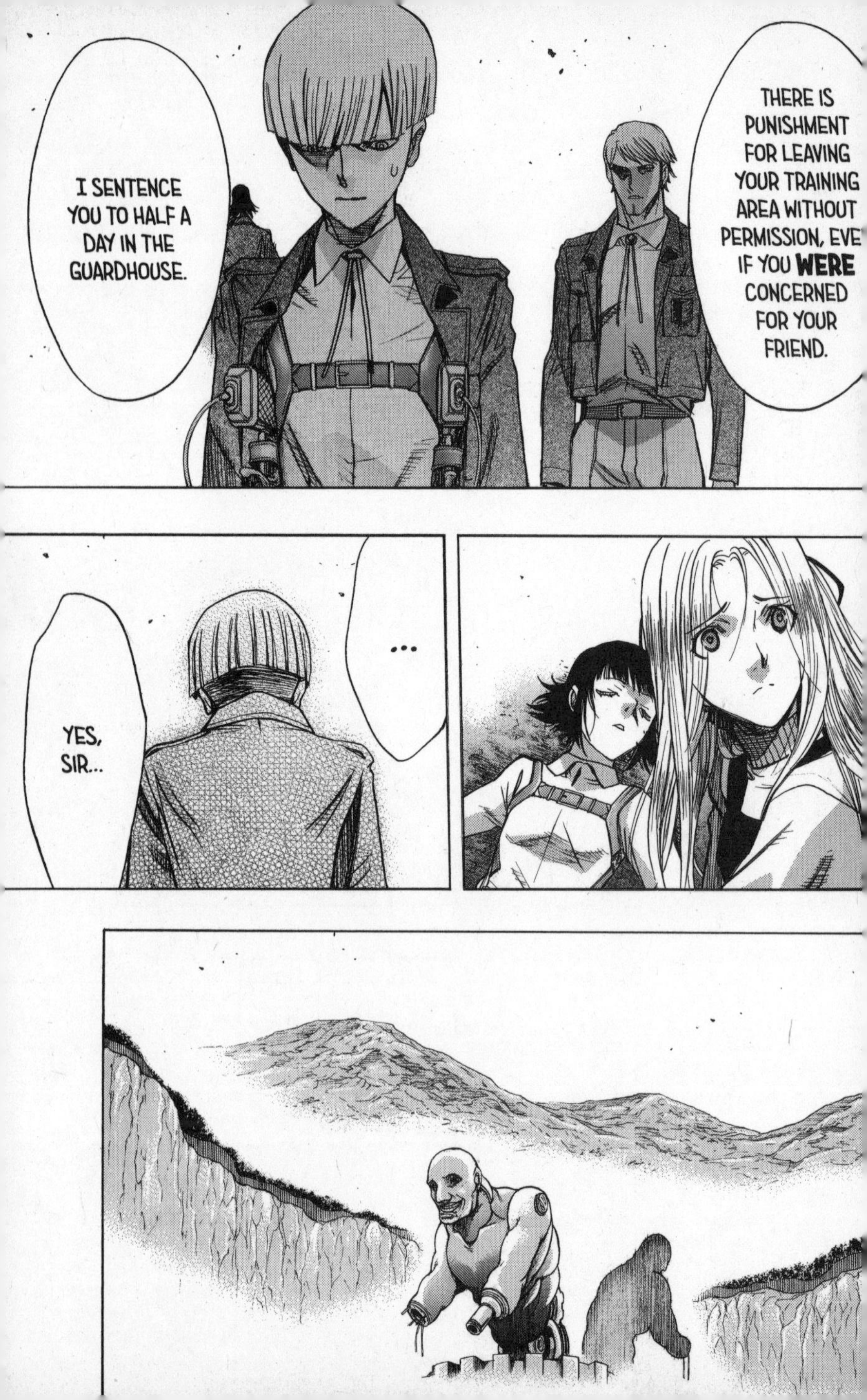
THERE IS PUNISHMENT FOR LEAVING YOUR TRAINING AREA WITHOUT PERMISSION, EVE IF YOU **WERE** CONCERNED FOR YOUR FRIEND.
I SENTENCE YOU TO HALF A DAY IN THE GUARDHOUSE.
...
YES, SIR...

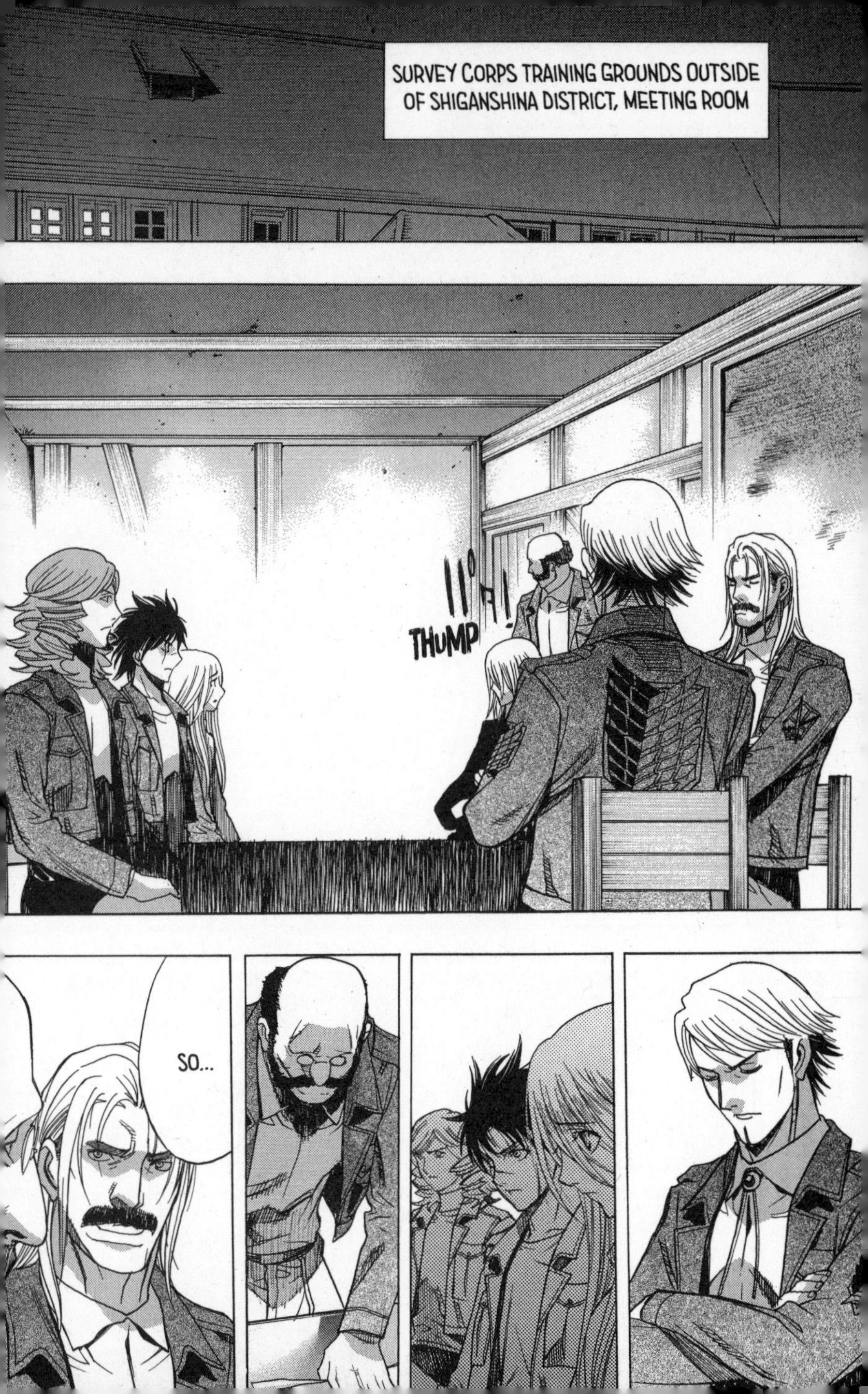
SURVEY CORPS TRAINING GROUNDS OUTSIDE OF SHIGANSHINA DISTRICT, MEETING ROOM
THUMP
SO...

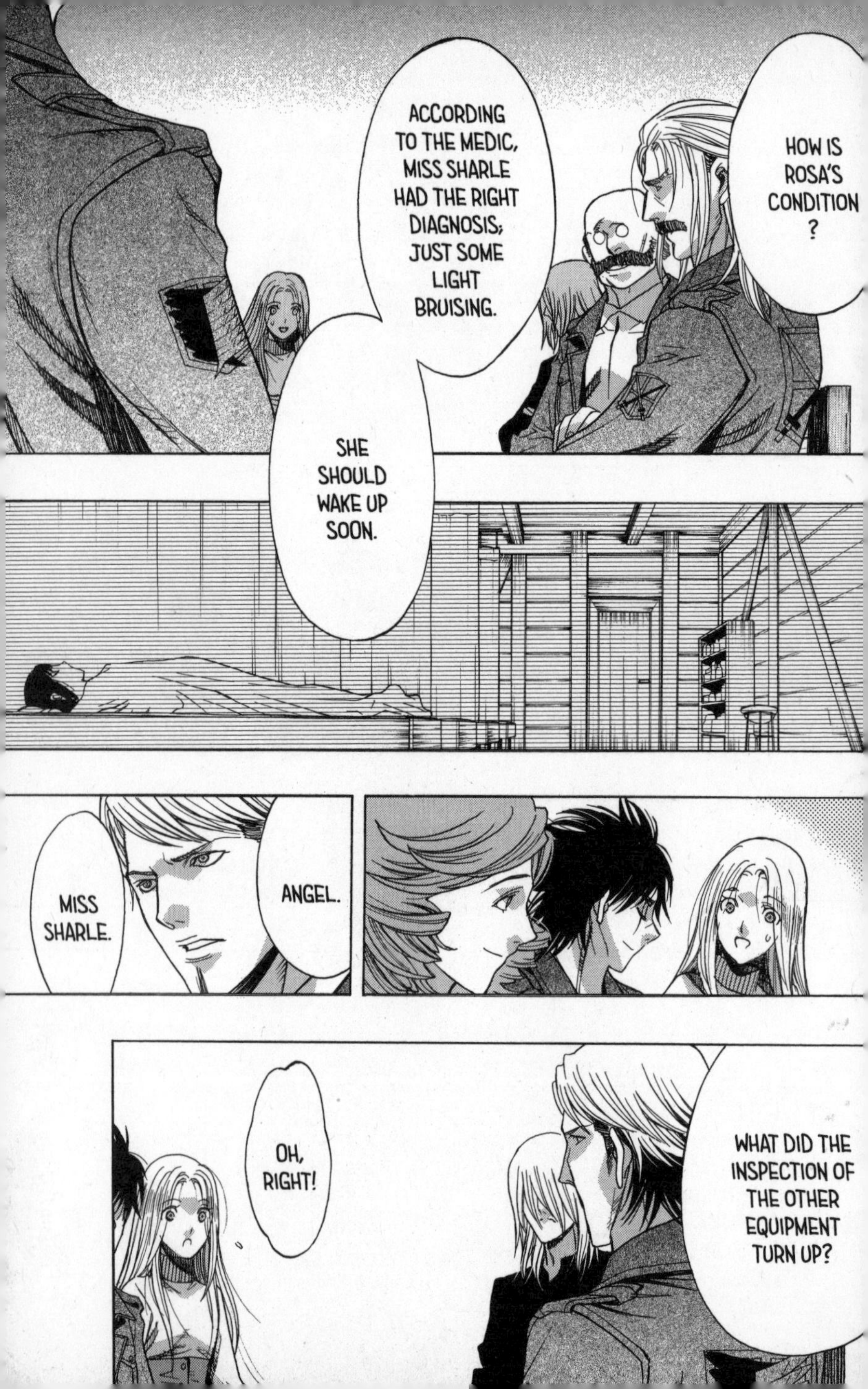
HOW IS ROSA'S CONDITION?
ACCORDING TO THE MEDIC, MISS SHARLE HAD THE RIGHT DIAGNOSIS; JUST SOME LIGHT BRUISING.
SHE SHOULD WAKE UP SOON.
ANGEL.
MISS SHARLE.
WHAT DID THE INSPECTION OF THE OTHER EQUIPMENT TURN UP?
OH, RIGHT!

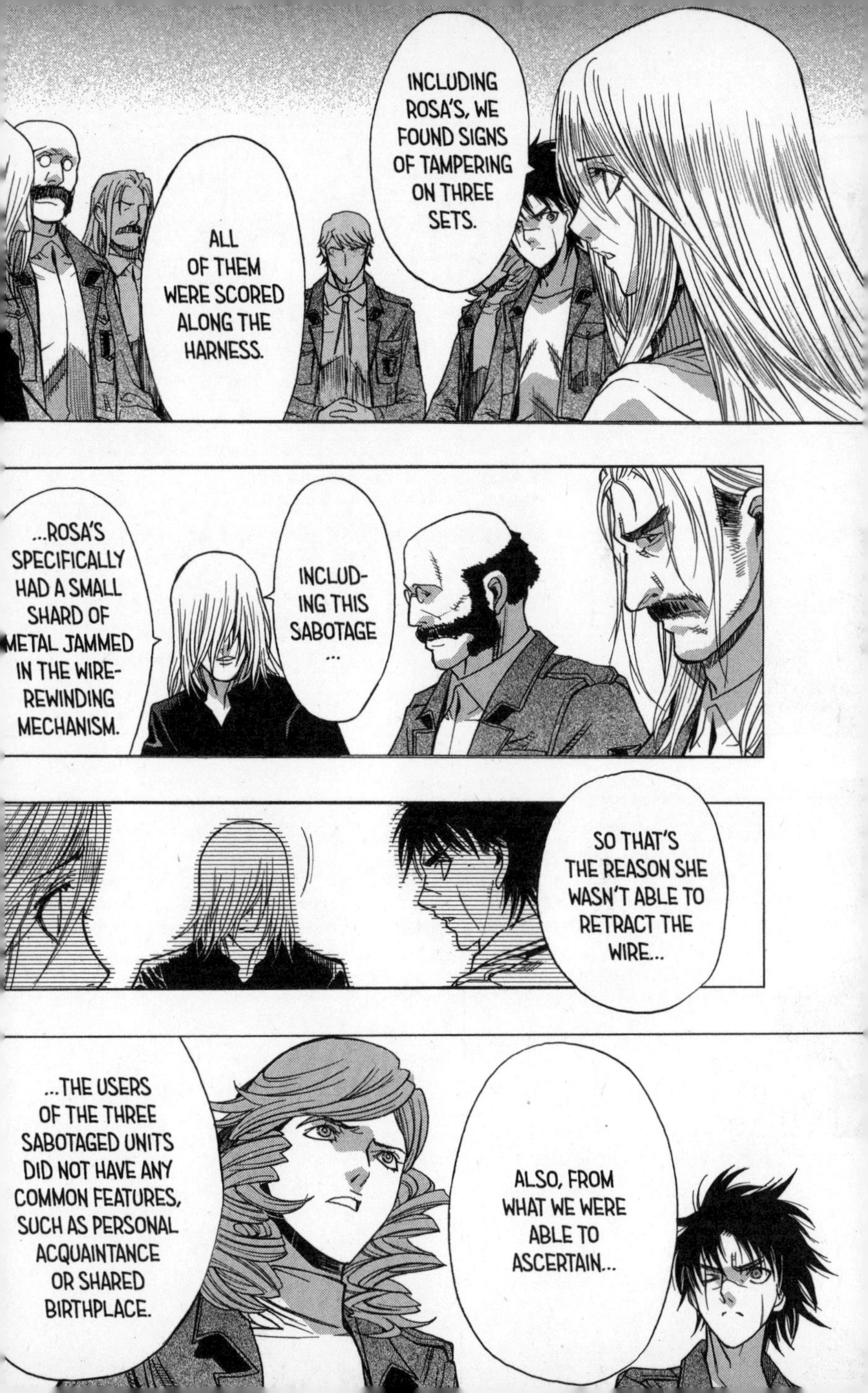
INCLUDING ROSA'S, WE FOUND SIGNS OF TAMPERING ON THREE SETS.
ALL OF THEM WERE SCORED ALONG THE HARNESS.
INCLUDING THIS SABOTAGE...
...ROSA'S SPECIFICALLY HAD A SMALL SHARD OF METAL JAMMED IN THE WIRE-REWINDING MECHANISM.
SO THAT'S THE REASON SHE WASN'T ABLE TO RETRACT THE WIRE...
ALSO, FROM WHAT WE WERE ABLE TO ASCERTAIN...
...THE USERS OF THE THREE SABOTAGED UNITS DID NOT HAVE ANY COMMON FEATURES, SUCH AS PERSONAL ACQUAINTANCE OR SHARED BIRTHPLACE.

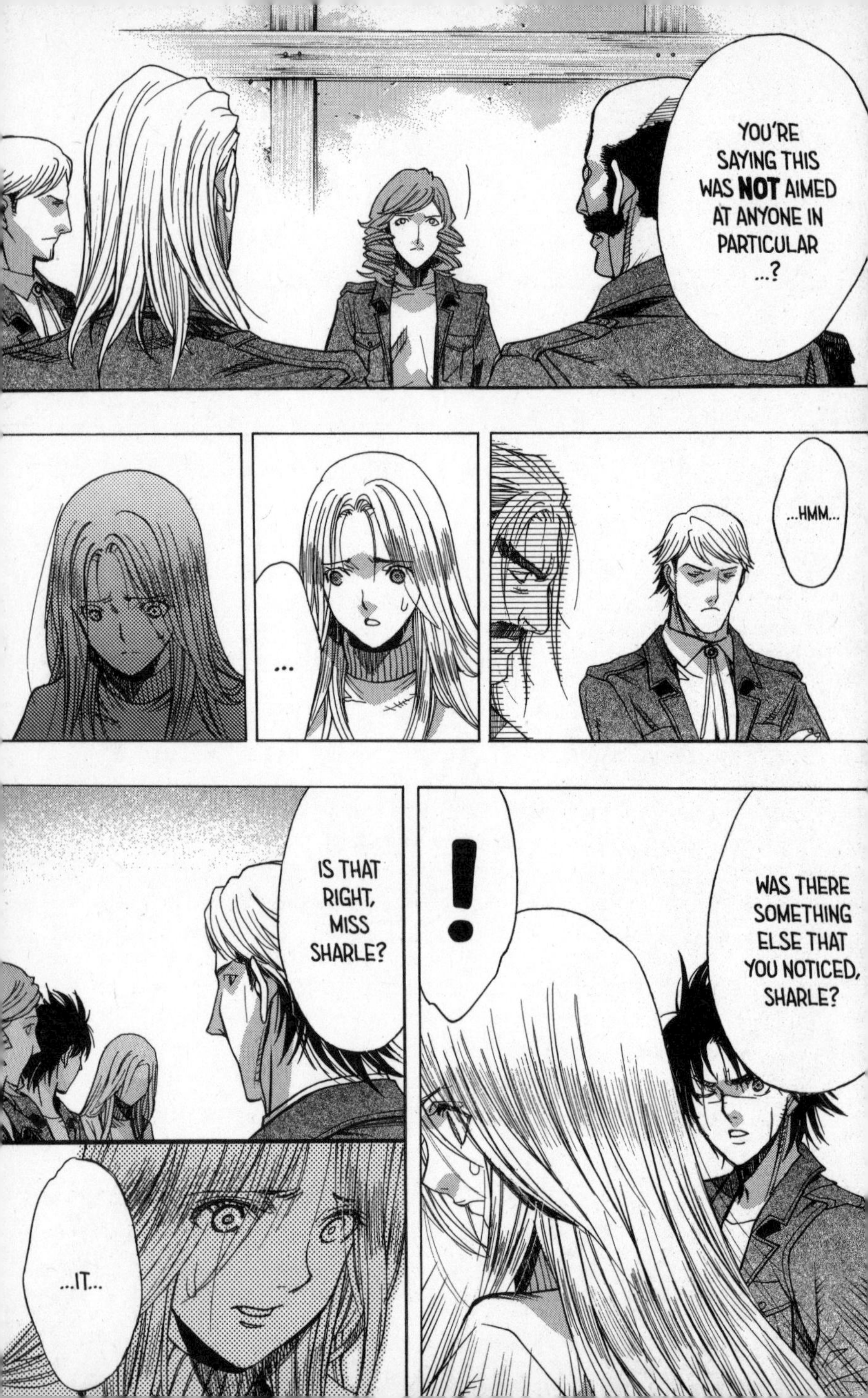
YOU'RE SAYING THIS WAS **NOT** AIMED AT ANYONE IN PARTICULAR ...?
...HMM...
...
WAS THERE SOMETHING ELSE THAT YOU NOTICED, SHARLE?
!
IS THAT RIGHT, MISS SHARLE?
...IT...

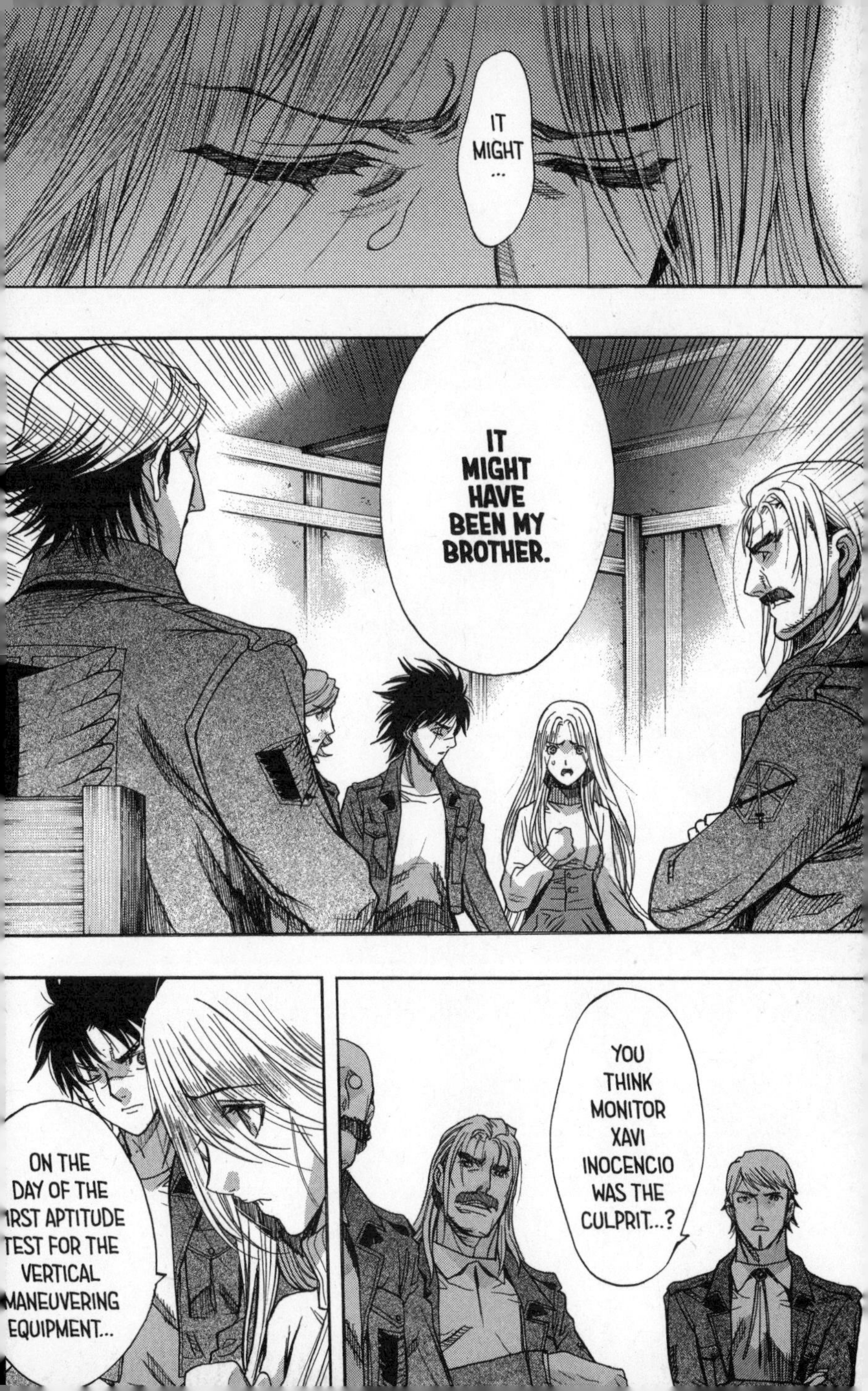
IT MIGHT ...
IT MIGHT HAVE BEEN MY BROTHER.
YOU THINK MONITOR XAVI INOCENCIO WAS THE CULPRIT...?
ON THE DAY OF THE IRST APTITUDE TEST FOR THE VERTICAL MANEUVERING EQUIPMENT...

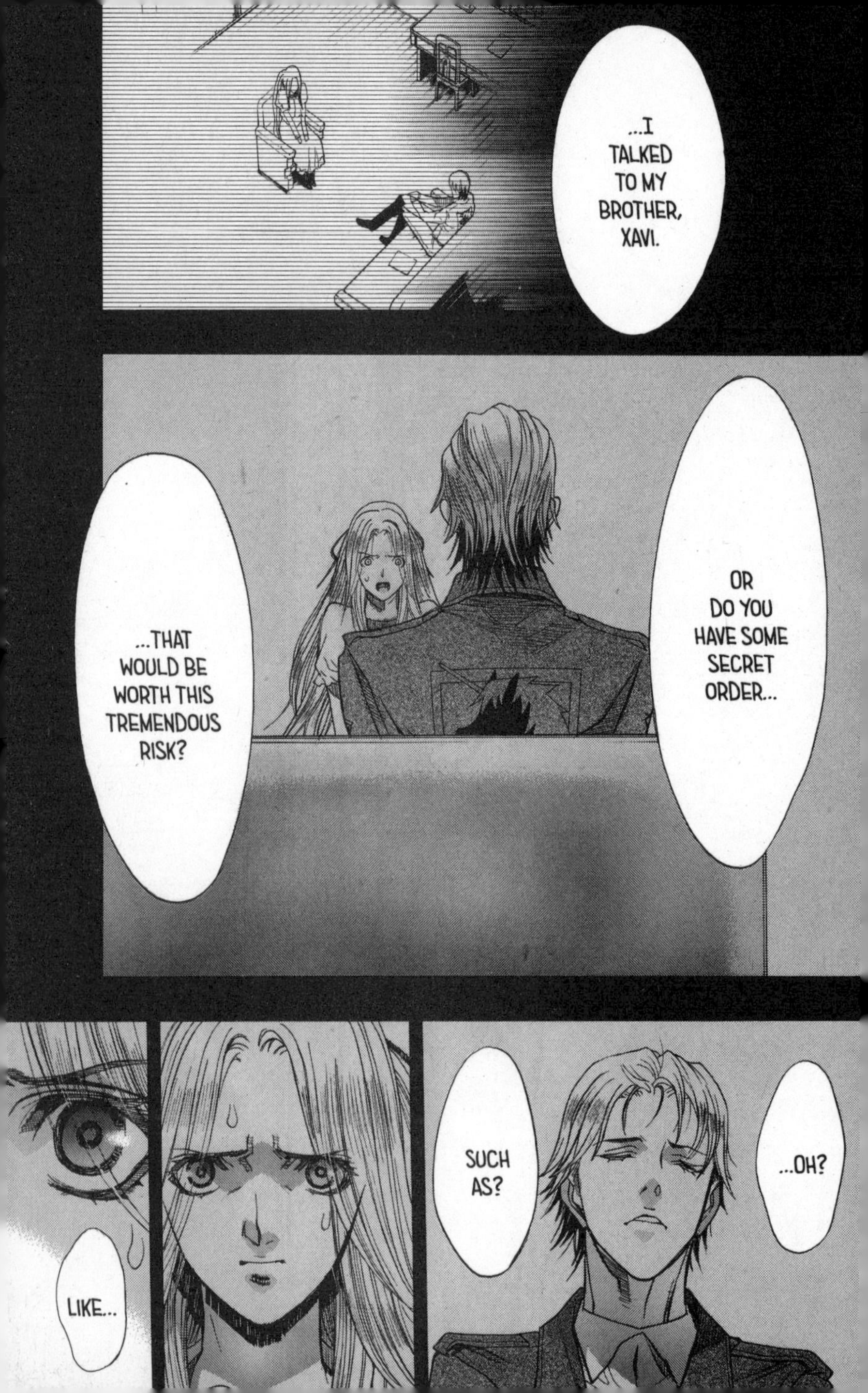
...I TALKED TO MY BROTHER, XAVI.
OR DO YOU HAVE SOME SECRET ORDER...
...THAT WOULD BE WORTH THIS TREMENDOUS RISK?
...OH?
SUCH AS?
LIKE...

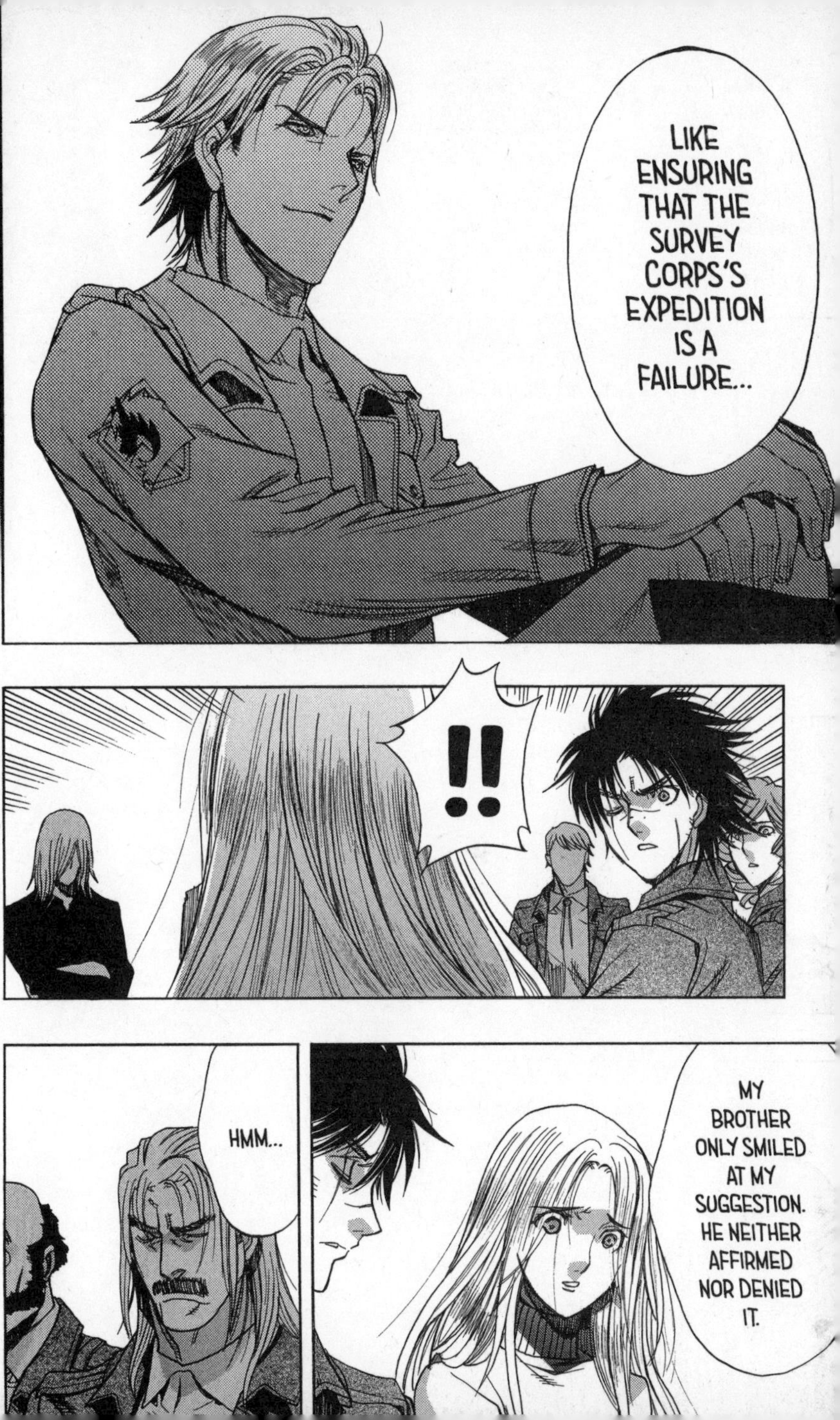
LIKE ENSURING THAT THE SURVEY CORPS'S EXPEDITION IS A FAILURE...
!!
MY BROTHER ONLY SMILED AT MY SUGGESTION. HE NEITHER AFFIRMED NOR DENIED IT.
HMM...

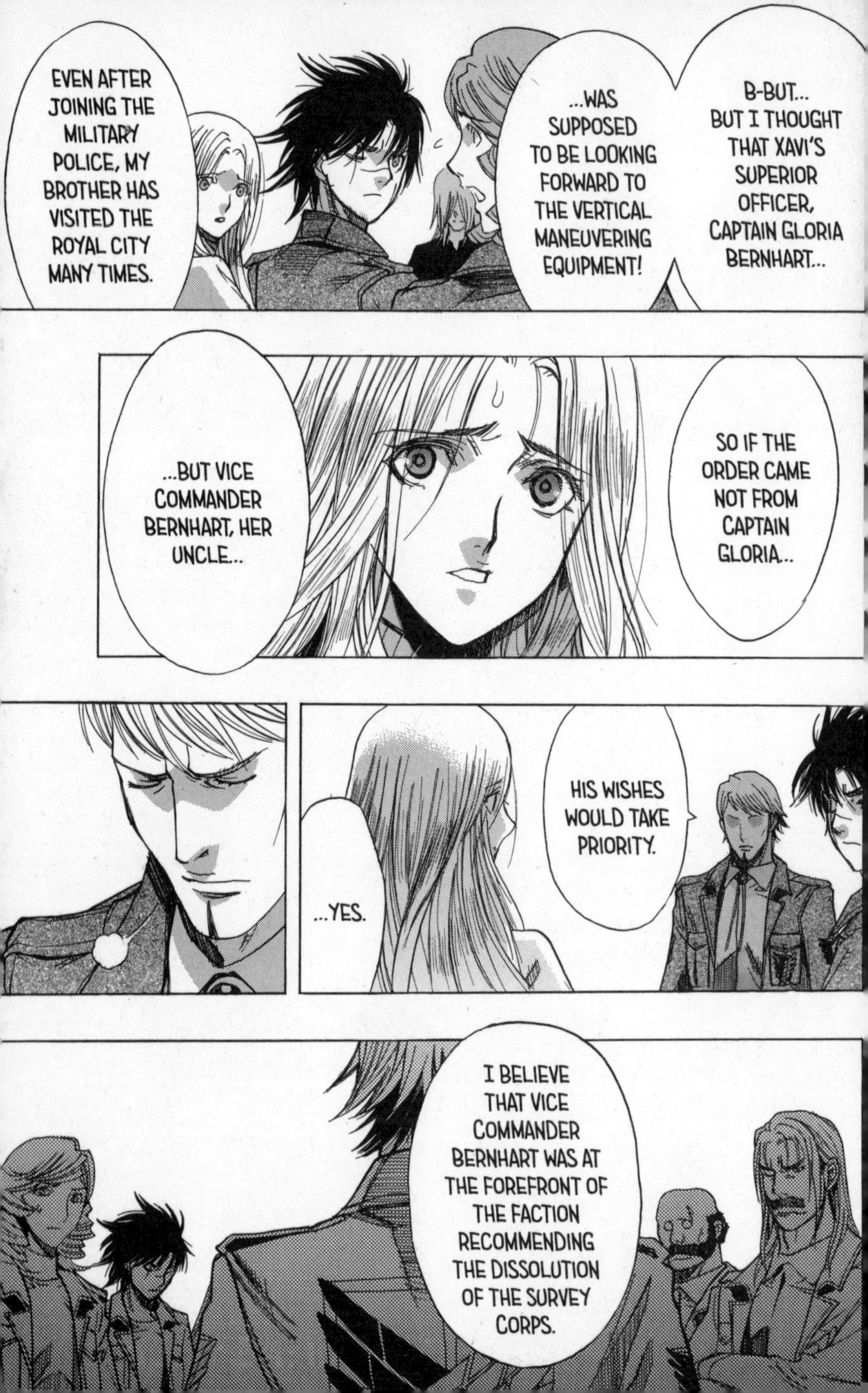
B-BUT... BUT I THOUGHT THAT XAVI'S SUPERIOR OFFICER, CAPTAIN GLORIA BERNHART...
...WAS SUPPOSED TO BE LOOKING FORWARD TO THE VERTICAL MANEUVERING EQUIPMENT!
EVEN AFTER JOINING THE MILITARY POLICE, MY BROTHER HAS VISITED THE ROYAL CITY MANY TIMES.
SO IF THE ORDER CAME NOT FROM CAPTAIN GLORIA...
...BUT VICE COMMANDER BERNHART, HER UNCLE...
HIS WISHES WOULD TAKE PRIORITY.
...YES.
I BELIEVE THAT VICE COMMANDER BERNHART WAS AT THE FOREFRONT OF THE FACTION RECOMMENDING THE DISSOLUTION OF THE SURVEY CORPS.

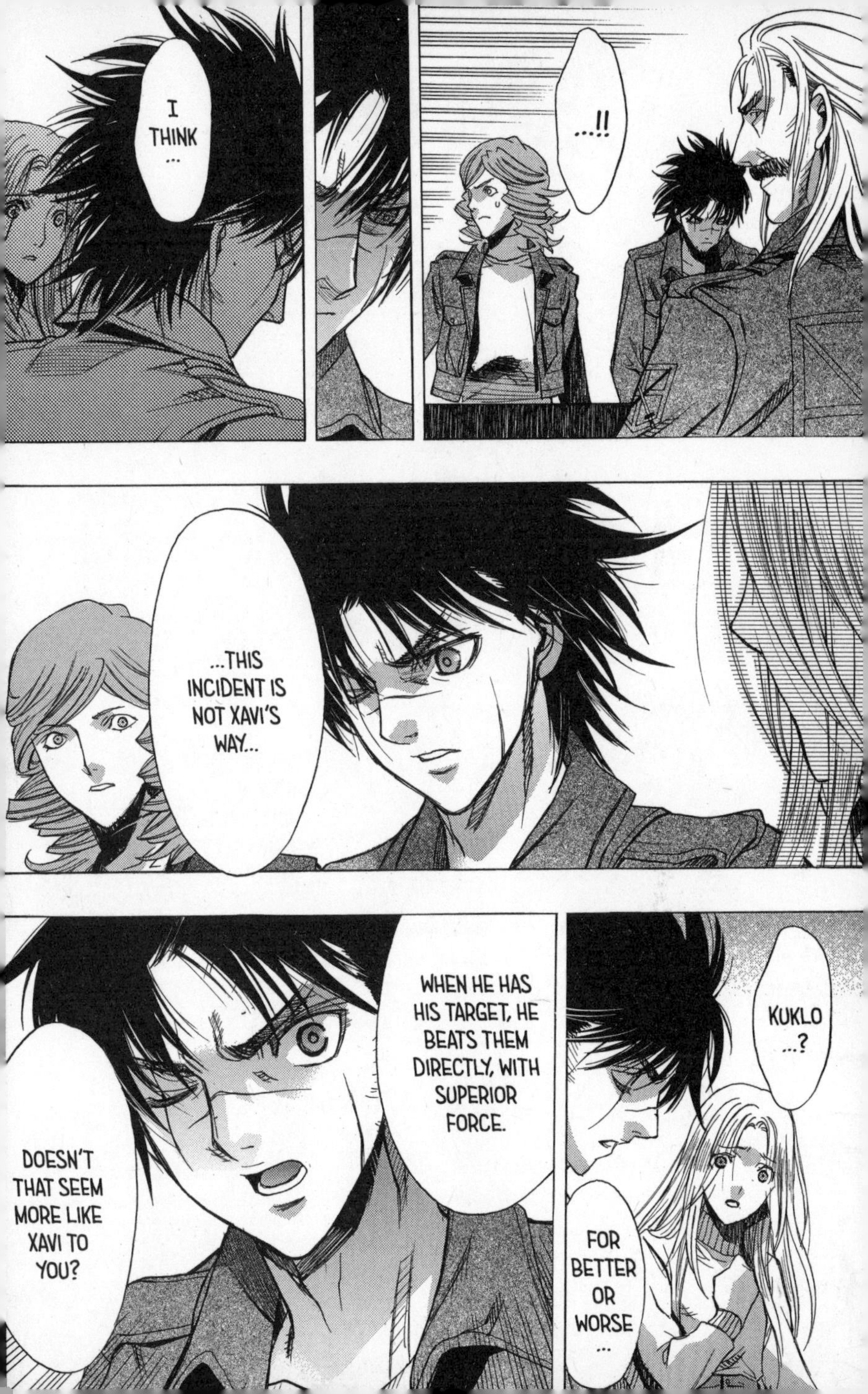

...!!
I THINK ...
...THIS INCIDENT IS NOT XAVI'S WAY...
KUKLO ...?
FOR BETTER OR WORSE ...
WHEN HE HAS HIS TARGET, HE BEATS THEM DIRECTLY, WITH SUPERIOR FORCE.
DOESN'T THAT SEEM MORE LIKE XAVI TO YOU?

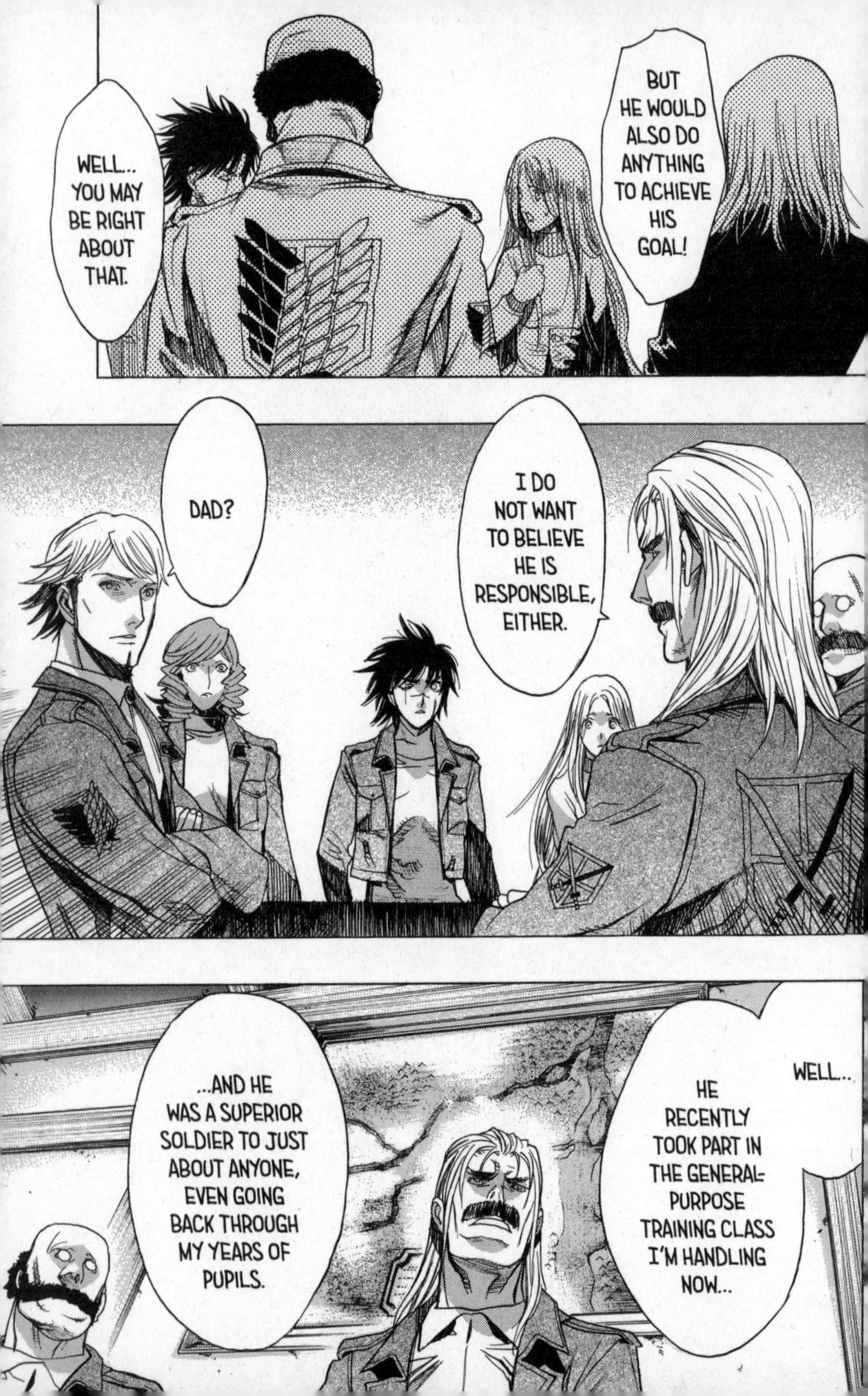
BUT HE WOULD ALSO DO ANYTHING TO ACHIEVE HIS GOAL!
WELL... YOU MAY BE RIGHT ABOUT THAT.
I DO NOT WANT TO BELIEVE HE IS RESPONSIBLE, EITHER.
DAD?
WELL...
HE RECENTLY TOOK PART IN THE GENERAL-PURPOSE TRAINING CLASS I'M HANDLING NOW...
...AND HE WAS A SUPERIOR SOLDIER TO JUST ABOUT ANYONE, EVEN GOING BACK THROUGH MY YEARS OF PUPILS.

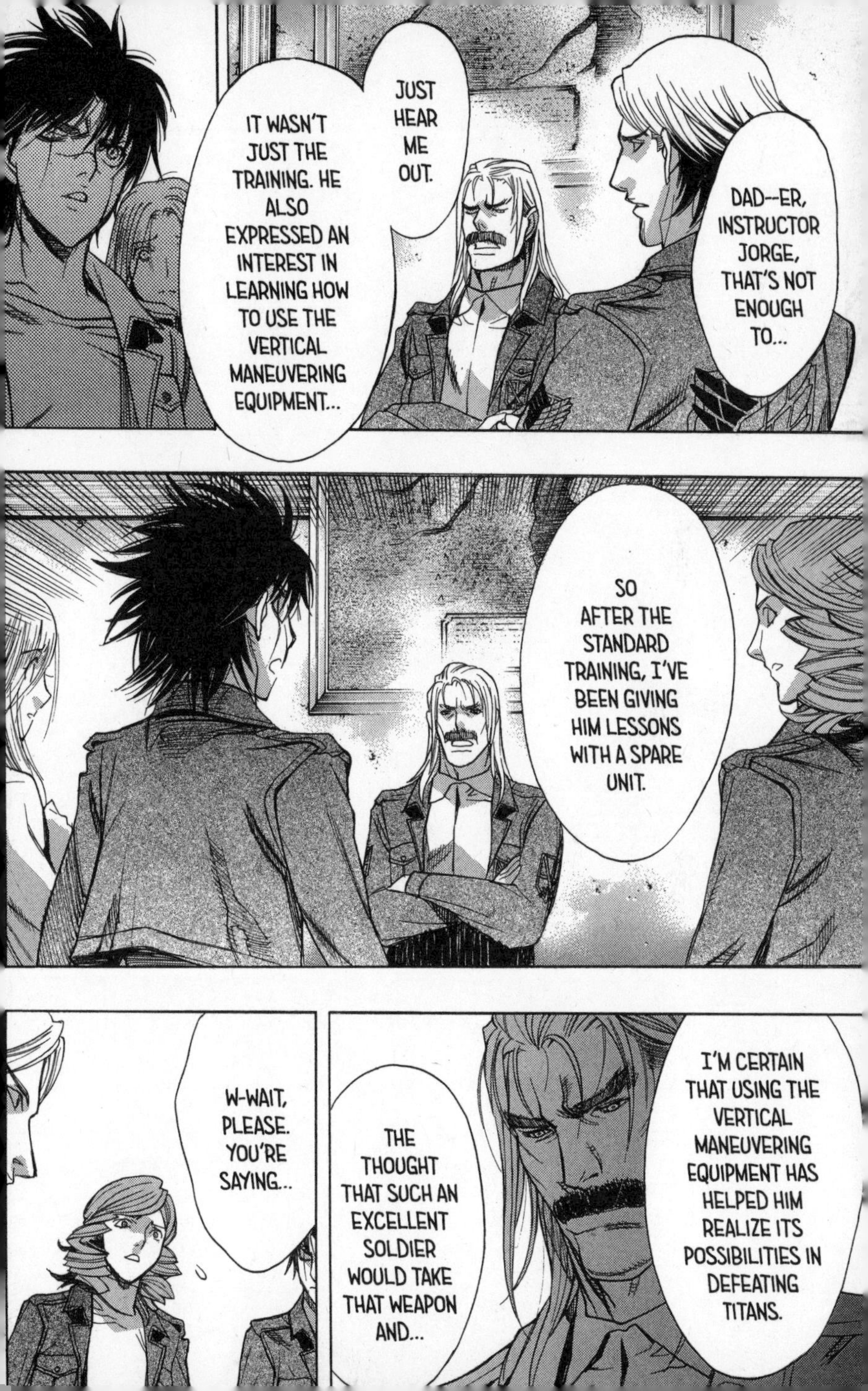
DAD--ER, INSTRUCTOR JORGE, THAT'S NOT ENOUGH TO...
JUST HEAR ME OUT.
IT WASN'T JUST THE TRAINING. HE ALSO EXPRESSED AN INTEREST IN LEARNING HOW TO USE THE VERTICAL MANEUVERING EQUIPMENT...
SO AFTER THE STANDARD TRAINING, I'VE BEEN GIVING HIM LESSONS WITH A SPARE UNIT.
I'M CERTAIN THAT USING THE VERTICAL MANEUVERING EQUIPMENT HAS HELPED HIM REALIZE ITS POSSIBILITIES IN DEFEATING TITANS.
THE THOUGHT THAT SUCH AN EXCELLENT SOLDIER WOULD TAKE THAT WEAPON AND...
W-WAIT, PLEASE. YOU'RE SAYING...

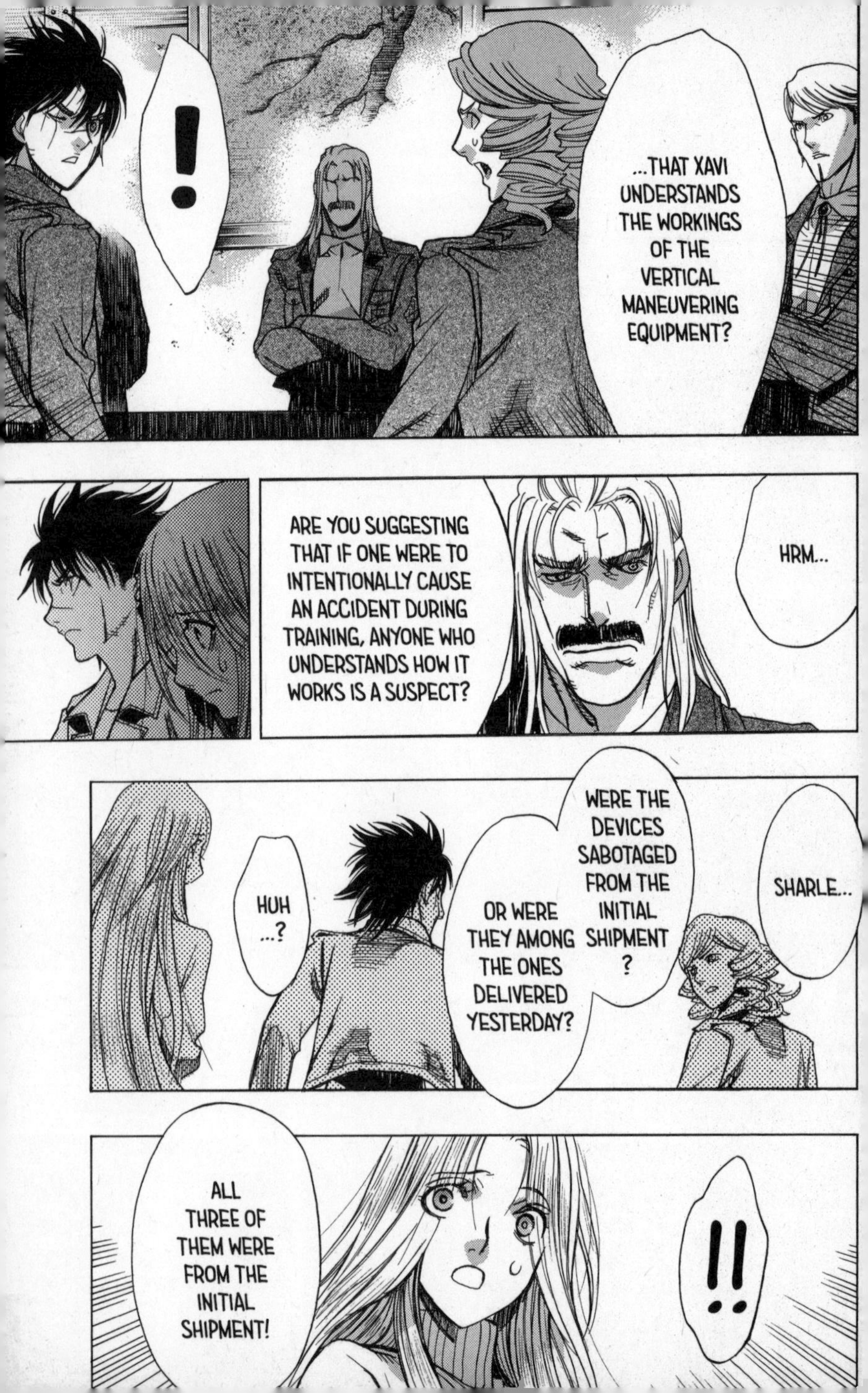
...THAT XAVI UNDERSTANDS THE WORKINGS OF THE VERTICAL MANEUVERING EQUIPMENT?
!
HRM...
ARE YOU SUGGESTING THAT IF ONE WERE TO INTENTIONALLY CAUSE AN ACCIDENT DURING TRAINING, ANYONE WHO UNDERSTANDS HOW IT WORKS IS A SUSPECT?
SHARLE...
WERE THE DEVICES SABOTAGED FROM THE INITIAL SHIPMENT ?
OR WERE THEY AMONG THE ONES DELIVERED YESTERDAY?
HUH ...?
!!
ALL THREE OF THEM WERE FROM THE INITIAL SHIPMENT!

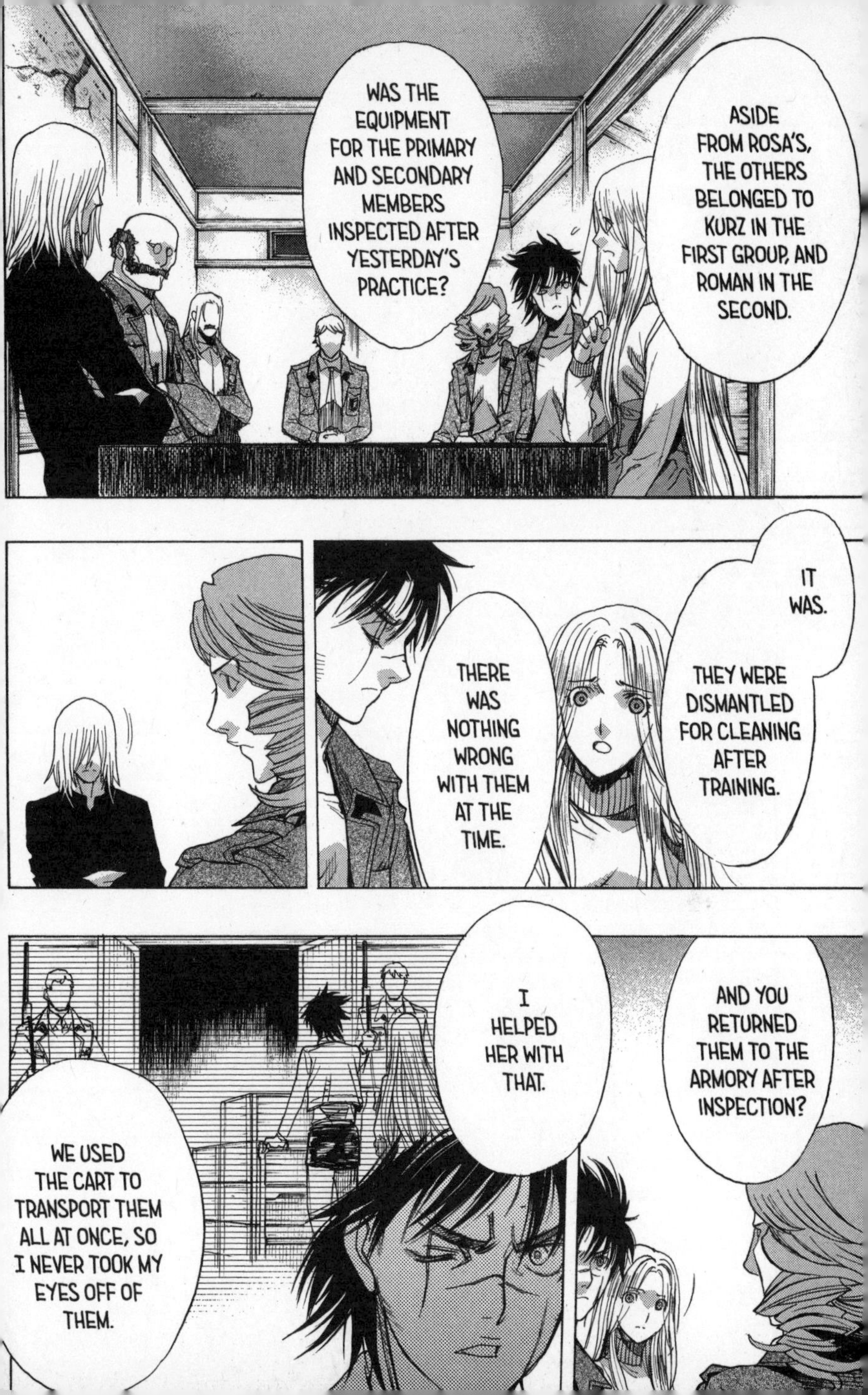
ASIDE FROM ROSA'S, THE OTHERS BELONGED TO KURZ IN THE FIRST GROUP, AND ROMAN IN THE SECOND.
WAS THE EQUIPMENT FOR THE PRIMARY AND SECONDARY MEMBERS INSPECTED AFTER YESTERDAY'S PRACTICE?
IT WAS.
THEY WERE DISMANTLED FOR CLEANING AFTER TRAINING.
THERE WAS NOTHING WRONG WITH THEM AT THE TIME.
AND YOU RETURNED THEM TO THE ARMORY AFTER INSPECTION?
I HELPED HER WITH THAT.
WE USED THE CART TO TRANSPORT THEM ALL AT ONCE, SO I NEVER TOOK MY EYES OFF OF THEM.

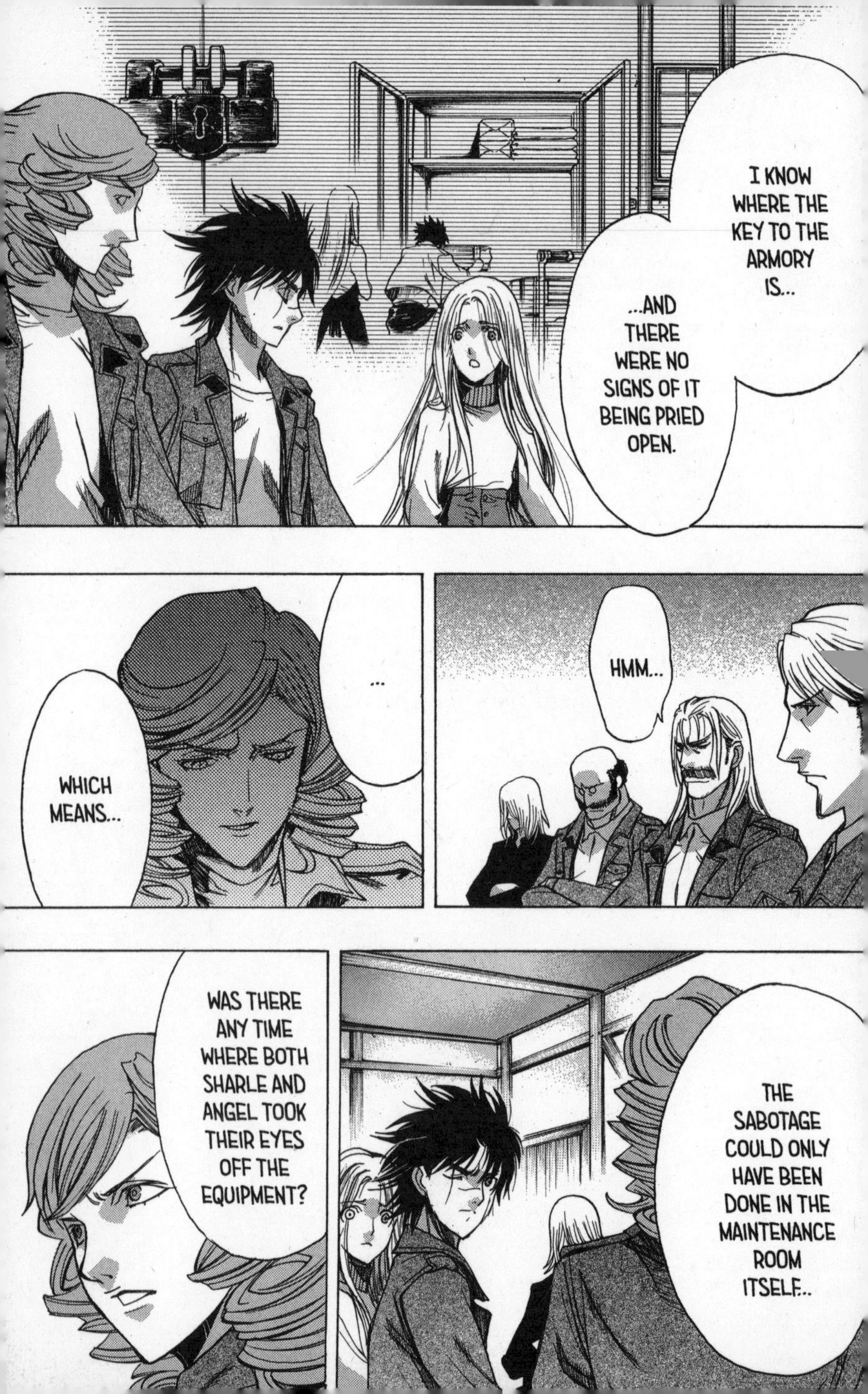
I KNOW WHERE THE KEY TO THE ARMORY IS...
...AND THERE WERE NO SIGNS OF IT BEING PRIED OPEN.
HMM...
...
WHICH MEANS...
THE SABOTAGE COULD ONLY HAVE BEEN DONE IN THE MAINTENANCE ROOM ITSELF...
WAS THERE ANY TIME WHERE BOTH SHARLE AND ANGEL TOOK THEIR EYES OFF THE EQUIPMENT?

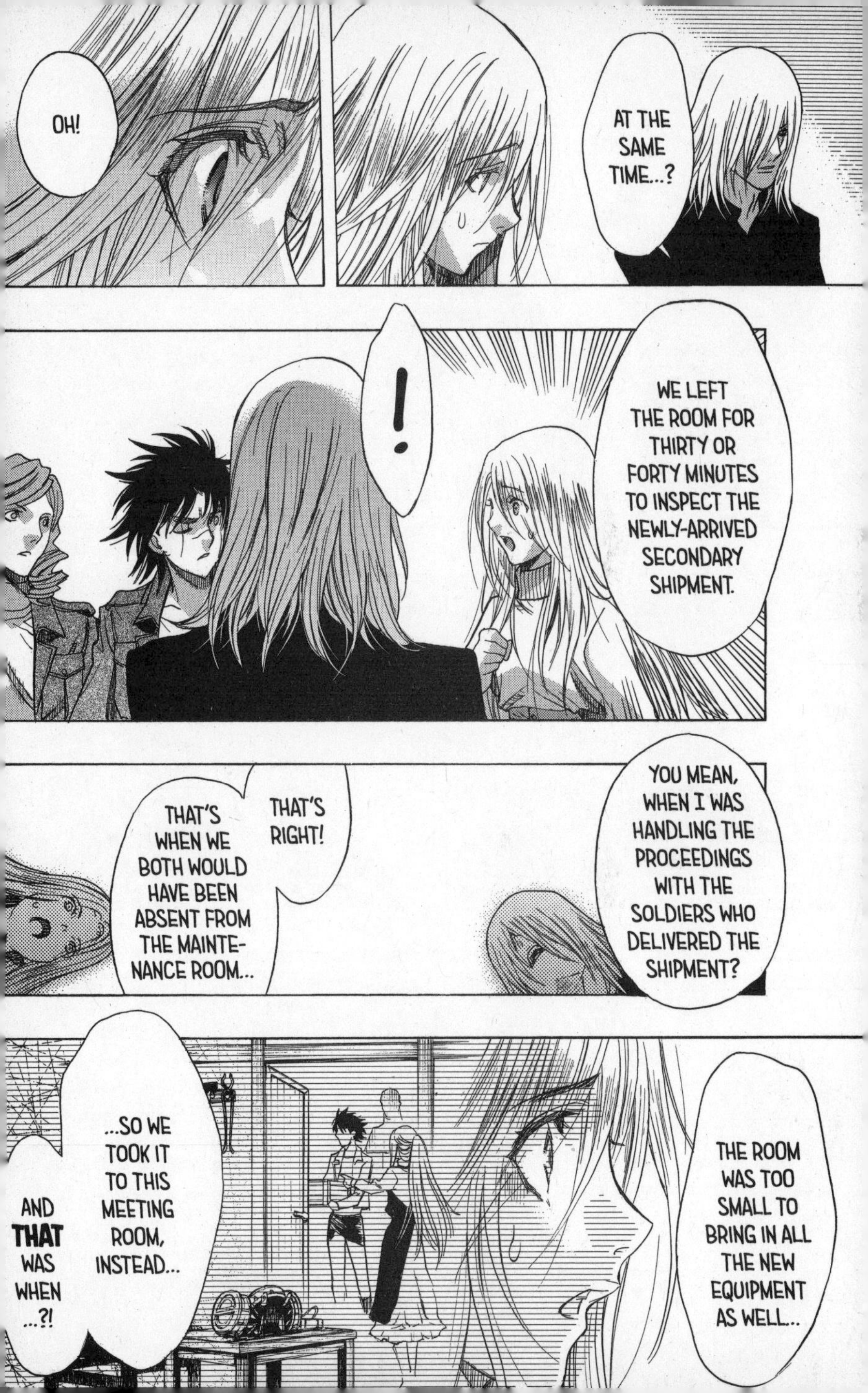
AT THE SAME TIME...?
OH!
WE LEFT THE ROOM FOR THIRTY OR FORTY MINUTES TO INSPECT THE NEWLY-ARRIVED SECONDARY SHIPMENT.
!
YOU MEAN, WHEN I WAS HANDLING THE PROCEEDINGS WITH THE SOLDIERS WHO DELIVERED THE SHIPMENT?
THAT'S RIGHT!
THAT'S WHEN WE BOTH WOULD HAVE BEEN ABSENT FROM THE MAINTE-NANCE ROOM...
THE ROOM WAS TOO SMALL TO BRING IN ALL THE NEW EQUIPMENT AS WELL...
...SO WE TOOK IT TO THIS MEETING ROOM, INSTEAD...
AND **THAT** WAS WHEN ...?!

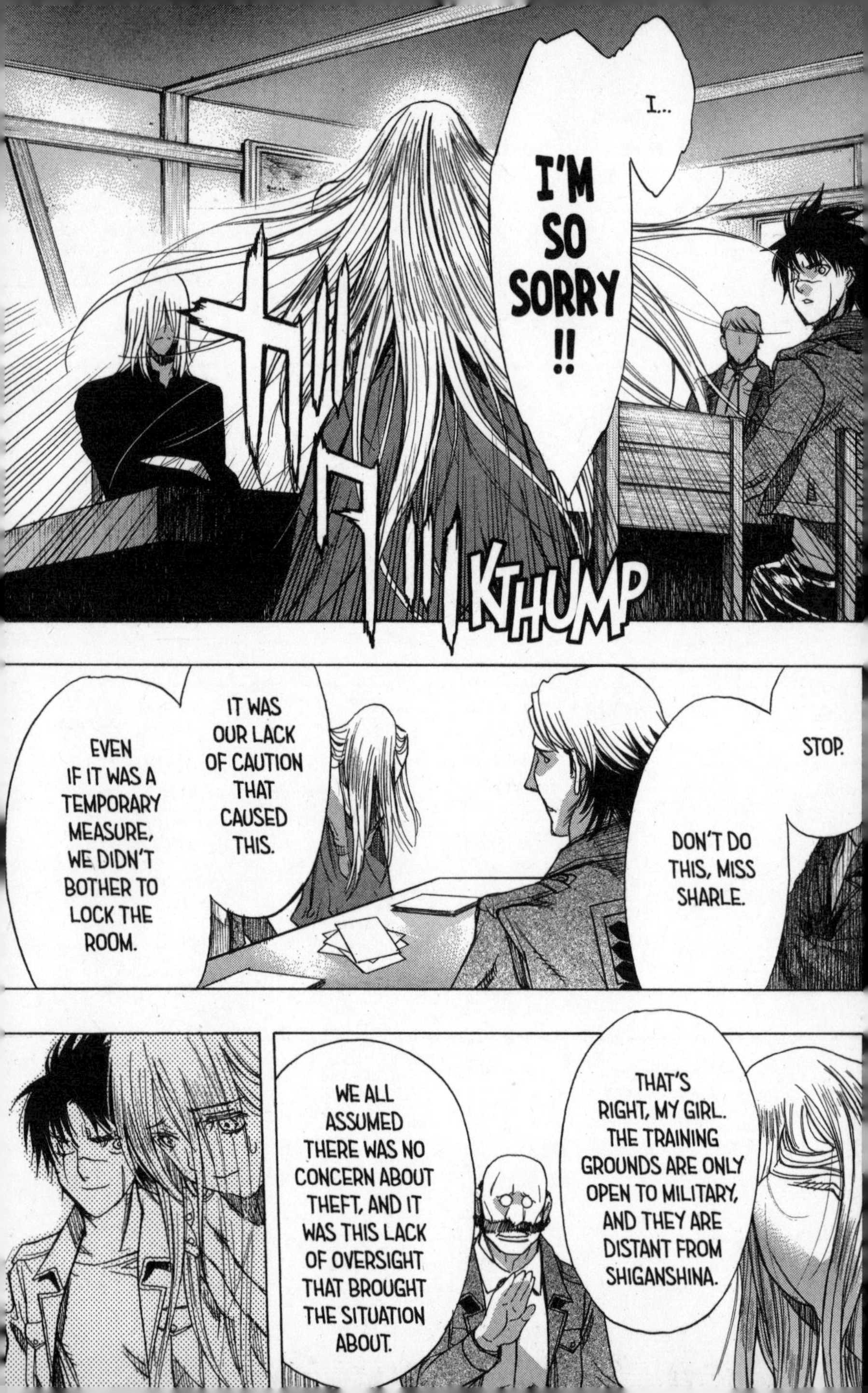
I...
I'M SO SORRY!!
KTHUMP
STOP.
DON'T DO THIS, MISS SHARLE.
IT WAS OUR LACK OF CAUTION THAT CAUSED THIS.
EVEN IF IT WAS A TEMPORARY MEASURE, WE DIDN'T BOTHER TO LOCK THE ROOM.
THAT'S RIGHT, MY GIRL. THE TRAINING GROUNDS ARE ONLY OPEN TO MILITARY, AND THEY ARE DISTANT FROM SHIGANSHINA.
WE ALL ASSUMED THERE WAS NO CONCERN ABOUT THEFT, AND IT WAS THIS LACK OF OVERSIGHT THAT BROUGHT THE SITUATION ABOUT.

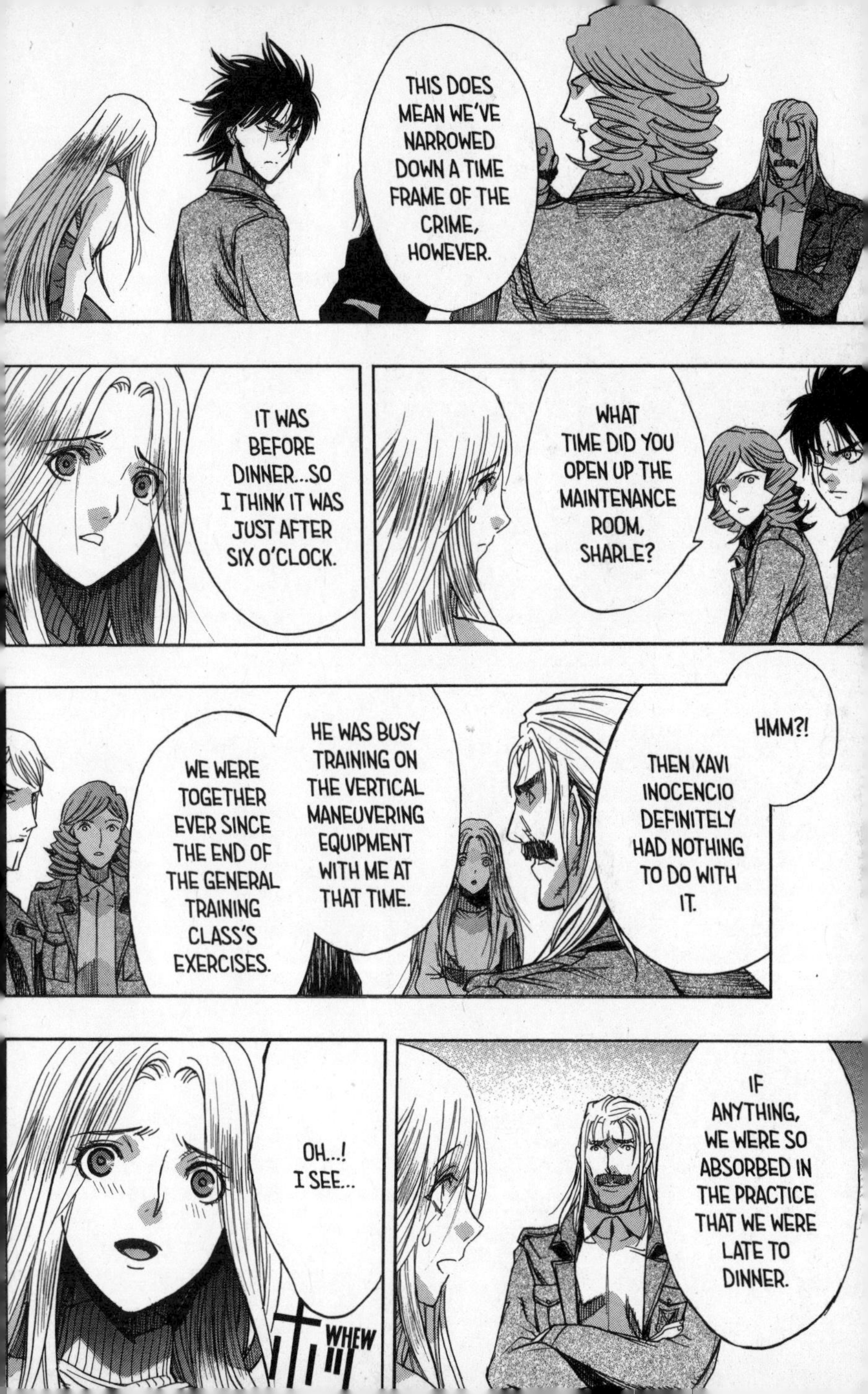
THIS DOES MEAN WE'VE NARROWED DOWN A TIME FRAME OF THE CRIME, HOWEVER.
WHAT TIME DID YOU OPEN UP THE MAINTENANCE ROOM, SHARLE?
IT WAS BEFORE DINNER...SO I THINK IT WAS JUST AFTER SIX O'CLOCK.
HMM?!
THEN XAVI INOCENCIO DEFINITELY HAD NOTHING TO DO WITH IT.
HE WAS BUSY TRAINING ON THE VERTICAL MANEUVERING EQUIPMENT WITH ME AT THAT TIME.
WE WERE TOGETHER EVER SINCE THE END OF THE GENERAL TRAINING CLASS'S EXERCISES.
IF ANYTHING, WE WERE SO ABSORBED IN THE PRACTICE THAT WE WERE LATE TO DINNER.
OH...! I SEE...
WHEW

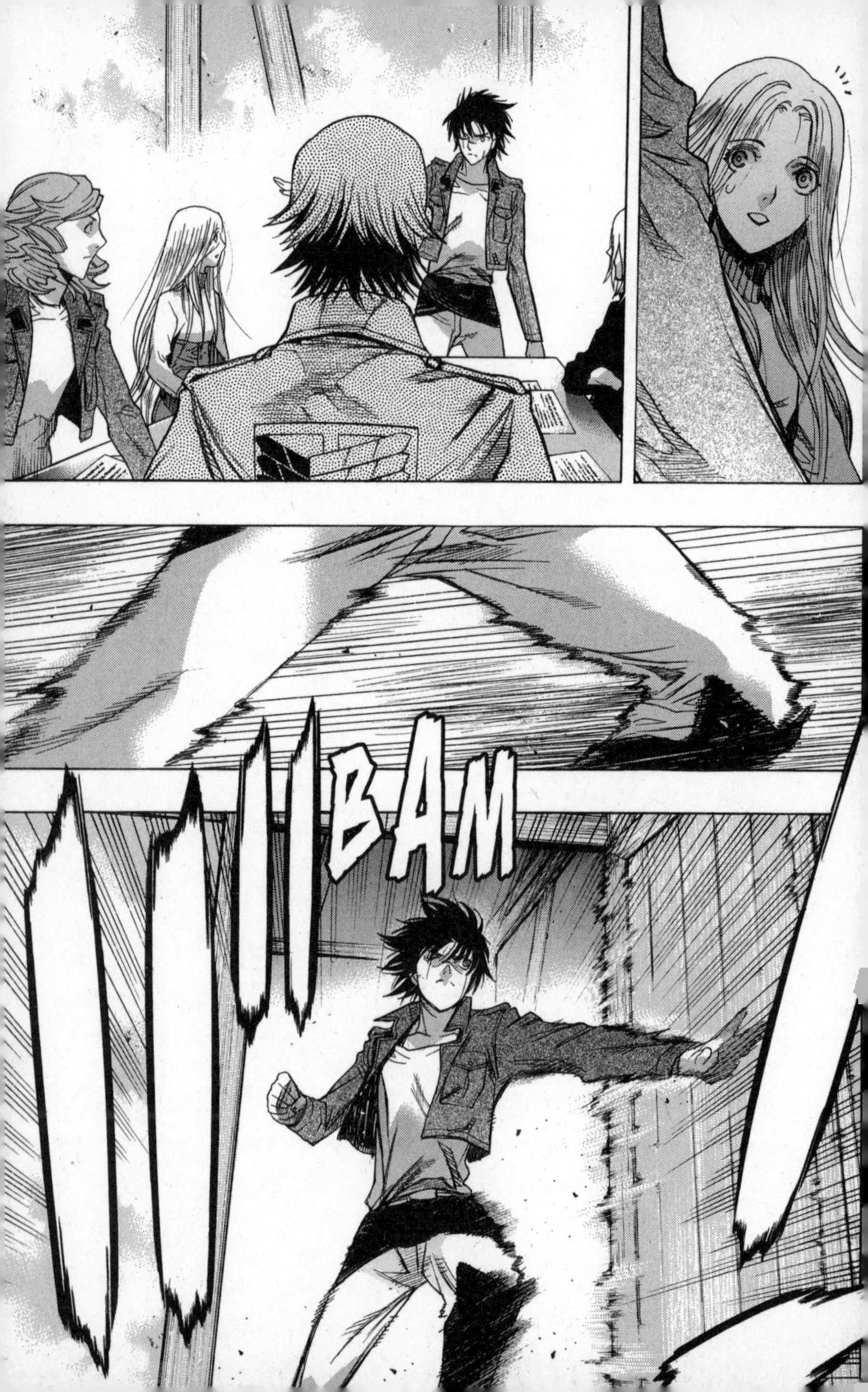
BAM

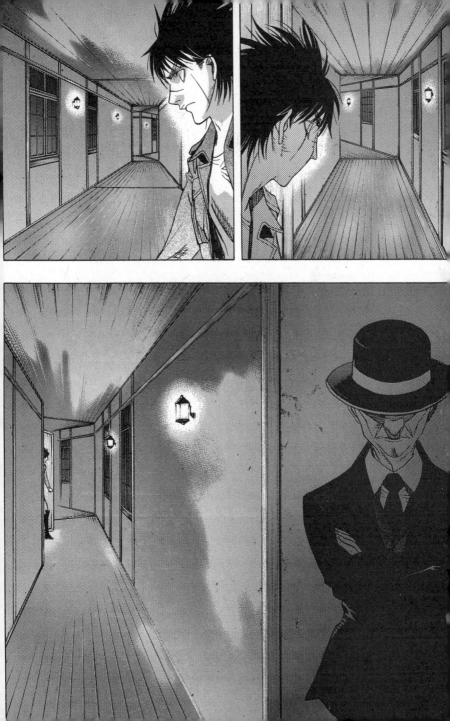

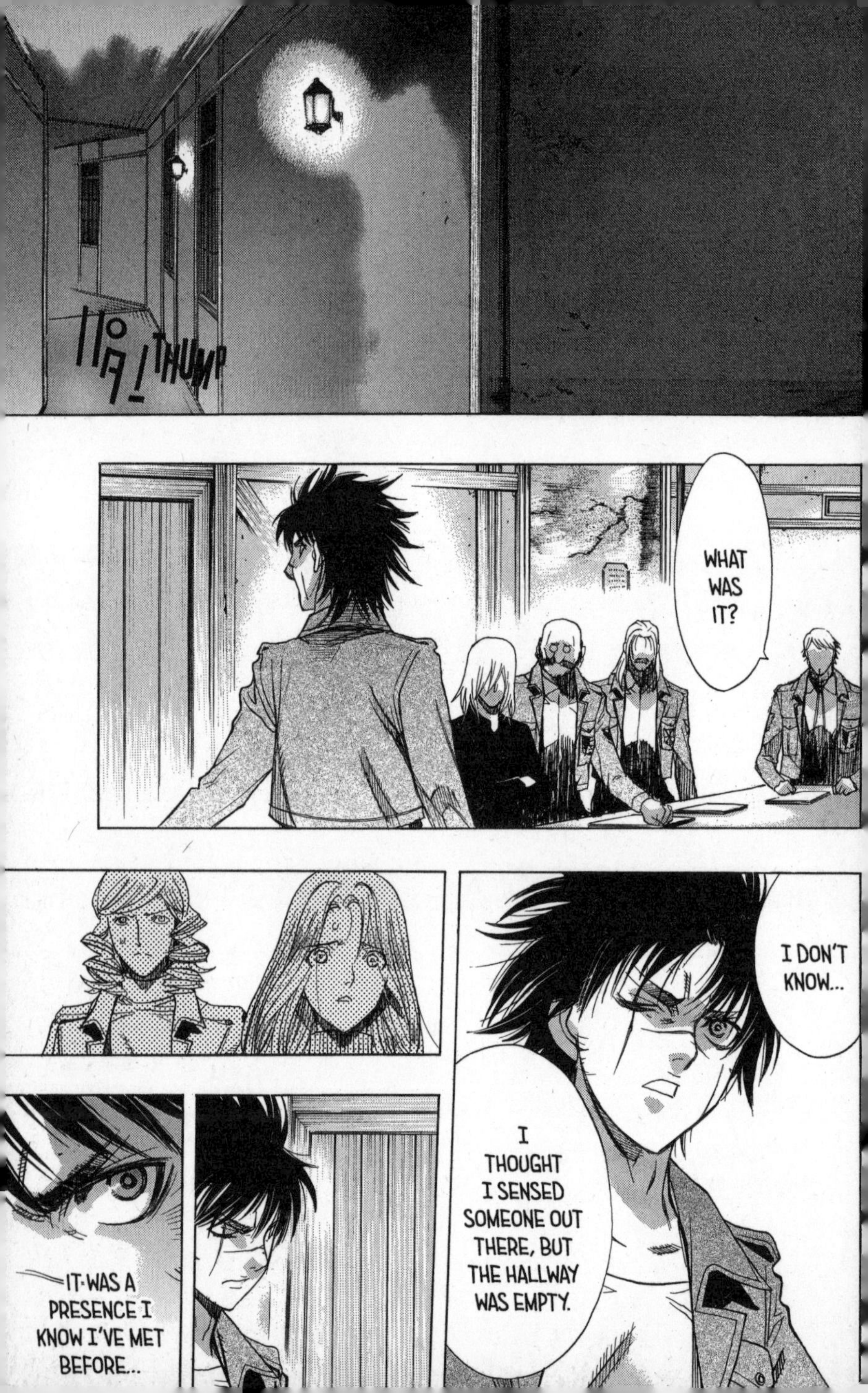
THUMP
WHAT WAS IT?
I DON'T KNOW...
I THOUGHT I SENSED SOMEONE OUT THERE, BUT THE HALLWAY WAS EMPTY.
IT WAS A PRESENCE I KNOW I'VE MET BEFORE...

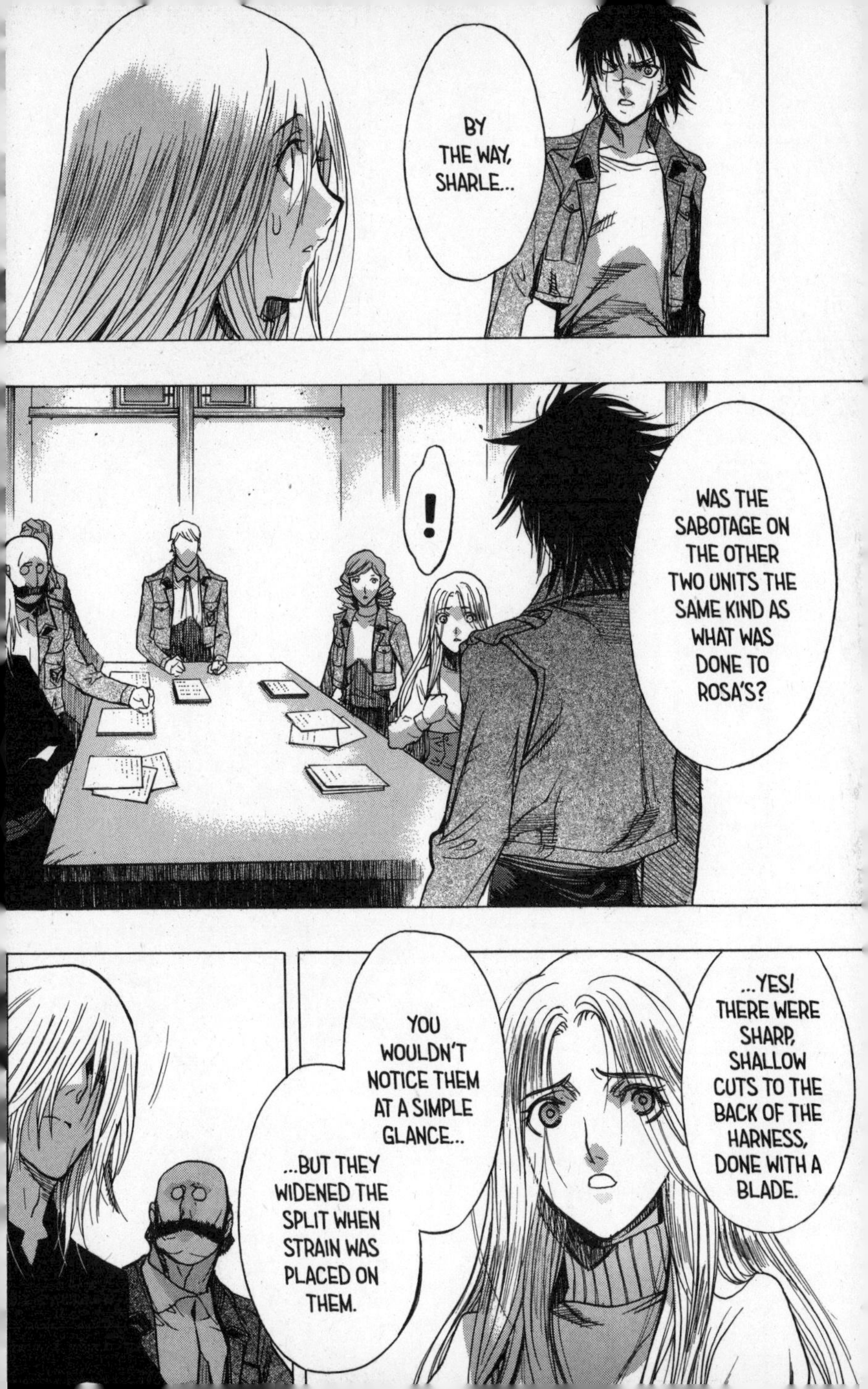
BY THE WAY, SHARLE...
WAS THE SABOTAGE ON THE OTHER TWO UNITS THE SAME KIND AS WHAT WAS DONE TO ROSA'S?
!
...YES! THERE WERE SHARP, SHALLOW CUTS TO THE BACK OF THE HARNESS, DONE WITH A BLADE.
YOU WOULDN'T NOTICE THEM AT A SIMPLE GLANCE...
...BUT THEY WIDENED THE SPLIT WHEN STRAIN WAS PLACED ON THEM.

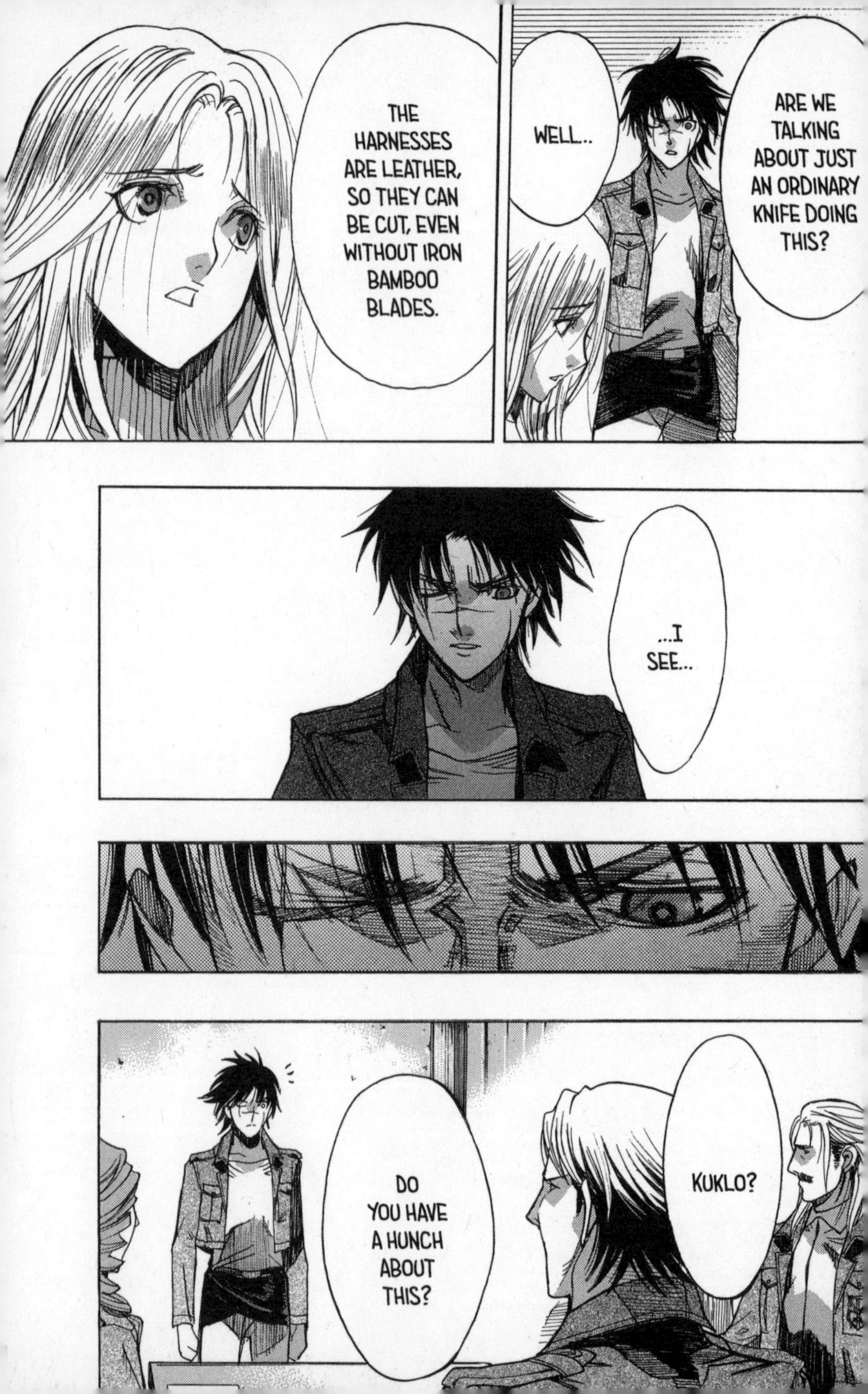
ARE WE TALKING ABOUT JUST AN ORDINARY KNIFE DOING THIS?
WELL...
THE HARNESSES ARE LEATHER, SO THEY CAN BE CUT, EVEN WITHOUT IRON BAMBOO BLADES.
...I SEE...
KUKLO?
DO YOU HAVE A HUNCH ABOUT THIS?

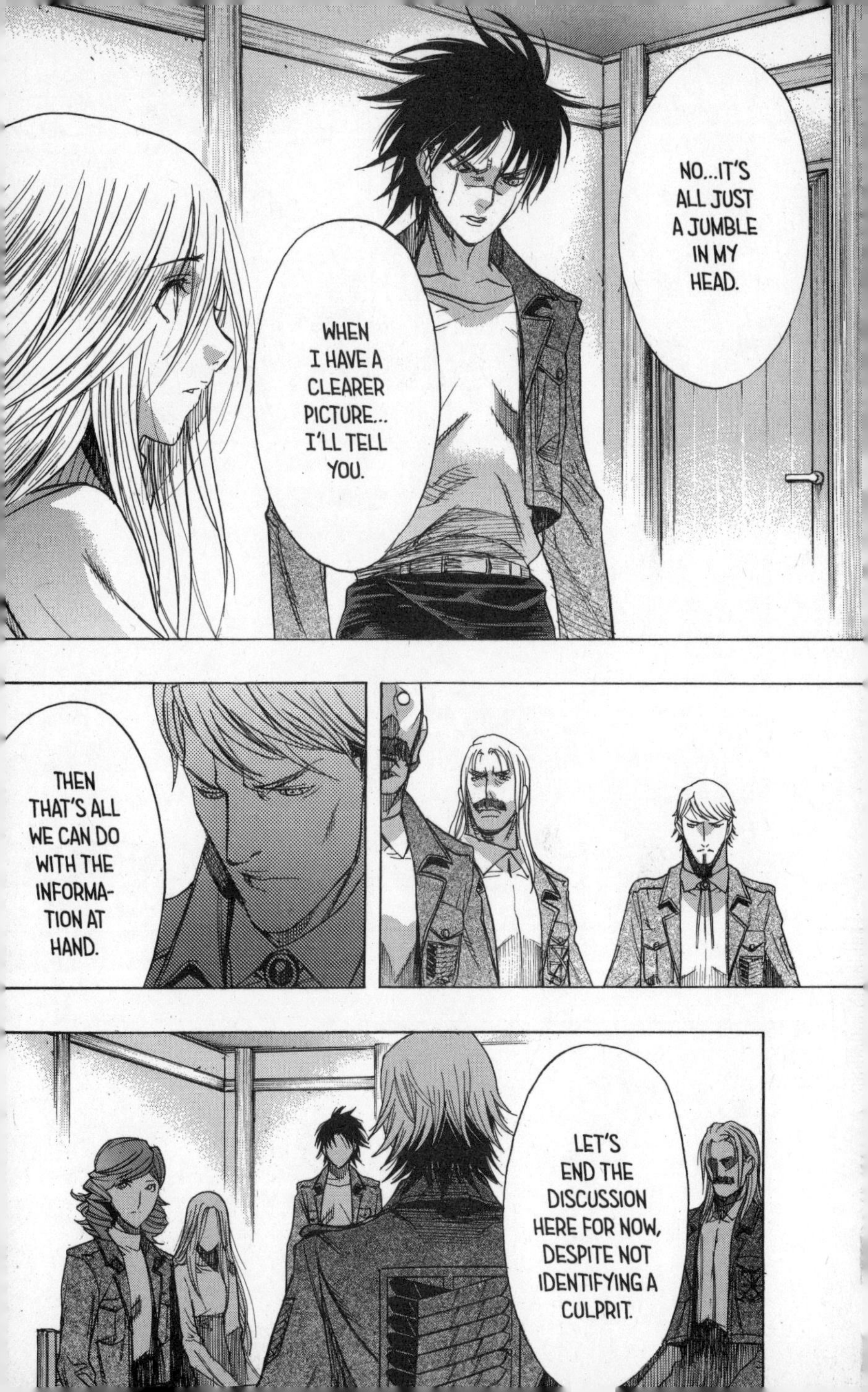
NO...IT'S ALL JUST A JUMBLE IN MY HEAD.
WHEN I HAVE A CLEARER PICTURE... I'LL TELL YOU.
THEN THAT'S ALL WE CAN DO WITH THE INFORMATION AT HAND.
LET'S END THE DISCUSSION HERE FOR NOW, DESPITE NOT IDENTIFYING A CULPRIT.

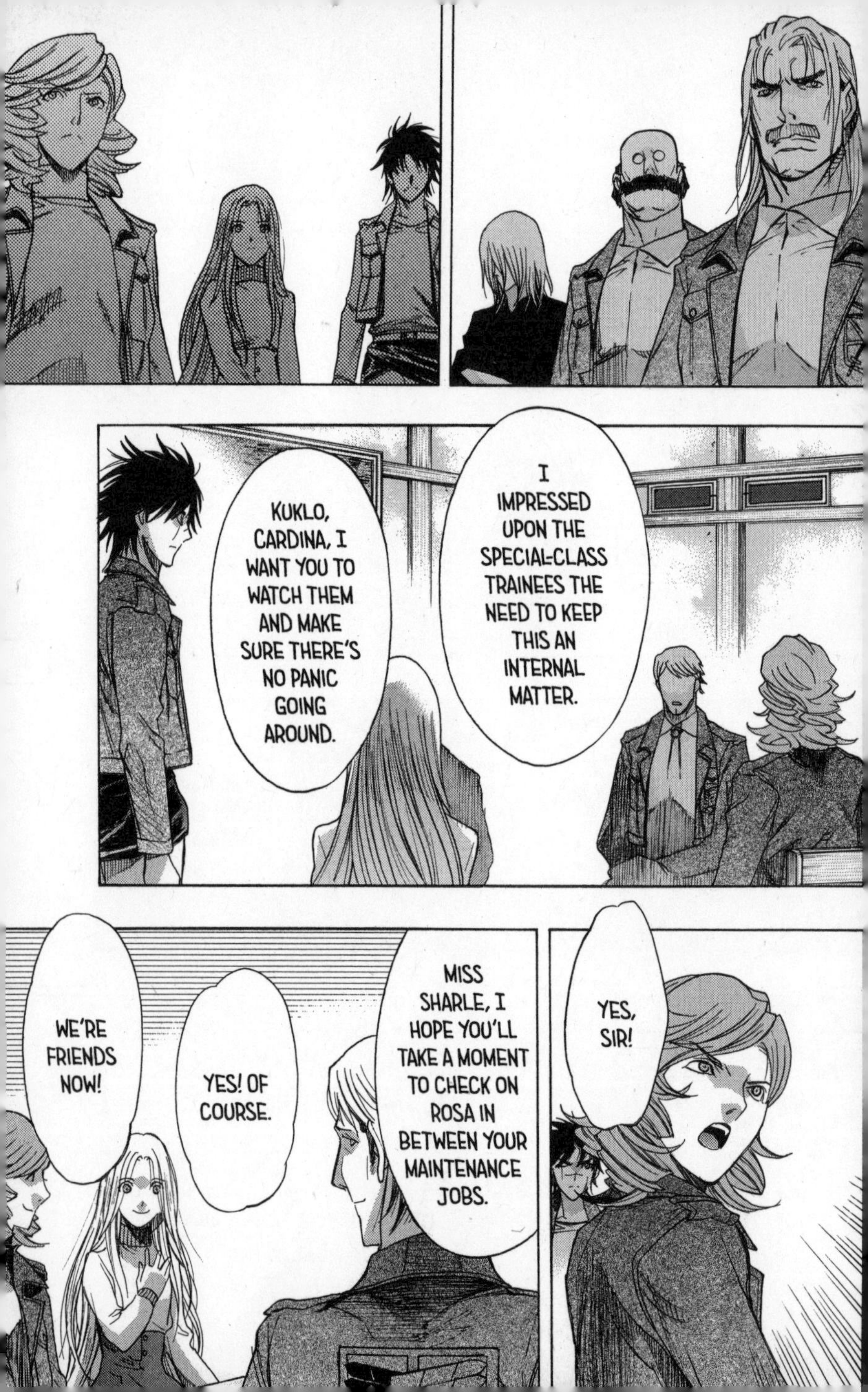
I IMPRESSED UPON THE SPECIAL-CLASS TRAINEES THE NEED TO KEEP THIS AN INTERNAL MATTER.
KUKLO, CARDINA, I WANT YOU TO WATCH THEM AND MAKE SURE THERE'S NO PANIC GOING AROUND.
YES, SIR!
MISS SHARLE, I HOPE YOU'LL TAKE A MOMENT TO CHECK ON ROSA IN BETWEEN YOUR MAINTENANCE JOBS.
YES! OF COURSE.
WE'RE FRIENDS NOW!

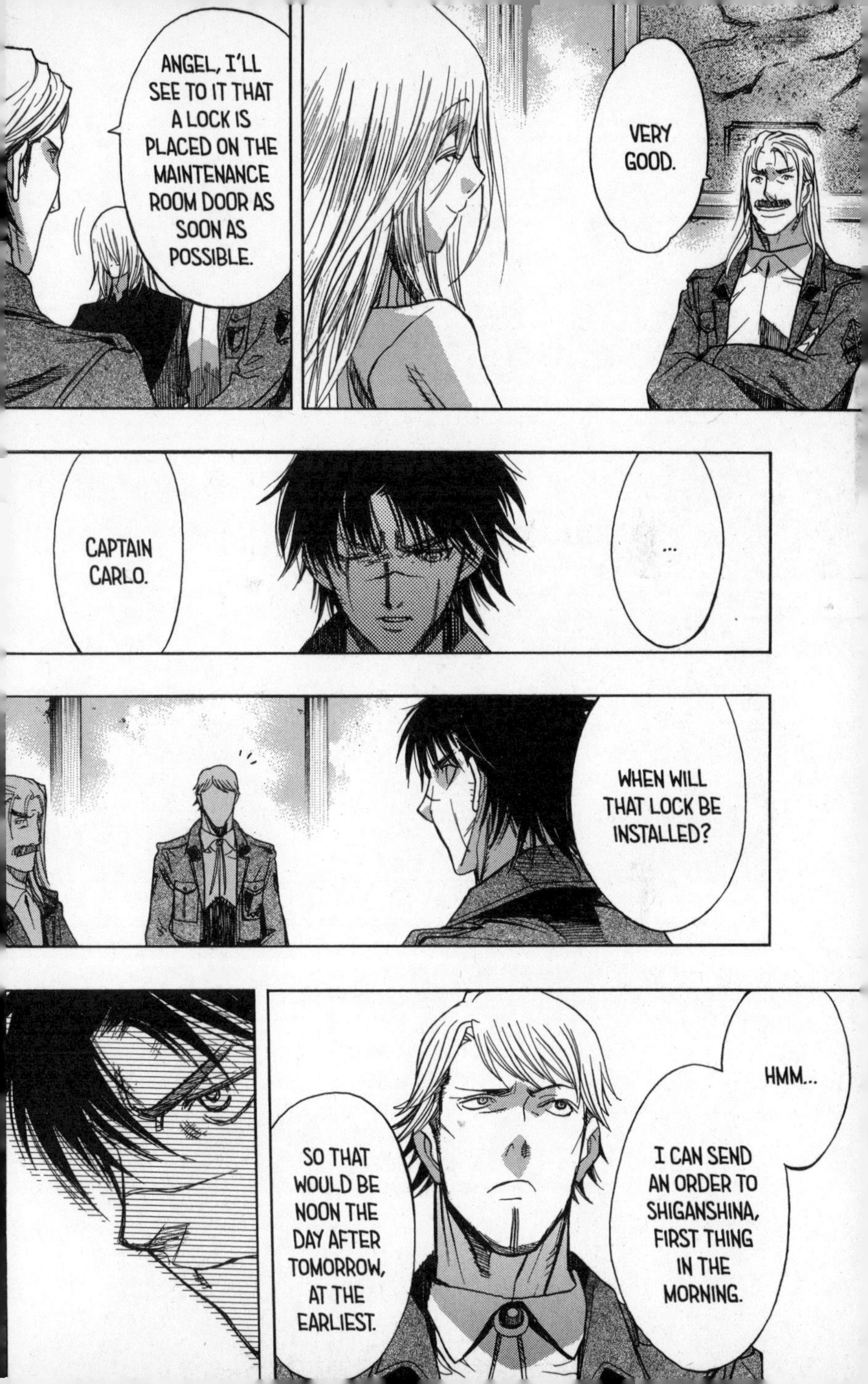
VERY GOOD.
ANGEL, I'LL SEE TO IT THAT A LOCK IS PLACED ON THE MAINTENANCE ROOM DOOR AS SOON AS POSSIBLE.
...
CAPTAIN CARLO.
WHEN WILL THAT LOCK BE INSTALLED?
HMM...
I CAN SEND AN ORDER TO SHIGANSHINA, FIRST THING IN THE MORNING.
SO THAT WOULD BE NOON THE DAY AFTER TOMORROW, AT THE EARLIEST.

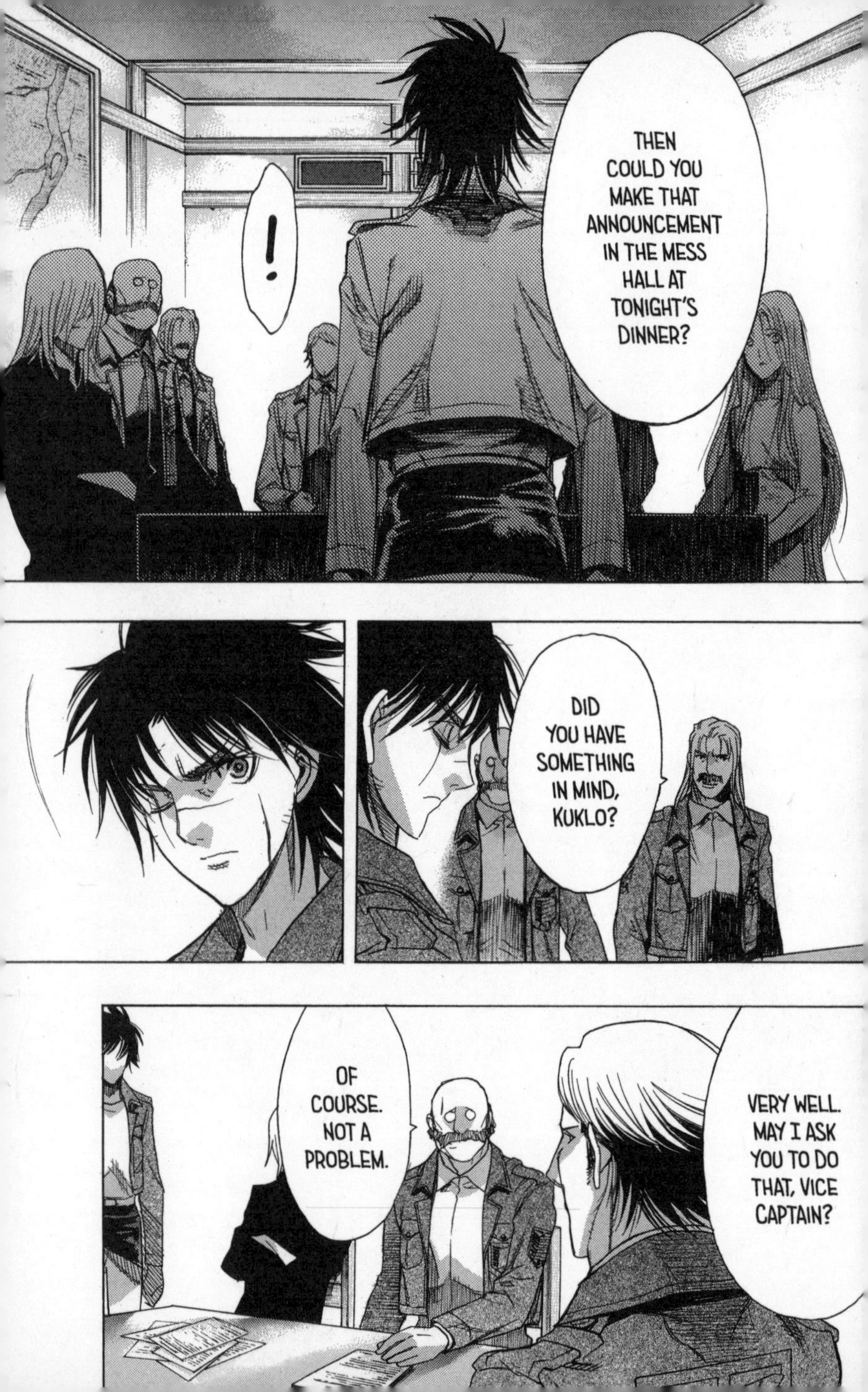
THEN COULD YOU MAKE THAT ANNOUNCEMENT IN THE MESS HALL AT TONIGHT'S DINNER?
!
DID YOU HAVE SOMETHING IN MIND, KUKLO?
VERY WELL. MAY I ASK YOU TO DO THAT, VICE CAPTAIN?
OF COURSE. NOT A PROBLEM.

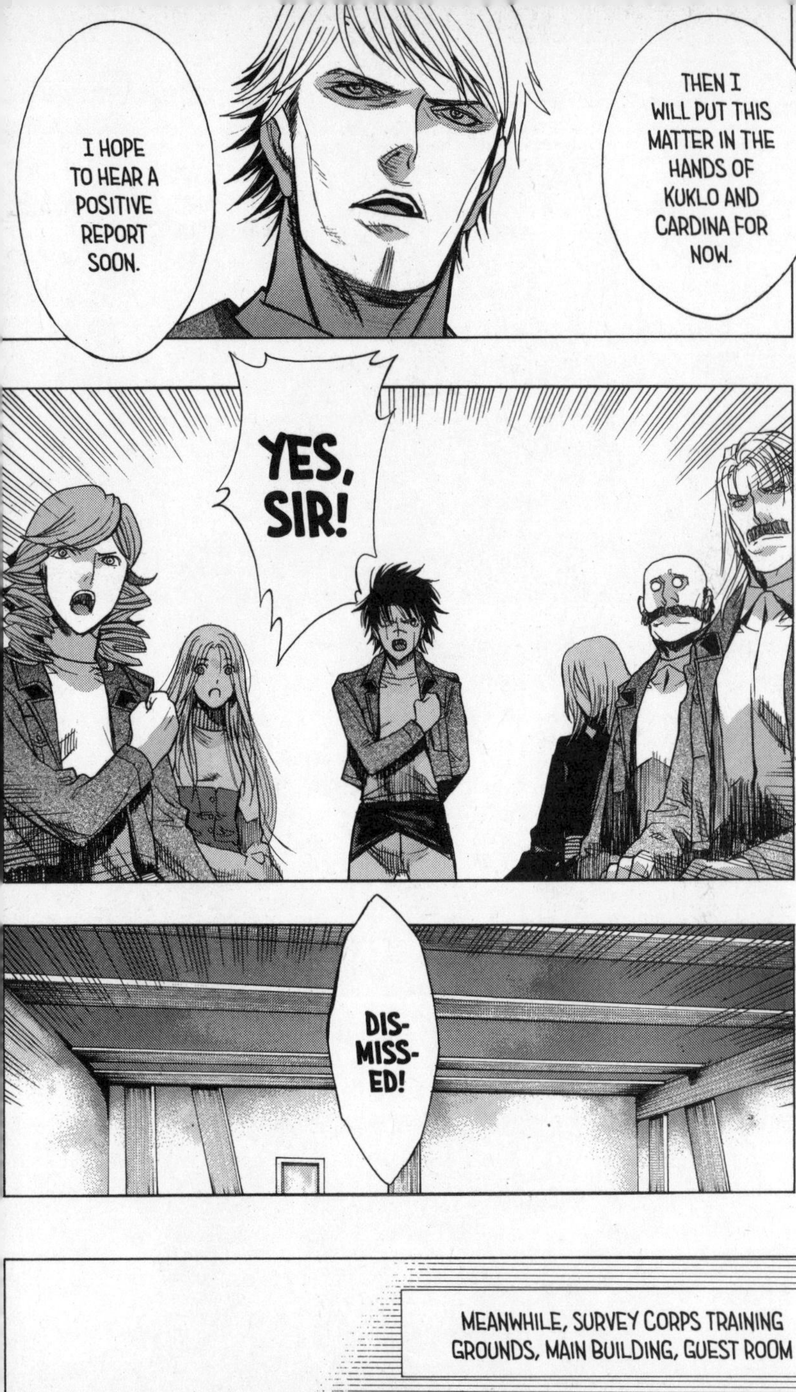
THEN I WILL PUT THIS MATTER IN THE HANDS OF KUKLO AND CARDINA FOR NOW.
I HOPE TO HEAR A POSITIVE REPORT SOON.
YES, SIR!
DIS-MISS-ED!
MEANWHILE, SURVEY CORPS TRAINING GROUNDS, MAIN BUILDING, GUEST ROOM

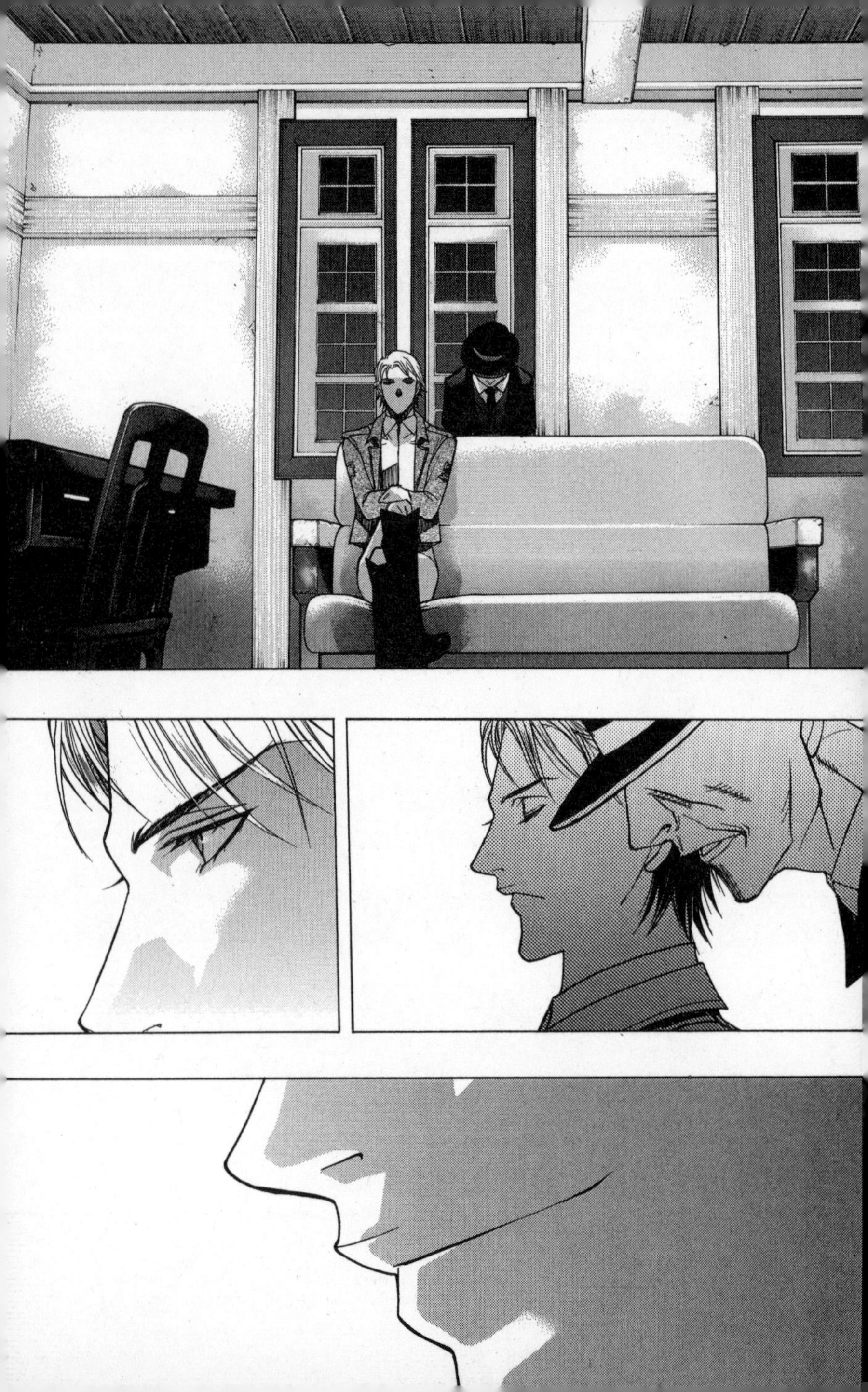

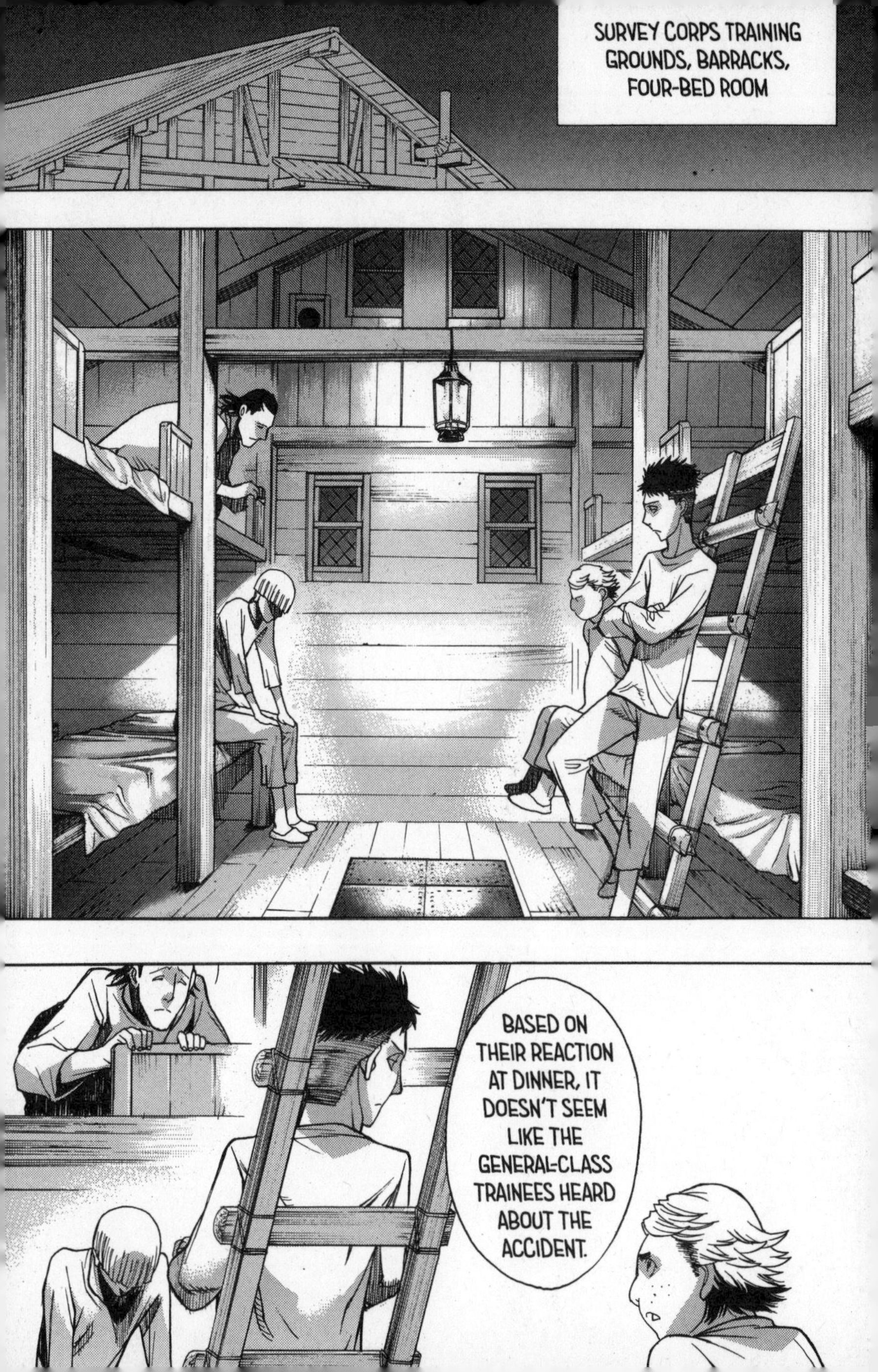
SURVEY CORPS TRAINING GROUNDS, BARRACKS, FOUR-BED ROOM
BASED ON THEIR REACTION AT DINNER, IT DOESN'T SEEM LIKE THE GENERAL-CLASS TRAINEES HEARD ABOUT THE ACCIDENT.

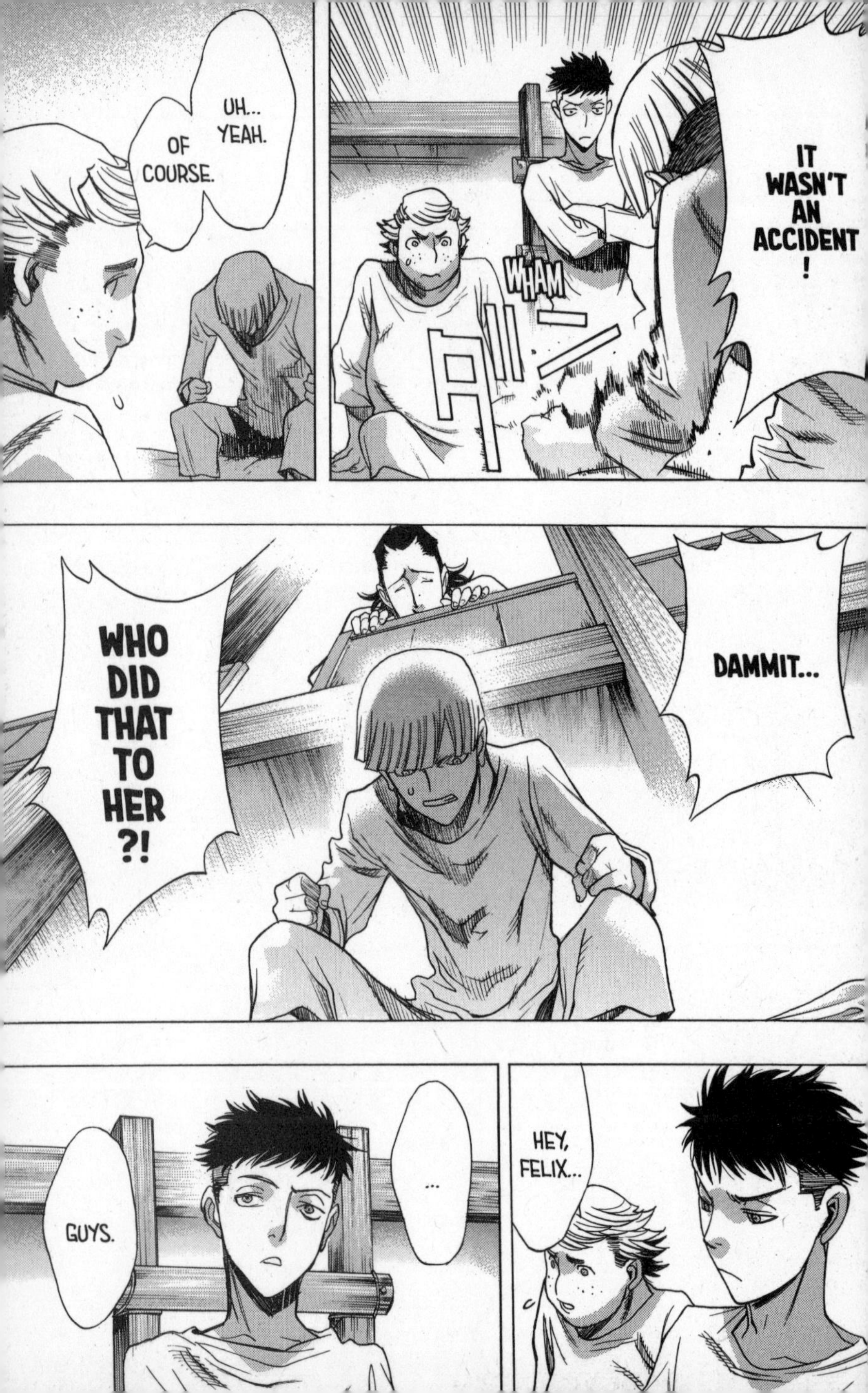
IT WASN'T AN ACCIDENT!
WHAM
UH... YEAH.
OF COURSE.
DAMMIT...
WHO DID THAT TO HER?!
HEY, FELIX...
...
GUYS.

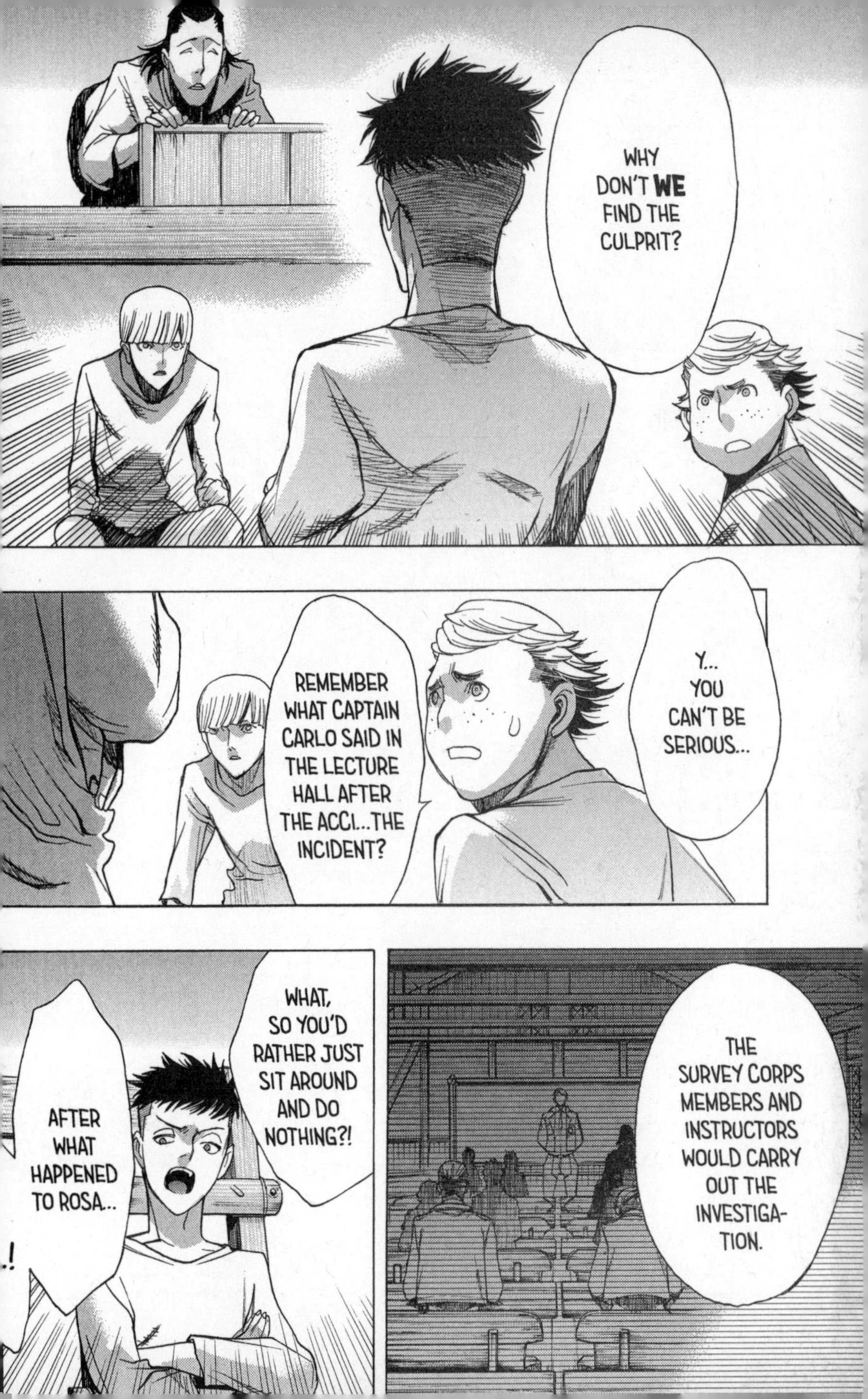
WHY DON'T **WE** FIND THE CULPRIT?
Y... YOU CAN'T BE SERIOUS...
REMEMBER WHAT CAPTAIN CARLO SAID IN THE LECTURE HALL AFTER THE ACCI...THE INCIDENT?
THE SURVEY CORPS MEMBERS AND INSTRUCTORS WOULD CARRY OUT THE INVESTIGA-TION.
WHAT, SO YOU'D RATHER JUST SIT AROUND AND DO NOTHING?!
AFTER WHAT HAPPENED TO ROSA...

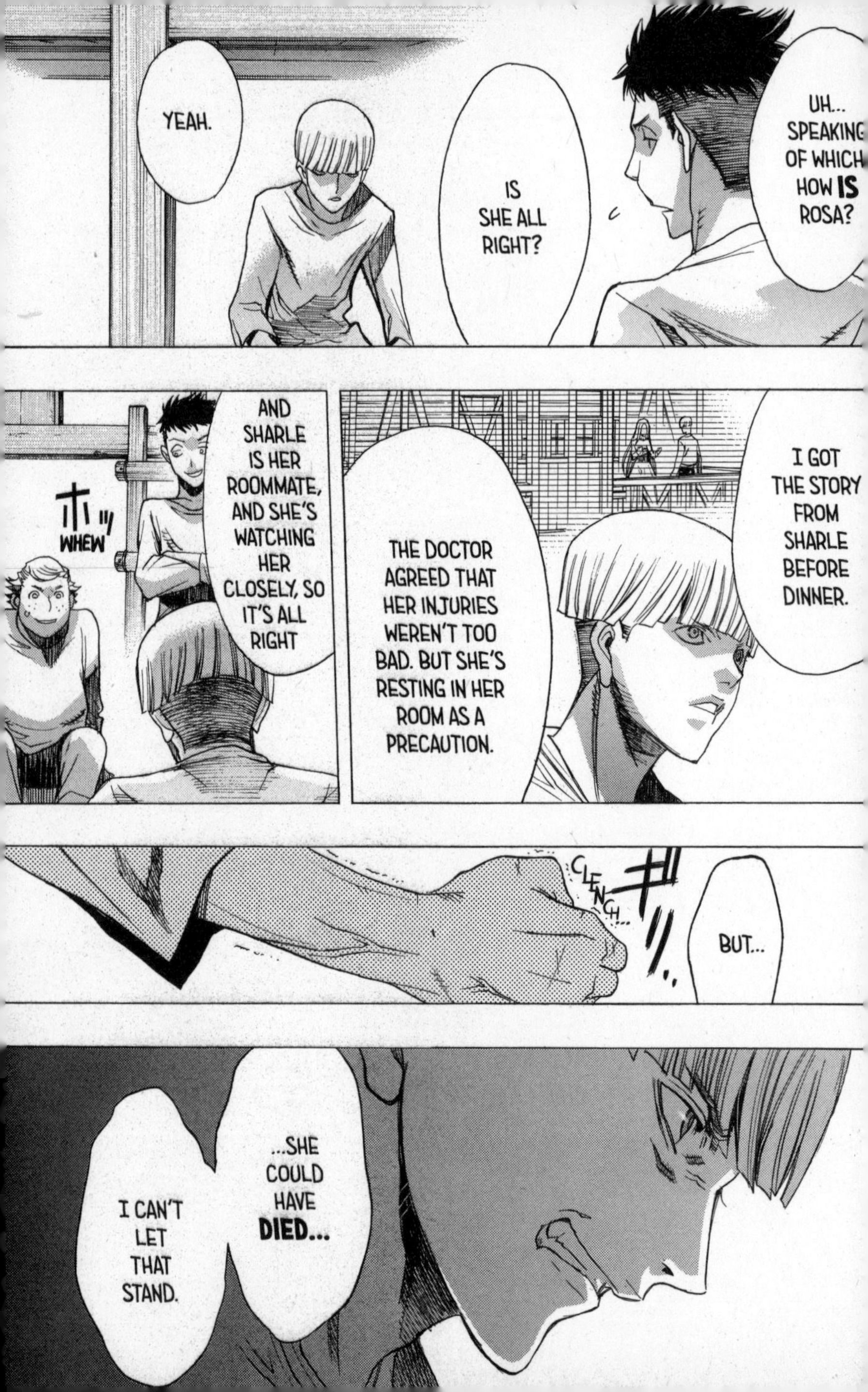
UH... SPEAKING OF WHICH HOW **IS** ROSA?
IS SHE ALL RIGHT?
YEAH.
I GOT THE STORY FROM SHARLE BEFORE DINNER.
THE DOCTOR AGREED THAT HER INJURIES WEREN'T TOO BAD. BUT SHE'S RESTING IN HER ROOM AS A PRECAUTION.
AND SHARLE IS HER ROOMMATE, AND SHE'S WATCHING HER CLOSELY, SO IT'S ALL RIGHT
ホッ
WHEW
BUT...
CLENCH...
...SHE COULD HAVE **DIED...**
I CAN'T LET THAT STAND.

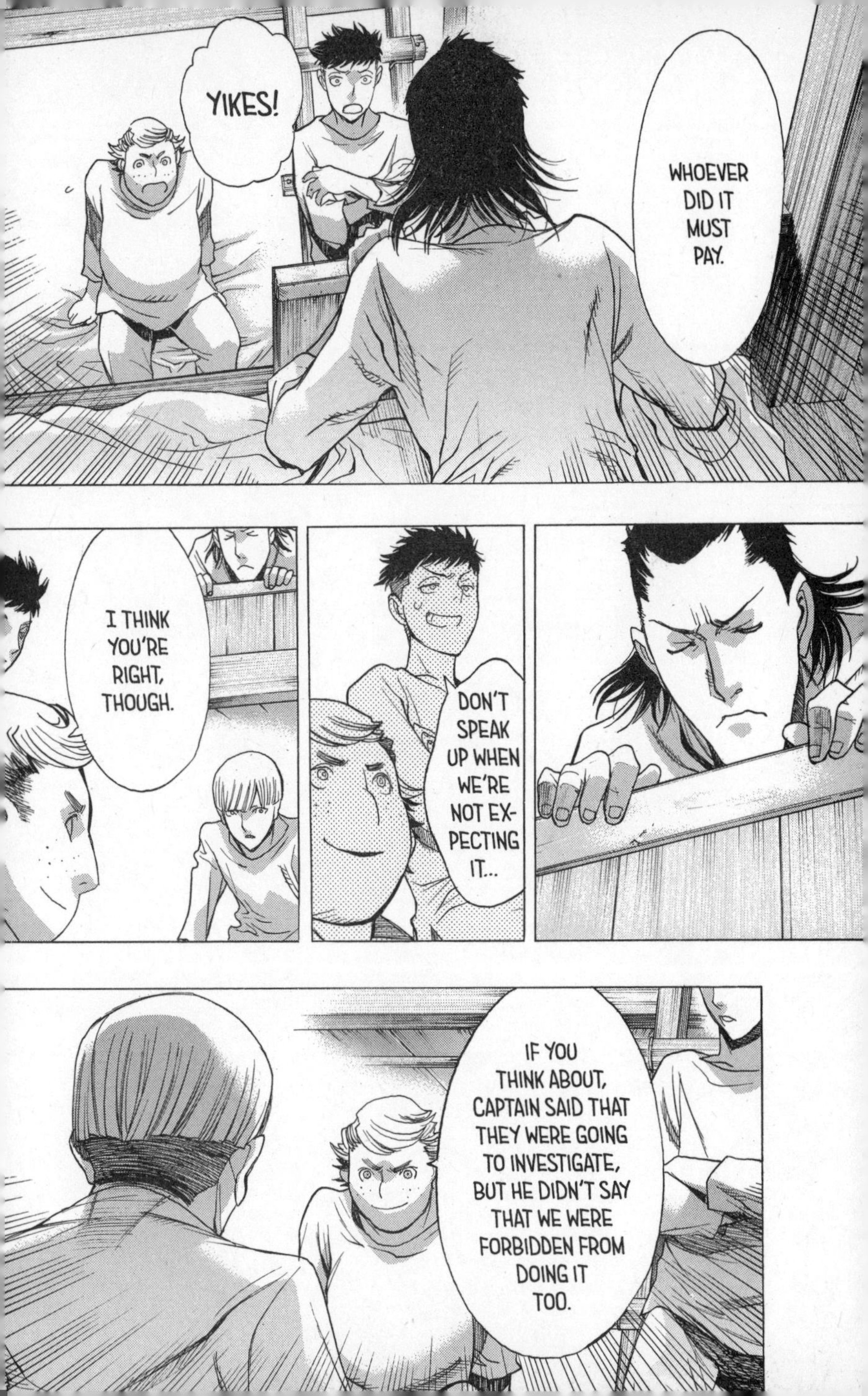
WHOEVER DID IT MUST PAY.
YIKES!
DON'T SPEAK UP WHEN WE'RE NOT EX-PECTING IT...
I THINK YOU'RE RIGHT, THOUGH.
IF YOU THINK ABOUT, CAPTAIN SAID THAT THEY WERE GOING TO INVESTIGATE, BUT HE DIDN'T SAY THAT WE WERE FORBIDDEN FROM DOING IT TOO.

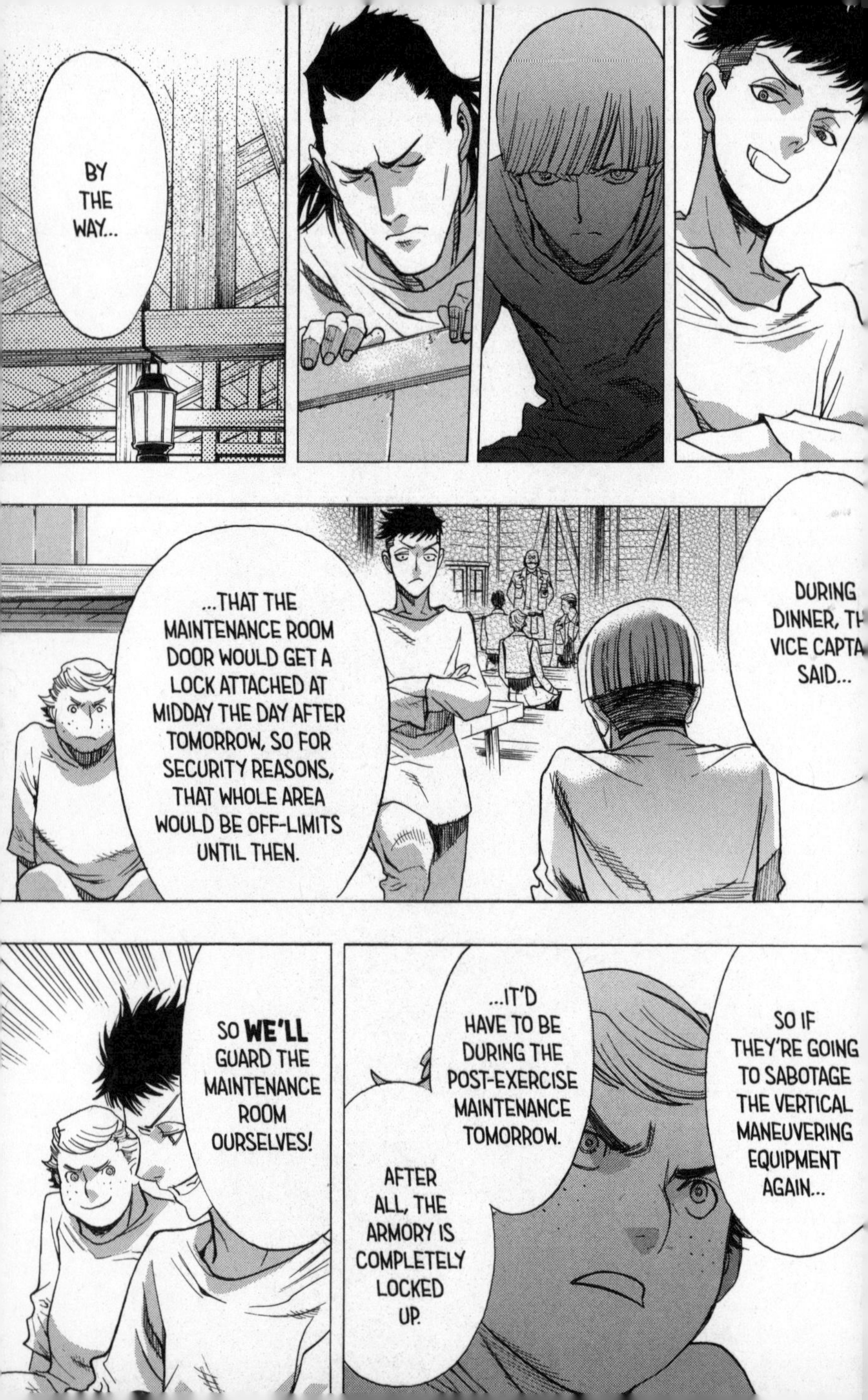
BY THE WAY...
DURING DINNER, TH
VICE CAPTA
SAID...
...THAT THE MAINTENANCE ROOM DOOR WOULD GET A LOCK ATTACHED AT MIDDAY THE DAY AFTER TOMORROW, SO FOR SECURITY REASONS, THAT WHOLE AREA WOULD BE OFF-LIMITS UNTIL THEN.
SO IF THEY'RE GOING TO SABOTAGE THE VERTICAL MANEUVERING EQUIPMENT AGAIN...
...IT'D HAVE TO BE DURING THE POST-EXERCISE MAINTENANCE TOMORROW.
AFTER ALL, THE ARMORY IS COMPLETELY LOCKED UP.
SO **WE'LL** GUARD THE MAINTENANCE ROOM OURSELVES!

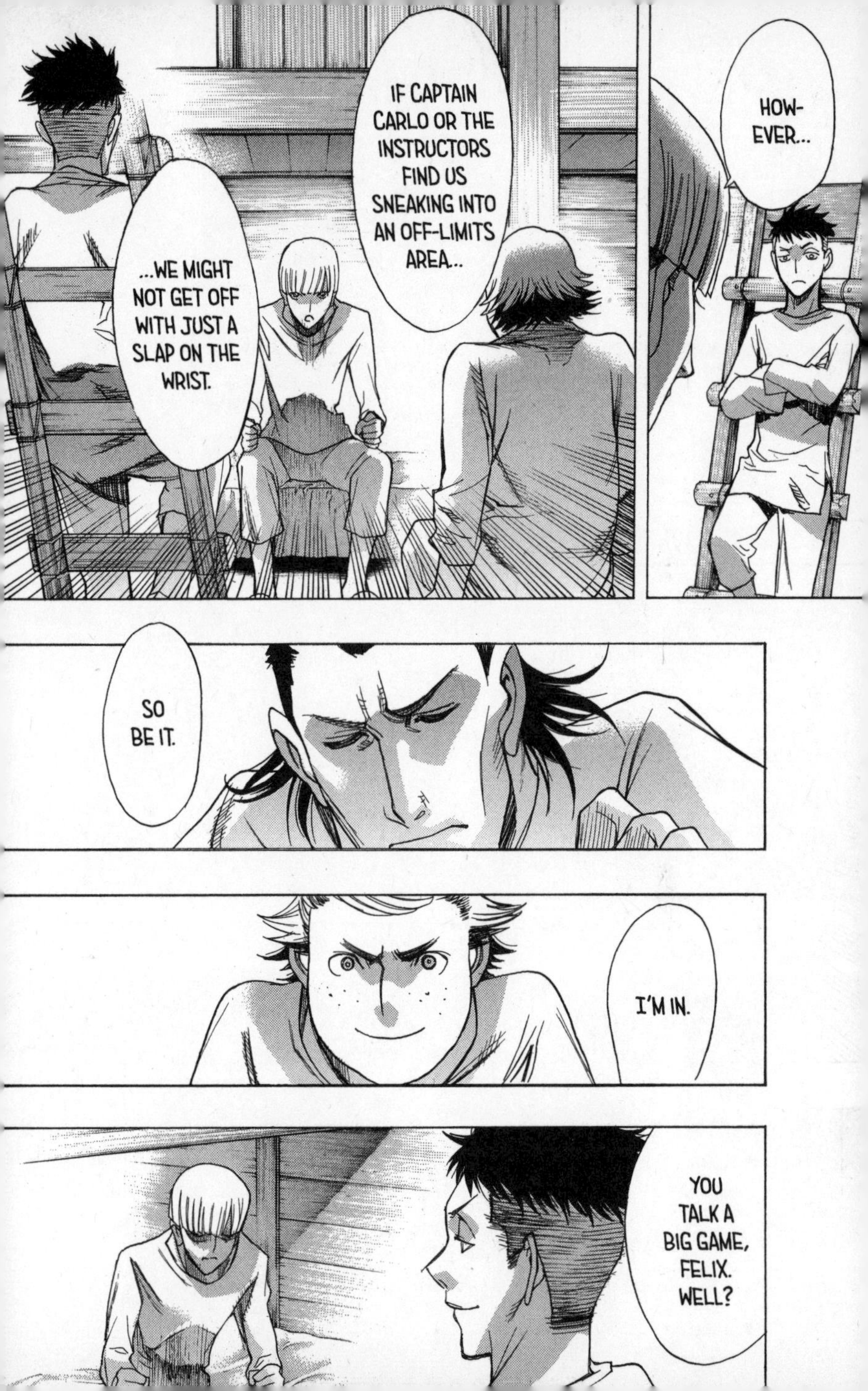
HOW-EVER...
IF CAPTAIN CARLO OR THE INSTRUCTORS FIND US SNEAKING INTO AN OFF-LIMITS AREA...
...WE MIGHT NOT GET OFF WITH JUST A SLAP ON THE WRIST.
SO BE IT.
I'M IN.
YOU TALK A BIG GAME, FELIX. WELL?

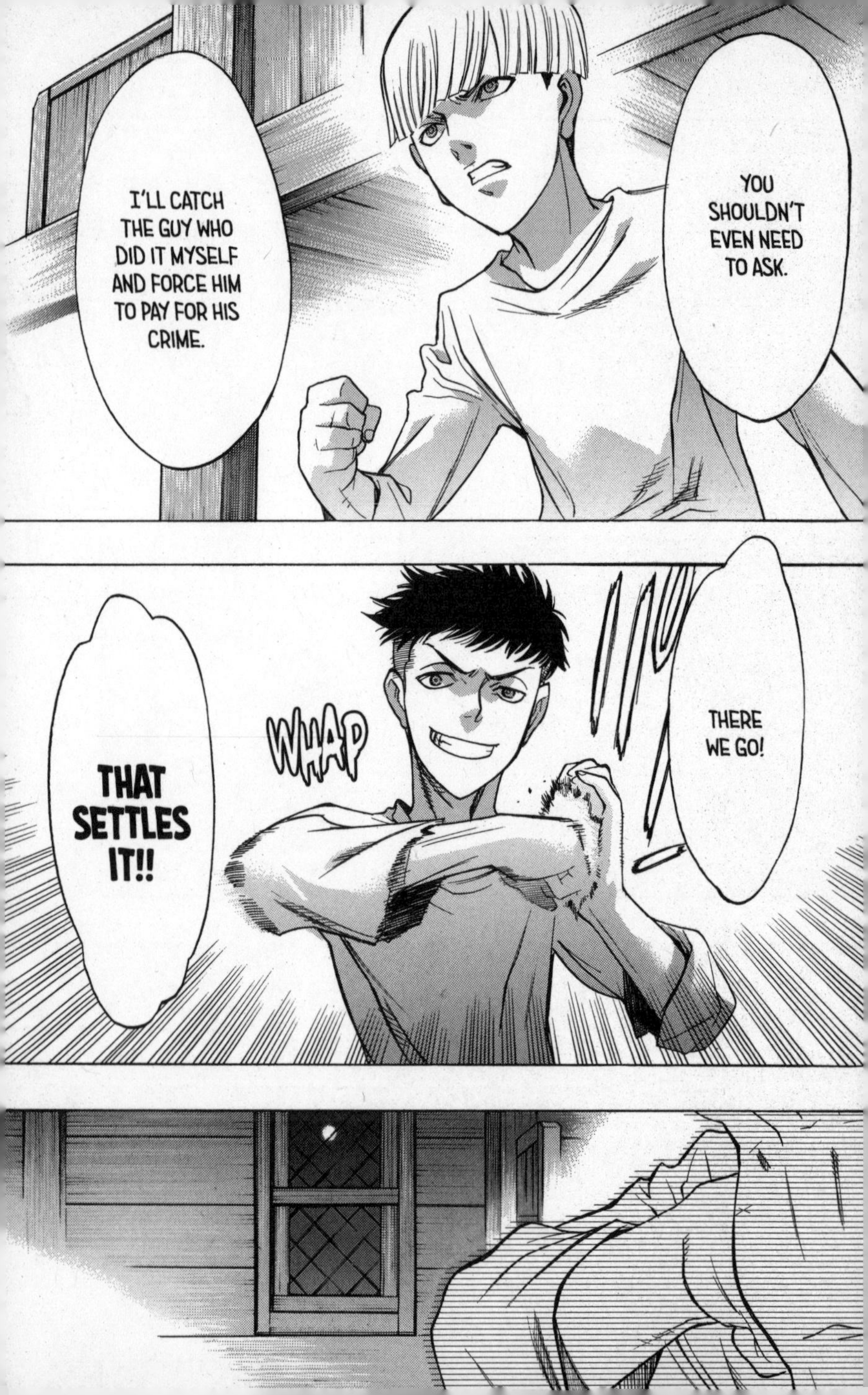
YOU SHOULDN'T EVEN NEED TO ASK.
I'LL CATCH THE GUY WHO DID IT MYSELF AND FORCE HIM TO PAY FOR HIS CRIME.
THERE WE GO!
WHAP
THAT SETTLES IT!!

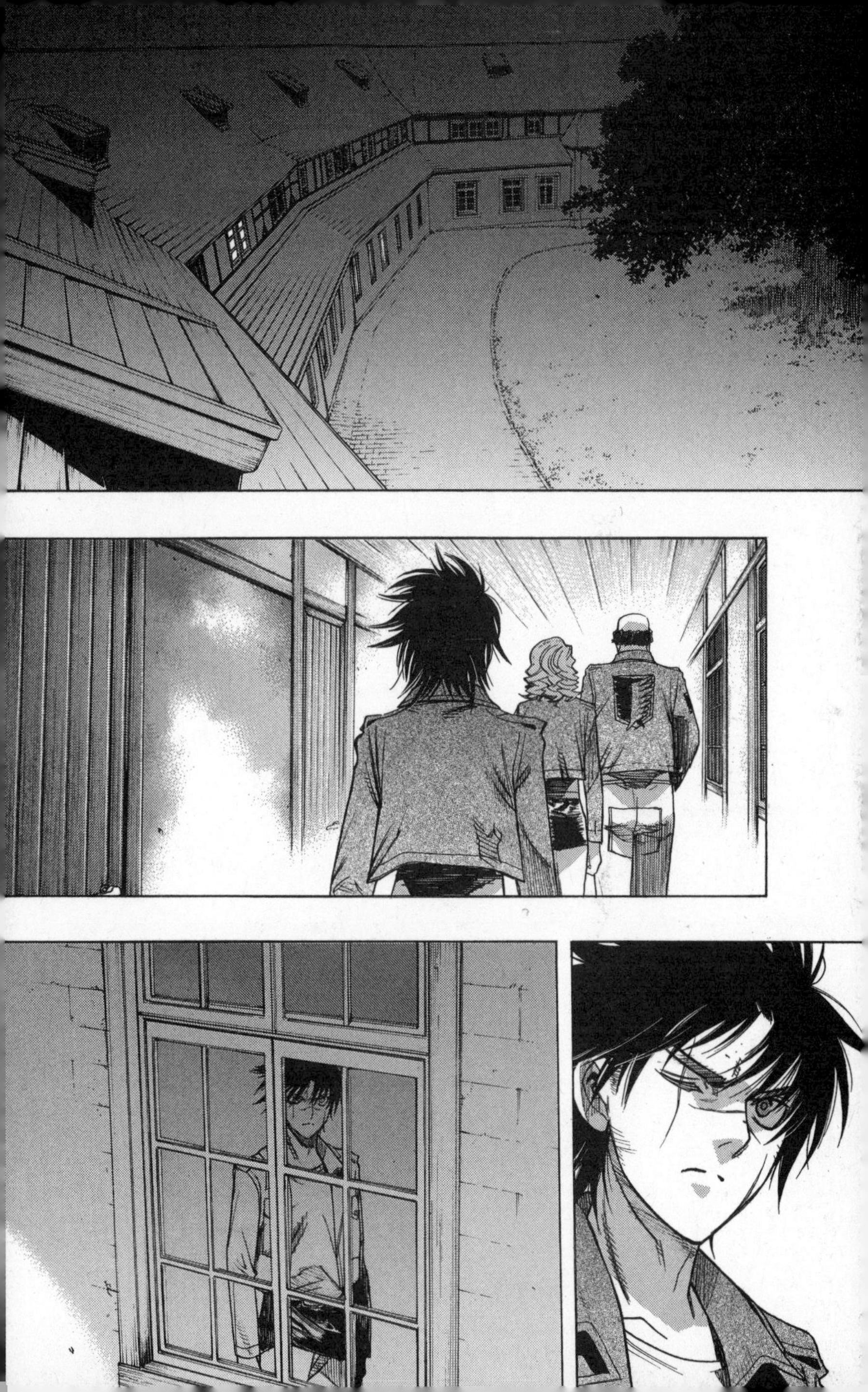

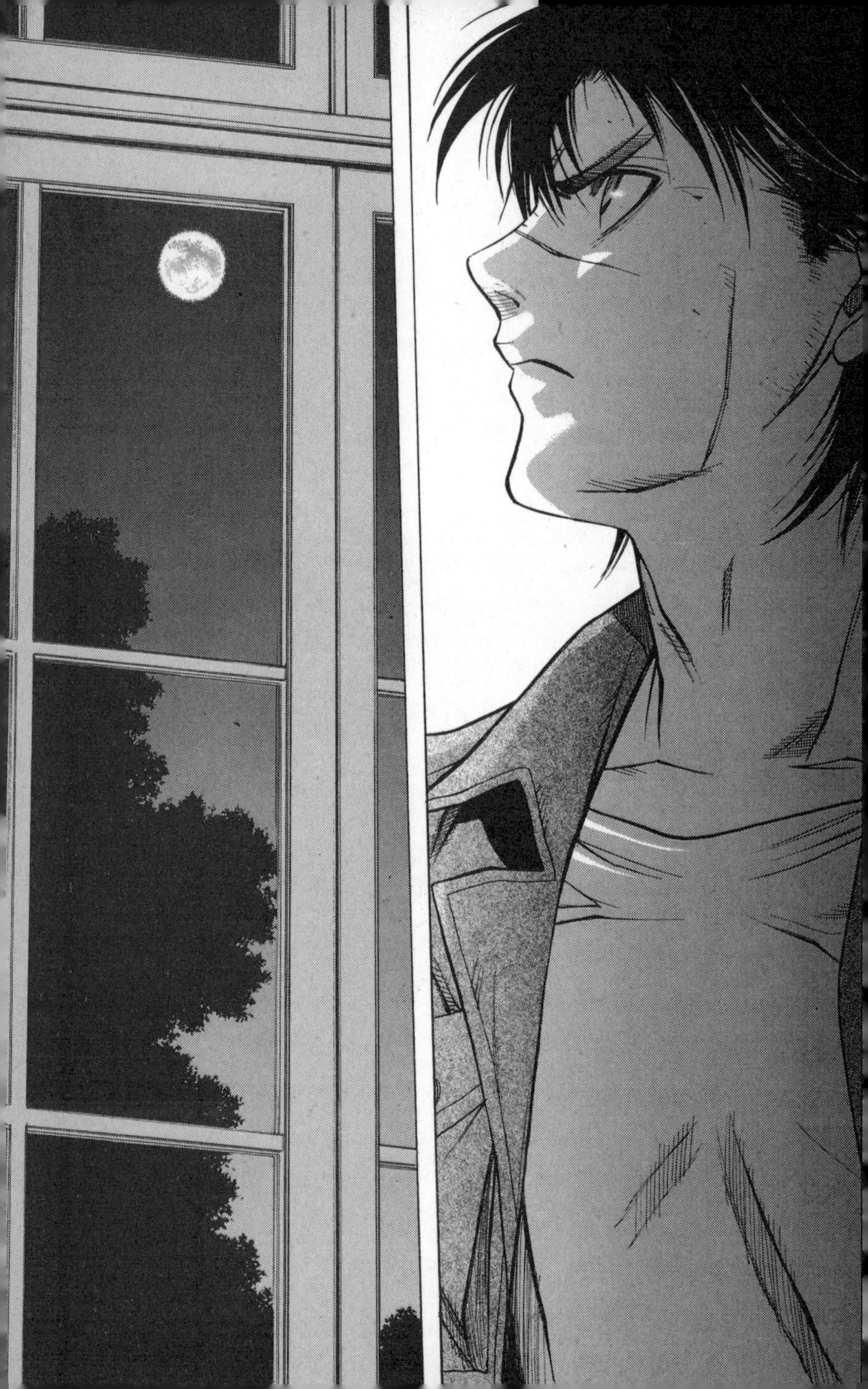

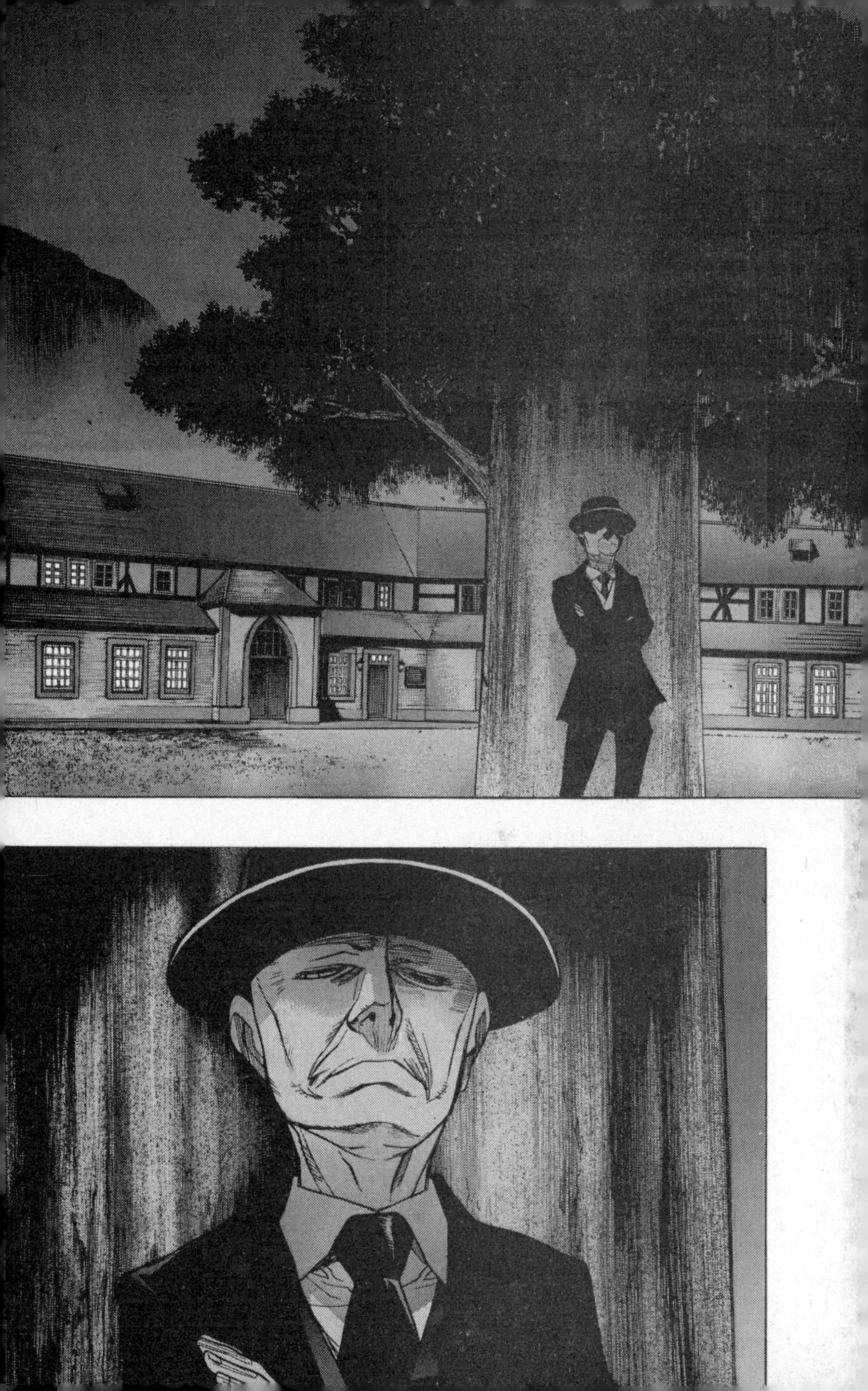

Chapter 54: In the Thick of Paranoia · End

ATTACK on TITAN

BEFORE THE FALL

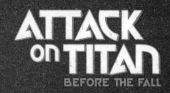

Chapter 55: Box of Delusions

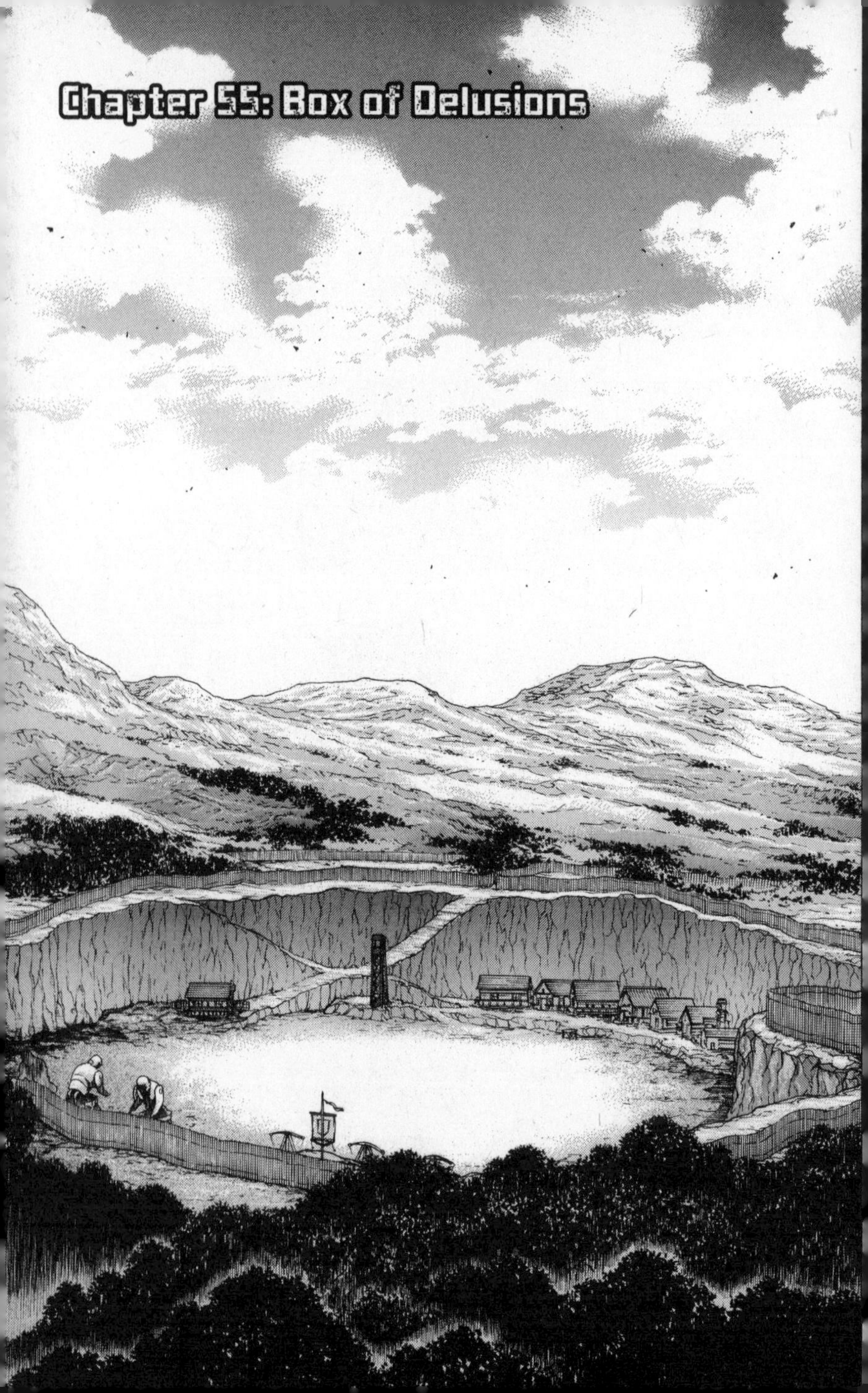

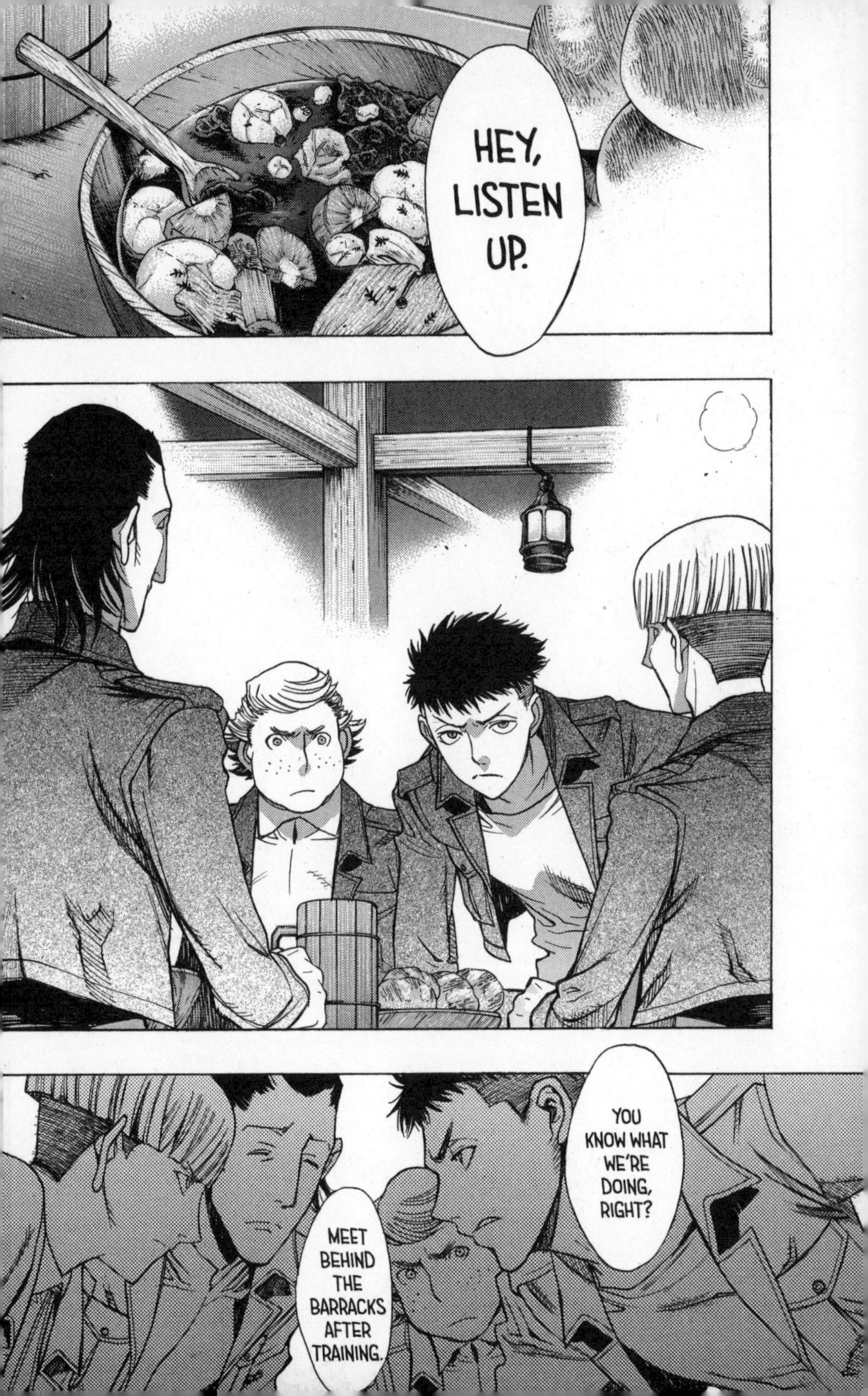
HEY, LISTEN UP.
YOU KNOW WHAT WE'RE DOING, RIGHT?
MEET BEHIND THE BARRACKS AFTER TRAINING.

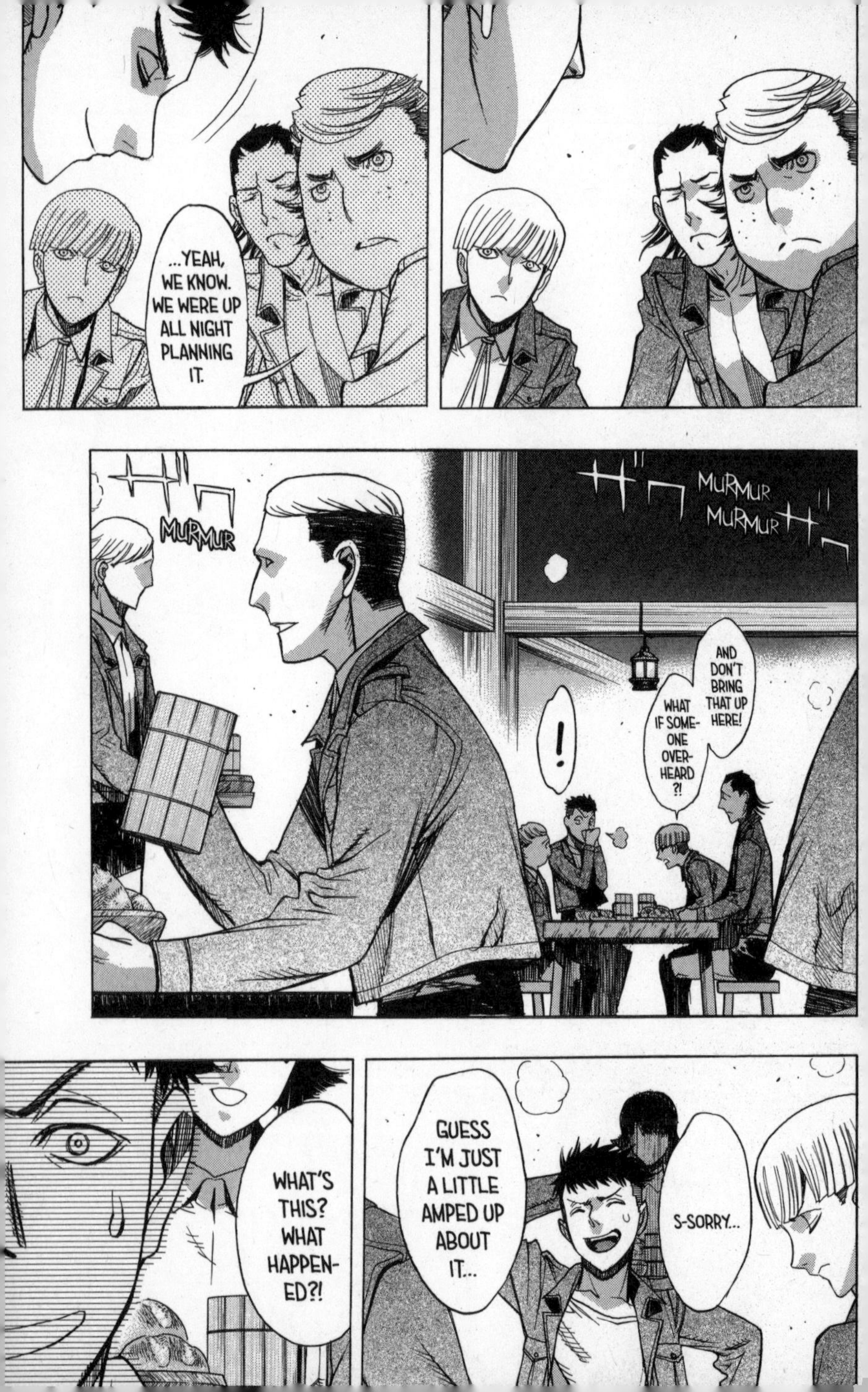
...YEAH, WE KNOW. WE WERE UP ALL NIGHT PLANNING IT.
MURMUR
MURMUR
AND DON'T BRING THAT UP HERE!
WHAT IF SOME-ONE OVER-HEARD?!
!
MURMUR
S-SORRY...
GUESS I'M JUST A LITTLE AMPED UP ABOUT IT...
WHAT'S THIS? WHAT HAPPEN-ED?!

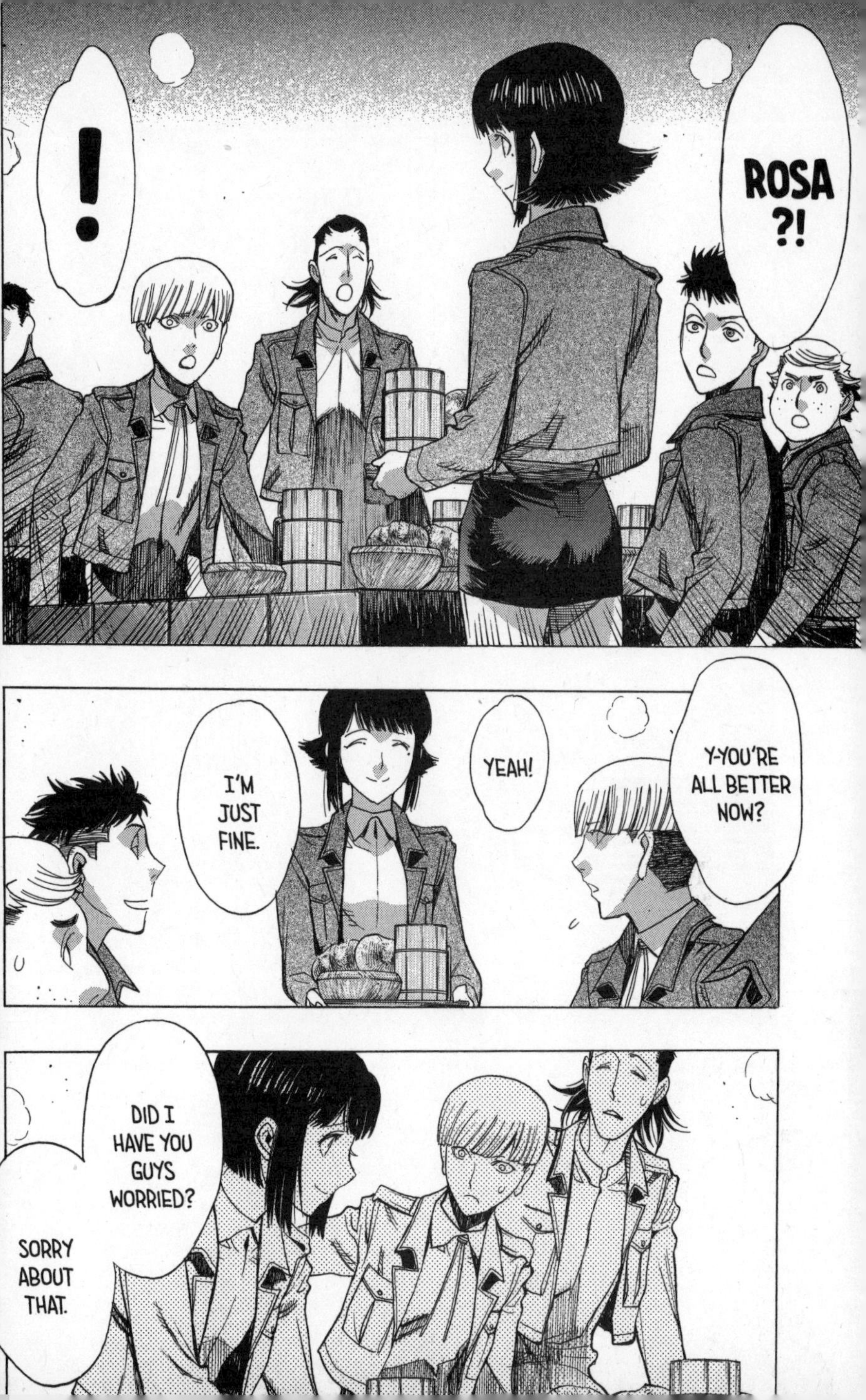
ROSA ?!
!
Y-YOU'RE ALL BETTER NOW?
YEAH!
I'M JUST FINE.
DID I HAVE YOU GUYS WORRIED?
SORRY ABOUT THAT.

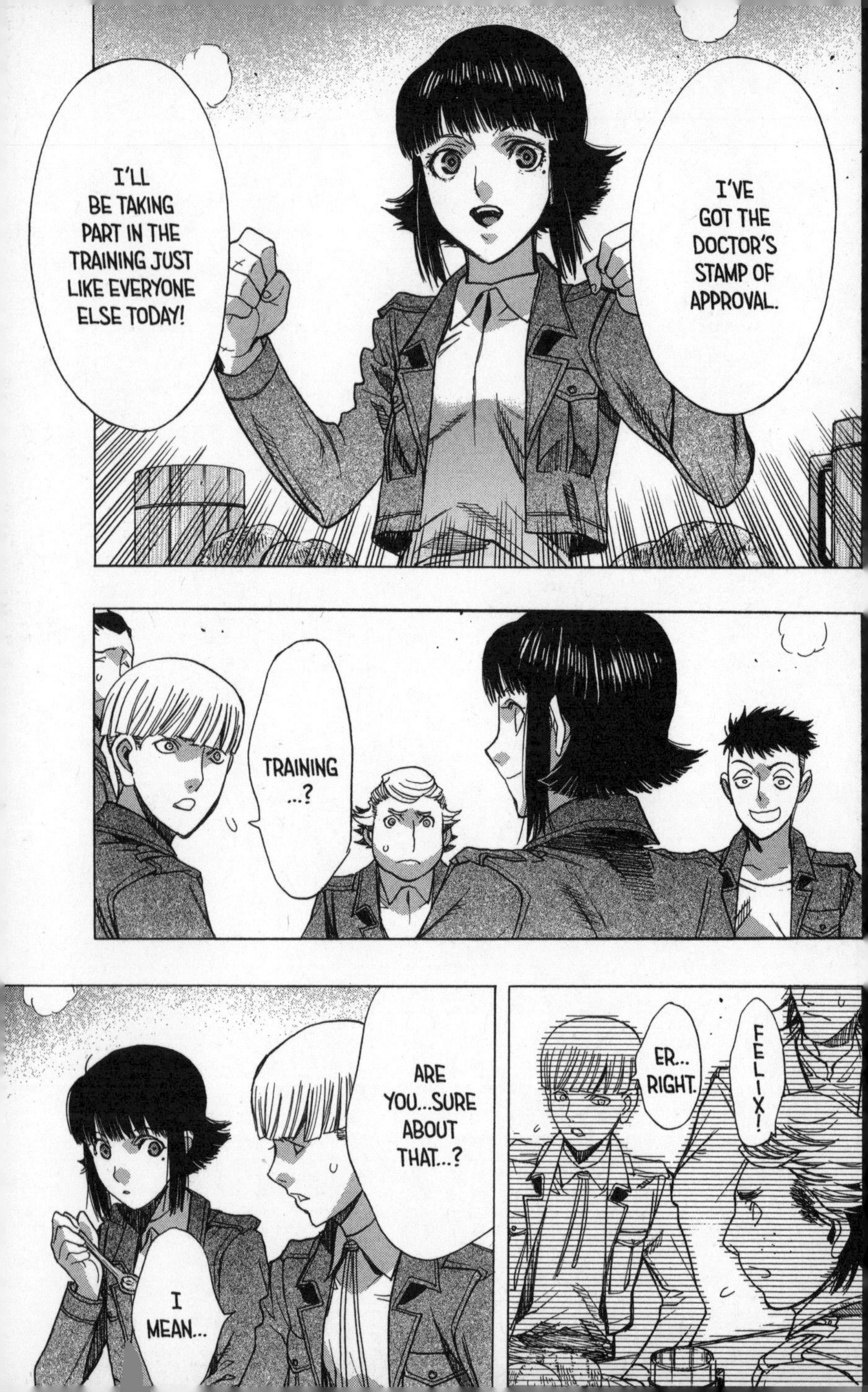
I'VE GOT THE DOCTOR'S STAMP OF APPROVAL.
I'LL BE TAKING PART IN THE TRAINING JUST LIKE EVERYONE ELSE TODAY!
TRAINING ...?
FELIX!
ER... RIGHT.
ARE YOU...SURE ABOUT THAT...?
I MEAN...

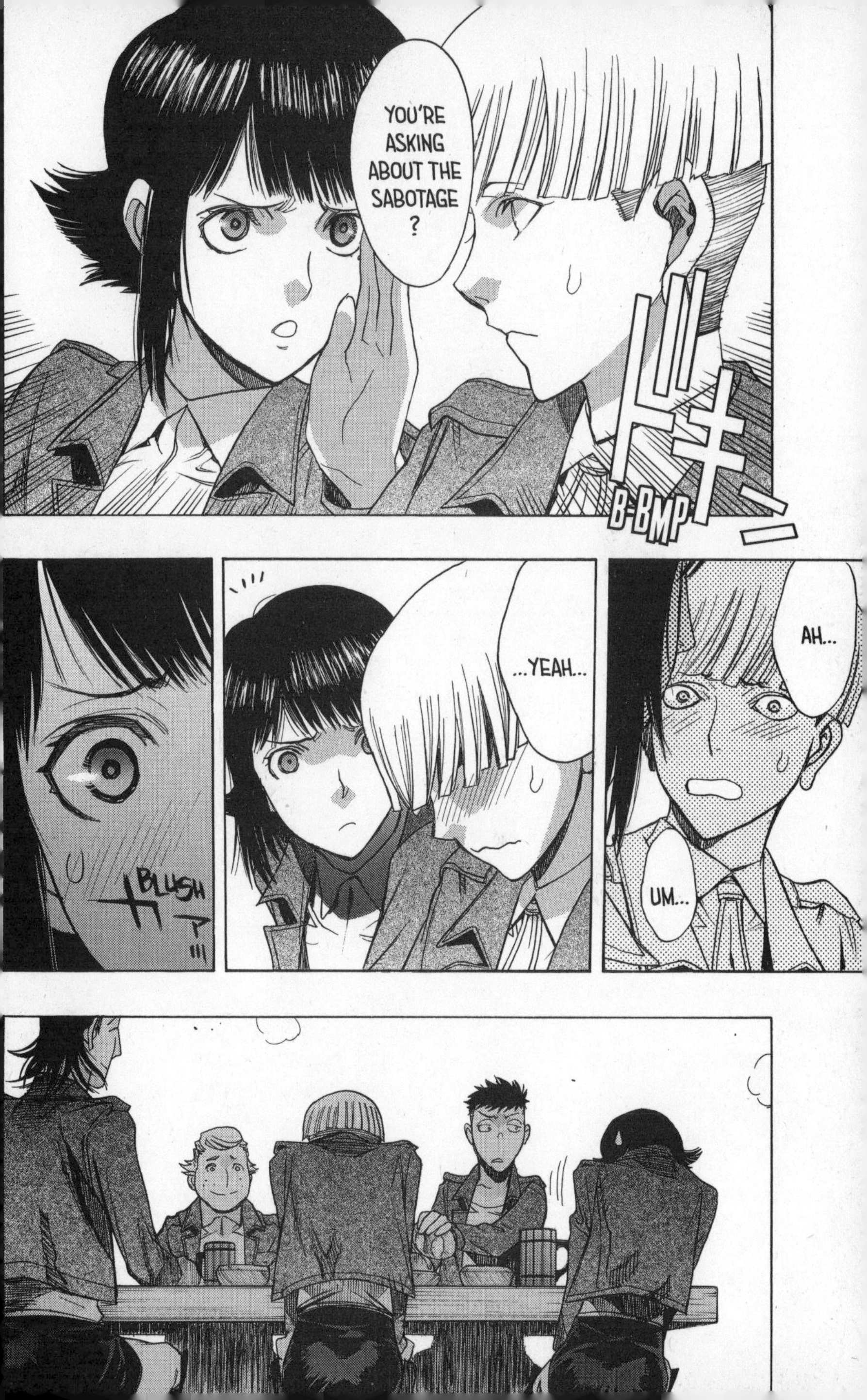
YOU'RE ASKING ABOUT THE SABOTAGE?
B-BMP
AH...
UM...
...YEAH...
BLUSH

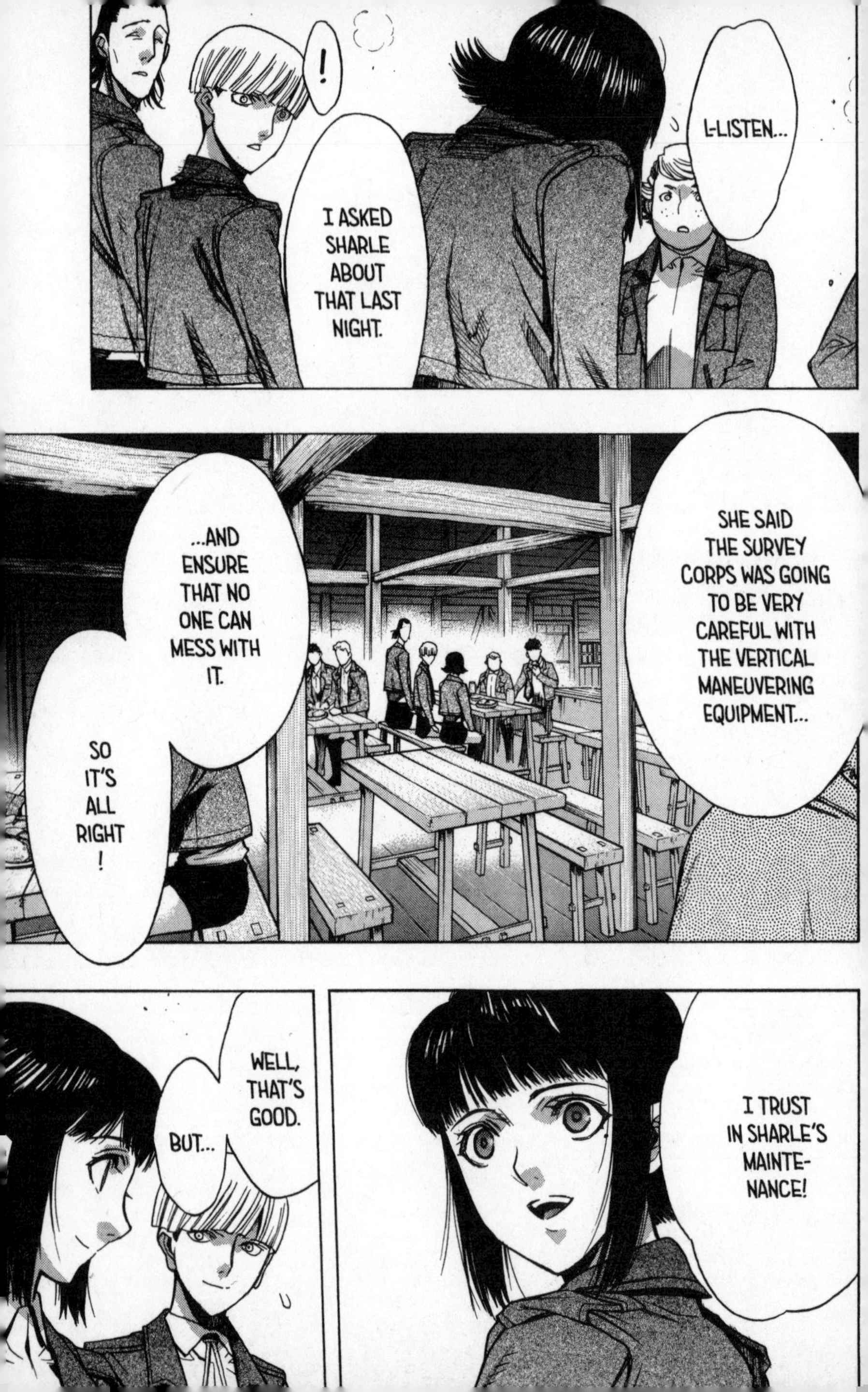
L-LISTEN...
!
I ASKED SHARLE ABOUT THAT LAST NIGHT.
SHE SAID THE SURVEY CORPS WAS GOING TO BE VERY CAREFUL WITH THE VERTICAL MANEUVERING EQUIPMENT...
...AND ENSURE THAT NO ONE CAN MESS WITH IT.
SO IT'S ALL RIGHT!
I TRUST IN SHARLE'S MAINTE-NANCE!
WELL, THAT'S GOOD.
BUT...

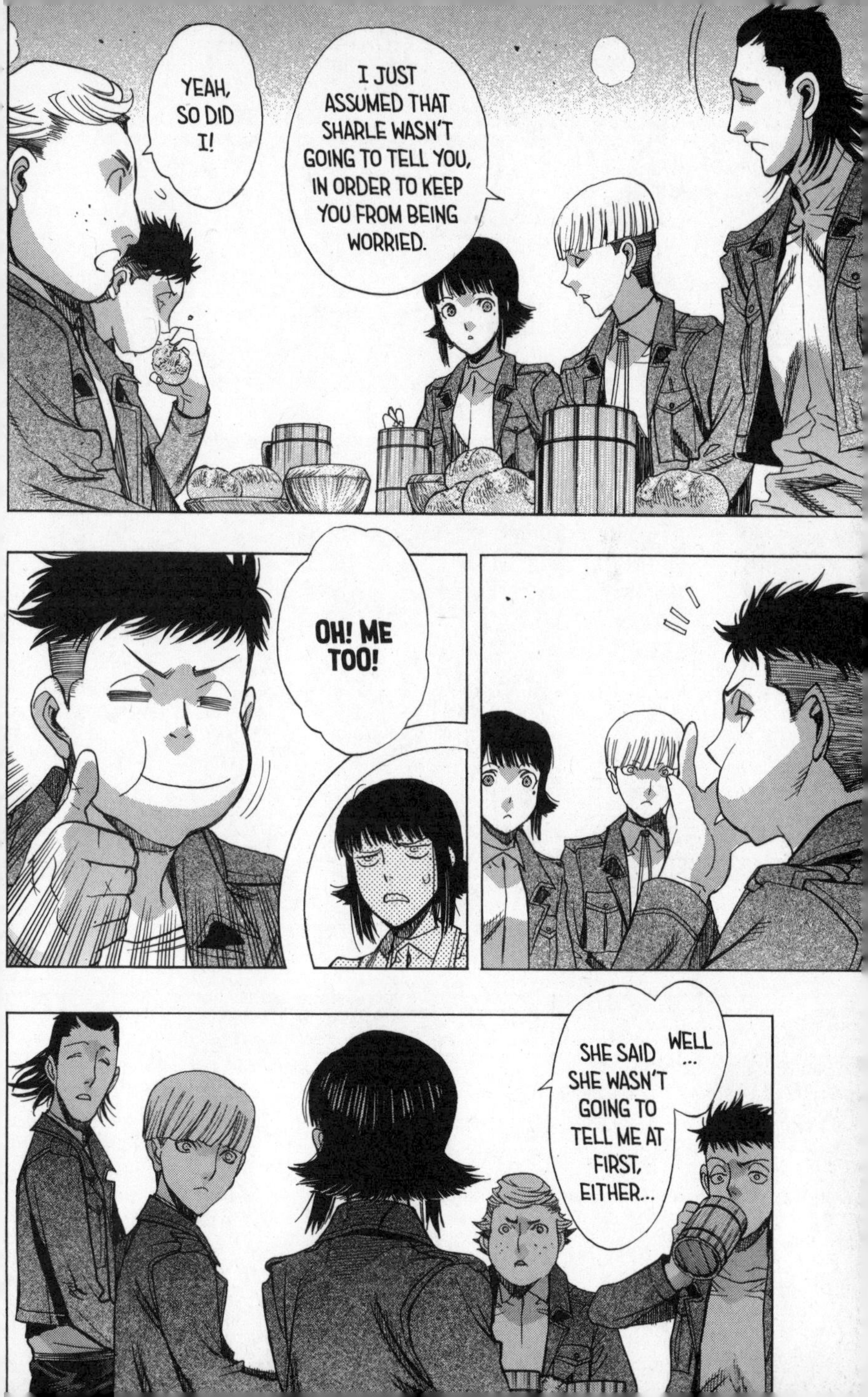
I JUST ASSUMED THAT SHARLE WASN'T GOING TO TELL YOU, IN ORDER TO KEEP YOU FROM BEING WORRIED.
YEAH, SO DID I!
OH! ME TOO!
WELL ...
SHE SAID SHE WASN'T GOING TO TELL ME AT FIRST, EITHER...

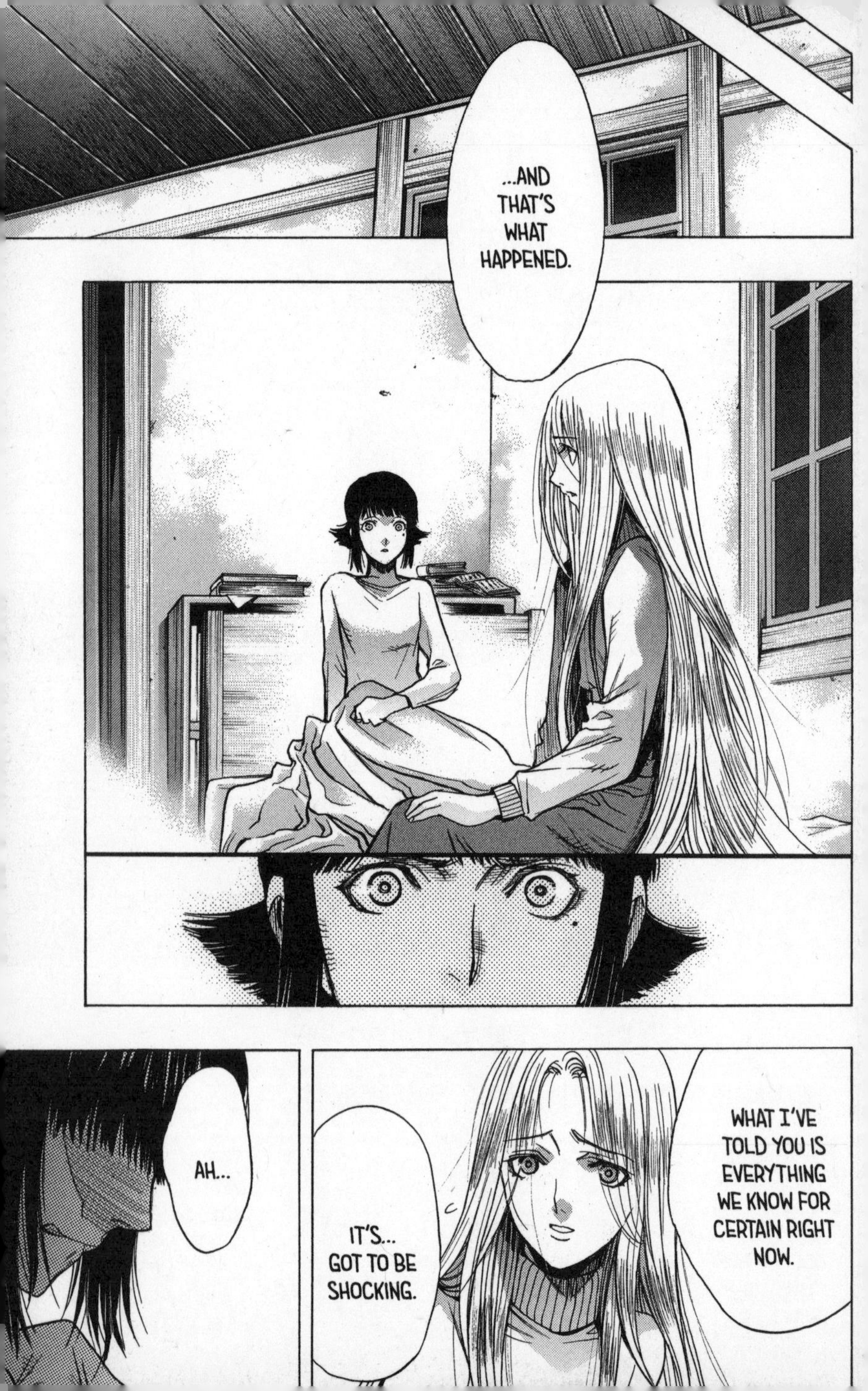
...AND THAT'S WHAT HAPPENED.
WHAT I'VE TOLD YOU IS EVERYTHING WE KNOW FOR CERTAIN RIGHT NOW.
IT'S... GOT TO BE SHOCKING.
AH...

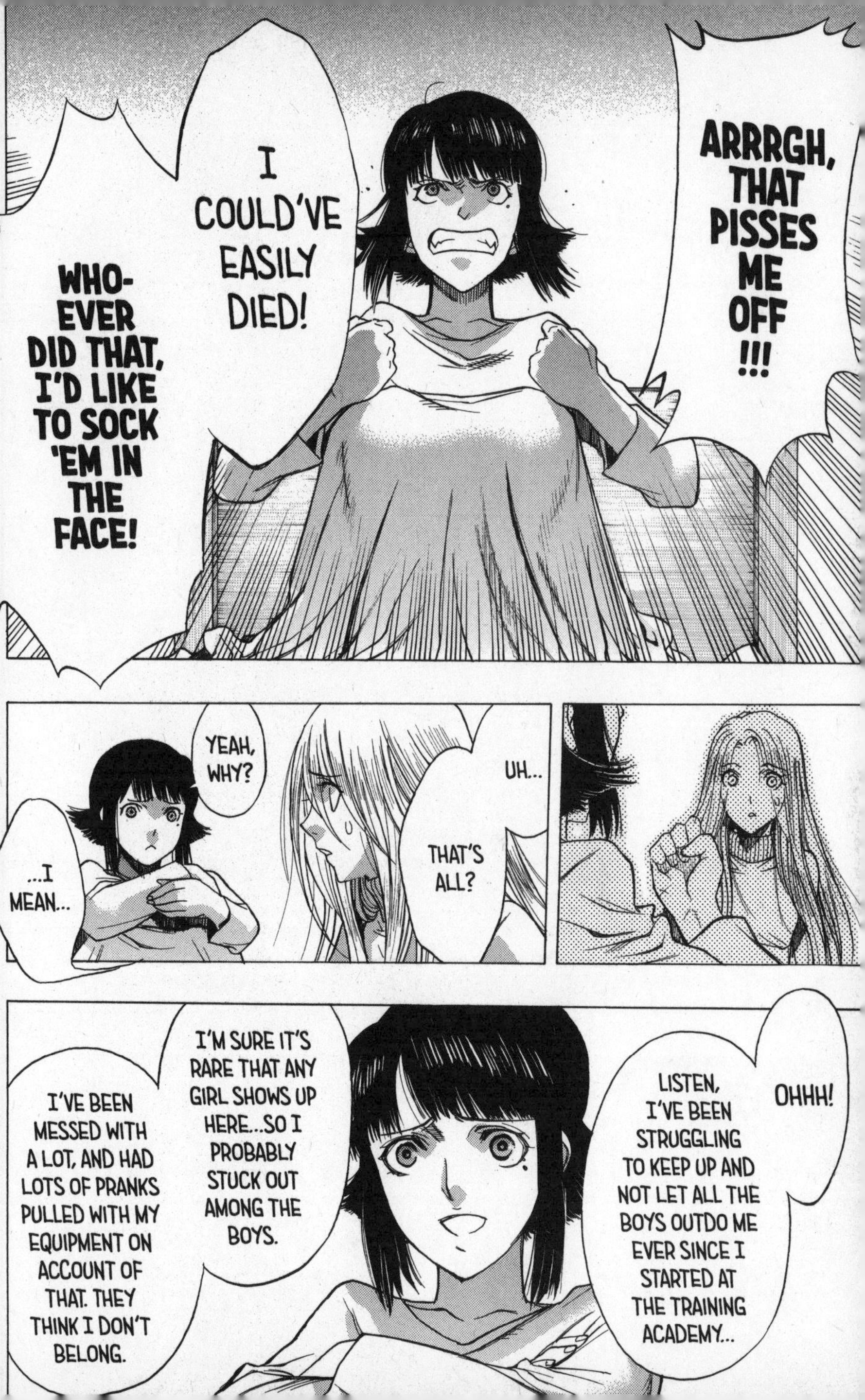
ARRRGH, THAT PISSES ME OFF!!!
I COULD'VE EASILY DIED!
WHO-EVER DID THAT, I'D LIKE TO SOCK 'EM IN THE FACE!
UH...
THAT'S ALL?
YEAH, WHY?
...I MEAN...
OHHH!
LISTEN, I'VE BEEN STRUGGLING TO KEEP UP AND NOT LET ALL THE BOYS OUTDO ME EVER SINCE I STARTED AT THE TRAINING ACADEMY...
I'M SURE IT'S RARE THAT ANY GIRL SHOWS UP HERE...SO I PROBABLY STUCK OUT AMONG THE BOYS.
I'VE BEEN MESSED WITH A LOT, AND HAD LOTS OF PRANKS PULLED WITH MY EQUIPMENT ON ACCOUNT OF THAT. THEY THINK I DON'T BELONG.

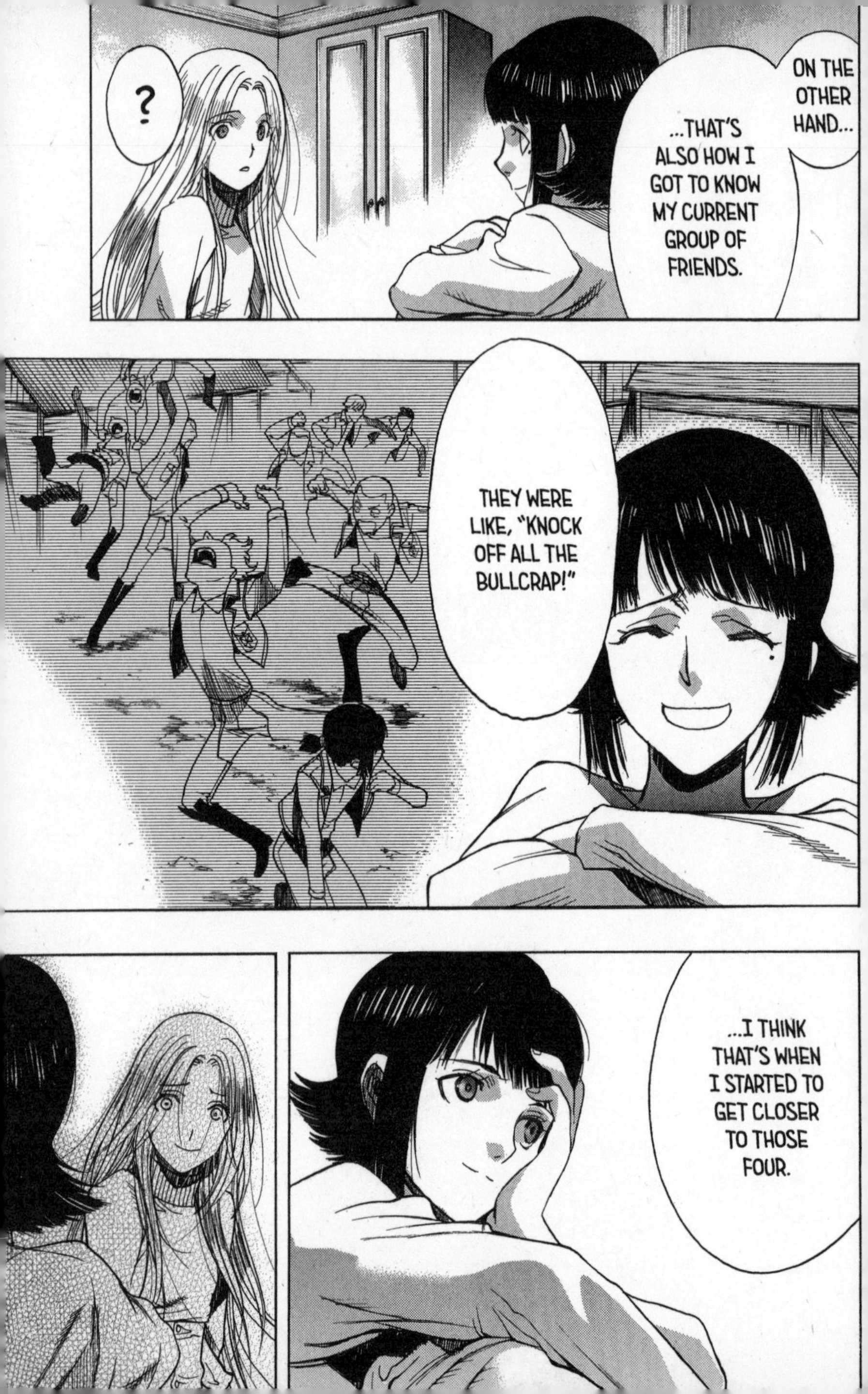
?
ON THE OTHER HAND...
...THAT'S ALSO HOW I GOT TO KNOW MY CURRENT GROUP OF FRIENDS.
THEY WERE LIKE, "KNOCK OFF ALL THE BULLCRAP!"
...I THINK THAT'S WHEN I STARTED TO GET CLOSER TO THOSE FOUR.

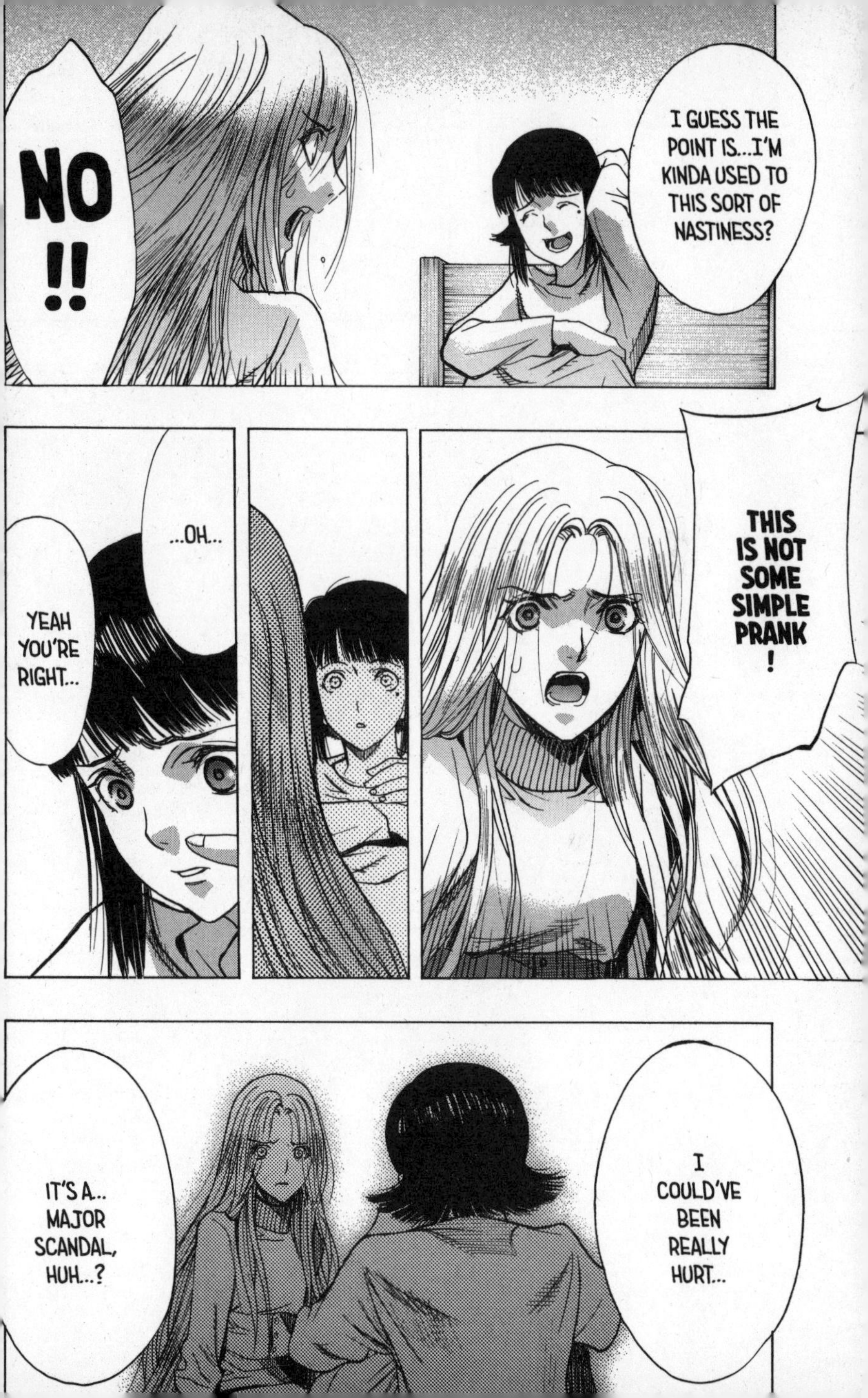
I GUESS THE POINT IS...I'M KINDA USED TO THIS SORT OF NASTINESS?
NO!!
THIS IS NOT SOME SIMPLE PRANK!
...OH...
YEAH YOU'RE RIGHT...
I COULD'VE BEEN REALLY HURT...
IT'S A... MAJOR SCANDAL, HUH...?

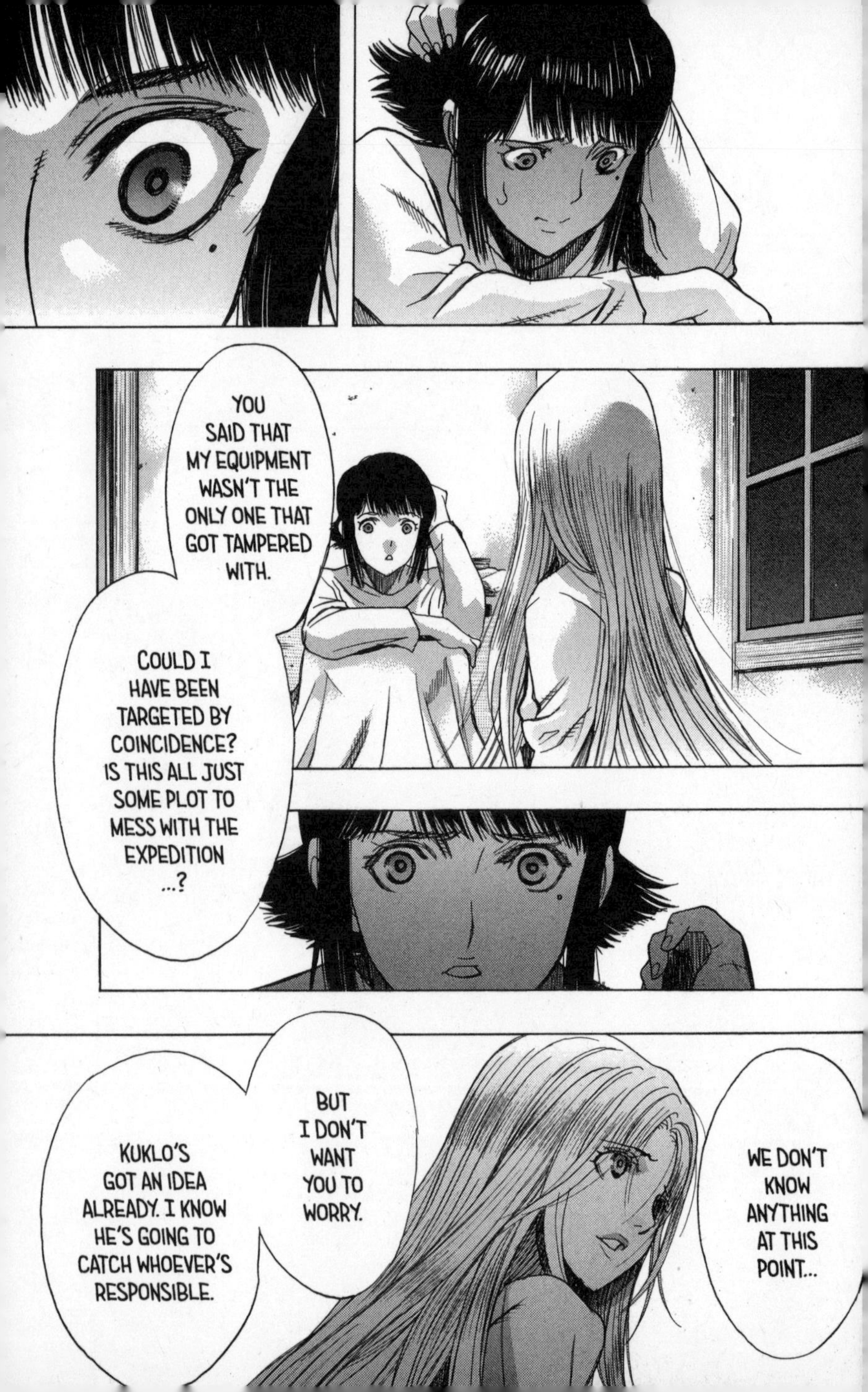
YOU SAID THAT MY EQUIPMENT WASN'T THE ONLY ONE THAT GOT TAMPERED WITH.
COULD I HAVE BEEN TARGETED BY COINCIDENCE? IS THIS ALL JUST SOME PLOT TO MESS WITH THE EXPEDITION ...?
WE DON'T KNOW ANYTHING AT THIS POINT...
BUT I DON'T WANT YOU TO WORRY.
KUKLO'S GOT AN IDEA ALREADY. I KNOW HE'S GOING TO CATCH WHOEVER'S RESPONSIBLE.

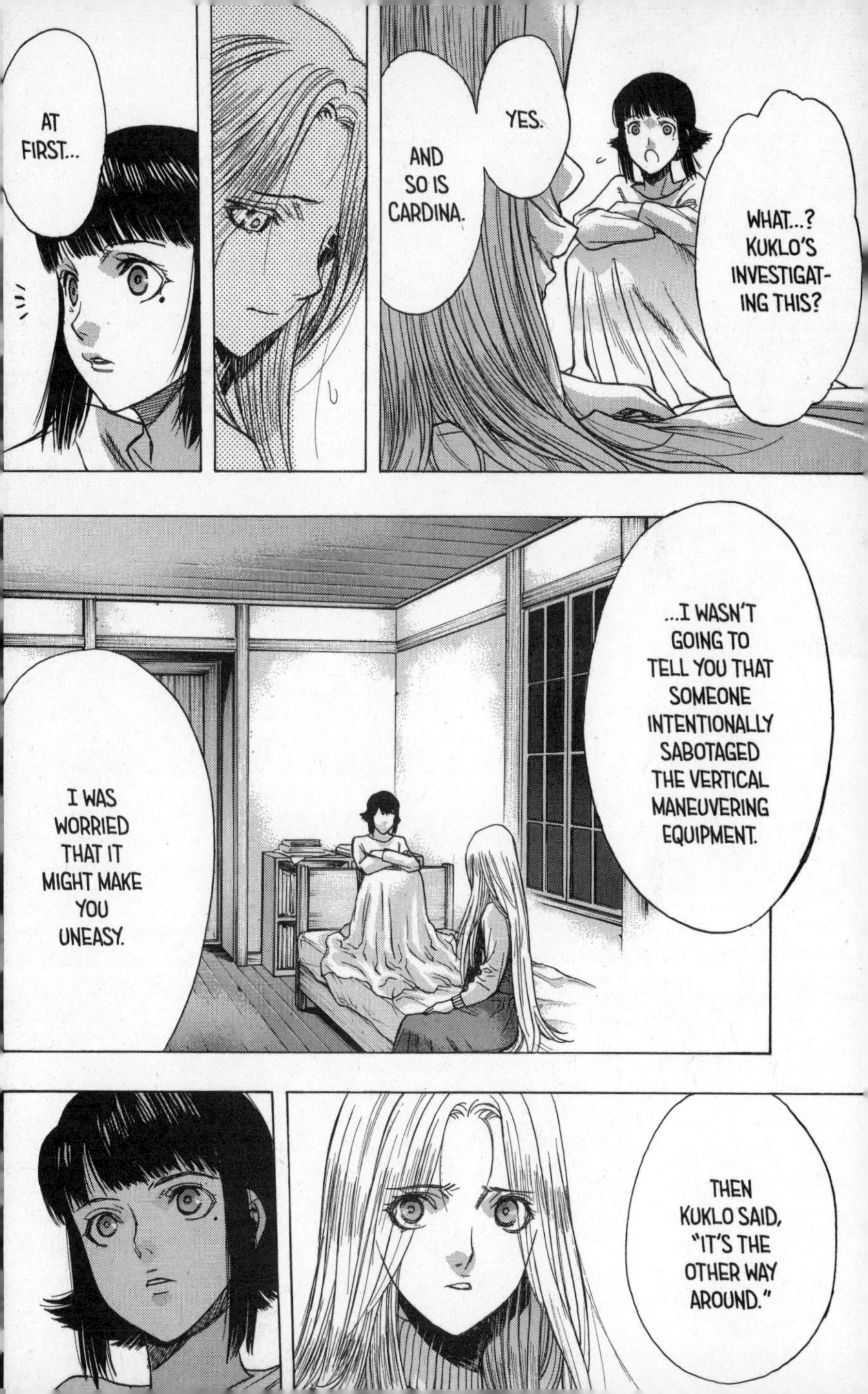
WHAT...? KUKLO'S INVESTIGAT-ING THIS?
YES.
AND SO IS CARDINA.
AT FIRST...
...I WASN'T GOING TO TELL YOU THAT SOMEONE INTENTIONALLY SABOTAGED THE VERTICAL MANEUVERING EQUIPMENT.
I WAS WORRIED THAT IT MIGHT MAKE YOU UNEASY.
THEN KUKLO SAID, "IT'S THE OTHER WAY AROUND."

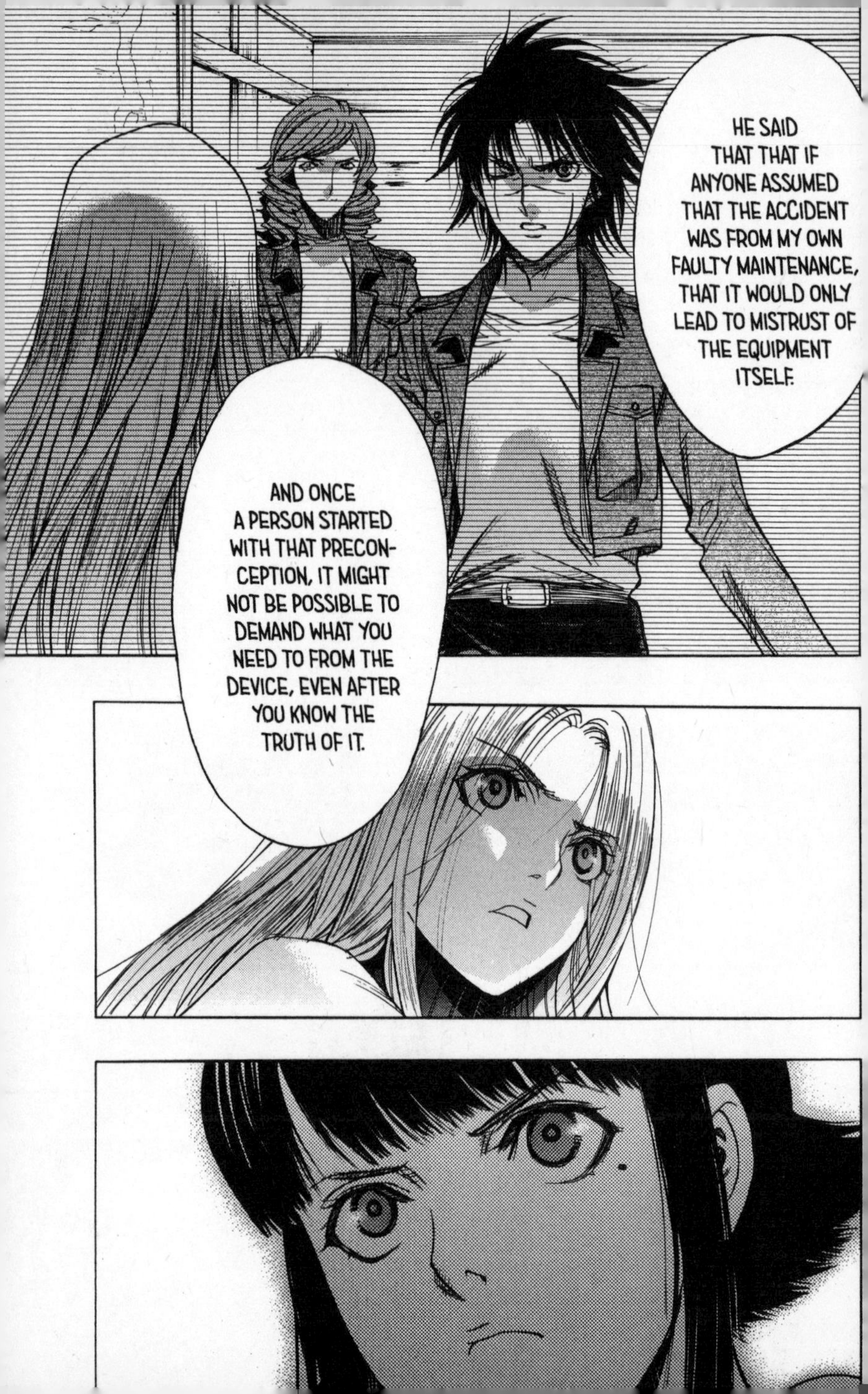
HE SAID THAT THAT IF ANYONE ASSUMED THAT THE ACCIDENT WAS FROM MY OWN FAULTY MAINTENANCE, THAT IT WOULD ONLY LEAD TO MISTRUST OF THE EQUIPMENT ITSELF.
AND ONCE A PERSON STARTED WITH THAT PRECON-CEPTION, IT MIGHT NOT BE POSSIBLE TO DEMAND WHAT YOU NEED TO FROM THE DEVICE, EVEN AFTER YOU KNOW THE TRUTH OF IT.

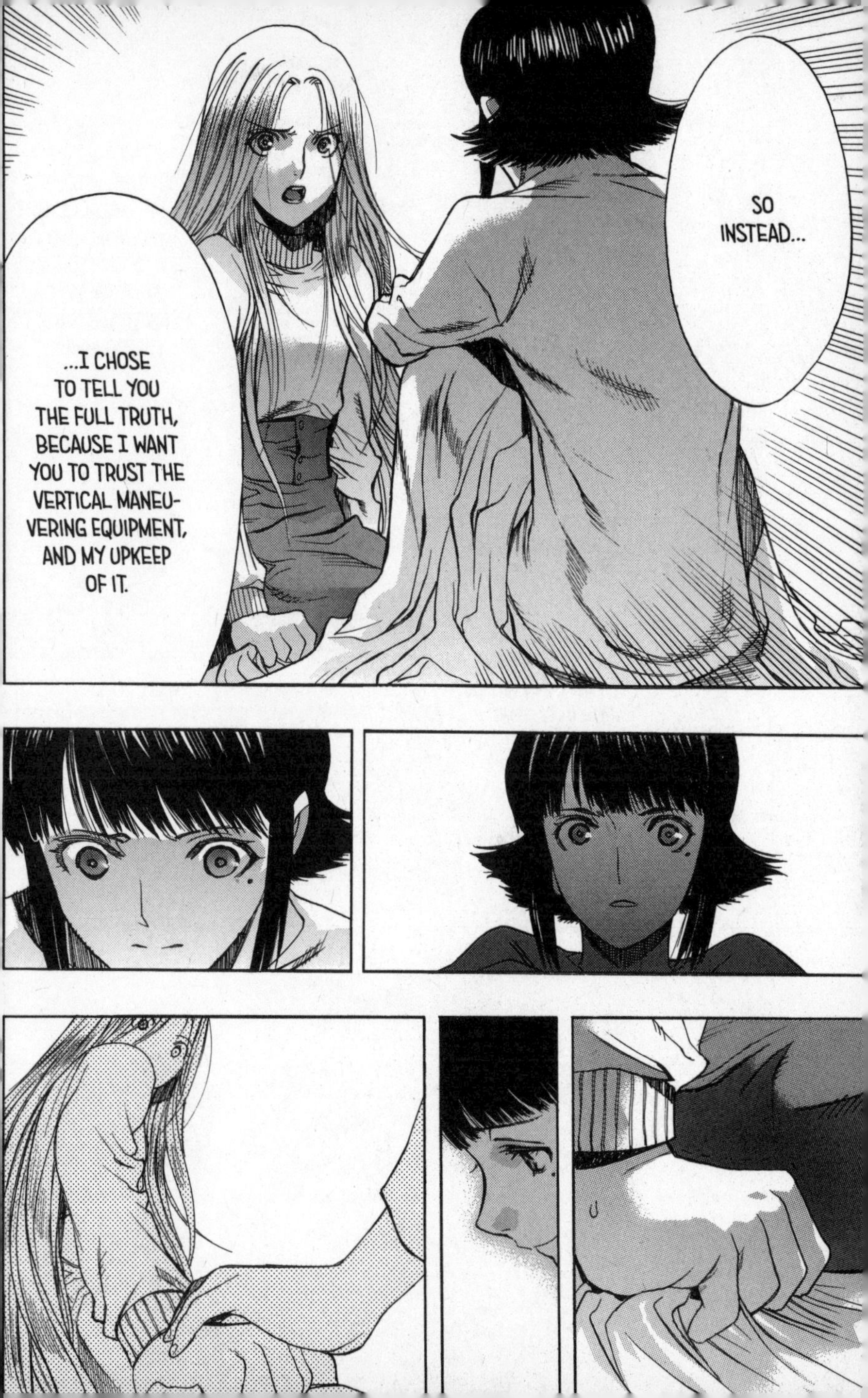
SO INSTEAD...
...I CHOSE TO TELL YOU THE FULL TRUTH, BECAUSE I WANT YOU TO TRUST THE VERTICAL MANEU-VERING EQUIPMENT, AND MY UPKEEP OF IT.

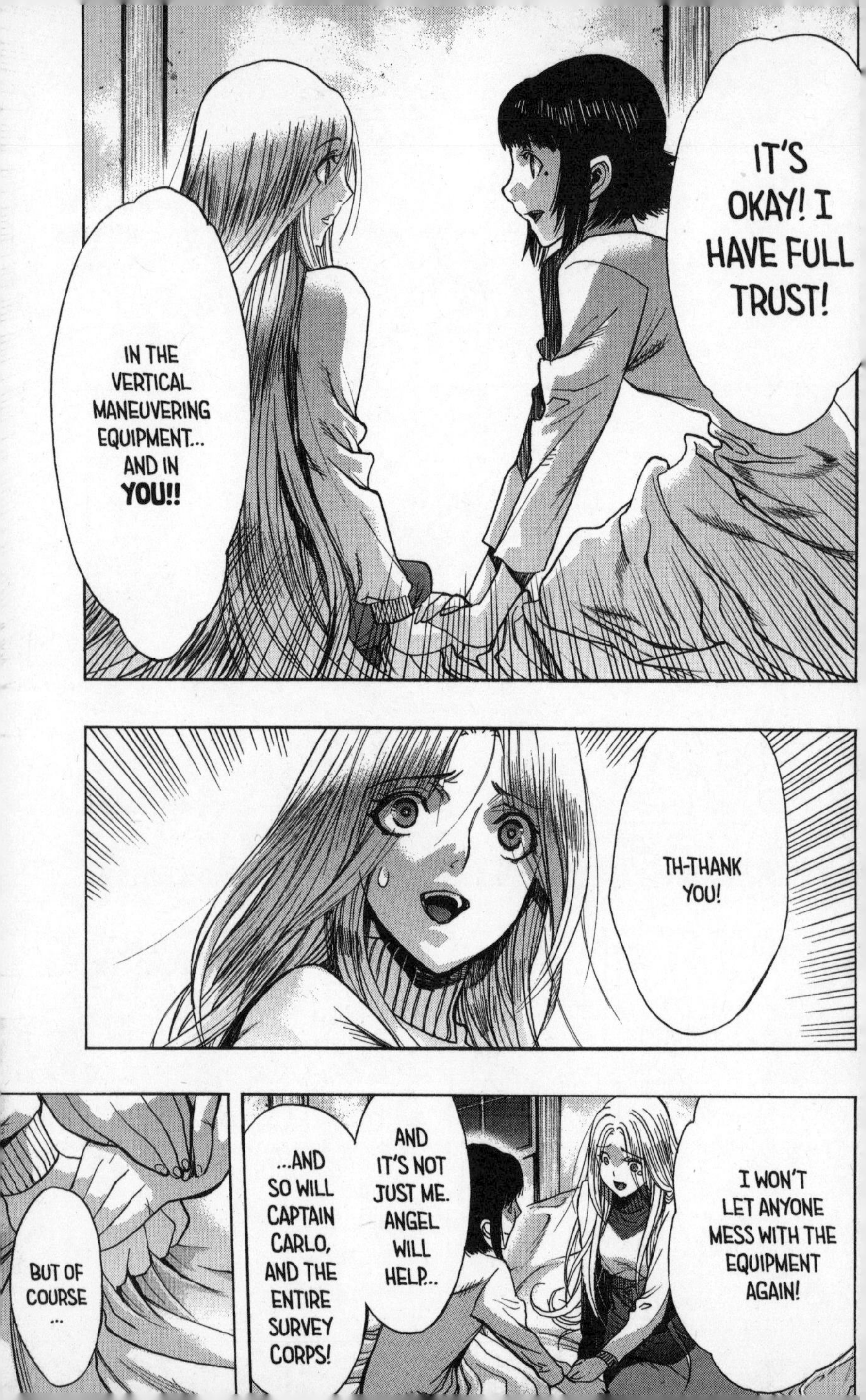
IT'S OKAY! I HAVE FULL TRUST!
IN THE VERTICAL MANEUVERING EQUIPMENT... AND IN YOU!!
TH-THANK YOU!
I WON'T LET ANYONE MESS WITH THE EQUIPMENT AGAIN!
AND IT'S NOT JUST ME. ANGEL WILL HELP...
...AND SO WILL CAPTAIN CARLO, AND THE ENTIRE SURVEY CORPS!
BUT OF COURSE ...

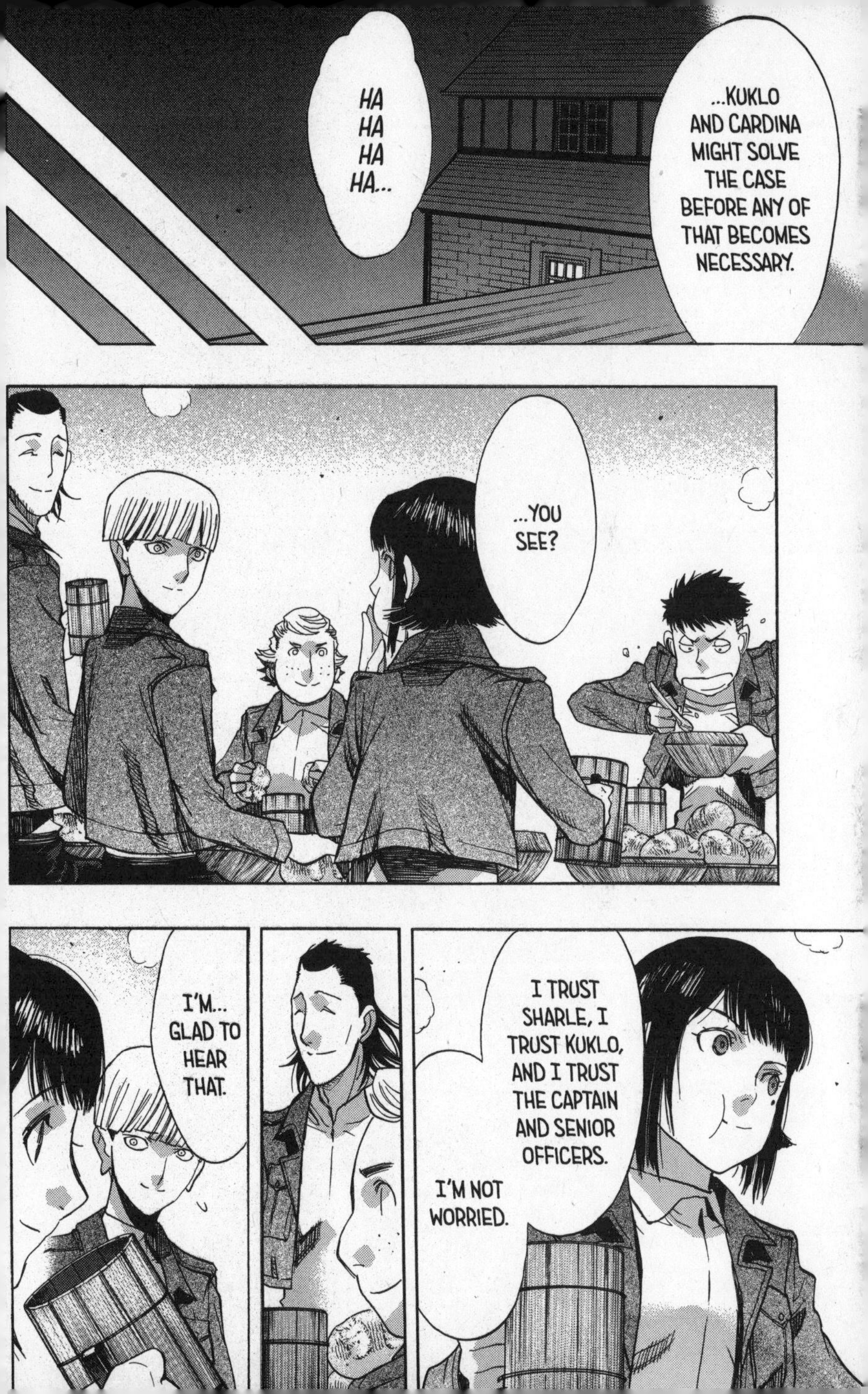
...KUKLO AND CARDINA MIGHT SOLVE THE CASE BEFORE ANY OF THAT BECOMES NECESSARY.
HA HA HA HA...
...YOU SEE?
I TRUST SHARLE, I TRUST KUKLO, AND I TRUST THE CAPTAIN AND SENIOR OFFICERS.
I'M NOT WORRIED.
I'M... GLAD TO HEAR THAT.

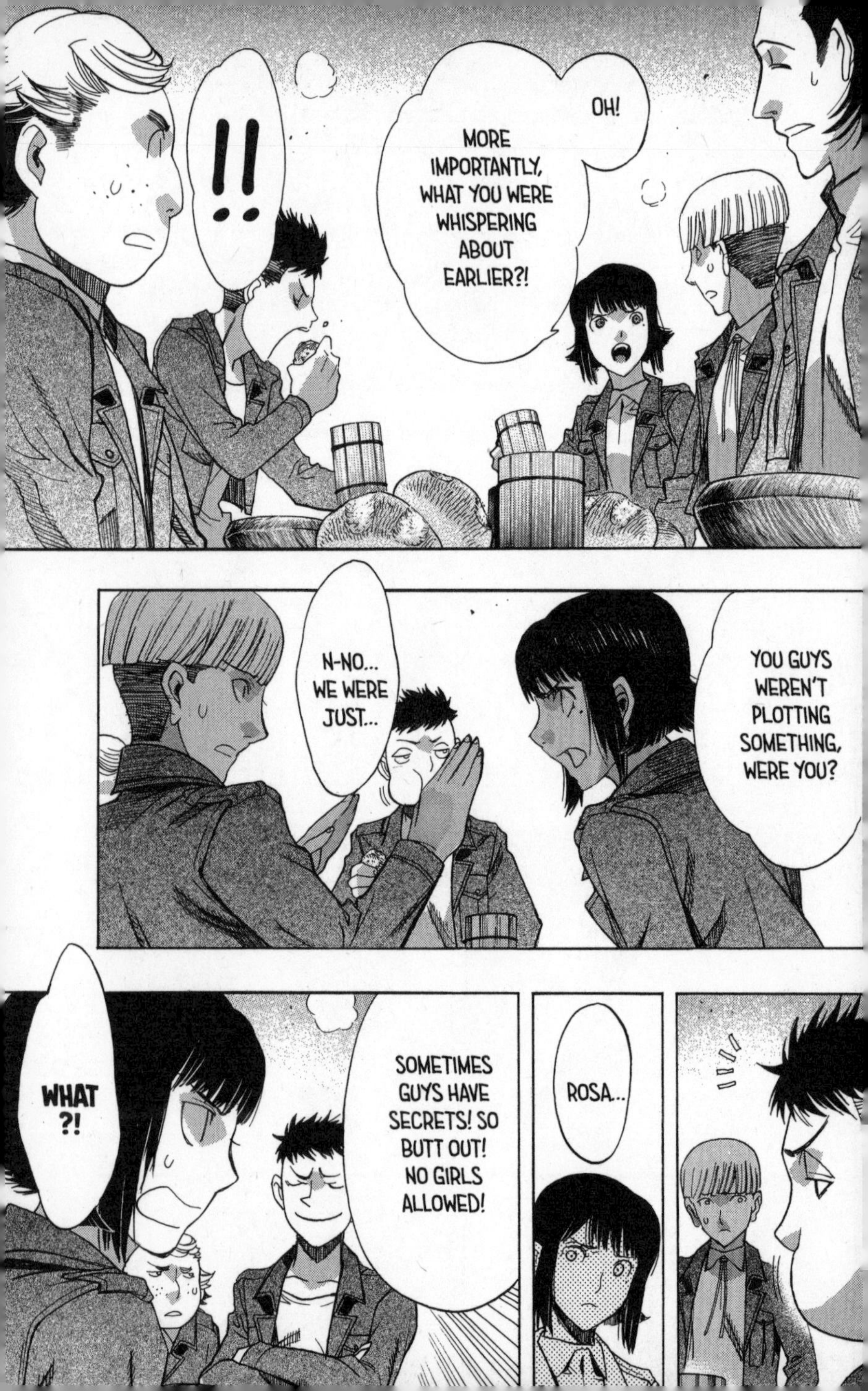
OH! MORE IMPORTANTLY, WHAT YOU WERE WHISPERING ABOUT EARLIER?!
!!
YOU GUYS WEREN'T PLOTTING SOMETHING, WERE YOU?
N-NO... WE WERE JUST...
ROSA...
SOMETIMES GUYS HAVE SECRETS! SO BUTT OUT! NO GIRLS ALLOWED!
WHAT?!

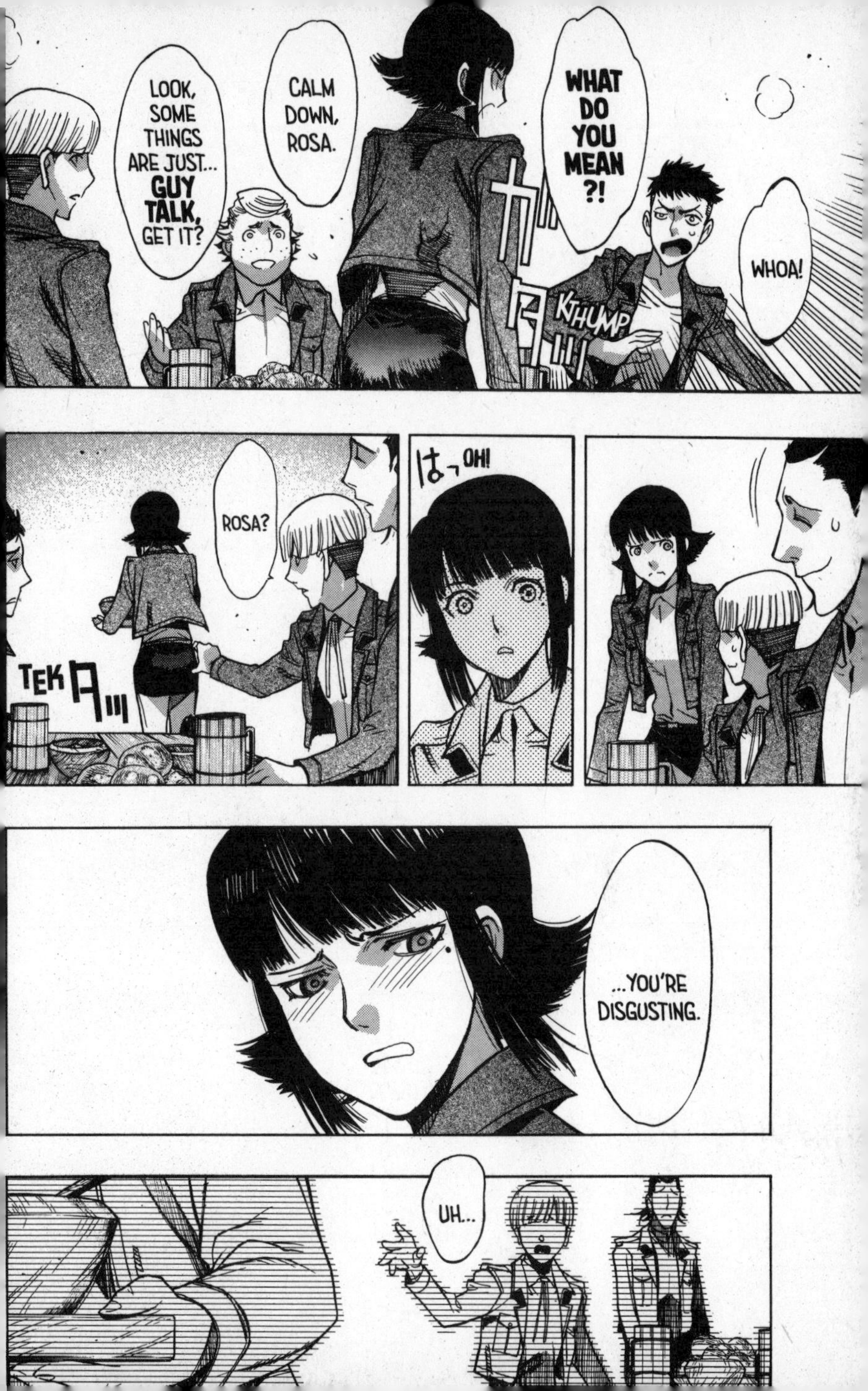
WHOA!
WHAT DO YOU MEAN?!
KTHUMP
CALM DOWN, ROSA.
LOOK, SOME THINGS ARE JUST... **GUY TALK,** GET IT?
はっ OH!
ROSA?
TEK
...YOU'RE DISGUSTING.
UH...

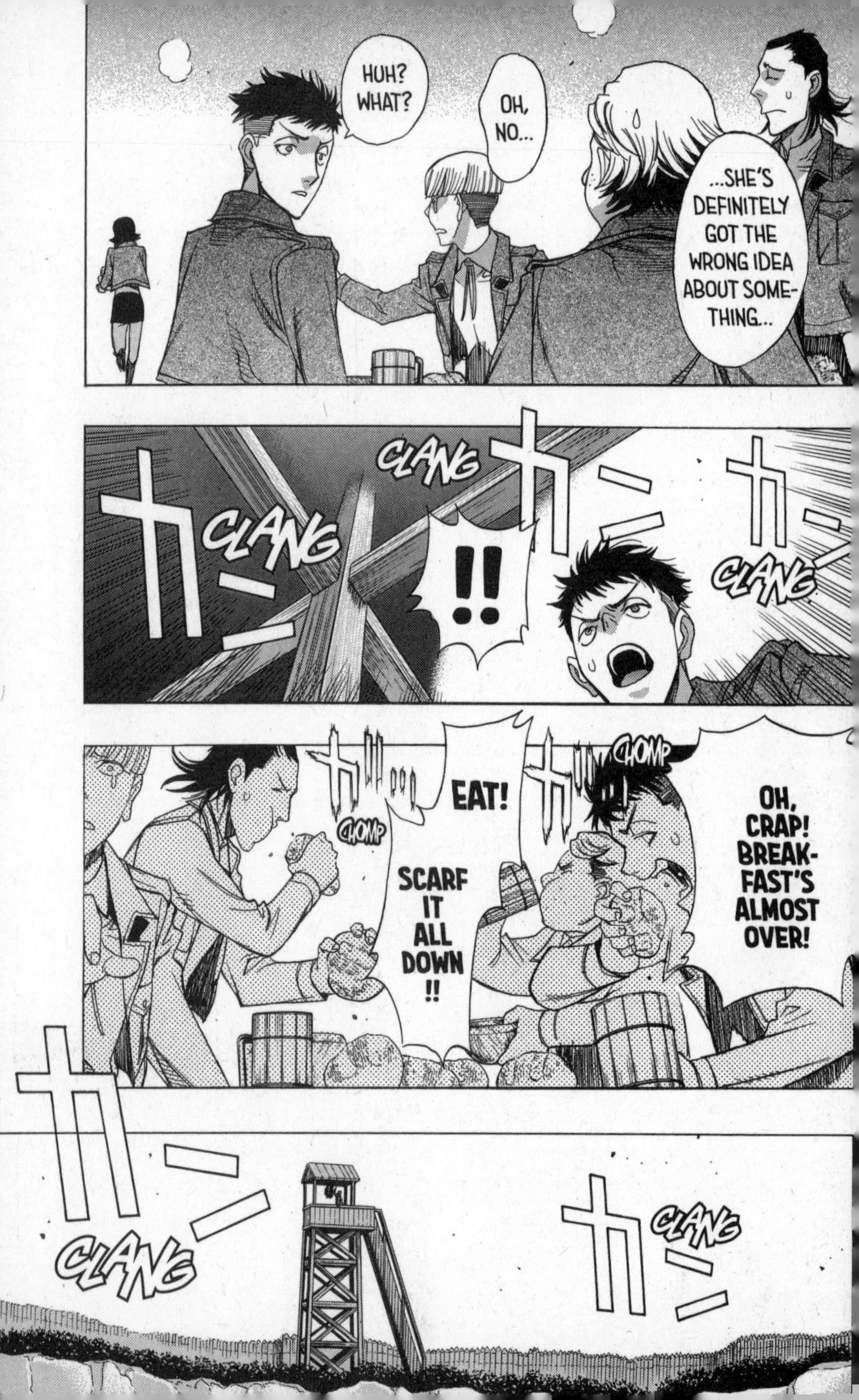
...SHE'S DEFINITELY GOT THE WRONG IDEA ABOUT SOME-THING...
OH, NO...
HUH? WHAT?
CLANG
CLANG
!!
CLANG
OH, CRAP! BREAK-FAST'S ALMOST OVER!
CHOMP
EAT!
SCARF IT ALL DOWN!!
CHOMP
CLANG
CLANG

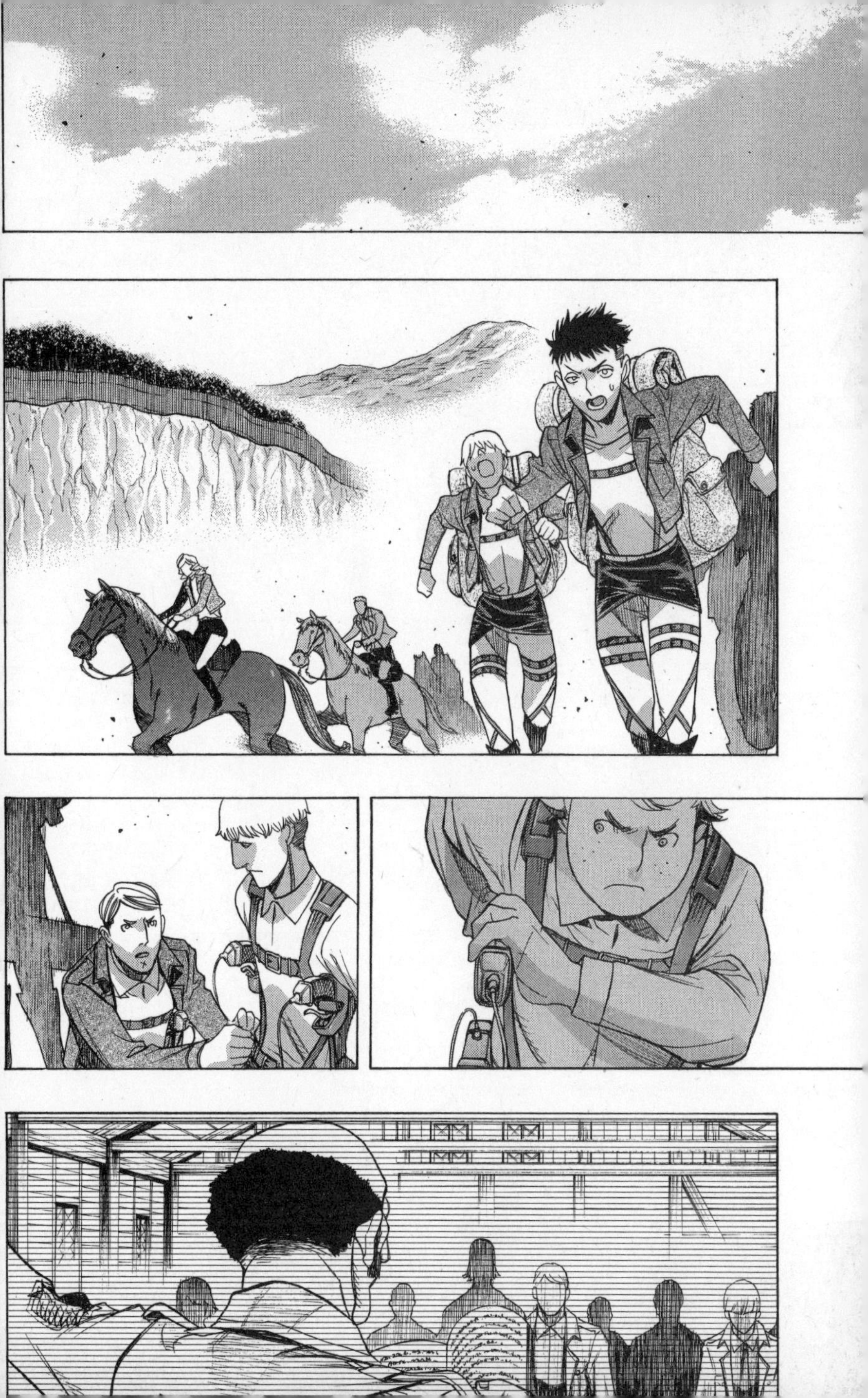

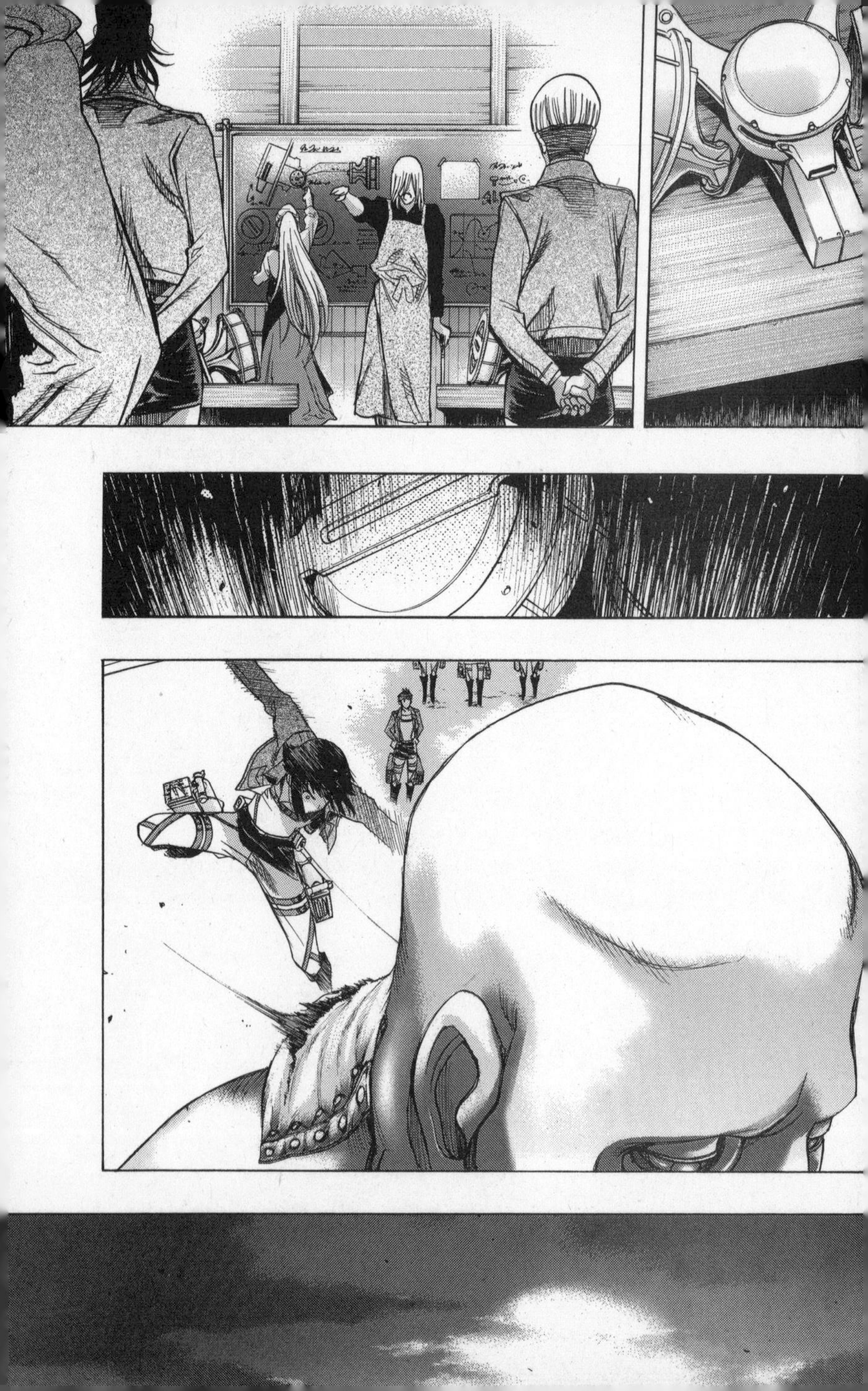

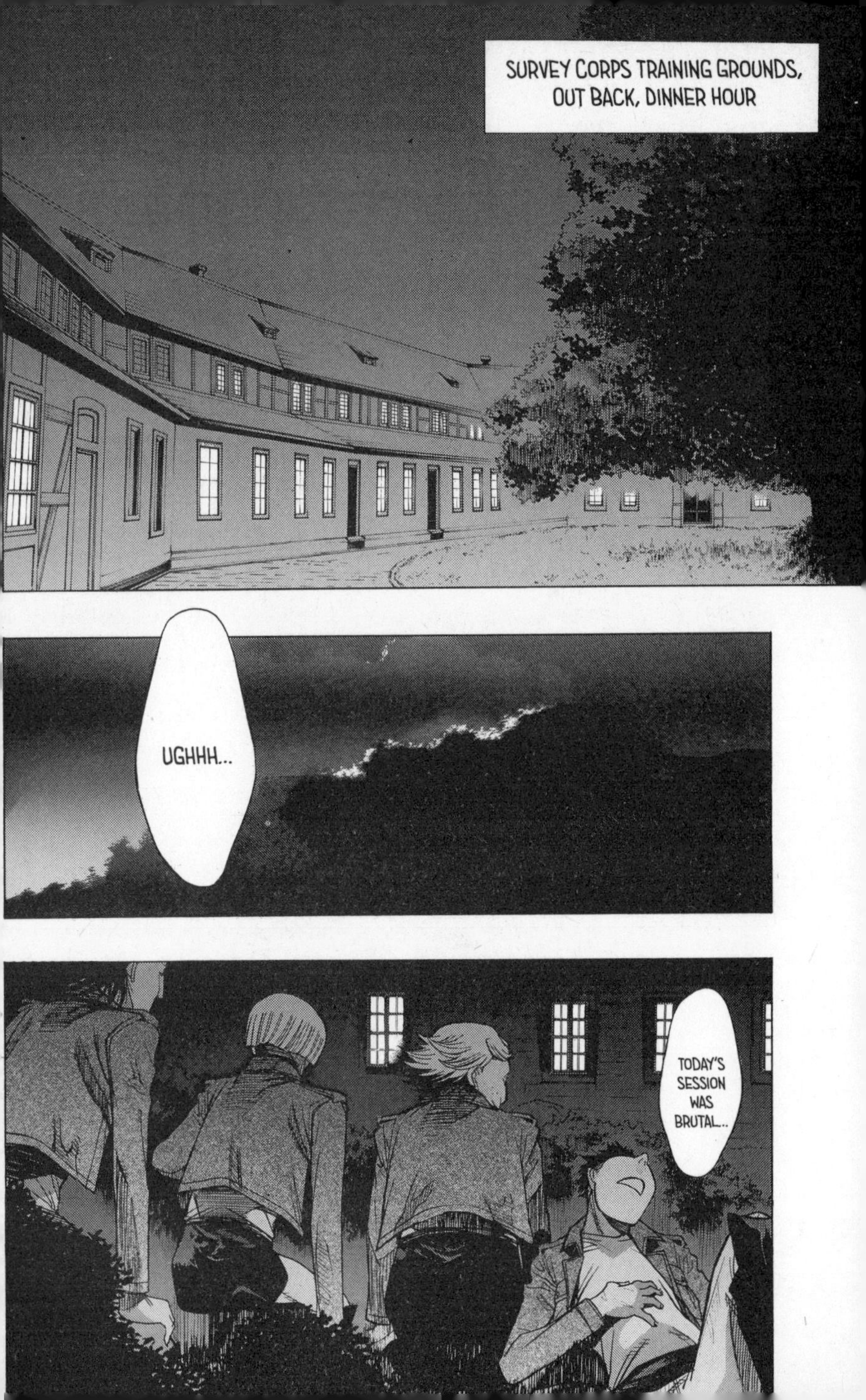
SURVEY CORPS TRAINING GROUNDS, OUT BACK, DINNER HOUR
UGHHH...
TODAY'S SESSION WAS BRUTAL...

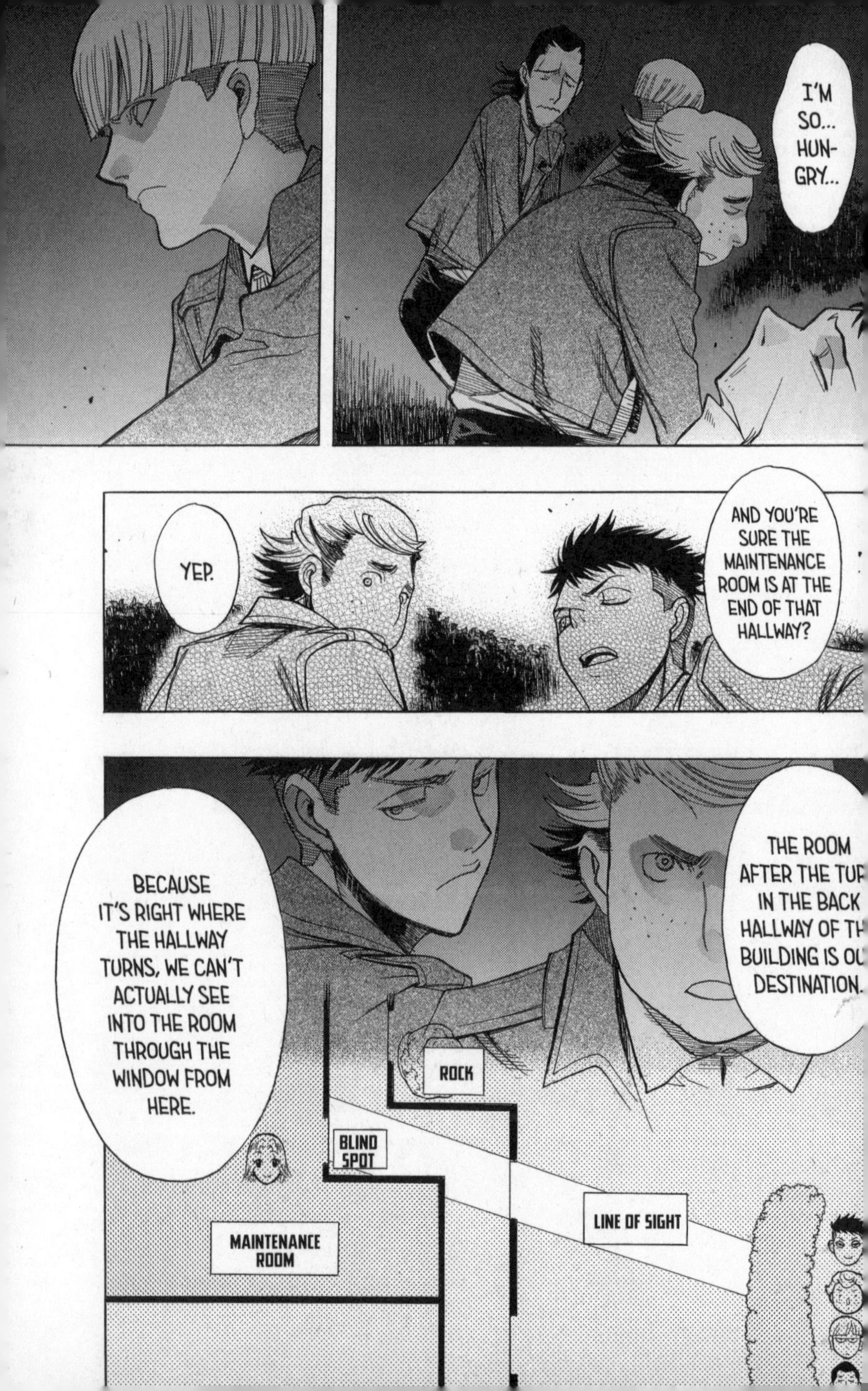

I'M SO... HUN-GRY...
AND YOU'RE SURE THE MAINTENANCE ROOM IS AT THE END OF THAT HALLWAY?
YEP.
THE ROOM AFTER THE TU IN THE BACK HALLWAY OF T BUILDING IS O DESTINATION.
BECAUSE IT'S RIGHT WHERE THE HALLWAY TURNS, WE CAN'T ACTUALLY SEE INTO THE ROOM THROUGH THE WINDOW FROM HERE.
ROCK
BLIND SPOT
LINE OF SIGHT
MAINTENANCE ROOM

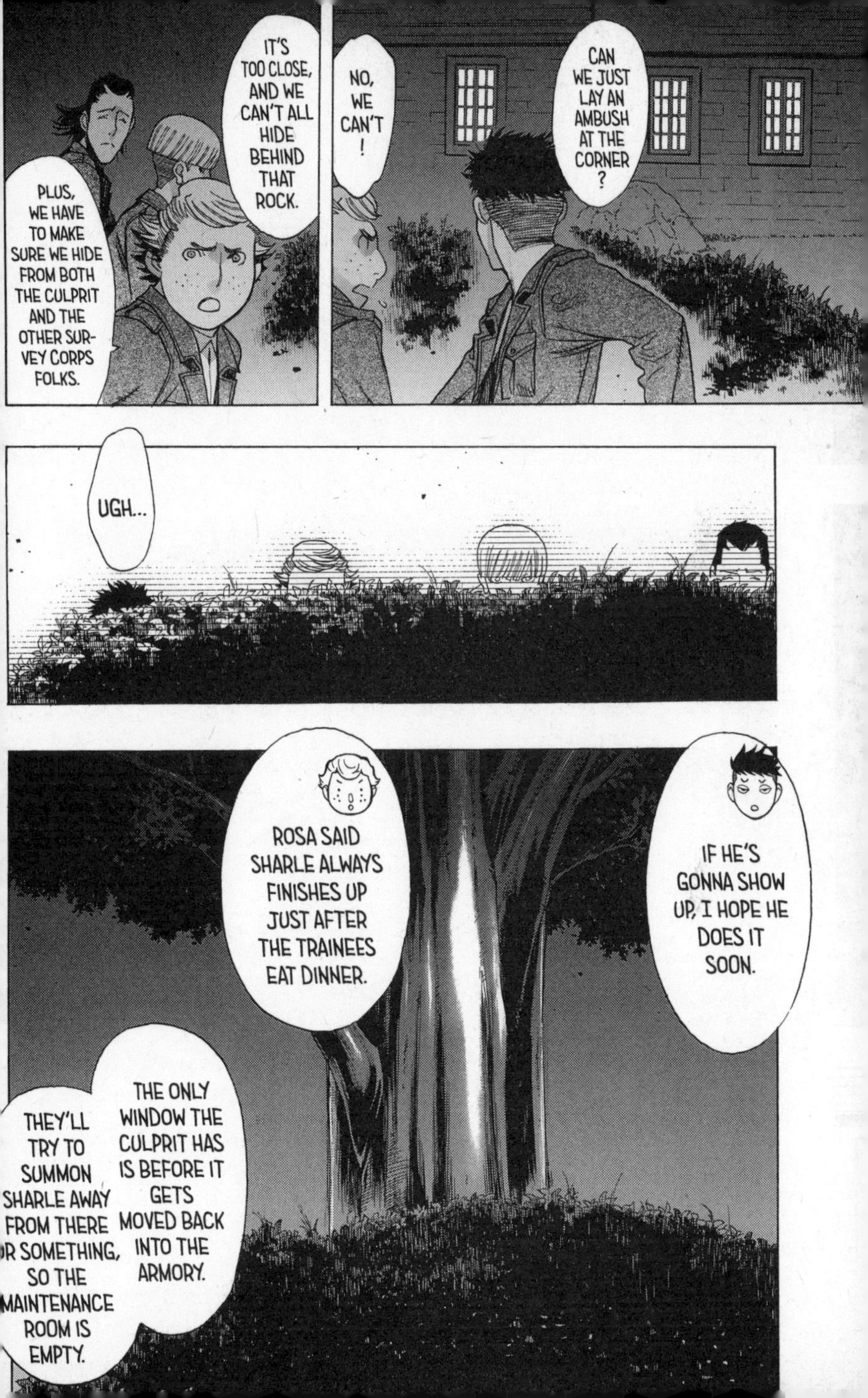
CAN WE JUST LAY AN AMBUSH AT THE CORNER?
NO, WE CAN'T!
IT'S TOO CLOSE, AND WE CAN'T ALL HIDE BEHIND THAT ROCK.
PLUS, WE HAVE TO MAKE SURE WE HIDE FROM BOTH THE CULPRIT AND THE OTHER SUR-VEY CORPS FOLKS.
UGH...
IF HE'S GONNA SHOW UP, I HOPE HE DOES IT SOON.
ROSA SAID SHARLE ALWAYS FINISHES UP JUST AFTER THE TRAINEES EAT DINNER.
THE ONLY WINDOW THE CULPRIT HAS IS BEFORE IT GETS MOVED BACK INTO THE ARMORY.
THEY'LL TRY TO SUMMON SHARLE AWAY FROM THERE OR SOMETHING, SO THE MAINTENANCE ROOM IS EMPTY.

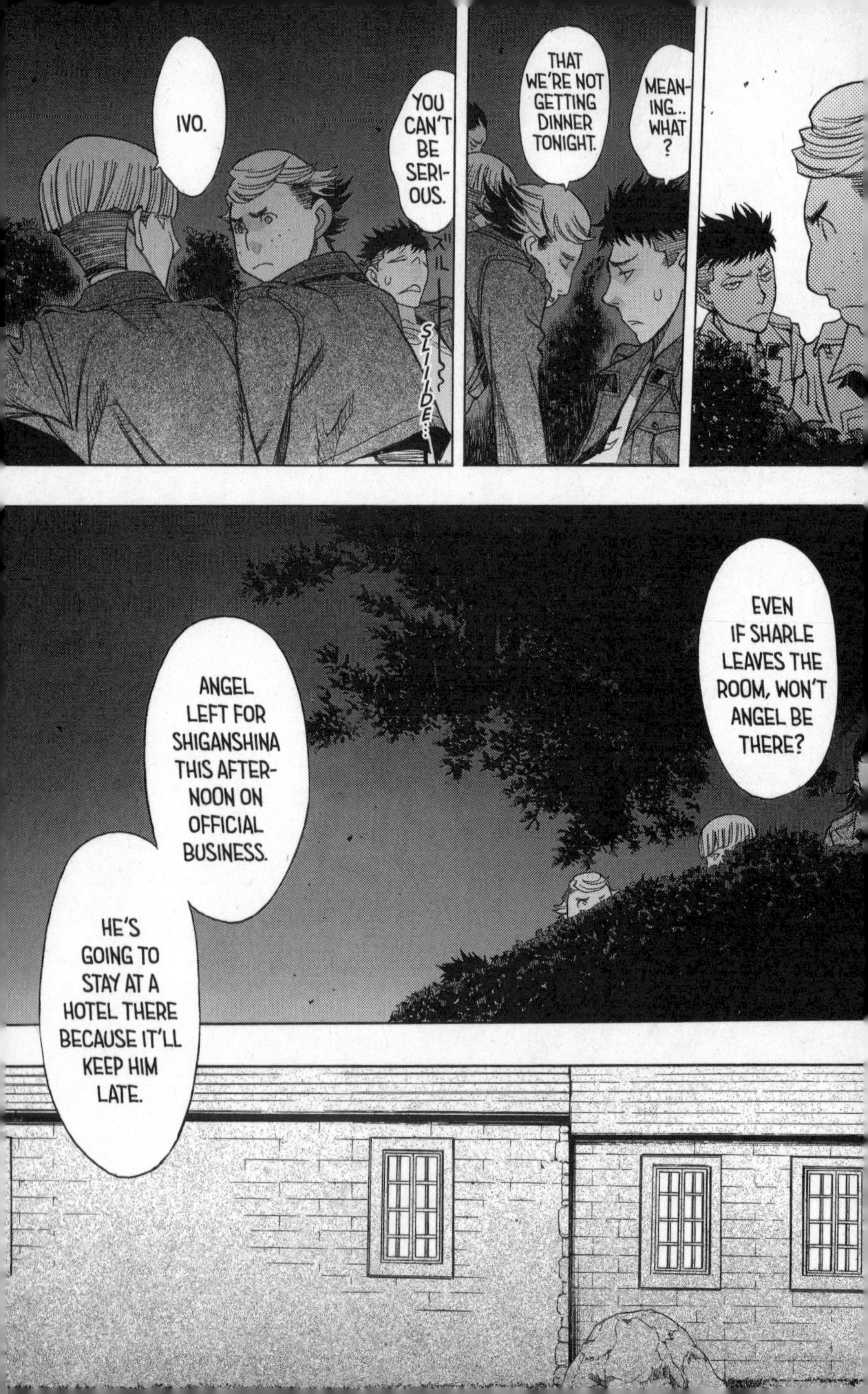
MEANING... WHAT?
THAT WE'RE NOT GETTING DINNER TONIGHT.
YOU CAN'T BE SERIOUS.
IVO.
SLIIIDE...
EVEN IF SHARLE LEAVES THE ROOM, WON'T ANGEL BE THERE?
ANGEL LEFT FOR SHIGANSHINA THIS AFTERNOON ON OFFICIAL BUSINESS.
HE'S GOING TO STAY AT A HOTEL THERE BECAUSE IT'LL KEEP HIM LATE.

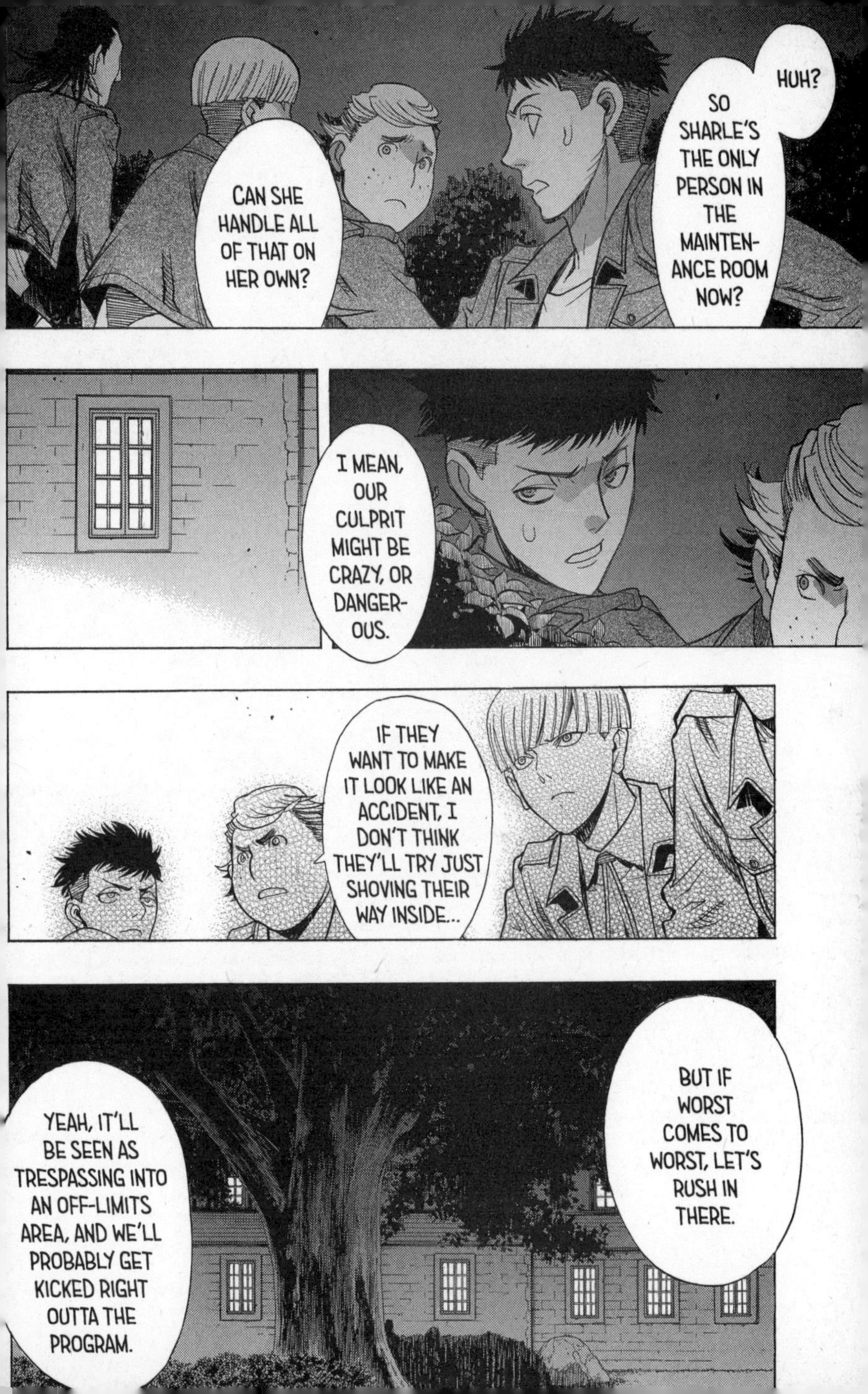
HUH?
SO SHARLE'S THE ONLY PERSON IN THE MAINTEN-ANCE ROOM NOW?
CAN SHE HANDLE ALL OF THAT ON HER OWN?
I MEAN, OUR CULPRIT MIGHT BE CRAZY, OR DANGER-OUS.
IF THEY WANT TO MAKE IT LOOK LIKE AN ACCIDENT, I DON'T THINK THEY'LL TRY JUST SHOVING THEIR WAY INSIDE...
BUT IF WORST COMES TO WORST, LET'S RUSH IN THERE.
YEAH, IT'LL BE SEEN AS TRESPASSING INTO AN OFF-LIMITS AREA, AND WE'LL PROBABLY GET KICKED RIGHT OUTTA THE PROGRAM.

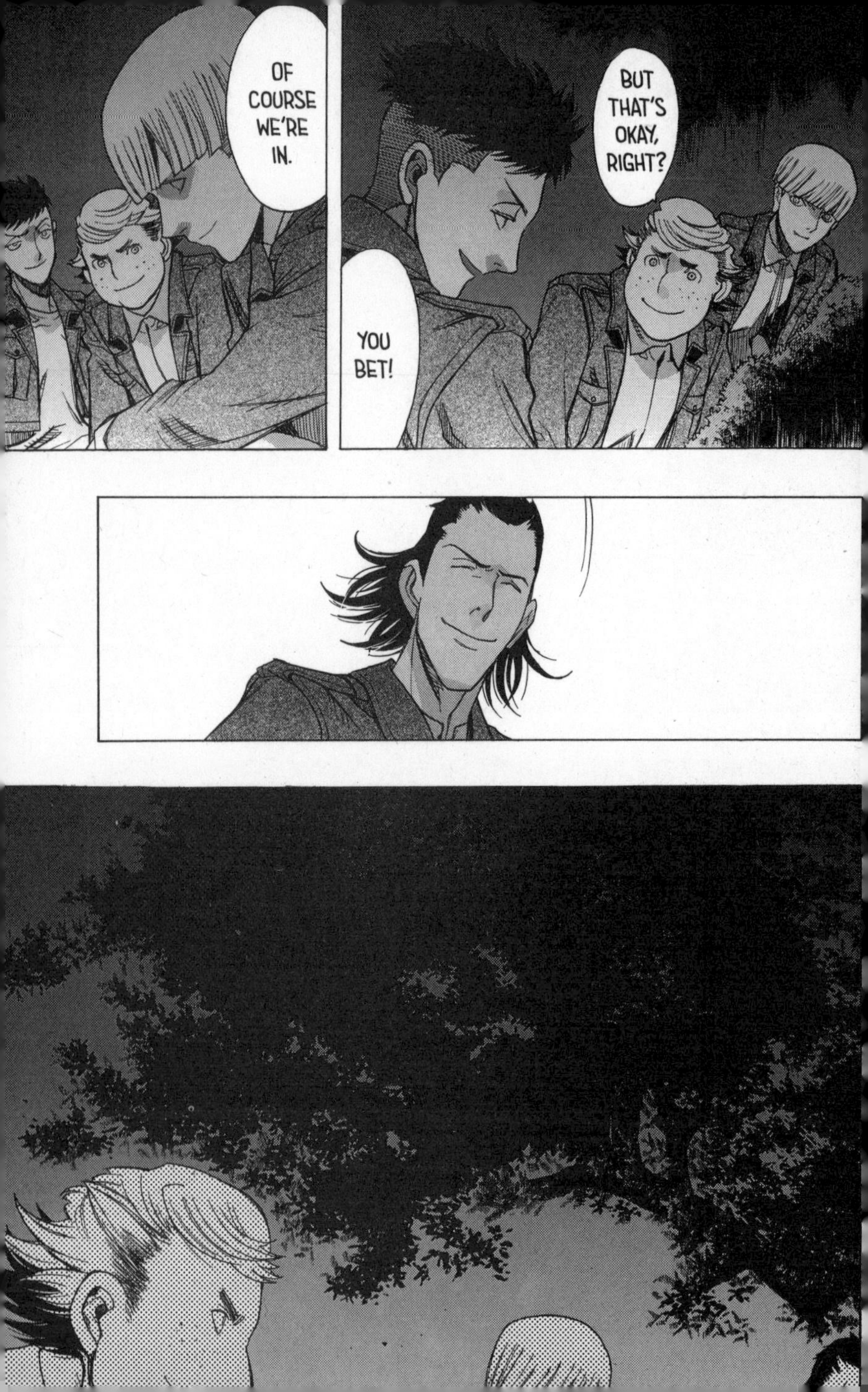
BUT THAT'S OKAY, RIGHT?
YOU BET!
OF COURSE WE'RE IN.

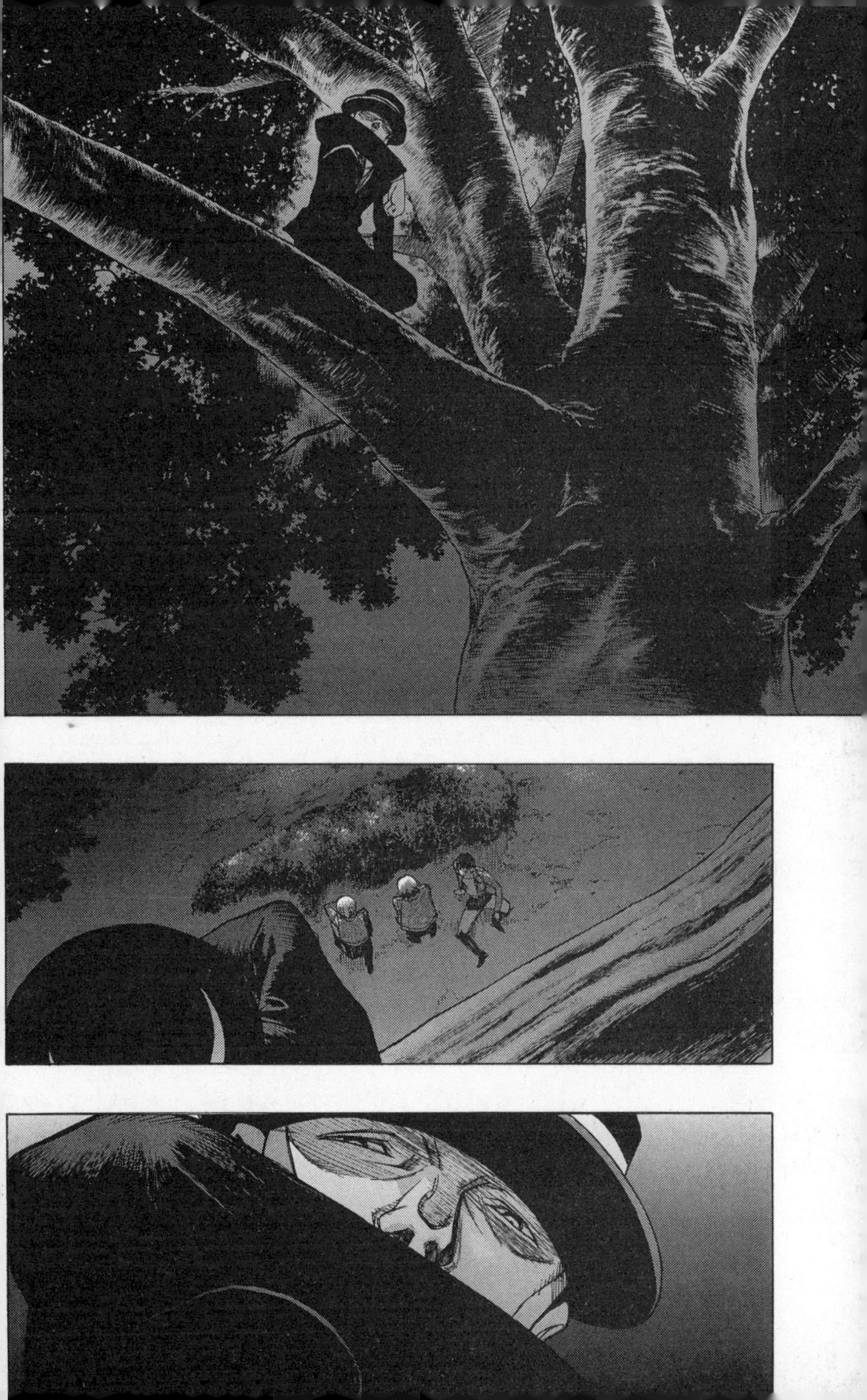

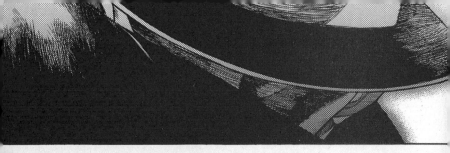

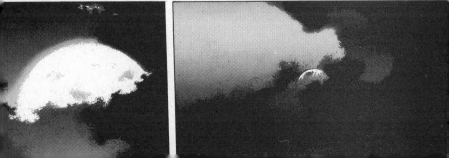

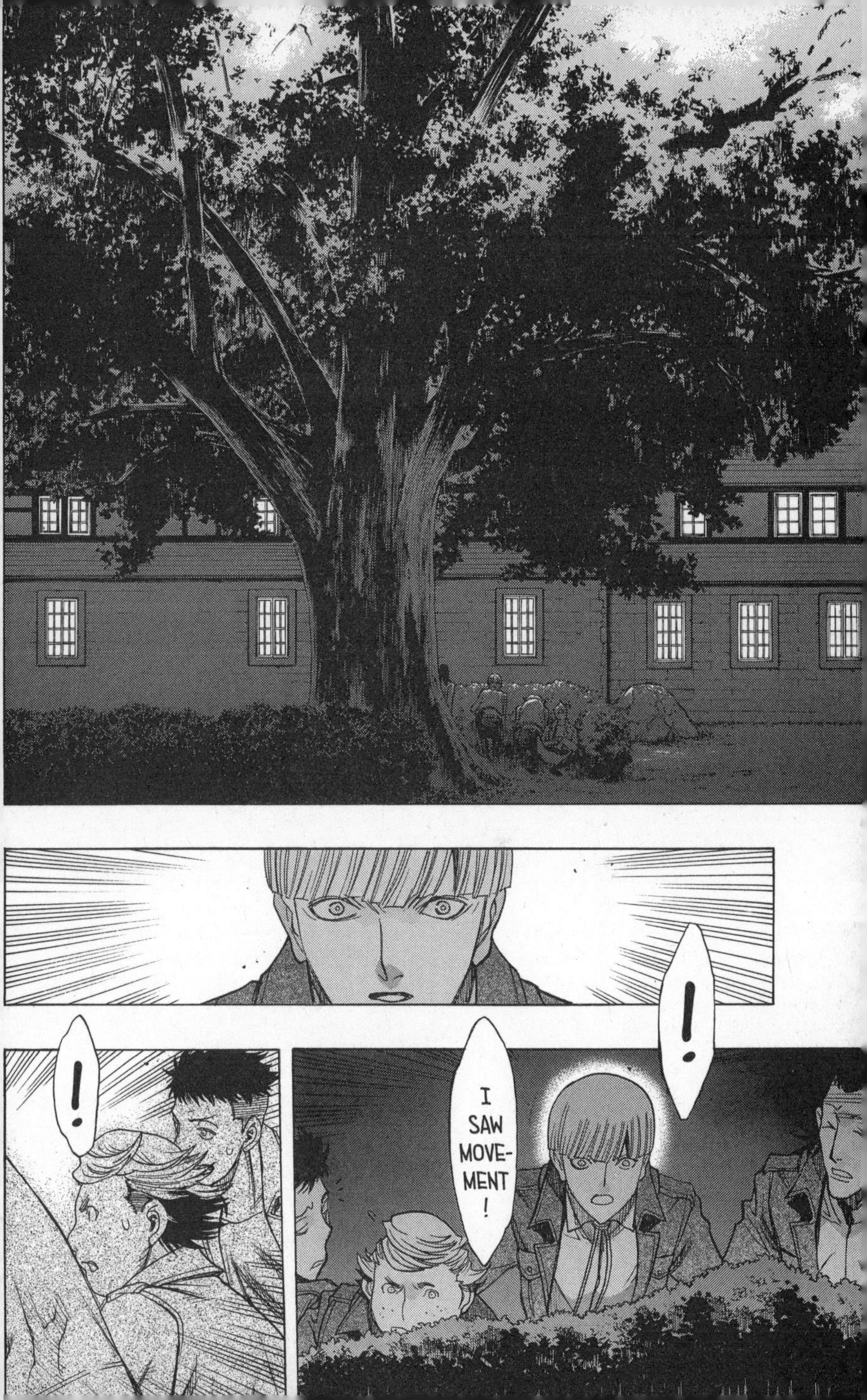
!
I SAW MOVE-MENT!
!

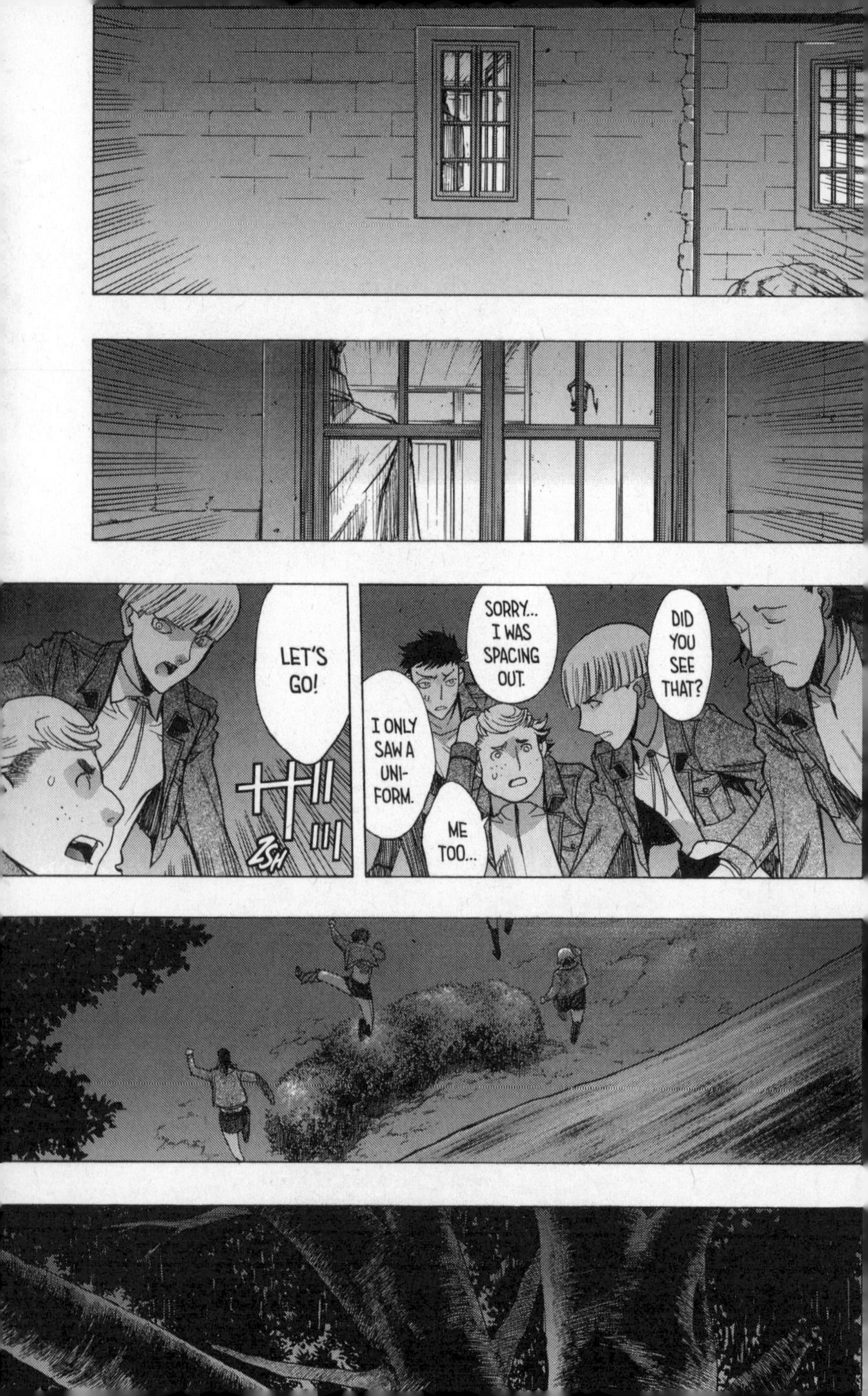
DID YOU SEE THAT?
SORRY... I WAS SPACING OUT.
I ONLY SAW A UNI-FORM.
ME TOO...
LET'S GO!
ZSH

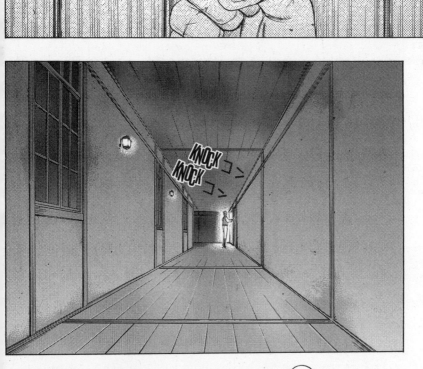

KNOCK
KNOCK
!
YES?
CAPTAIN CARLO WOULD LIKE TO SEE YOU.
PLEASE REPORT TO THE SPECIAL TRAINING AREA RIGHT AWAY.

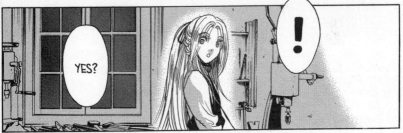

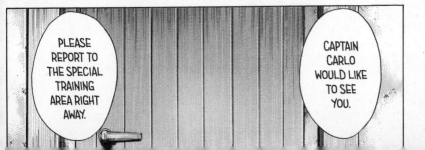

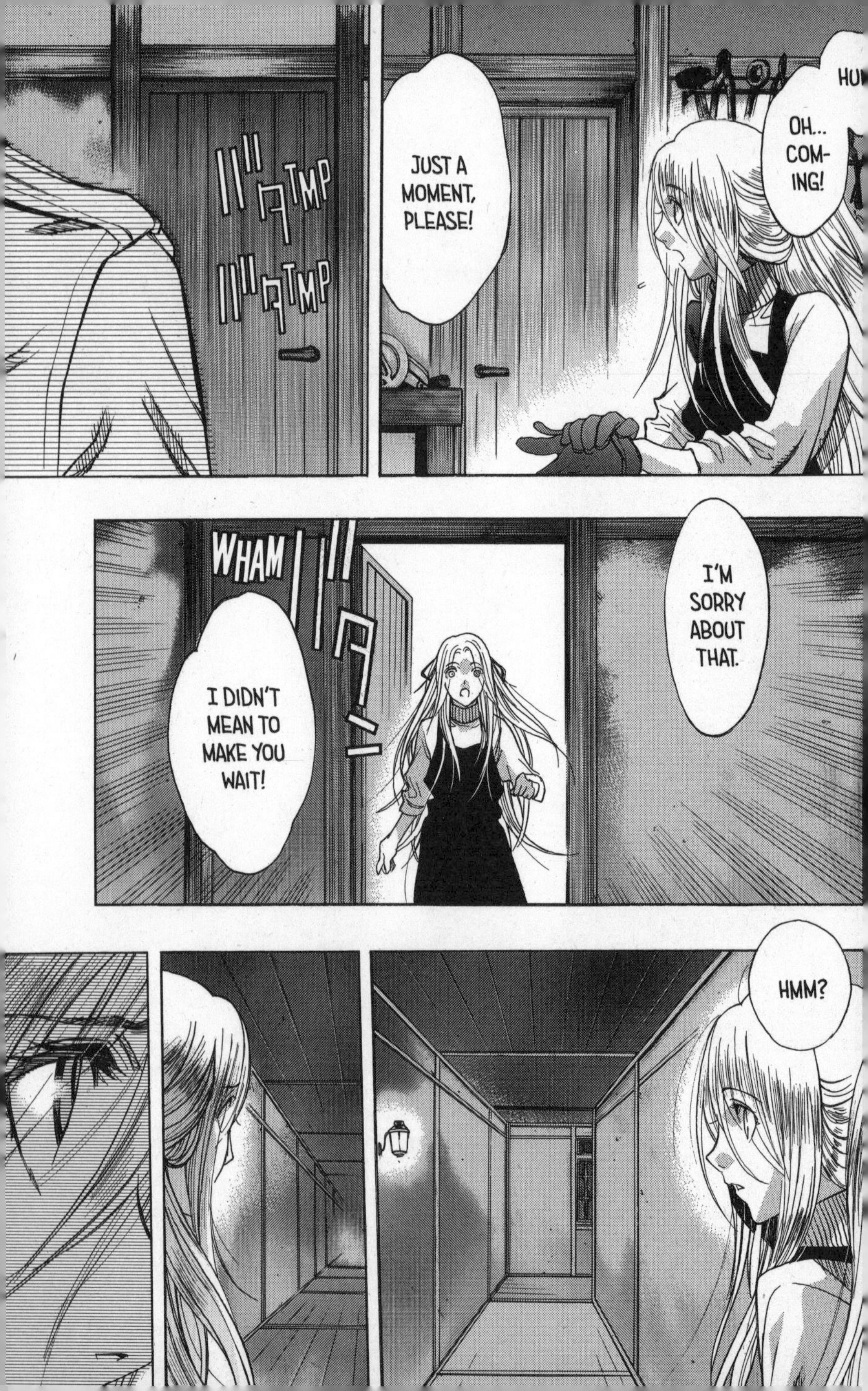
HU
OH... COM-ING!
JUST A MOMENT, PLEASE!
TMP
TMP
I'M SORRY ABOUT THAT.
WHAM
I DIDN'T MEAN TO MAKE YOU WAIT!
HMM?

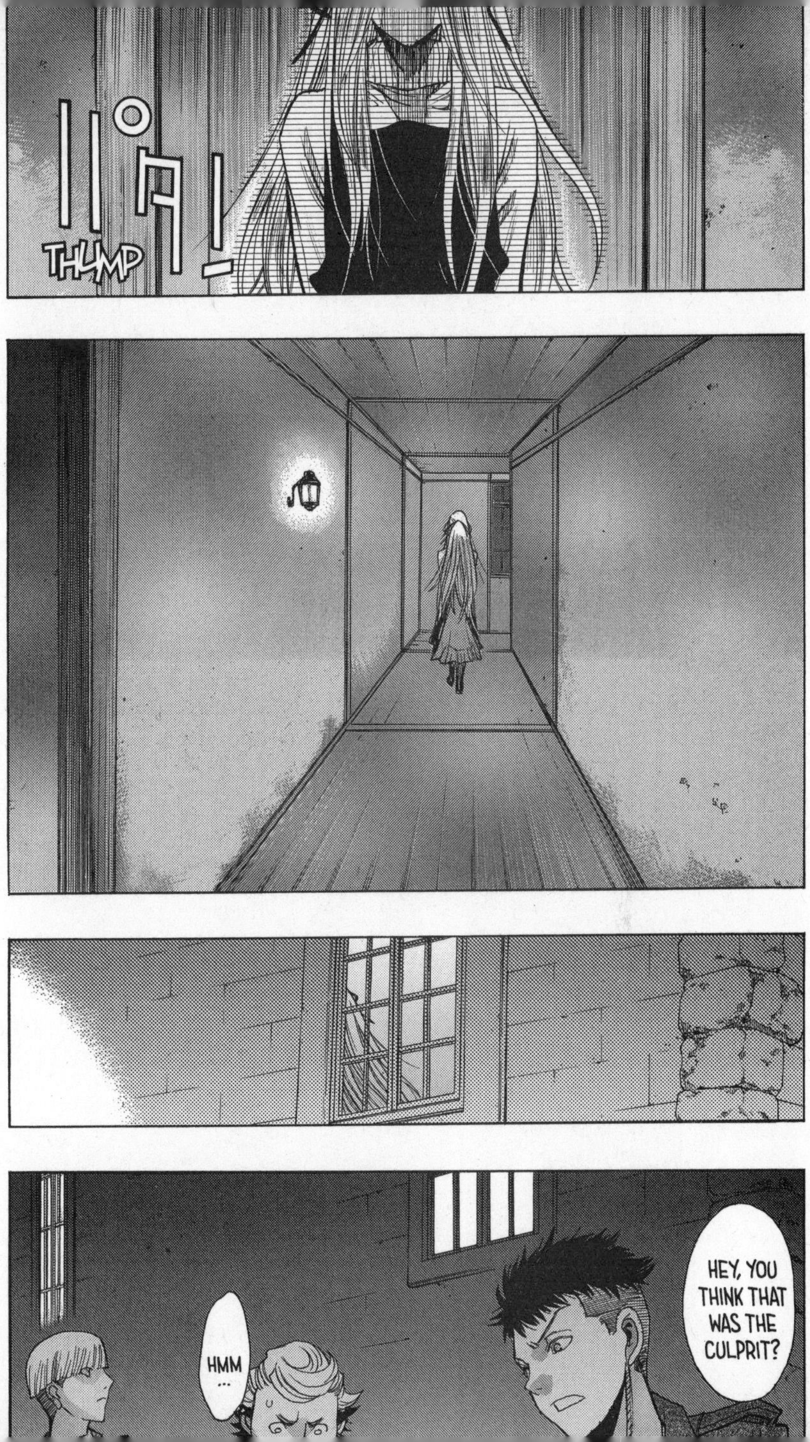
パタ…
THUMP
HEY, YOU THINK THAT WAS THE CULPRIT?
HMM ...

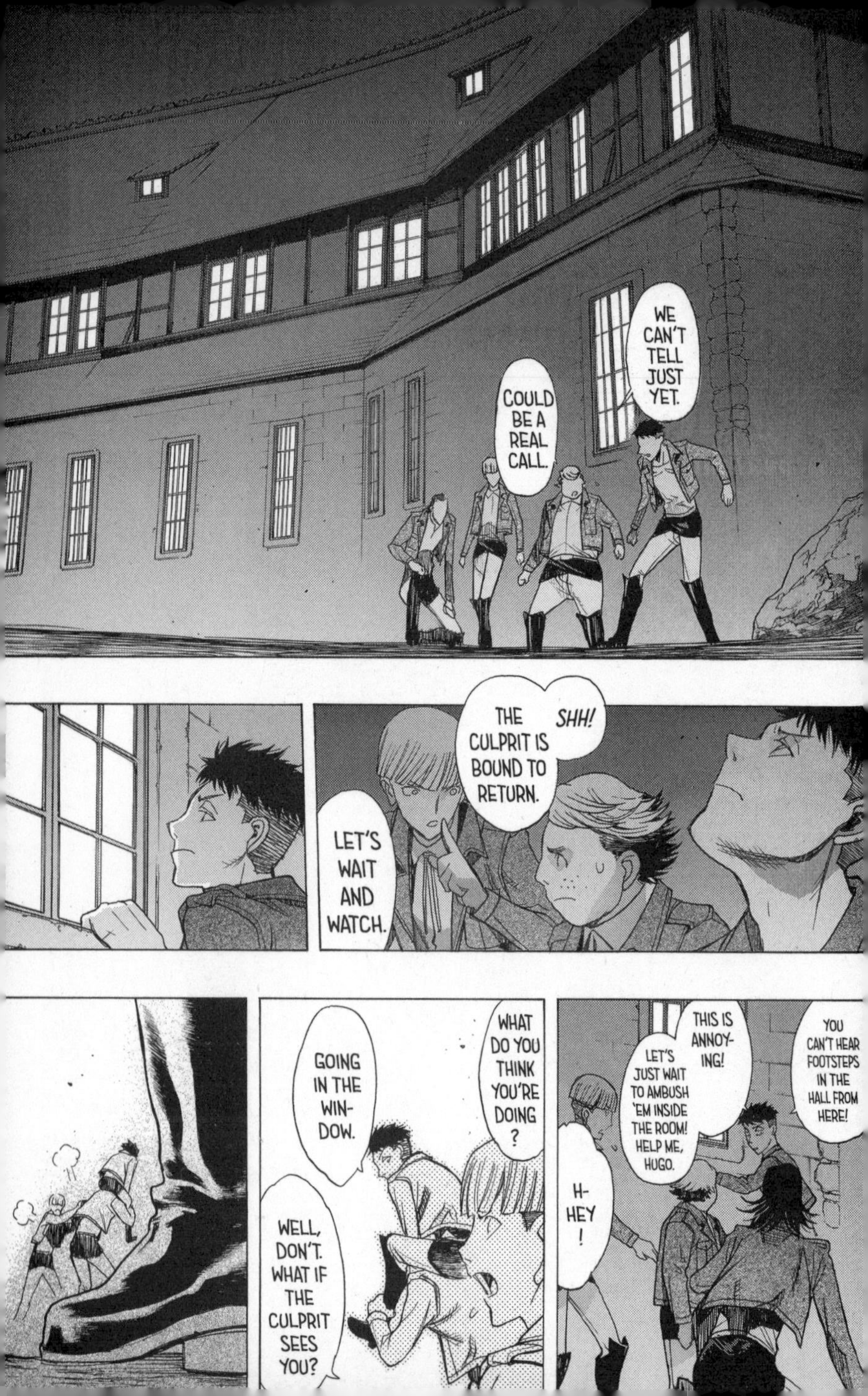
WE CAN'T TELL JUST YET.
COULD BE A REAL CALL.
SHH!
THE CULPRIT IS BOUND TO RETURN.
LET'S WAIT AND WATCH.
YOU CAN'T HEAR FOOTSTEPS IN THE HALL FROM HERE!
THIS IS ANNOY-ING!
LET'S JUST WAIT TO AMBUSH 'EM INSIDE THE ROOM! HELP ME, HUGO.
H-HEY!
WHAT DO YOU THINK YOU'RE DOING?
GOING IN THE WIN-DOW.
WELL, DON'T. WHAT IF THE CULPRIT SEES YOU?

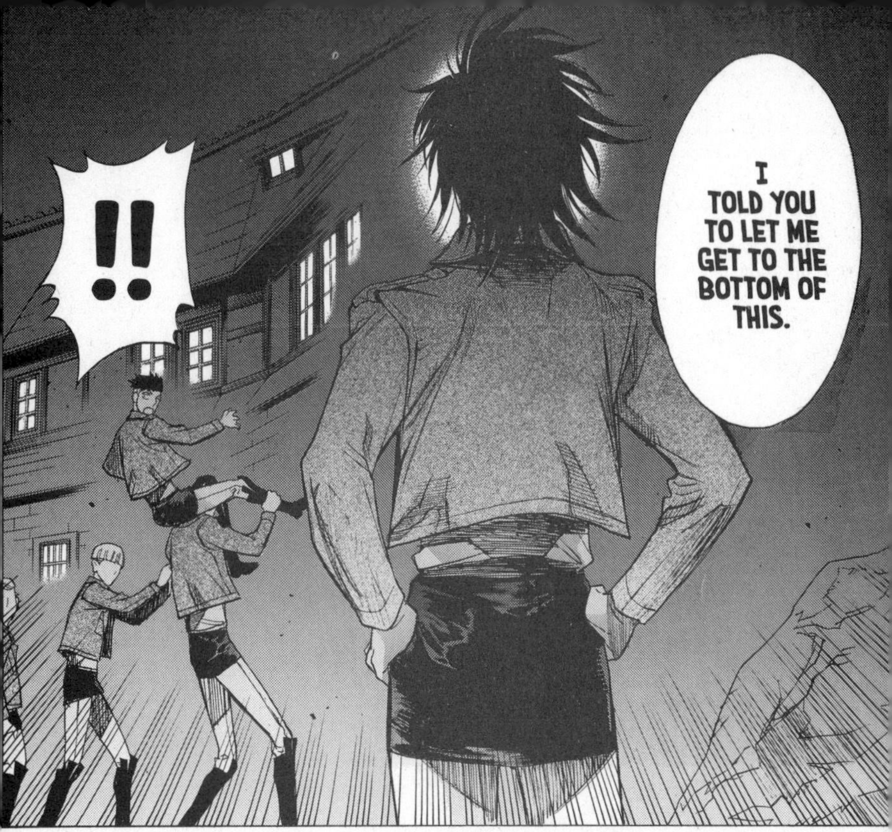
I TOLD YOU TO LET ME GET TO THE BOTTOM OF THIS.
!!
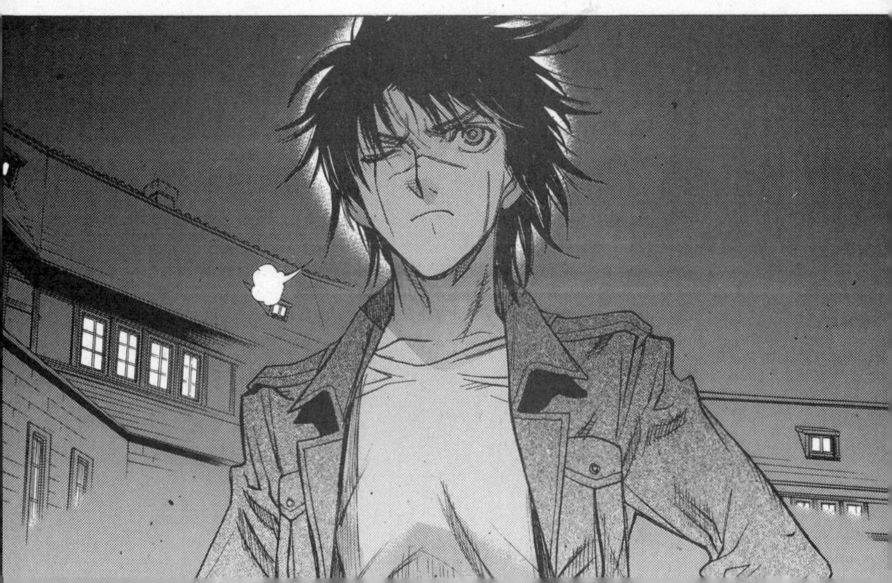

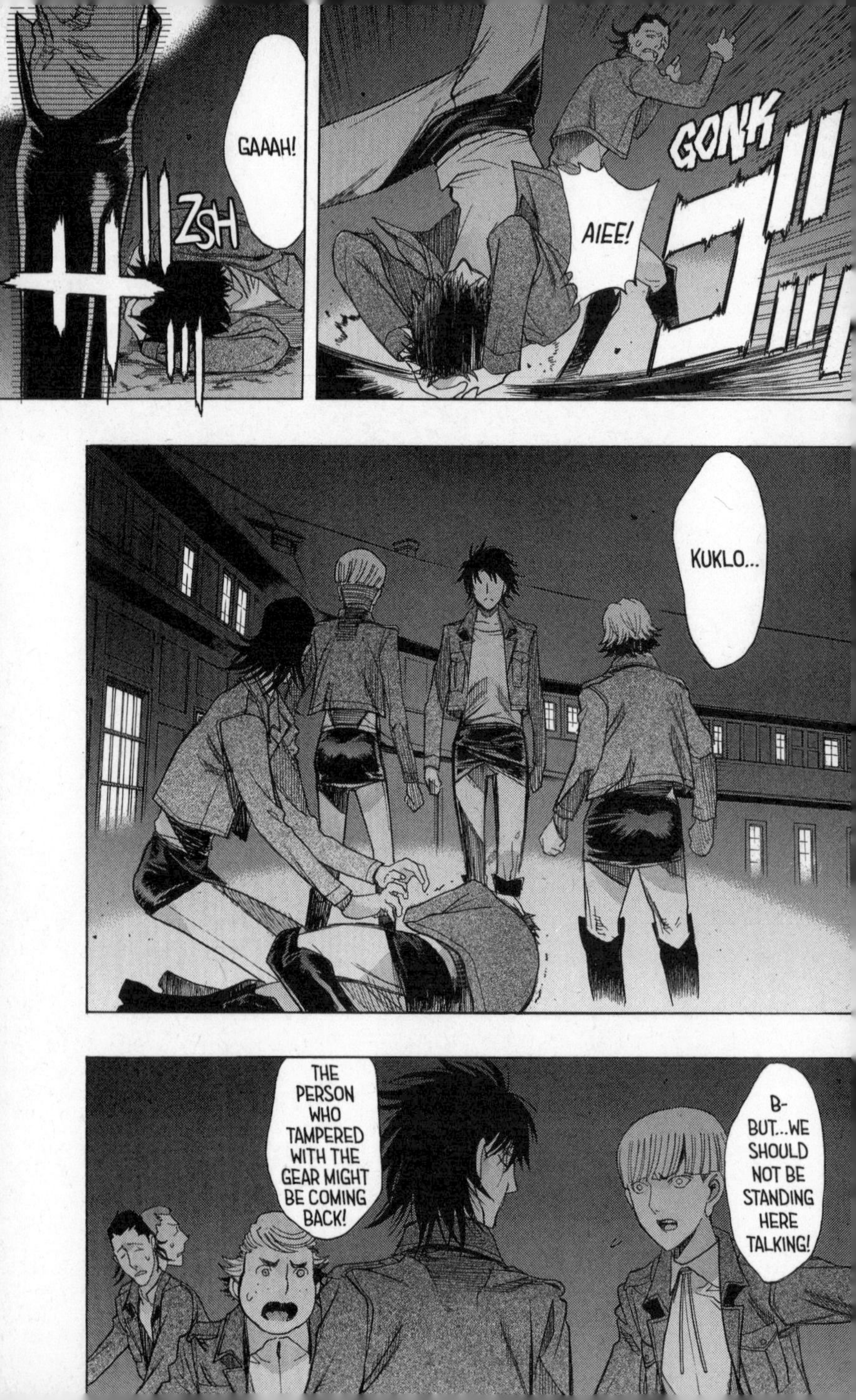
GONK
AIEE!
GAAAH!
ZSH
KUKLO...
B-BUT...WE SHOULD NOT BE STANDING HERE TALKING!
THE PERSON WHO TAMPERED WITH THE GEAR MIGHT BE COMING BACK!

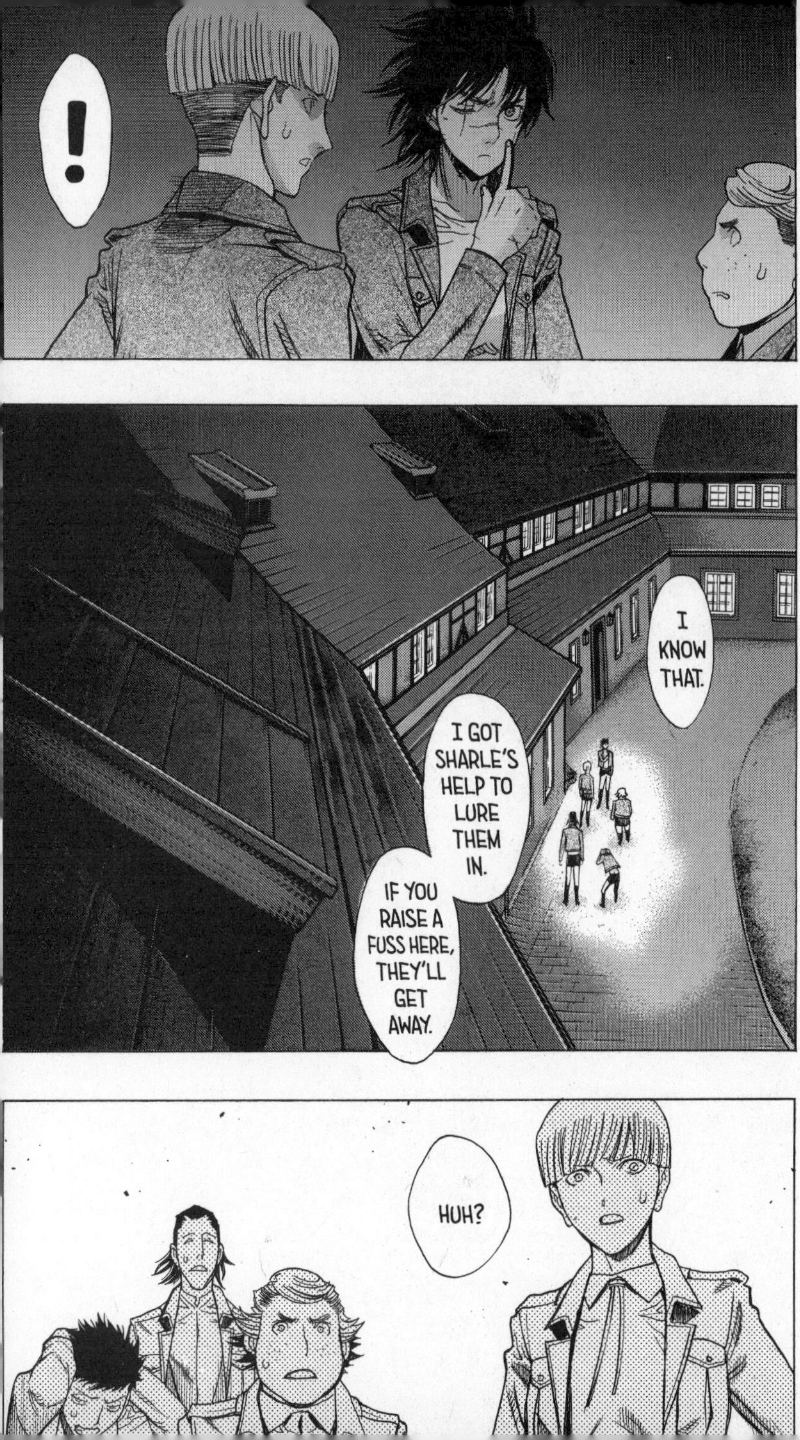
!
I KNOW THAT.
I GOT SHARLE'S HELP TO LURE THEM IN.
IF YOU RAISE A FUSS HERE, THEY'LL GET AWAY.
HUH?

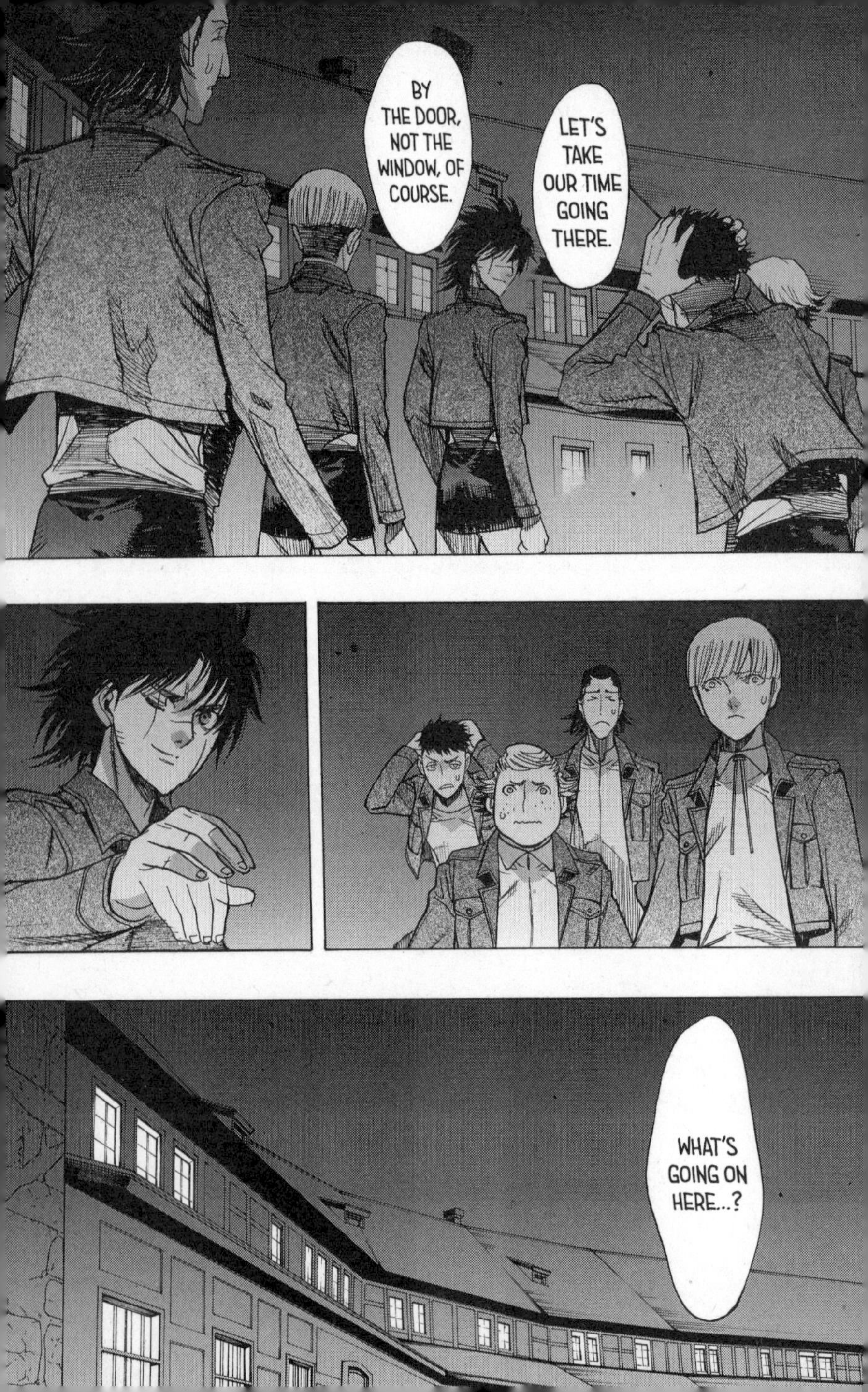
LET'S TAKE OUR TIME GOING THERE.
BY THE DOOR, NOT THE WINDOW, OF COURSE.
WHAT'S GOING ON HERE...?

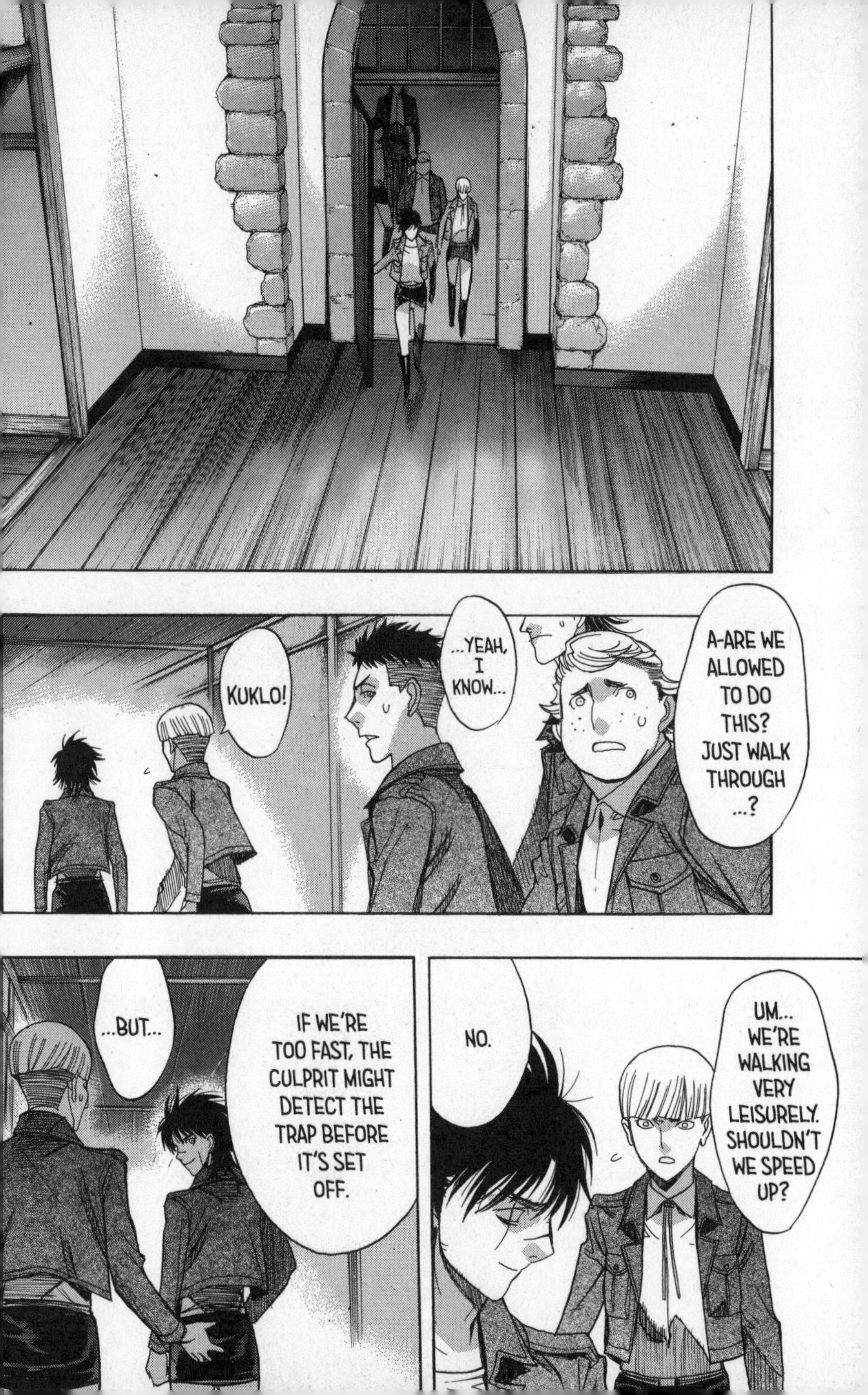
A-ARE WE ALLOWED TO DO THIS? JUST WALK THROUGH ...?
...YEAH, I KNOW...
KUKLO!
UM... WE'RE WALKING VERY LEISURELY. SHOULDN'T WE SPEED UP?
NO.
IF WE'RE TOO FAST, THE CULPRIT MIGHT DETECT THE TRAP BEFORE IT'S SET OFF.
...BUT...

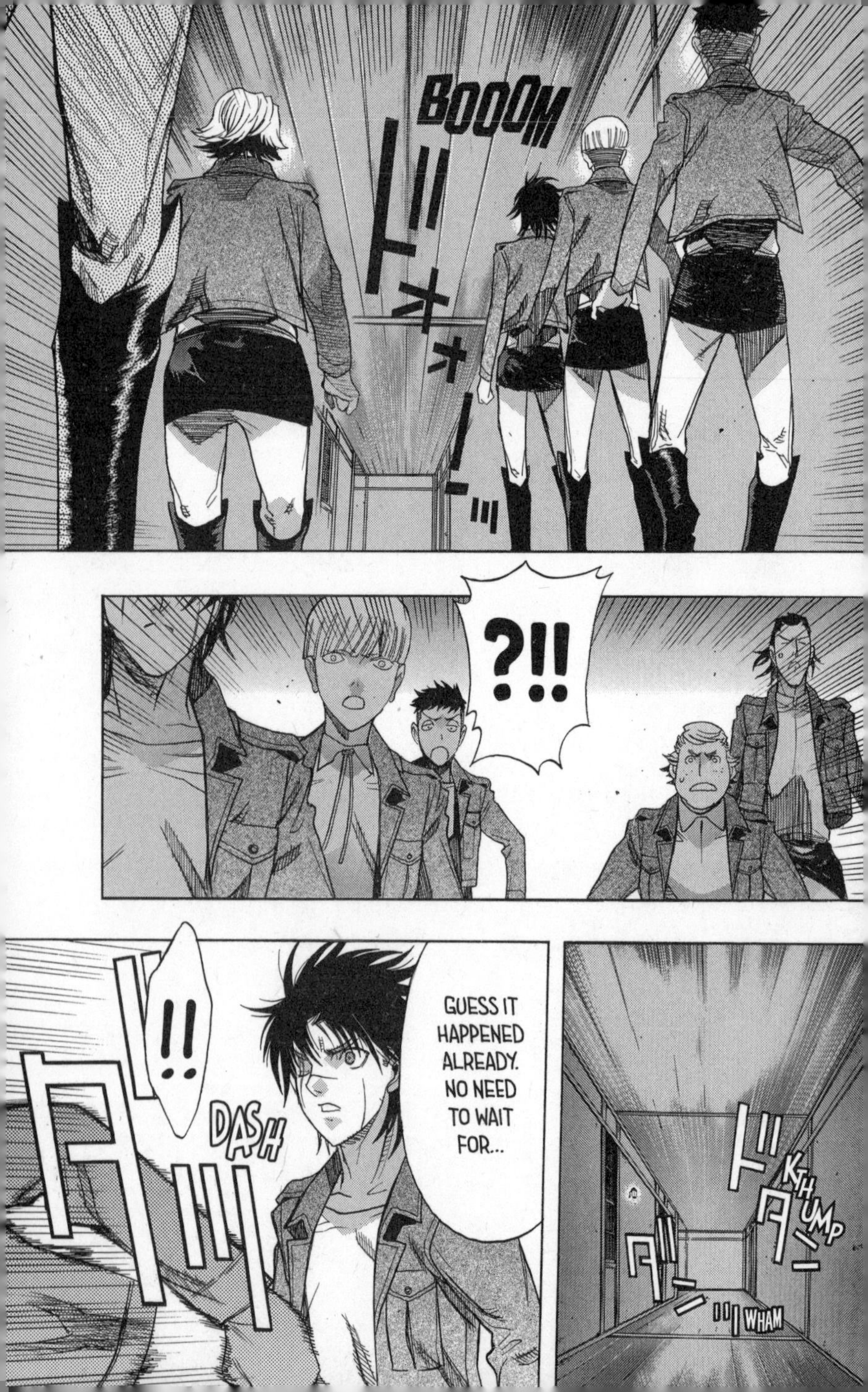
BOOOM
?!!
KTHUMP
WHAM
GUESS IT HAPPENED ALREADY. NO NEED TO WAIT FOR...
!!
DASH

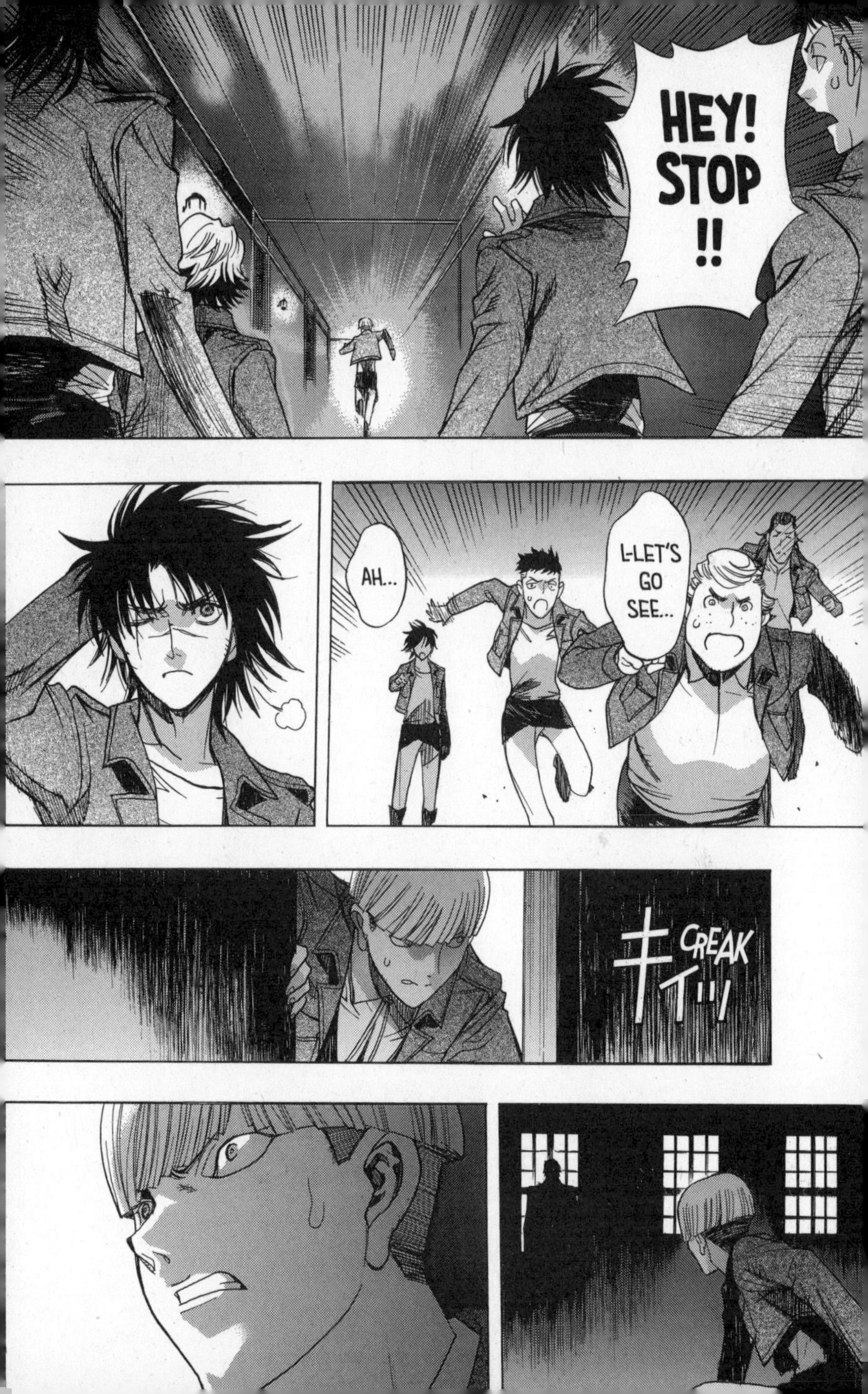
HEY! STOP !!
L-LET'S GO SEE...
AH...
CREAK
キイッ

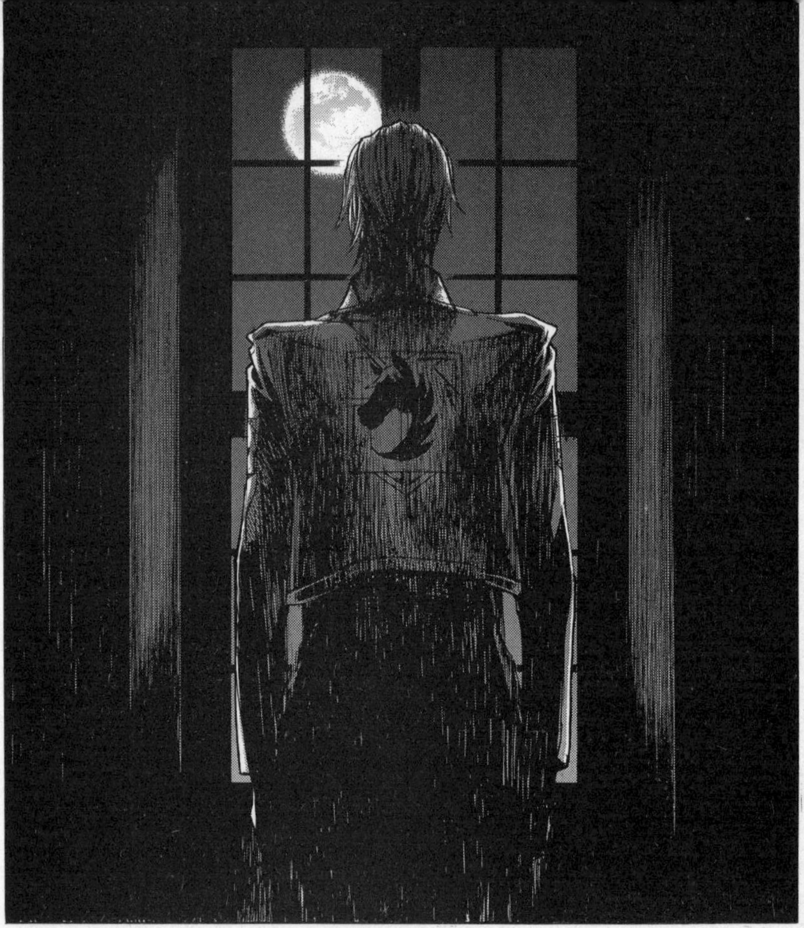
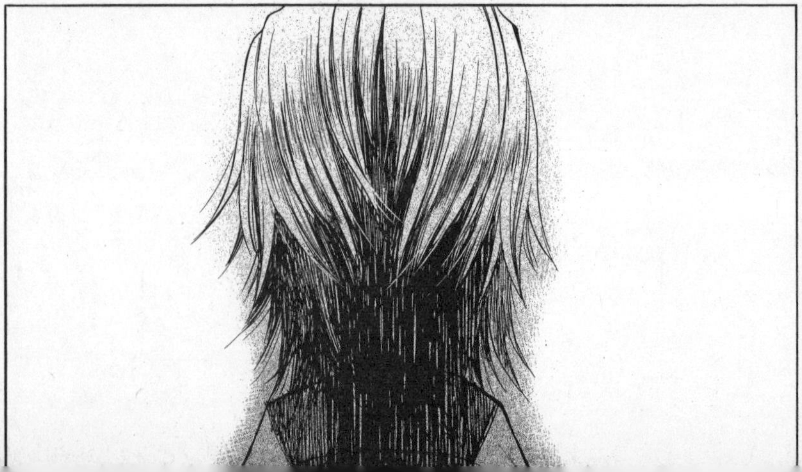

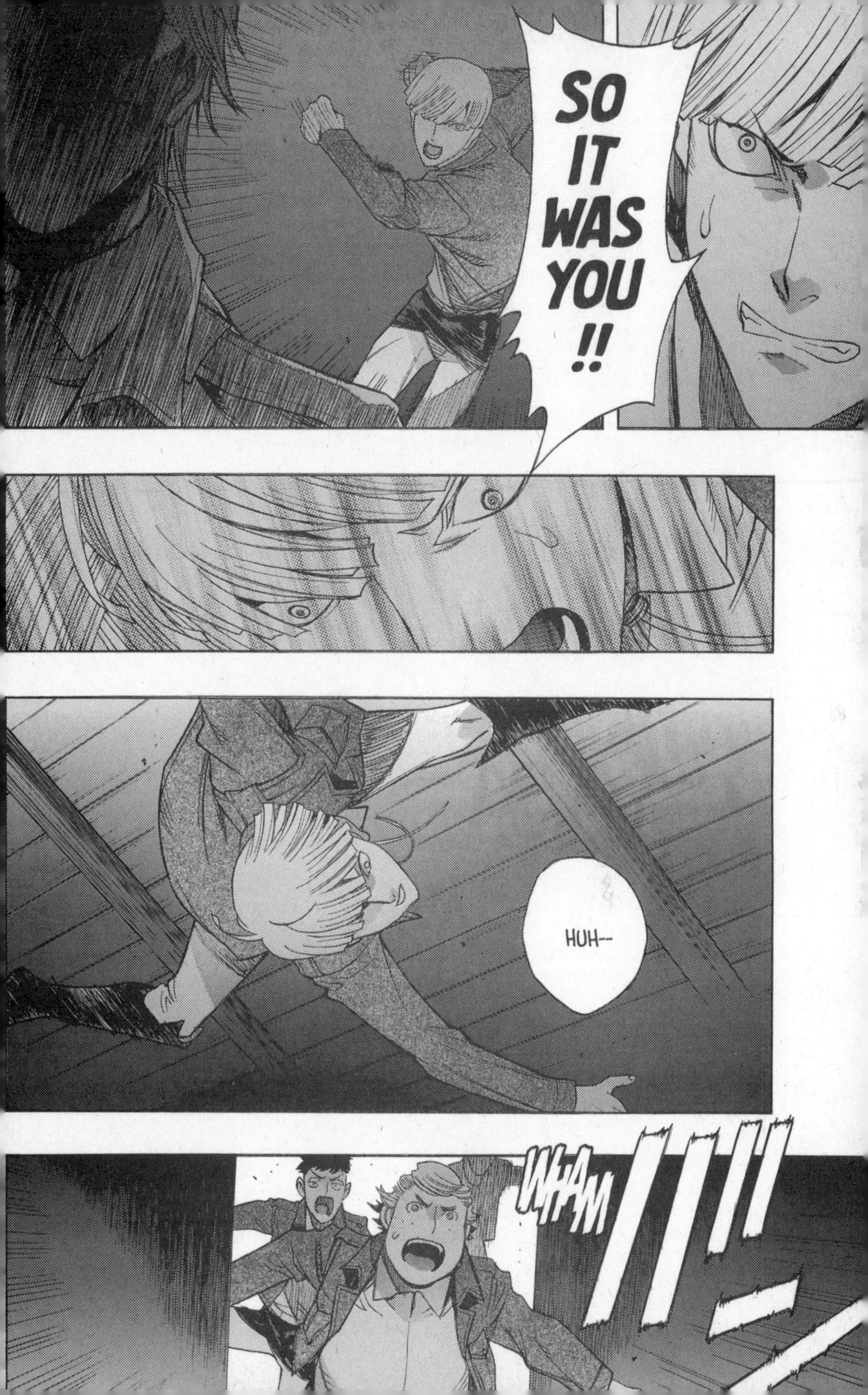
SO IT WAS YOU!!
HUH--
WHAM

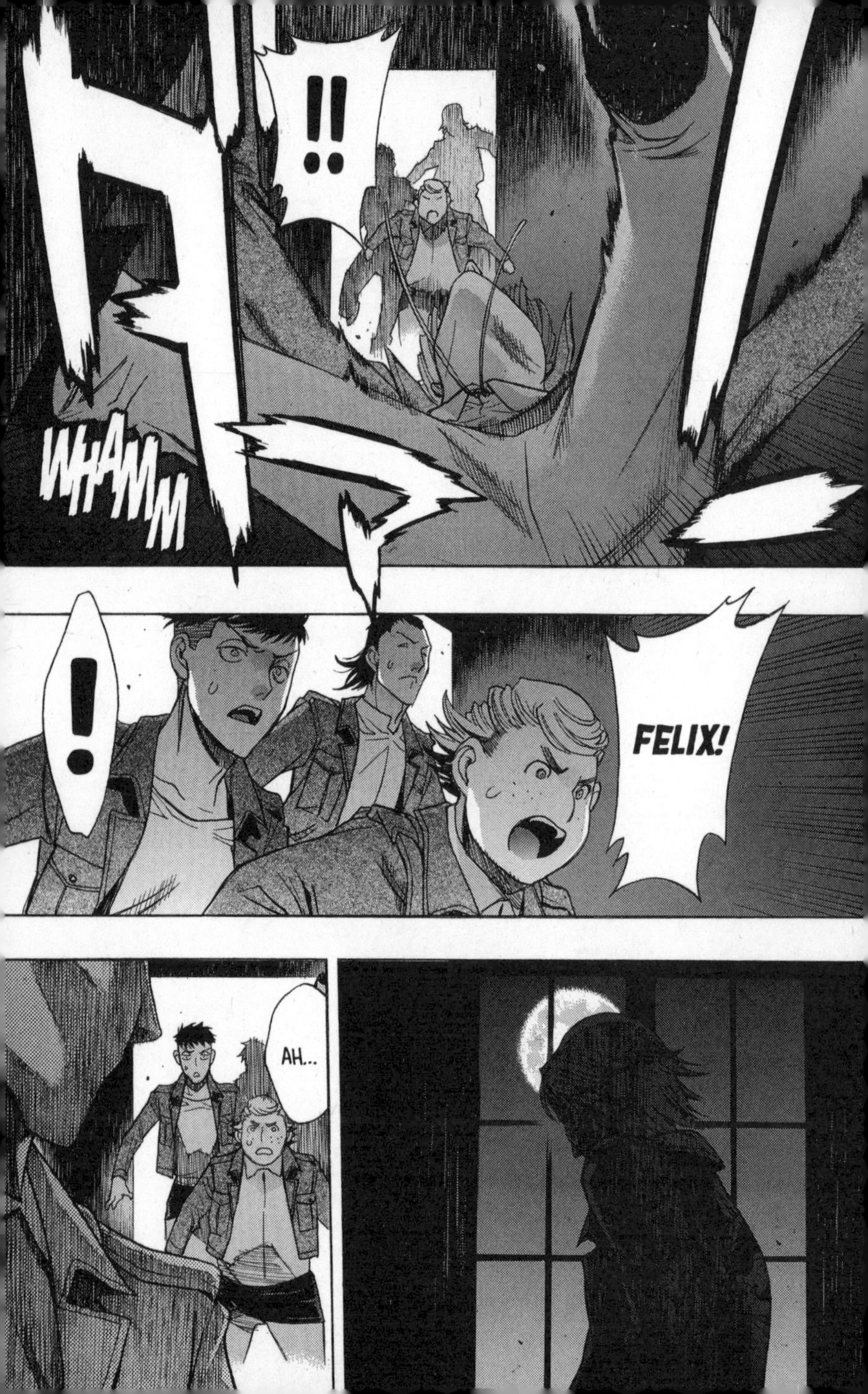

!!
WHAMM
FELIX!
!
AH...

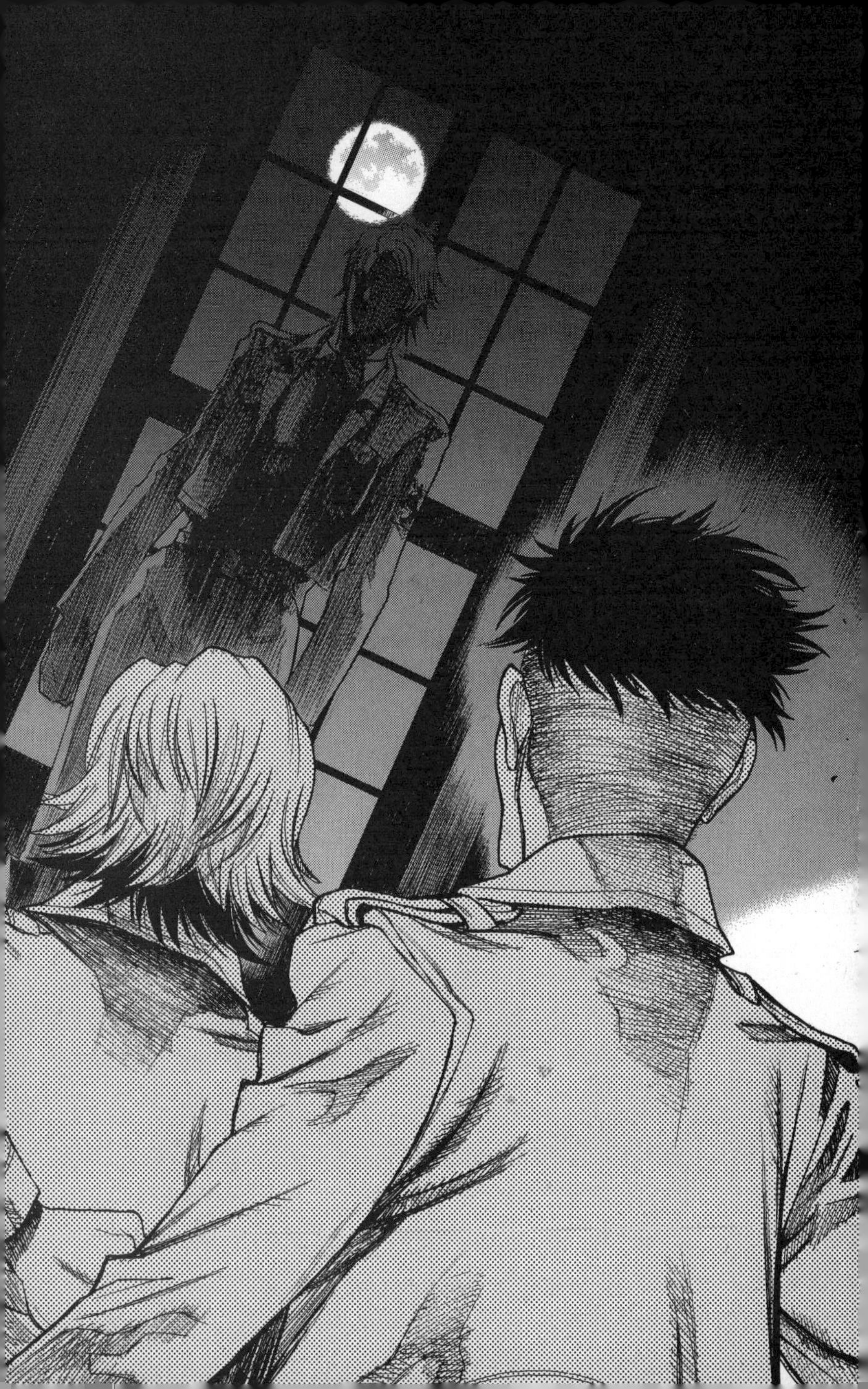

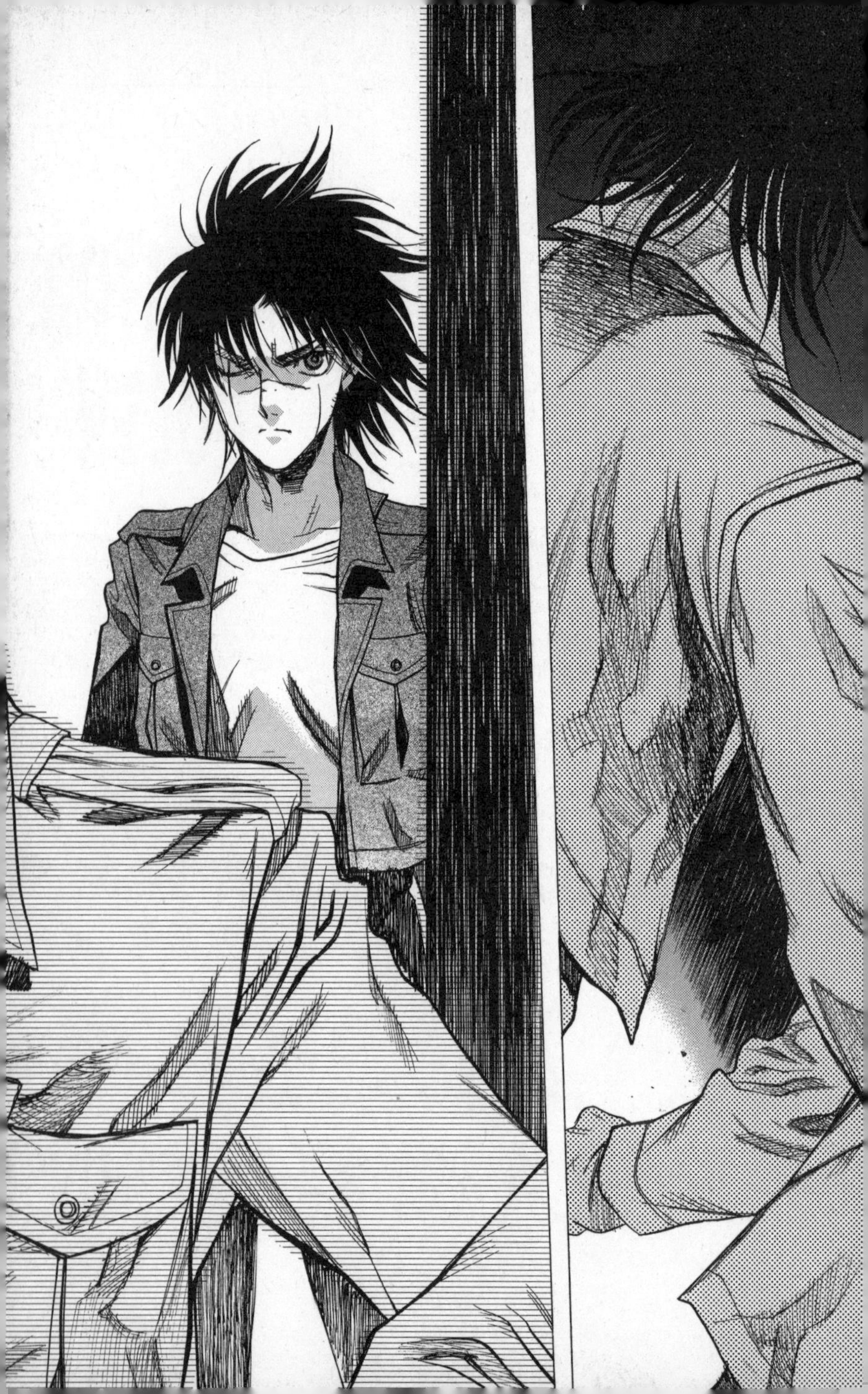

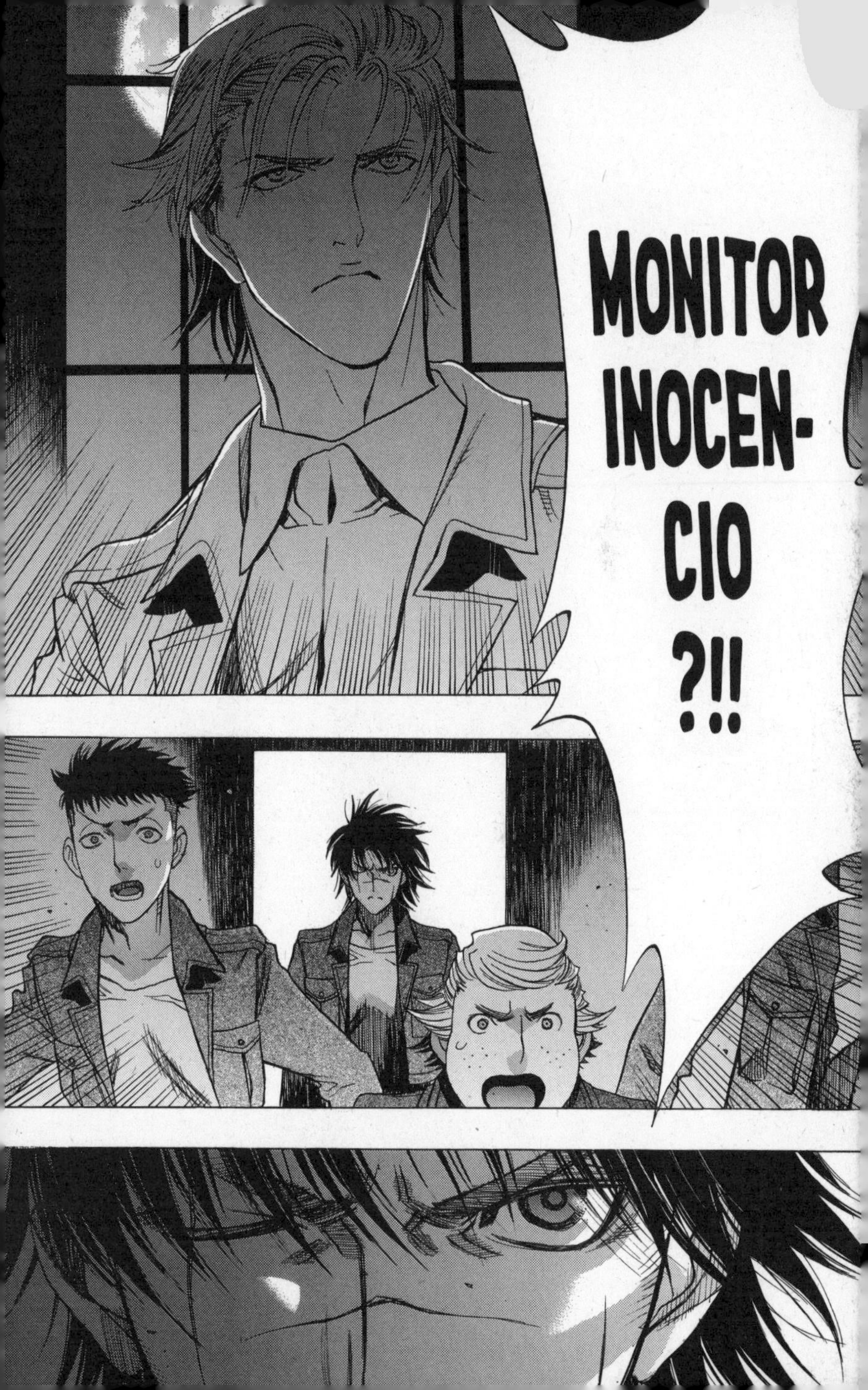
MONITOR INOCEN-CIO ?!!

Chapter 55: Box of Delusions · End

ATTACK on TITAN

BEFORE THE FALL

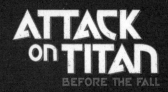

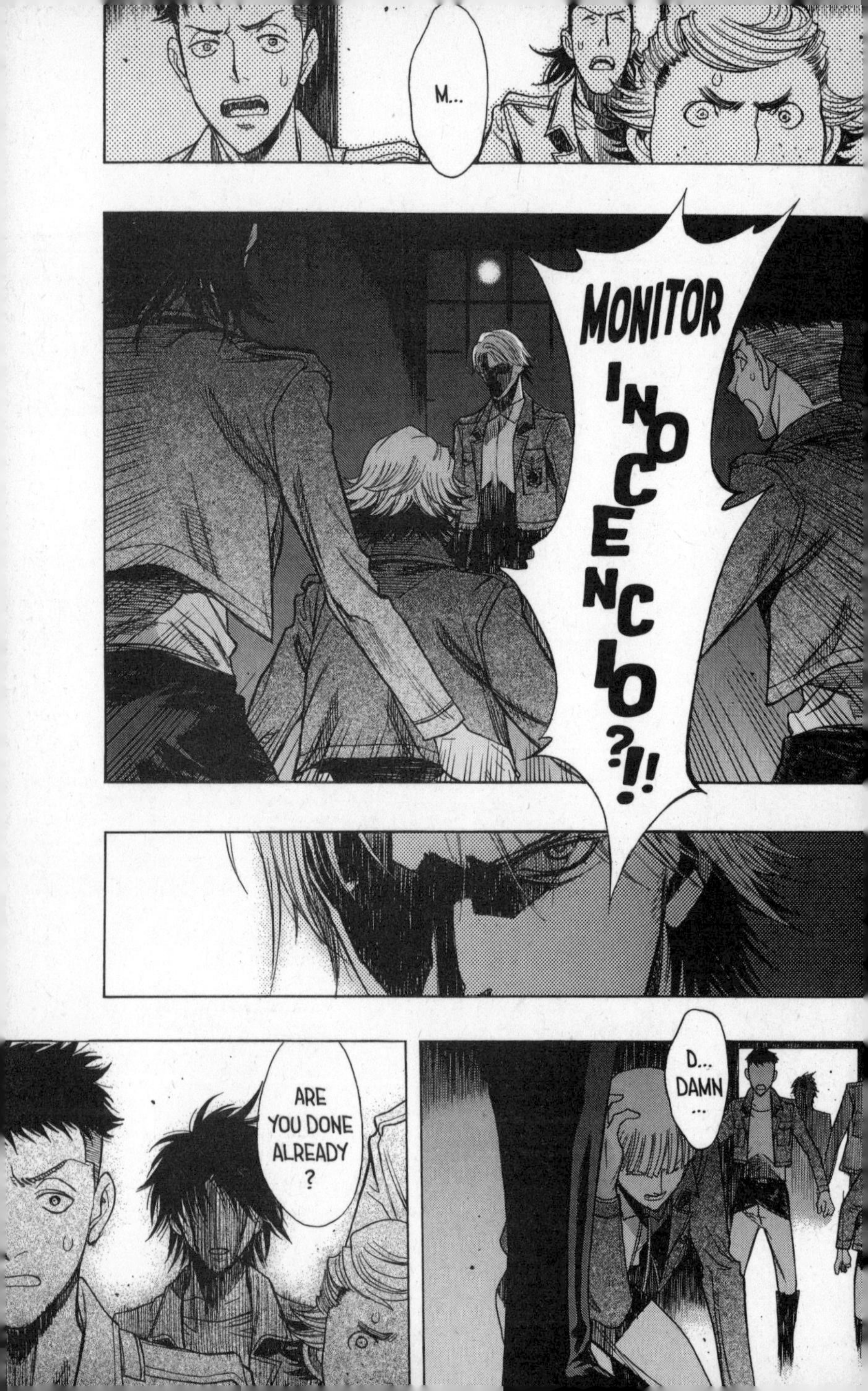
M...
MONITOR INOCENCIO?!!
D... DAMN...
ARE YOU DONE ALREADY?

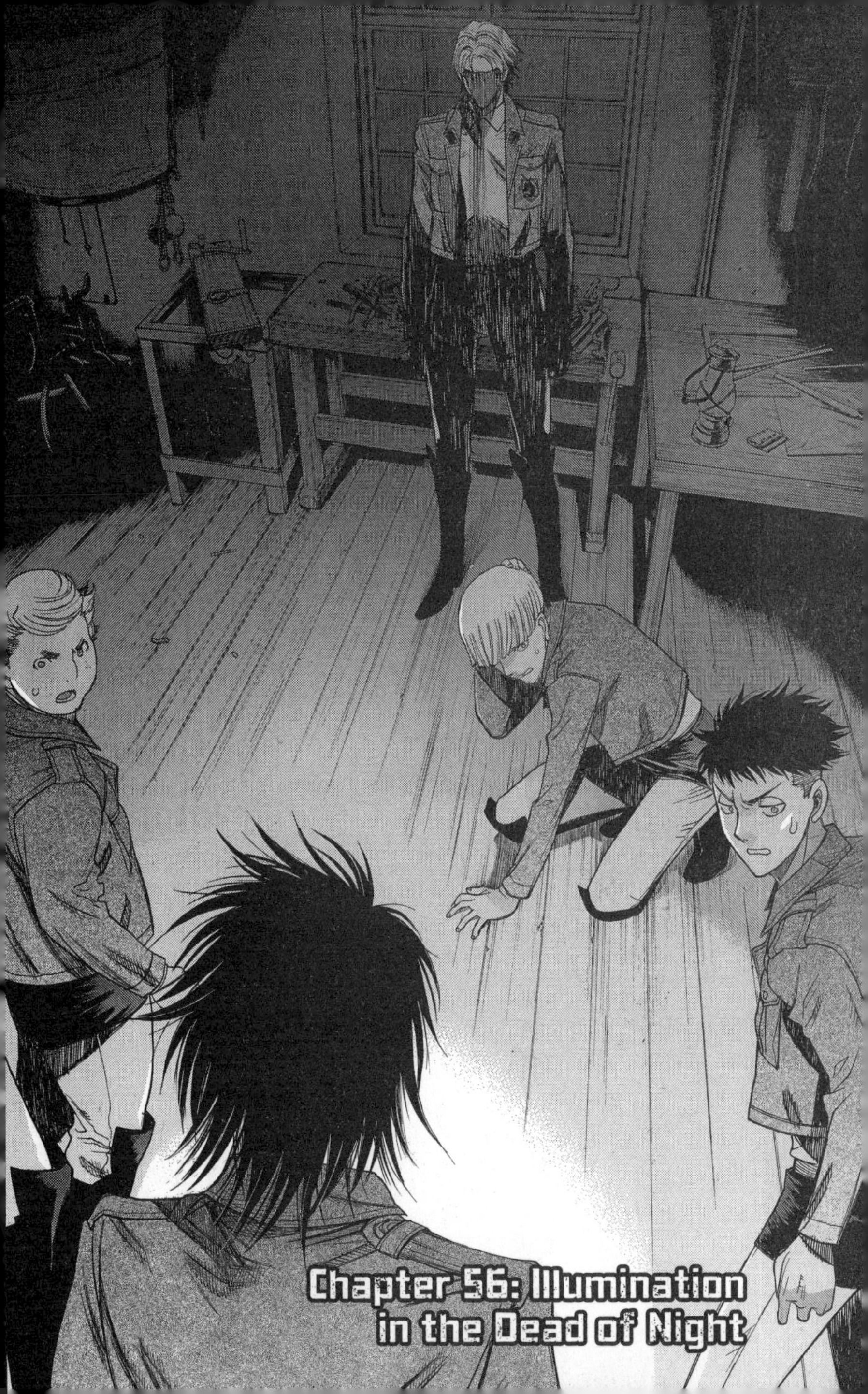
Chapter 56: Illumination in the Dead of Night

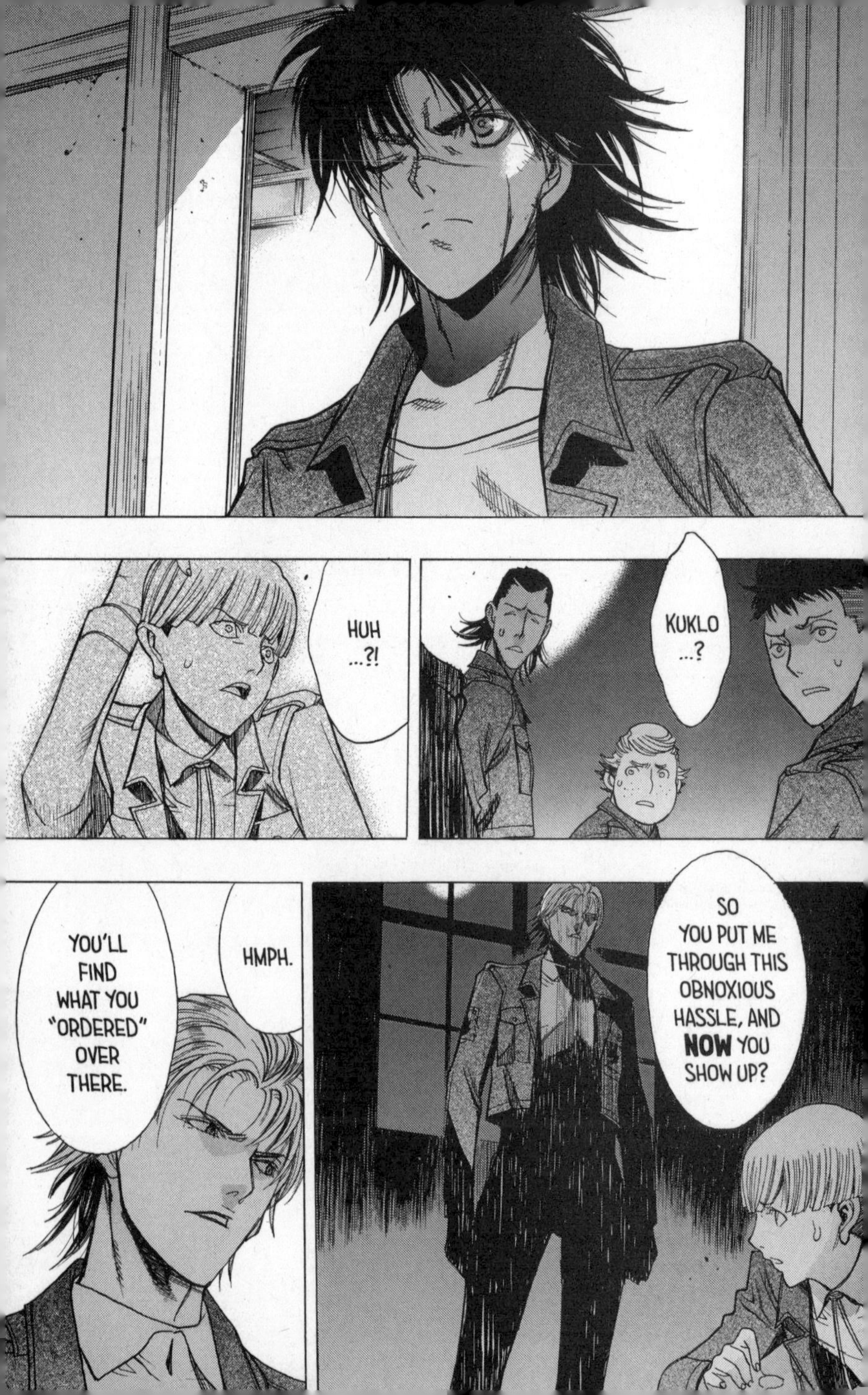
KUKLO ...?
HUH ...?!
SO YOU PUT ME THROUGH THIS OBNOXIOUS HASSLE, AND **NOW** YOU SHOW UP?
HMPH.
YOU'LL FIND WHAT YOU "ORDERED" OVER THERE.

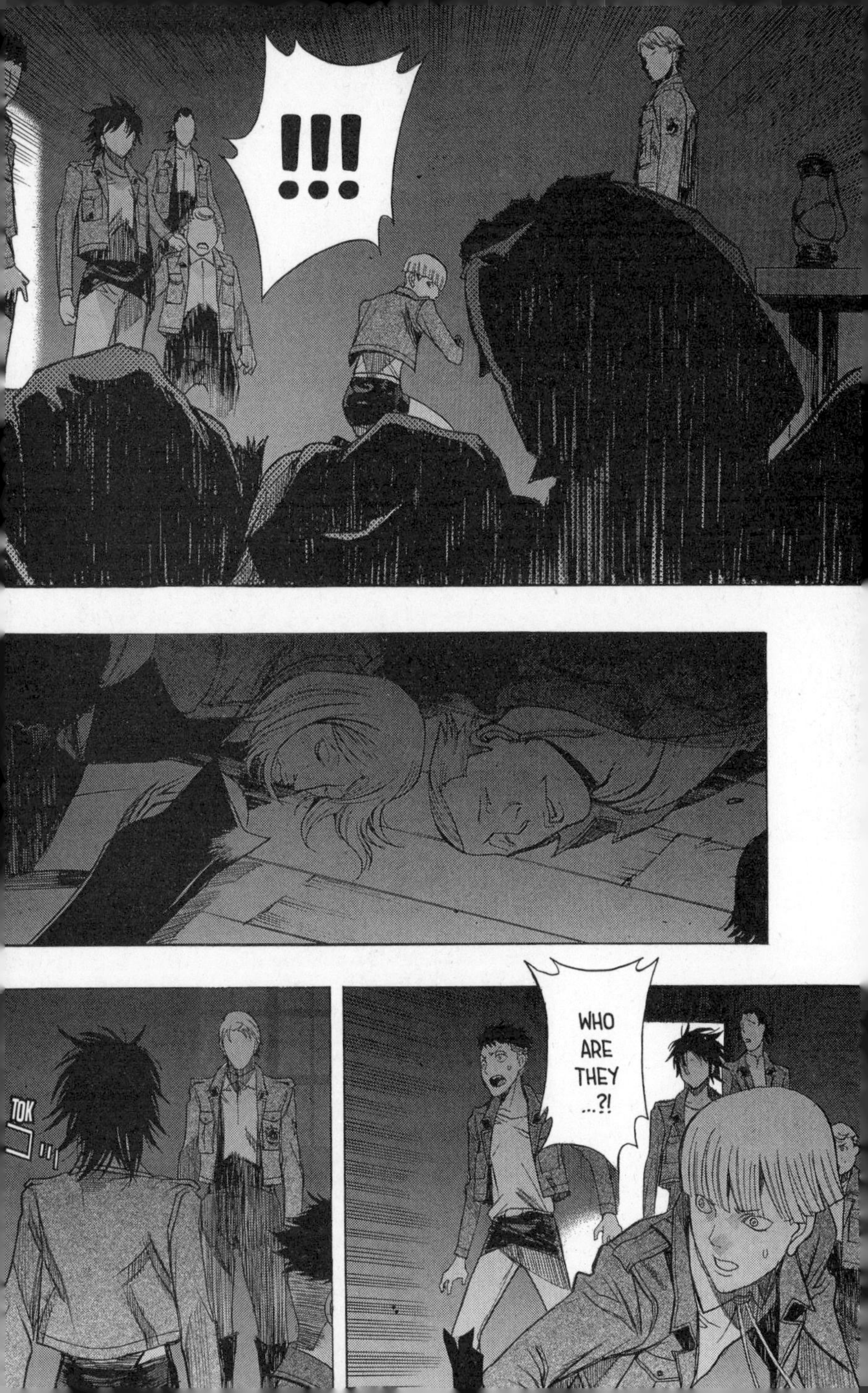
!!!
WHO ARE THEY ...?!
TOK

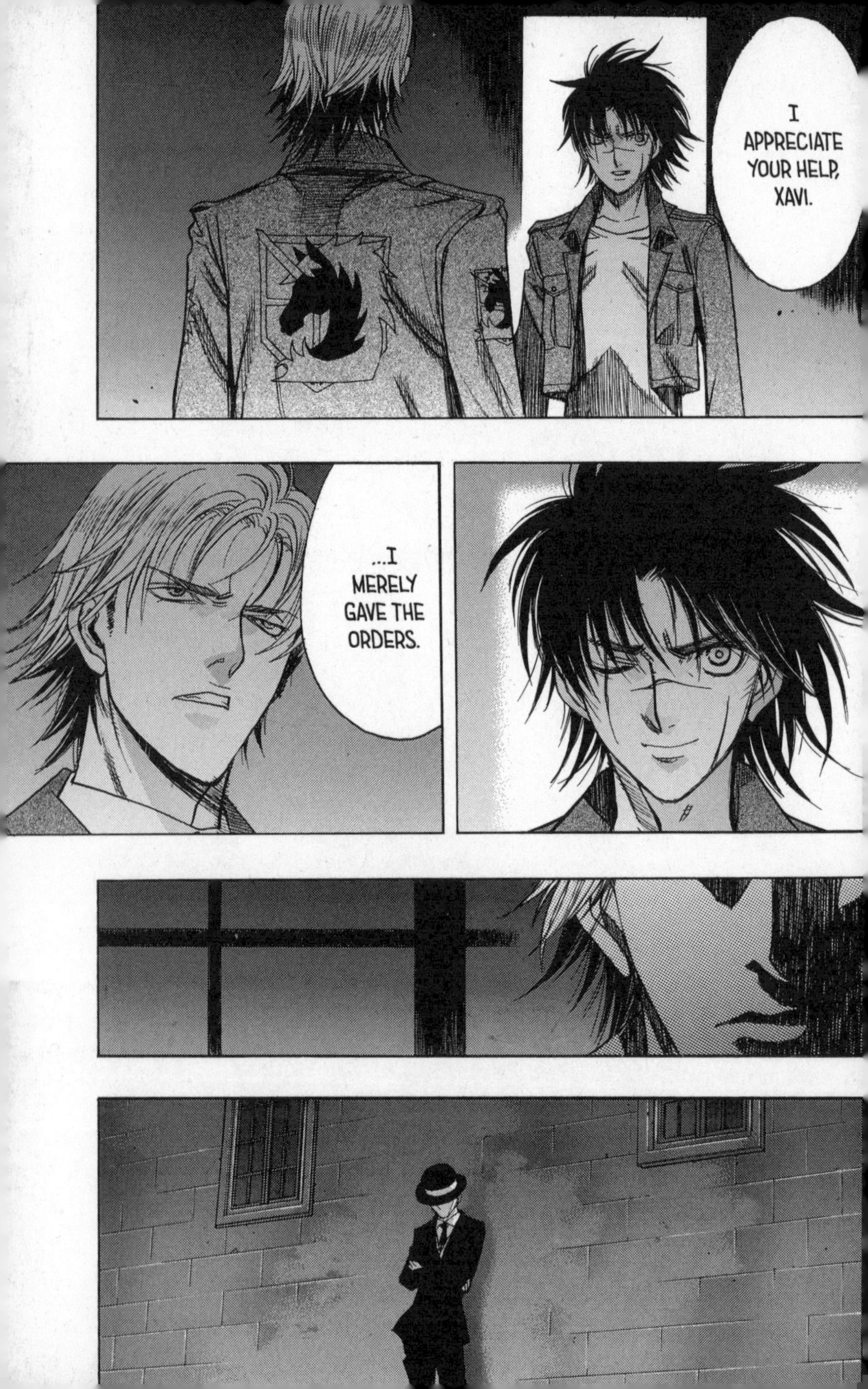
I APPRECIATE YOUR HELP, XAVI.
...I MERELY GAVE THE ORDERS.

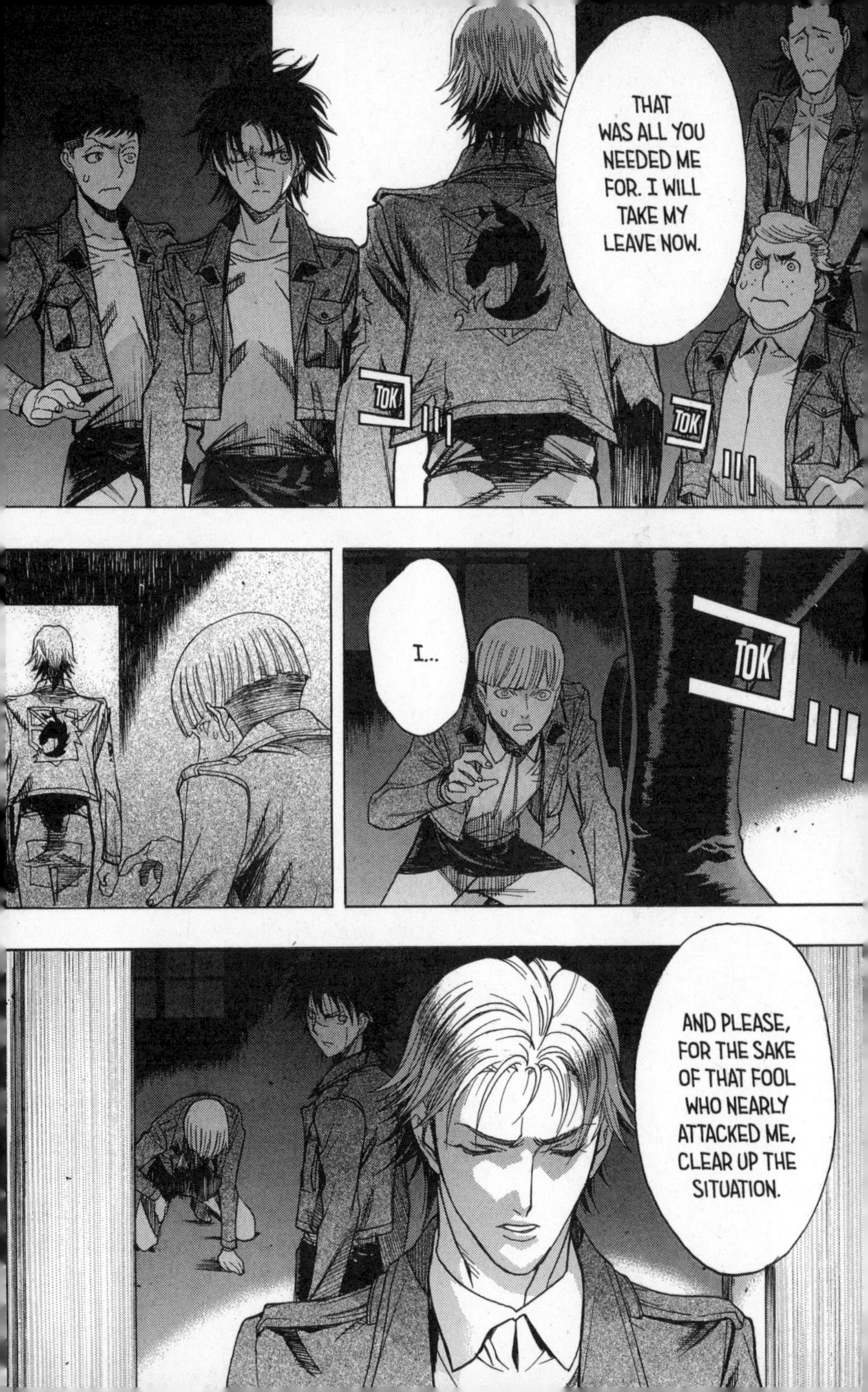
THAT WAS ALL YOU NEEDED ME FOR. I WILL TAKE MY LEAVE NOW.
TOK
TOK
TOK
I...
AND PLEASE, FOR THE SAKE OF THAT FOOL WHO NEARLY ATTACKED ME, CLEAR UP THE SITUATION.

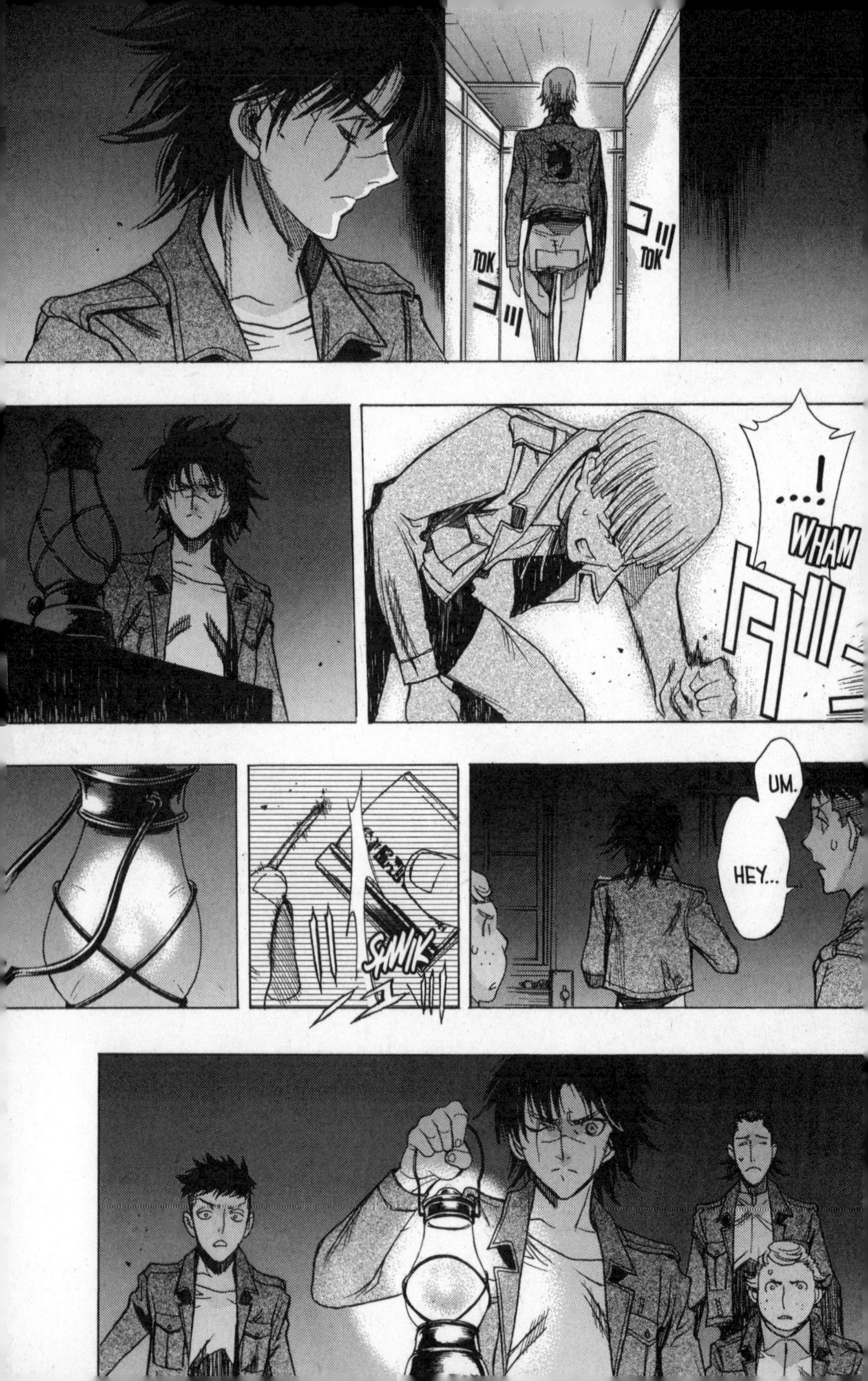
TOK
TOK
...!
WHAM
UM.
HEY...
SHWIK

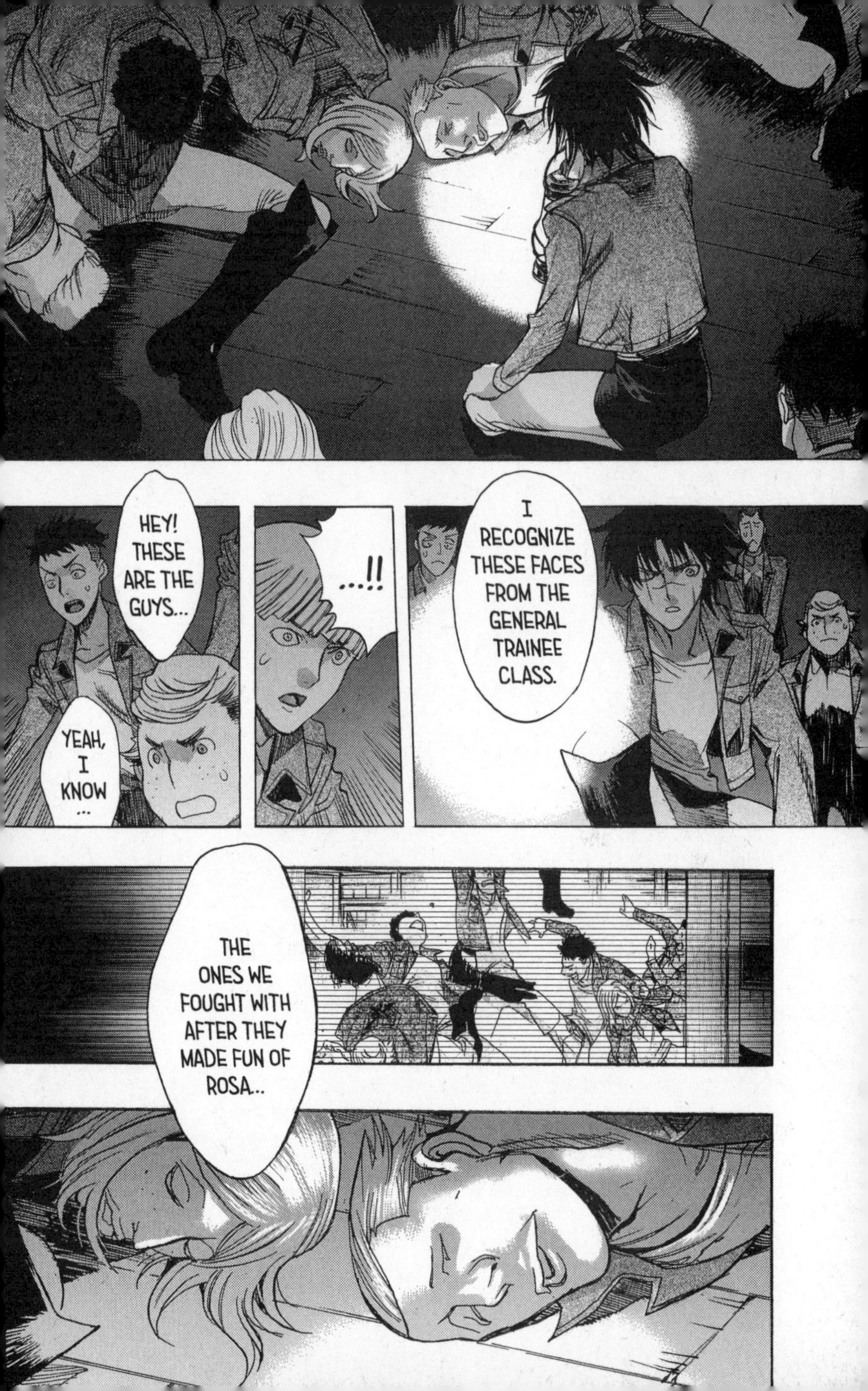
I RECOGNIZE THESE FACES FROM THE GENERAL TRAINEE CLASS.
...!!
HEY! THESE ARE THE GUYS...
YEAH, I KNOW...
THE ONES WE FOUGHT WITH AFTER THEY MADE FUN OF ROSA...

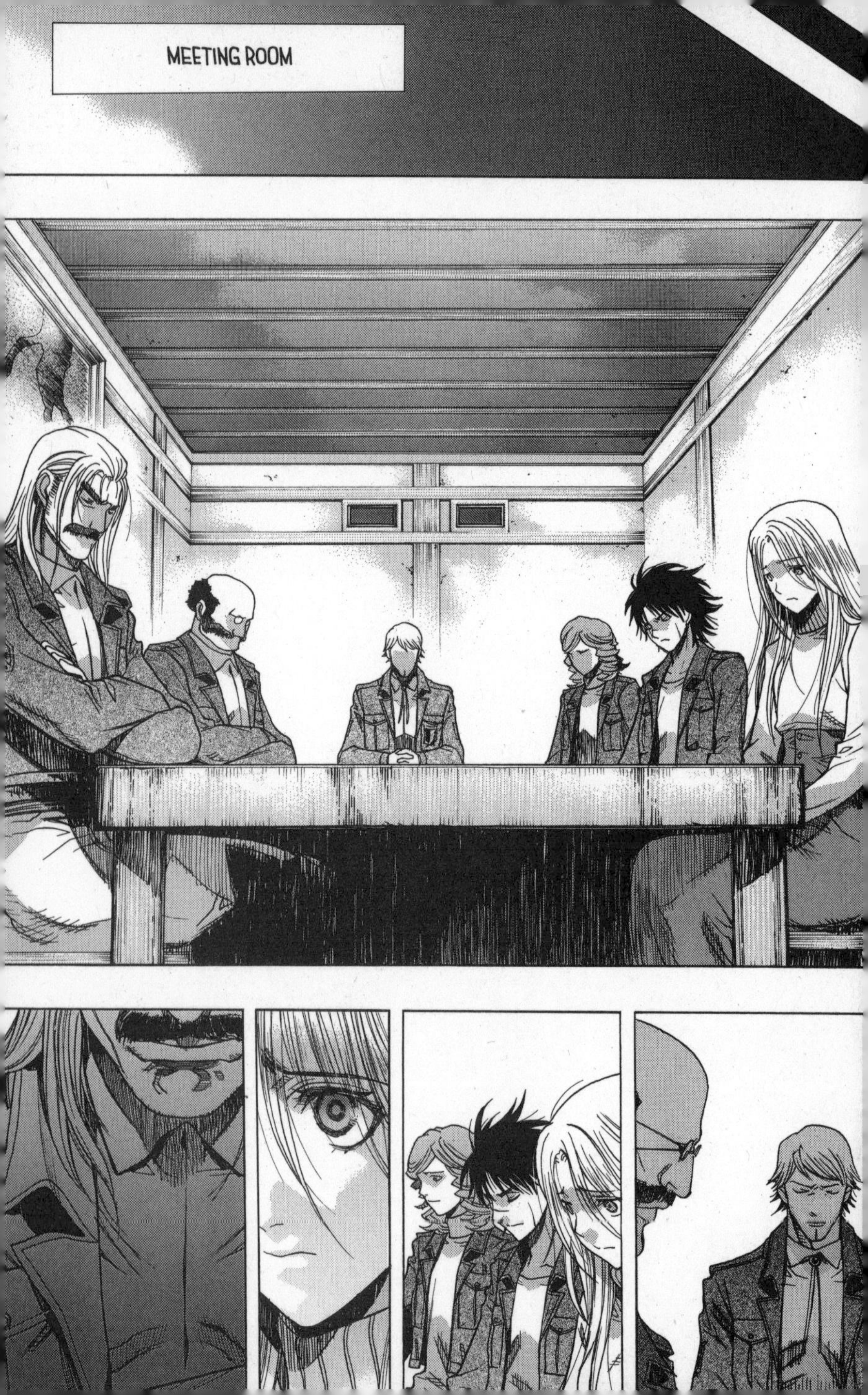
MEETING ROOM

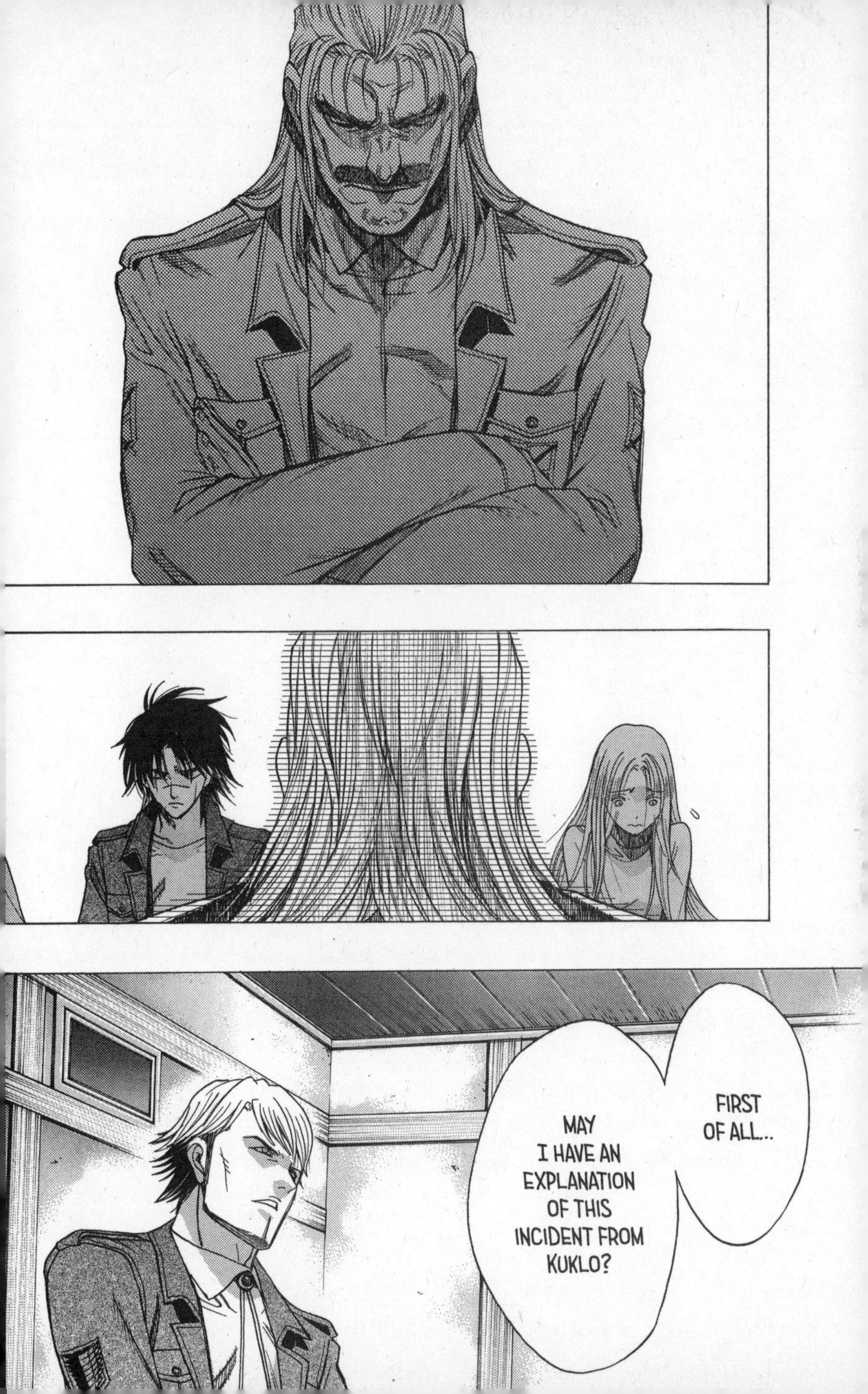
FIRST OF ALL...
MAY I HAVE AN EXPLANATION OF THIS INCIDENT FROM KUKLO?

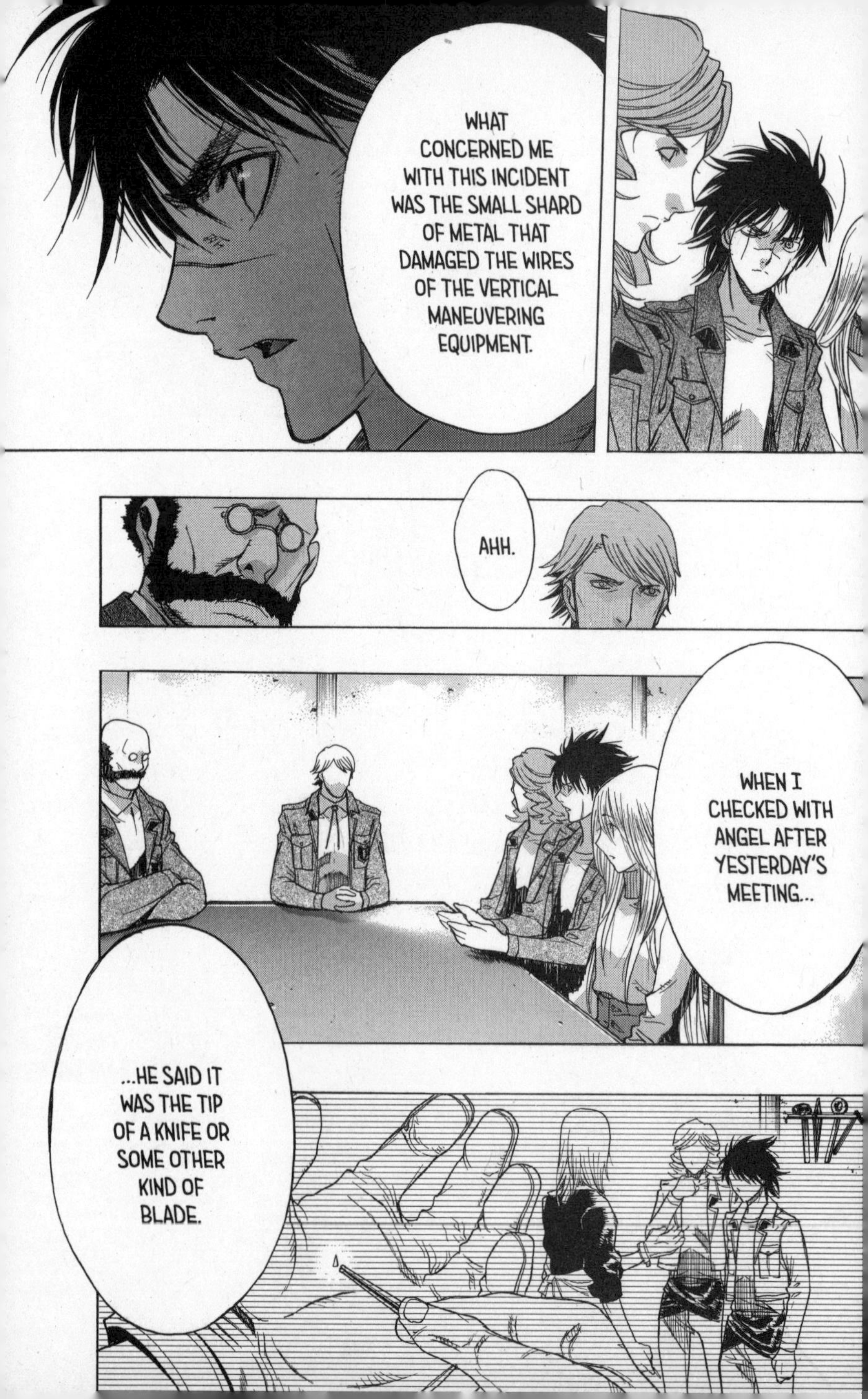
WHAT CONCERNED ME WITH THIS INCIDENT WAS THE SMALL SHARD OF METAL THAT DAMAGED THE WIRES OF THE VERTICAL MANEUVERING EQUIPMENT.
AHH.
WHEN I CHECKED WITH ANGEL AFTER YESTERDAY'S MEETING...
...HE SAID IT WAS THE TIP OF A KNIFE OR SOME OTHER KIND OF BLADE.

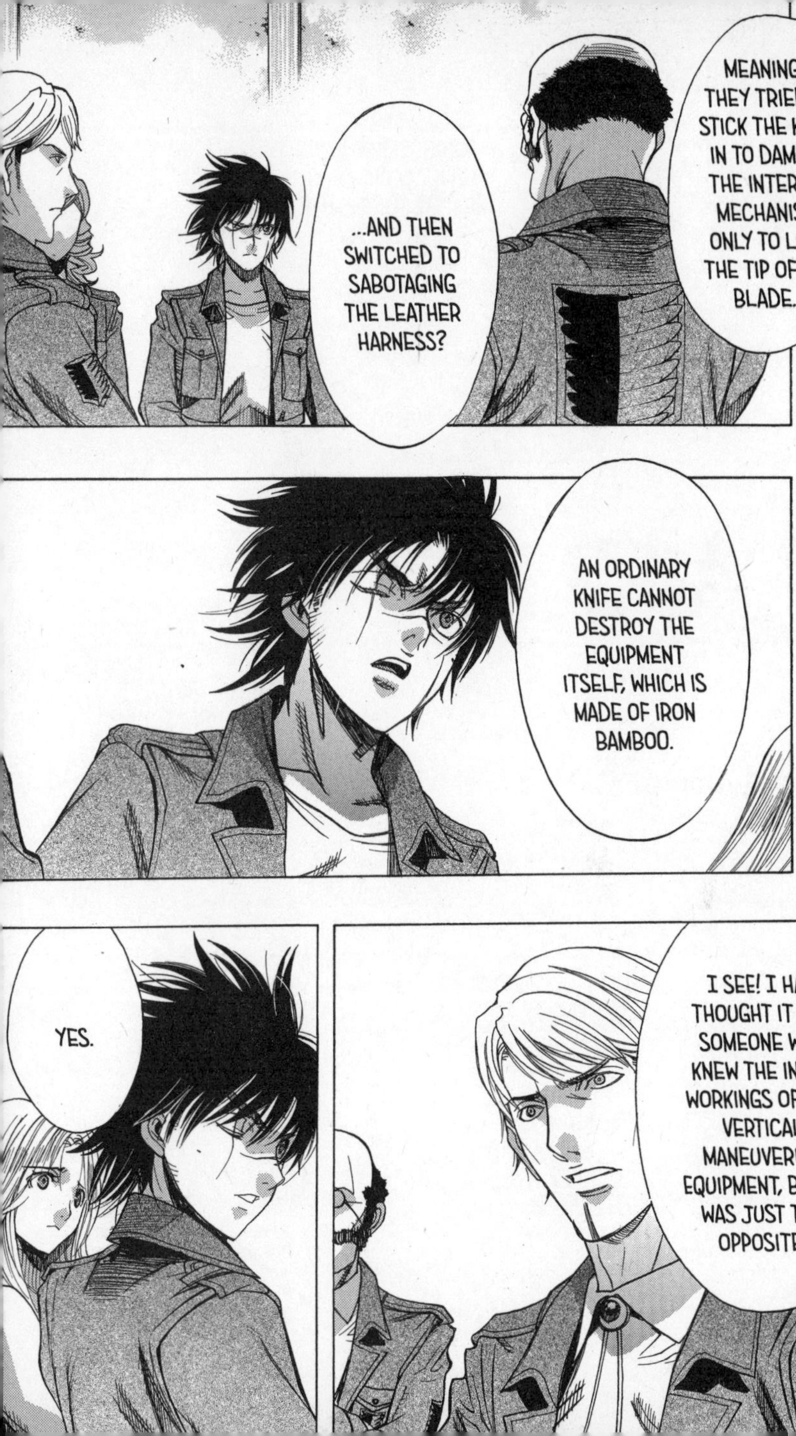
MEANING... THEY TRIED TO STICK THE KNIFE IN TO DAMAGE THE INTERNAL MECHANISM, ONLY TO LOSE THE TIP OF THE BLADE...
...AND THEN SWITCHED TO SABOTAGING THE LEATHER HARNESS?
AN ORDINARY KNIFE CANNOT DESTROY THE EQUIPMENT ITSELF, WHICH IS MADE OF IRON BAMBOO.
I SEE! I HAD THOUGHT IT WAS SOMEONE WHO KNEW THE INNER WORKINGS OF THE VERTICAL MANEUVERING EQUIPMENT, BUT IT WAS JUST THE OPPOSITE.
YES.

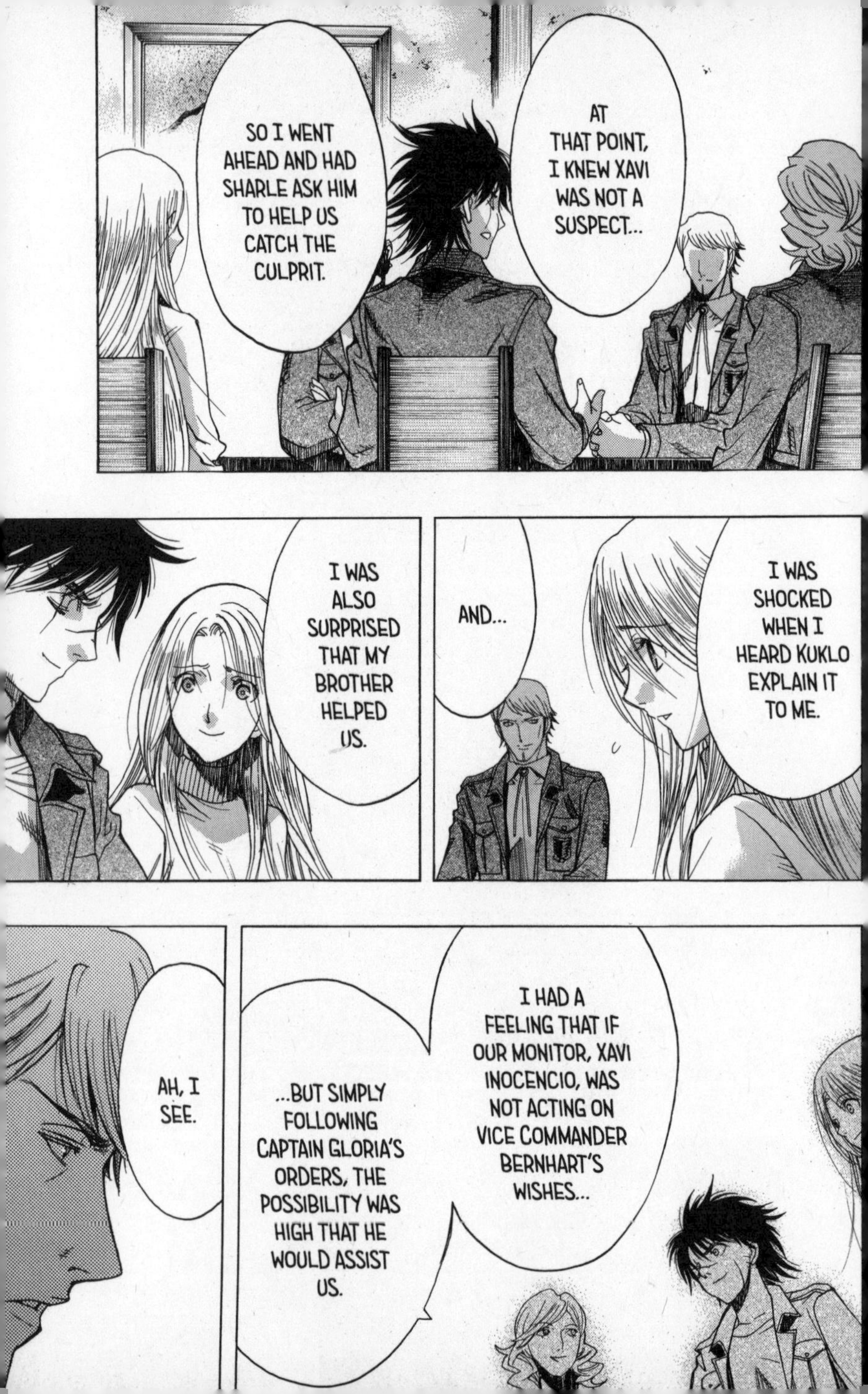
AT THAT POINT, I KNEW XAVI WAS NOT A SUSPECT...
SO I WENT AHEAD AND HAD SHARLE ASK HIM TO HELP US CATCH THE CULPRIT.
I WAS SHOCKED WHEN I HEARD KUKLO EXPLAIN IT TO ME.
AND...
I WAS ALSO SURPRISED THAT MY BROTHER HELPED US.
I HAD A FEELING THAT IF OUR MONITOR, XAVI INOCENCIO, WAS NOT ACTING ON VICE COMMANDER BERNHART'S WISHES...
...BUT SIMPLY FOLLOWING CAPTAIN GLORIA'S ORDERS, THE POSSIBILITY WAS HIGH THAT HE WOULD ASSIST US.
AH, I SEE.

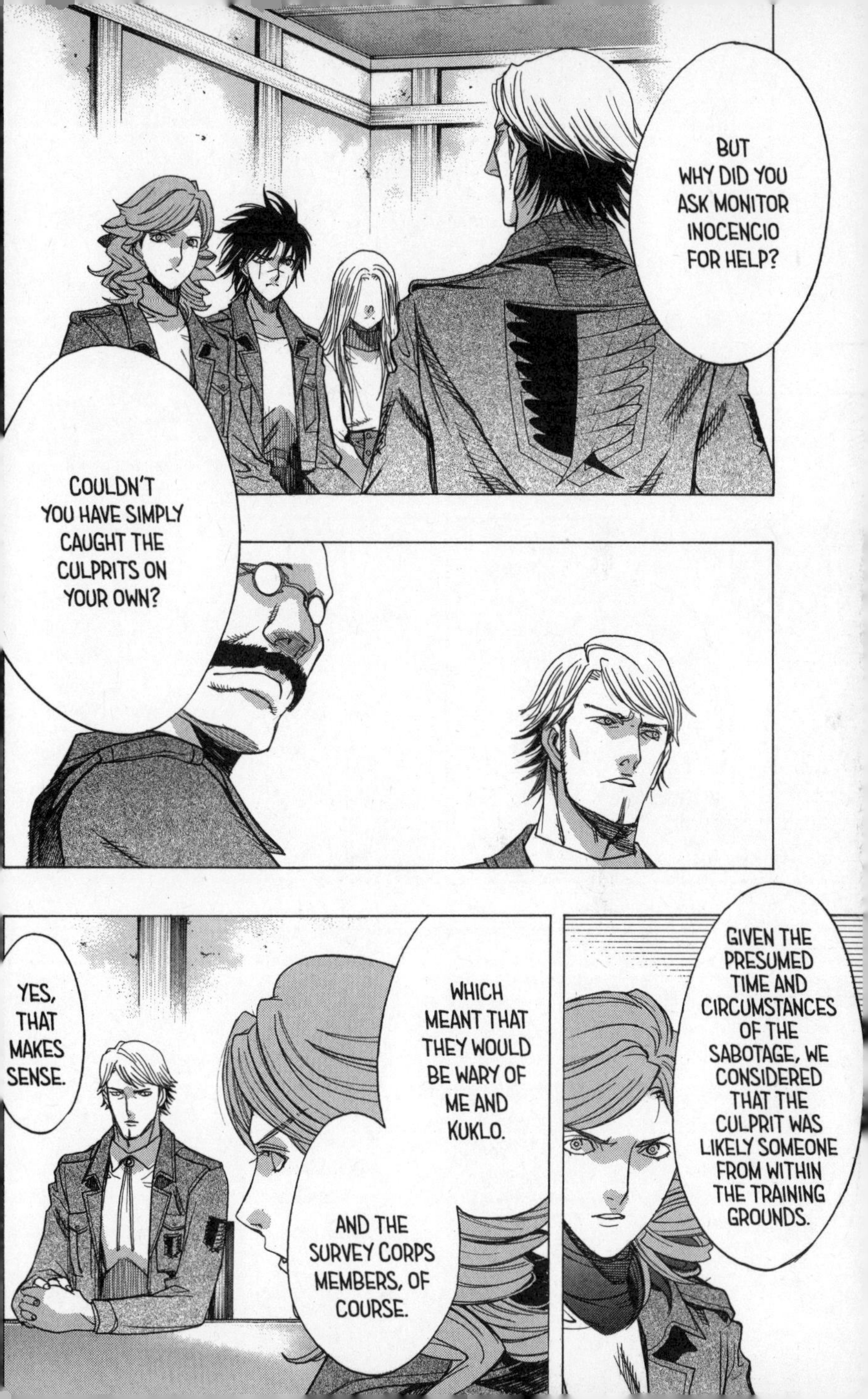
BUT WHY DID YOU ASK MONITOR INOCENCIO FOR HELP?
COULDN'T YOU HAVE SIMPLY CAUGHT THE CULPRITS ON YOUR OWN?
GIVEN THE PRESUMED TIME AND CIRCUMSTANCES OF THE SABOTAGE, WE CONSIDERED THAT THE CULPRIT WAS LIKELY SOMEONE FROM WITHIN THE TRAINING GROUNDS.
WHICH MEANT THAT THEY WOULD BE WARY OF ME AND KUKLO.
AND THE SURVEY CORPS MEMBERS, OF COURSE.
YES, THAT MAKES SENSE.

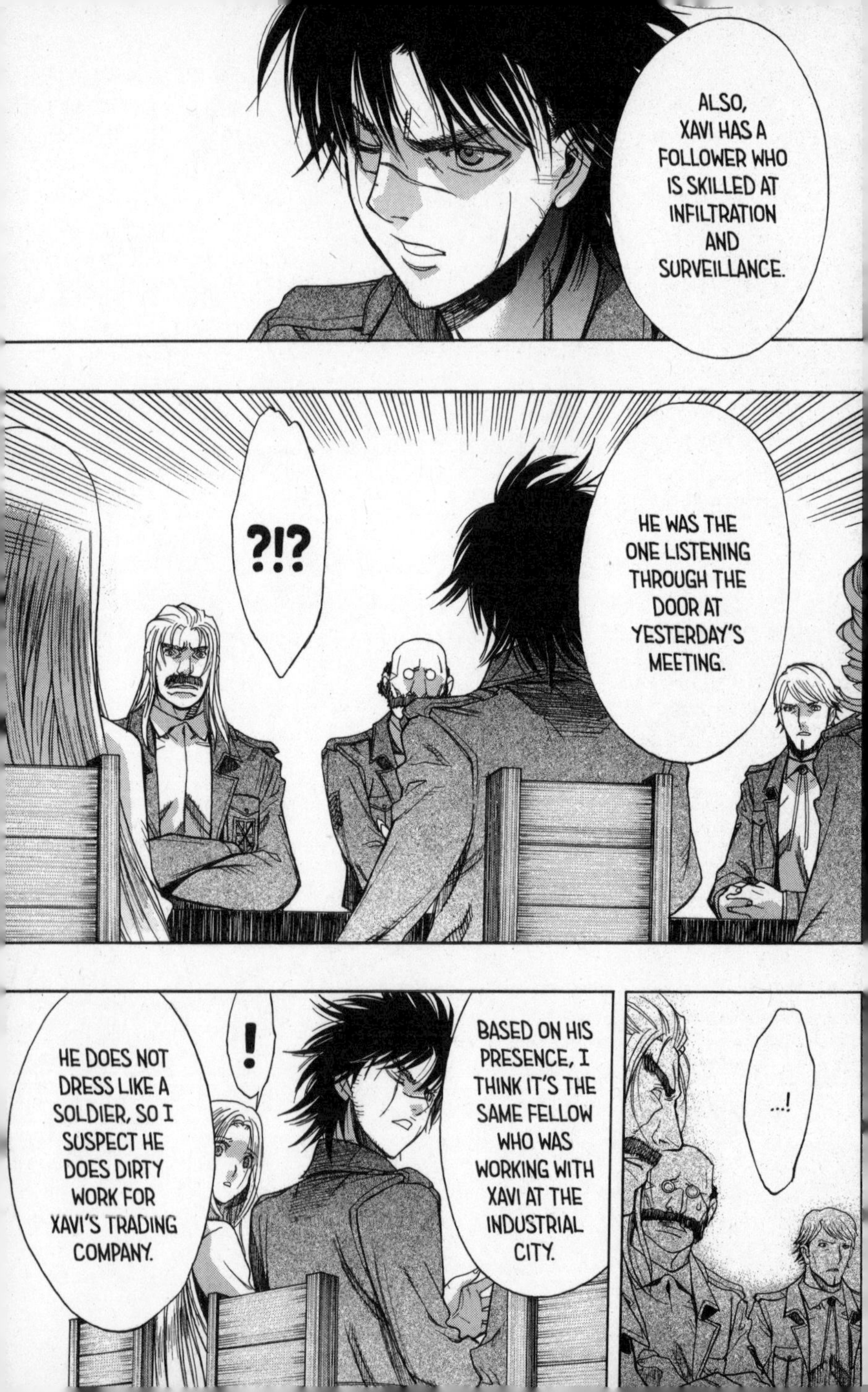
ALSO, XAVI HAS A FOLLOWER WHO IS SKILLED AT INFILTRATION AND SURVEILLANCE.
HE WAS THE ONE LISTENING THROUGH THE DOOR AT YESTERDAY'S MEETING.
?!?
...!
BASED ON HIS PRESENCE, I THINK IT'S THE SAME FELLOW WHO WAS WORKING WITH XAVI AT THE INDUSTRIAL CITY.
!
HE DOES NOT DRESS LIKE A SOLDIER, SO I SUSPECT HE DOES DIRTY WORK FOR XAVI'S TRADING COMPANY.

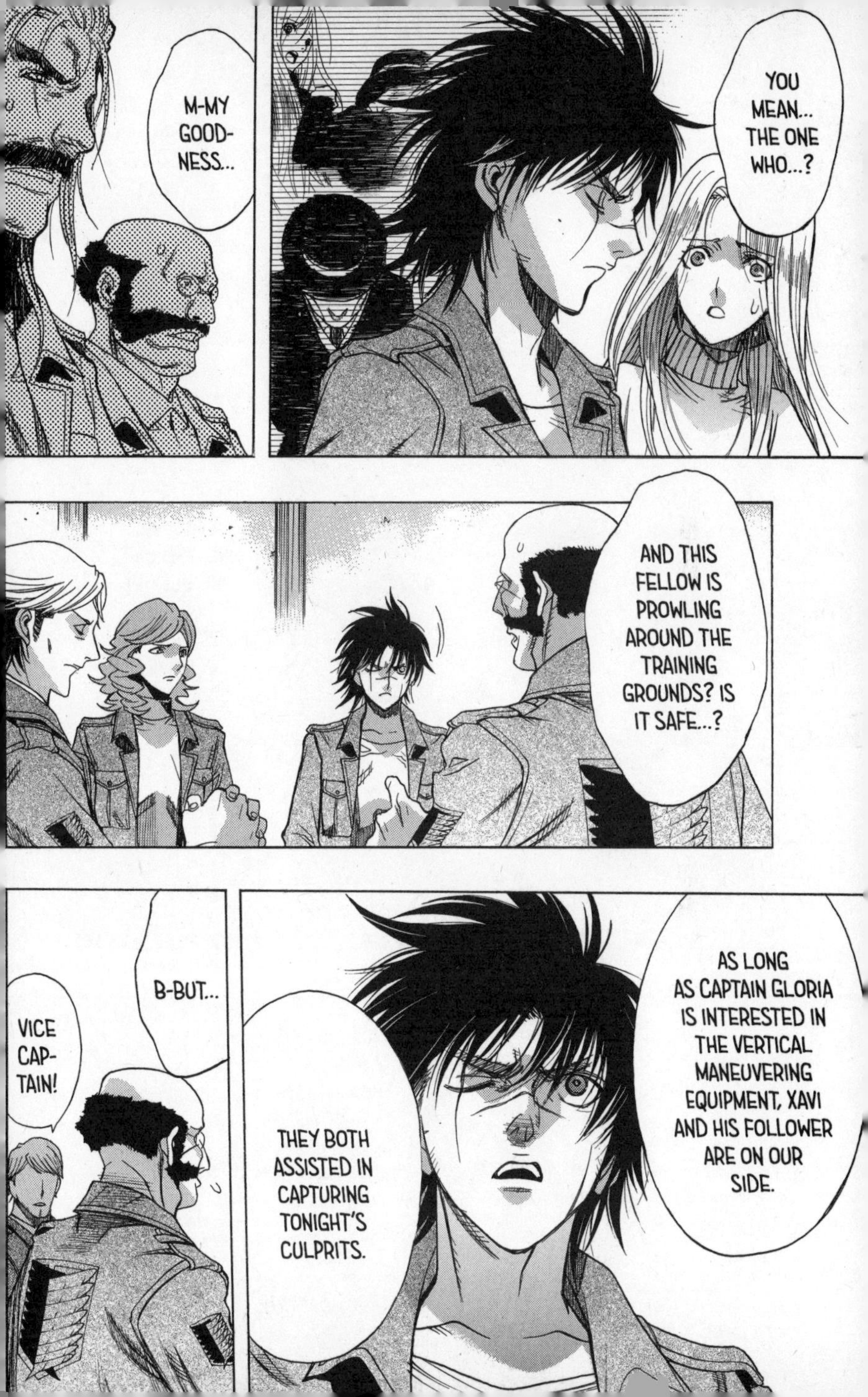
YOU MEAN... THE ONE WHO...?
M-MY GOOD-NESS...
AND THIS FELLOW IS PROWLING AROUND THE TRAINING GROUNDS? IS IT SAFE...?
AS LONG AS CAPTAIN GLORIA IS INTERESTED IN THE VERTICAL MANEUVERING EQUIPMENT, XAVI AND HIS FOLLOWER ARE ON OUR SIDE.
THEY BOTH ASSISTED IN CAPTURING TONIGHT'S CULPRITS.
B-BUT...
VICE CAP-TAIN!

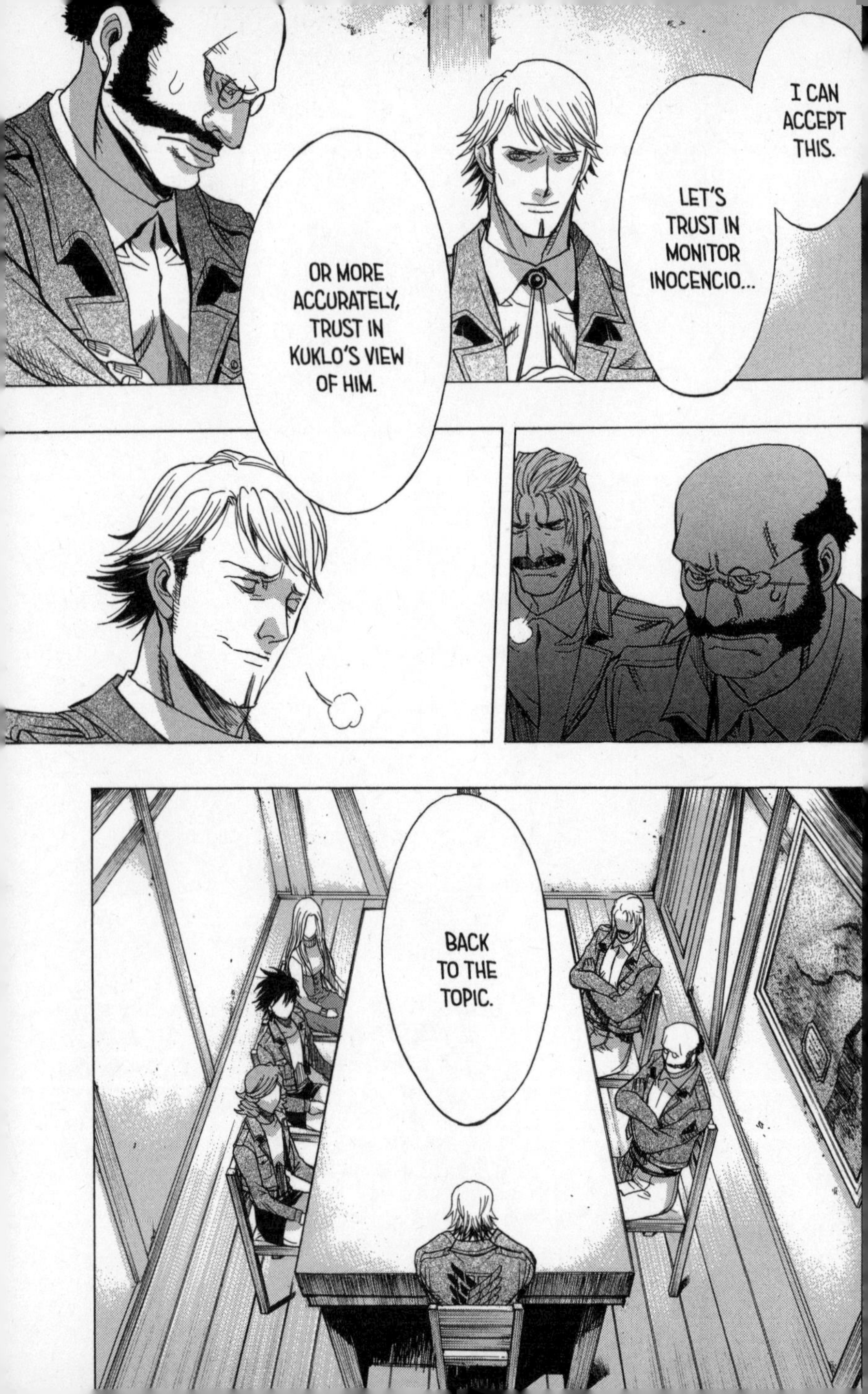
I CAN ACCEPT THIS.
LET'S TRUST IN MONITOR INOCENCIO...
OR MORE ACCURATELY, TRUST IN KUKLO'S VIEW OF HIM.
BACK TO THE TOPIC.

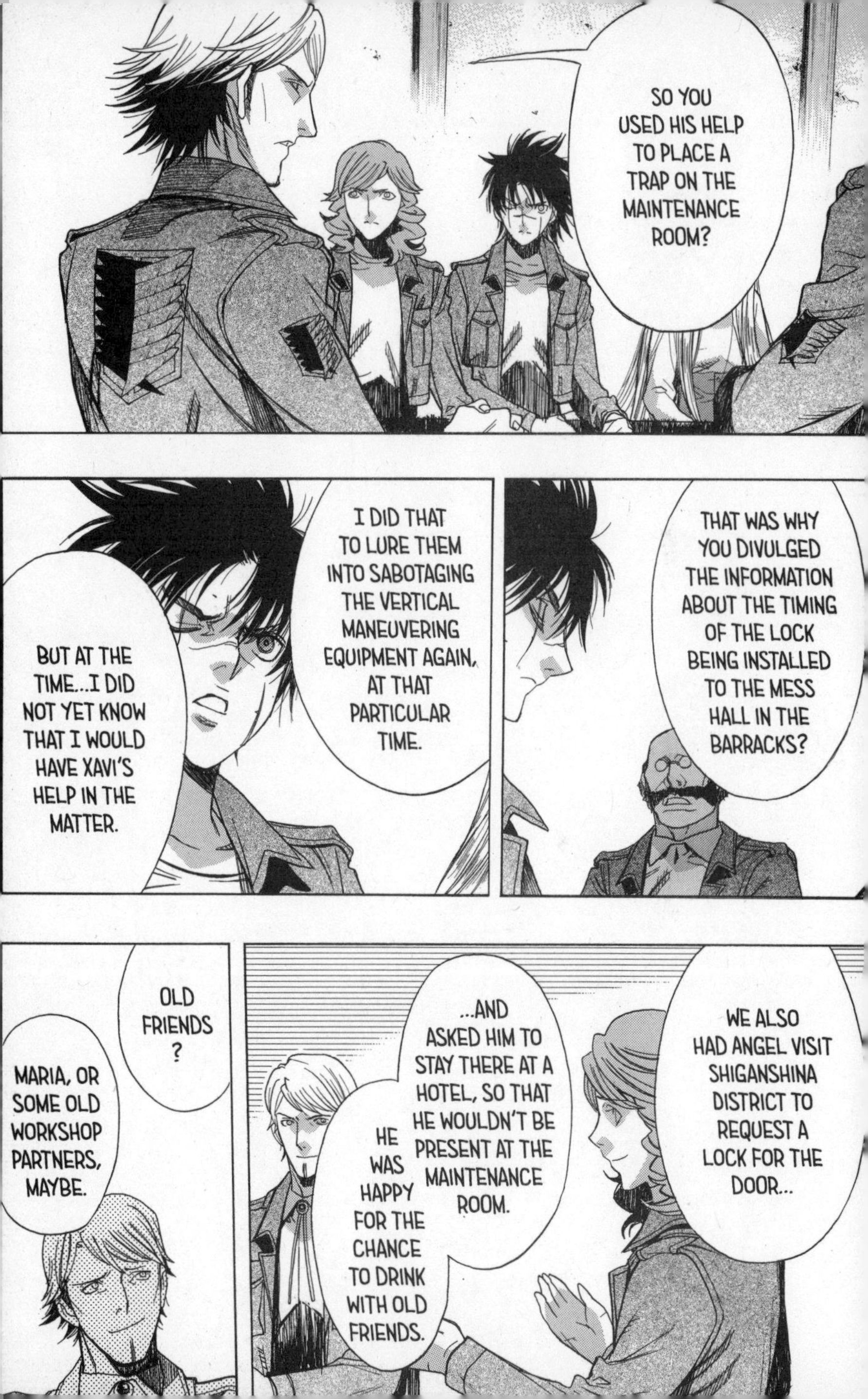
SO YOU USED HIS HELP TO PLACE A TRAP ON THE MAINTENANCE ROOM?
THAT WAS WHY YOU DIVULGED THE INFORMATION ABOUT THE TIMING OF THE LOCK BEING INSTALLED TO THE MESS HALL IN THE BARRACKS?
I DID THAT TO LURE THEM INTO SABOTAGING THE VERTICAL MANEUVERING EQUIPMENT AGAIN, AT THAT PARTICULAR TIME.
BUT AT THE TIME...I DID NOT YET KNOW THAT I WOULD HAVE XAVI'S HELP IN THE MATTER.
WE ALSO HAD ANGEL VISIT SHIGANSHINA DISTRICT TO REQUEST A LOCK FOR THE DOOR...
...AND ASKED HIM TO STAY THERE AT A HOTEL, SO THAT HE WOULDN'T BE PRESENT AT THE MAINTENANCE ROOM.
HE WAS HAPPY FOR THE CHANCE TO DRINK WITH OLD FRIENDS.
OLD FRIENDS?
MARIA, OR SOME OLD WORKSHOP PARTNERS, MAYBE.

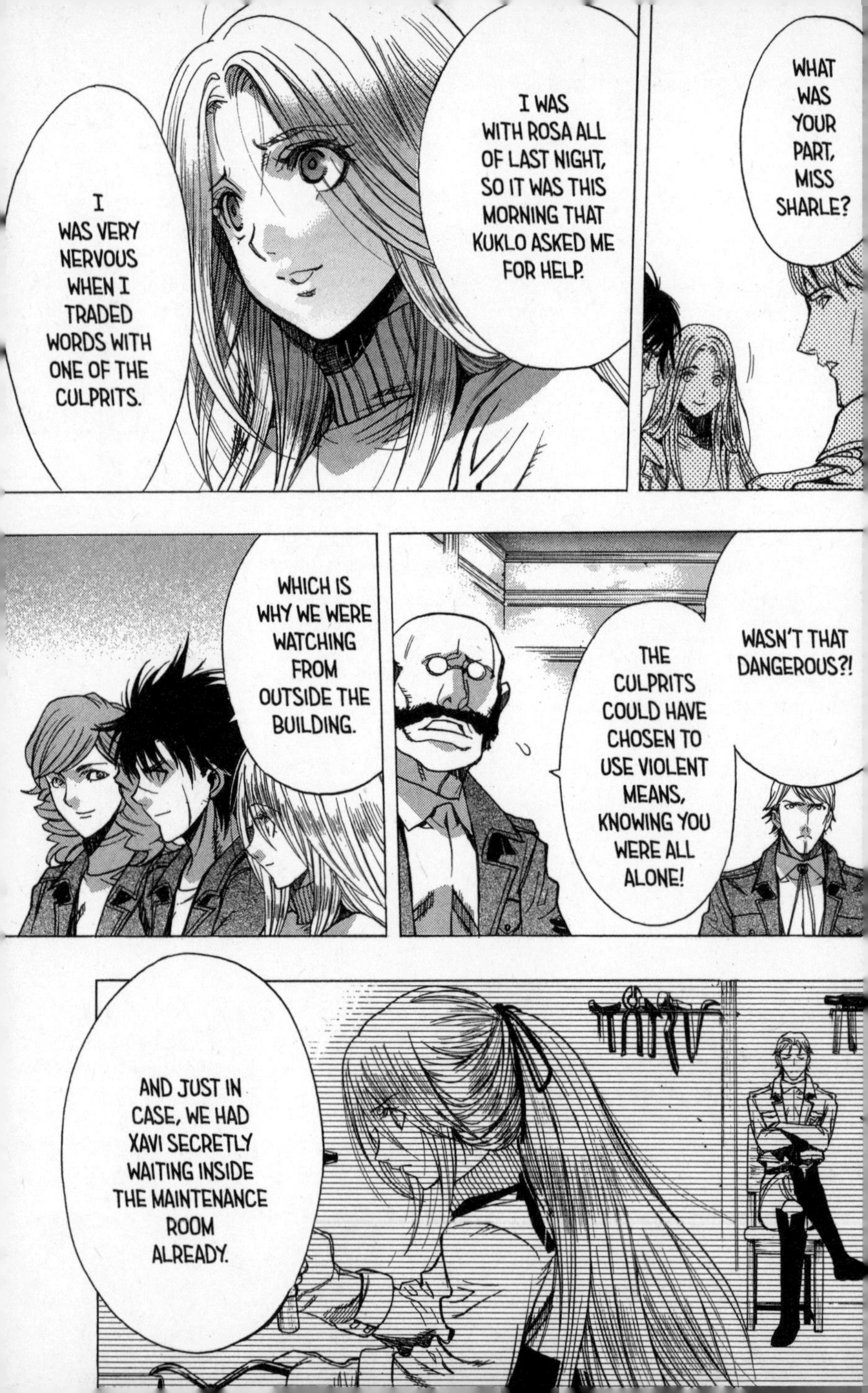
WHAT WAS YOUR PART, MISS SHARLE?
I WAS WITH ROSA ALL OF LAST NIGHT, SO IT WAS THIS MORNING THAT KUKLO ASKED ME FOR HELP.
I WAS VERY NERVOUS WHEN I TRADED WORDS WITH ONE OF THE CULPRITS.
WASN'T THAT DANGEROUS?!
THE CULPRITS COULD HAVE CHOSEN TO USE VIOLENT MEANS, KNOWING YOU WERE ALL ALONE!
WHICH IS WHY WE WERE WATCHING FROM OUTSIDE THE BUILDING.
AND JUST IN CASE, WE HAD XAVI SECRETLY WAITING INSIDE THE MAINTENANCE ROOM ALREADY.

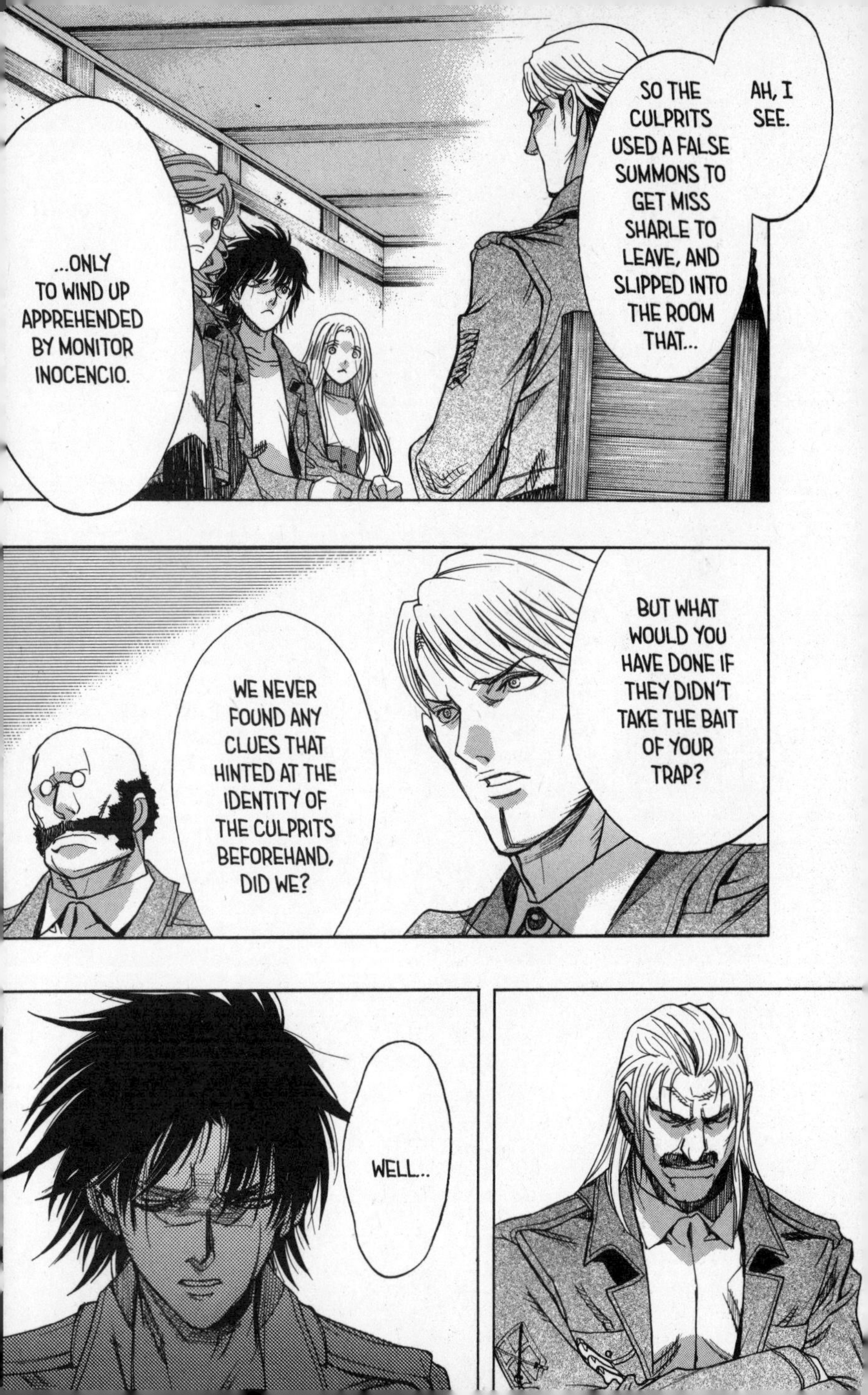
AH, I SEE.
SO THE CULPRITS USED A FALSE SUMMONS TO GET MISS SHARLE TO LEAVE, AND SLIPPED INTO THE ROOM THAT...
...ONLY TO WIND UP APPREHENDED BY MONITOR INOCENCIO.
BUT WHAT WOULD YOU HAVE DONE IF THEY DIDN'T TAKE THE BAIT OF YOUR TRAP?
WE NEVER FOUND ANY CLUES THAT HINTED AT THE IDENTITY OF THE CULPRITS BEFOREHAND, DID WE?
WELL...

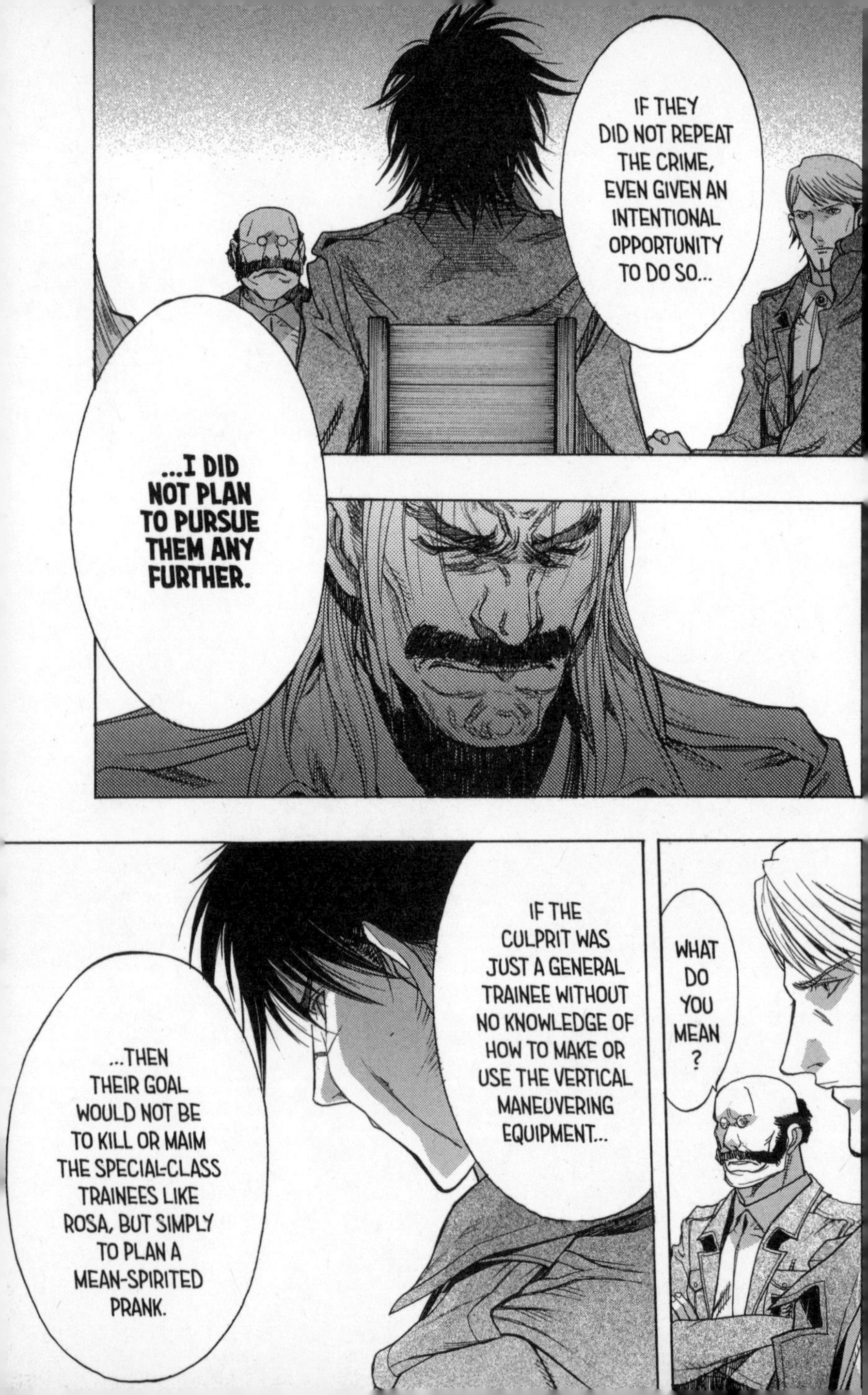
IF THEY DID NOT REPEAT THE CRIME, EVEN GIVEN AN INTENTIONAL OPPORTUNITY TO DO SO...
...I DID NOT PLAN TO PURSUE THEM ANY FURTHER.
WHAT DO YOU MEAN ?
IF THE CULPRIT WAS JUST A GENERAL TRAINEE WITHOUT NO KNOWLEDGE OF HOW TO MAKE OR USE THE VERTICAL MANEUVERING EQUIPMENT...
...THEN THEIR GOAL WOULD NOT BE TO KILL OR MAIM THE SPECIAL-CLASS TRAINEES LIKE ROSA, BUT SIMPLY TO PLAN A MEAN-SPIRITED PRANK.

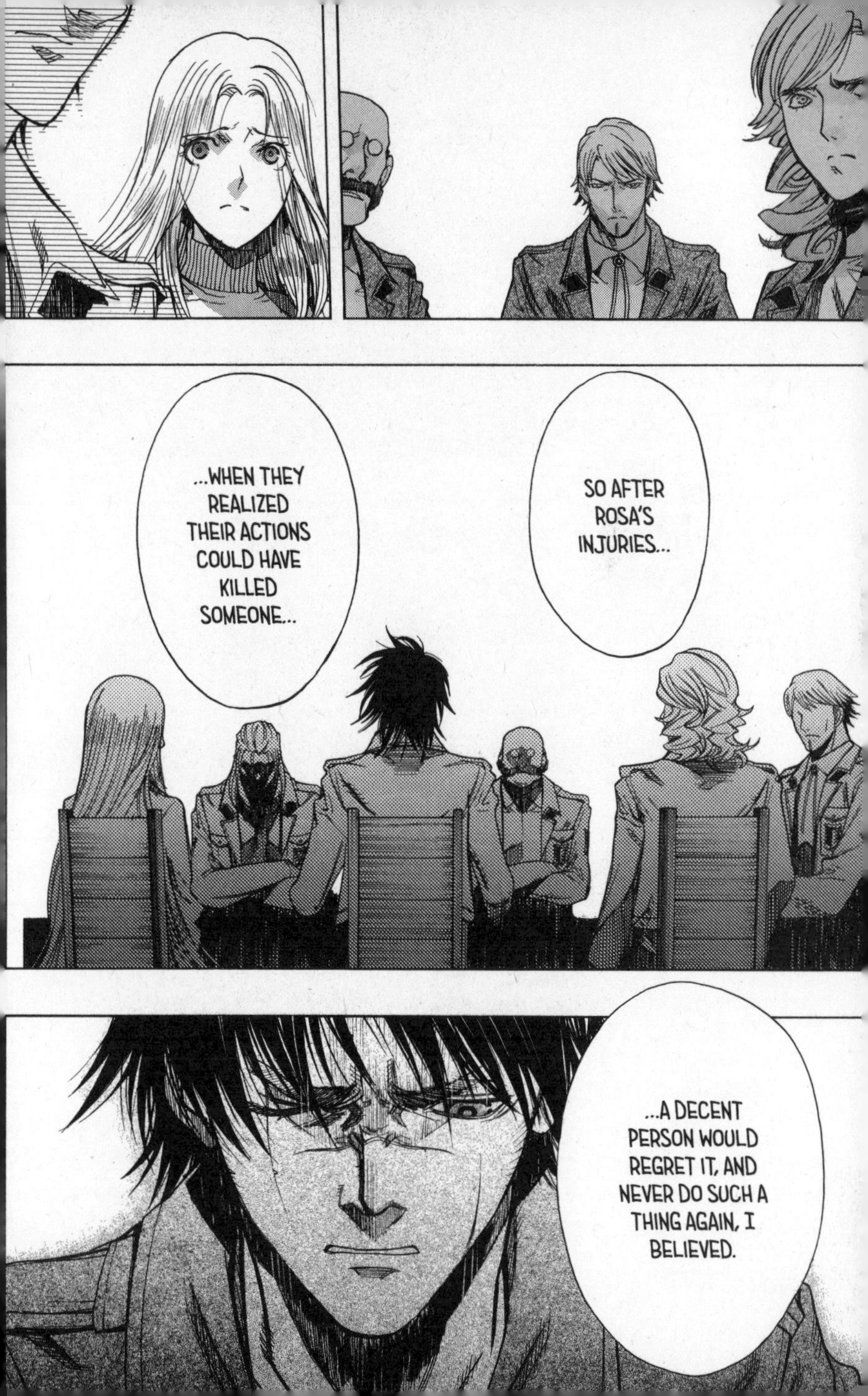
SO AFTER ROSA'S INJURIES...
...WHEN THEY REALIZED THEIR ACTIONS COULD HAVE KILLED SOMEONE...
...A DECENT PERSON WOULD REGRET IT, AND NEVER DO SUCH A THING AGAIN, I BELIEVED.

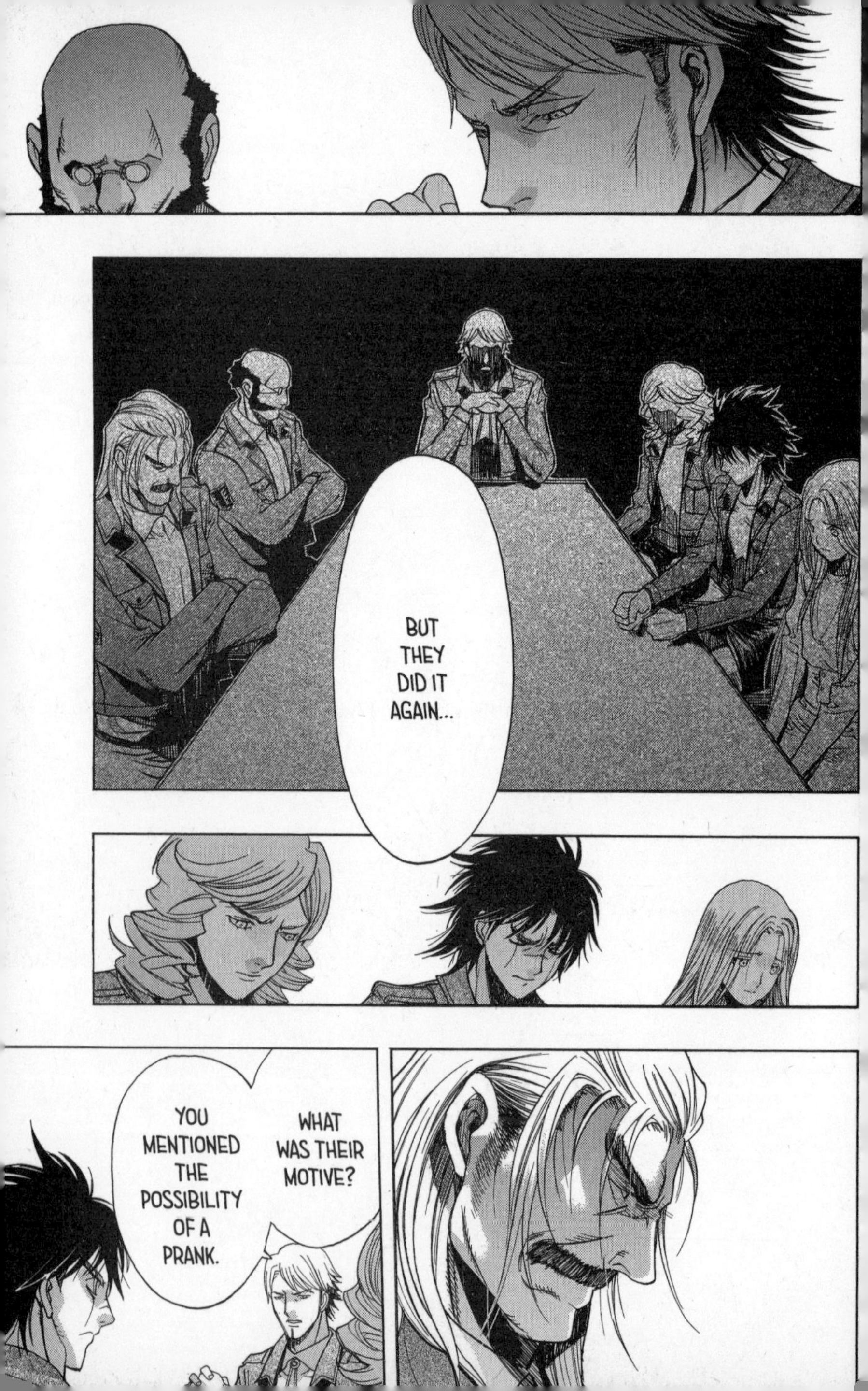
BUT THEY DID IT AGAIN...
WHAT WAS THEIR MOTIVE?
YOU MENTIONED THE POSSIBILITY OF A PRANK.

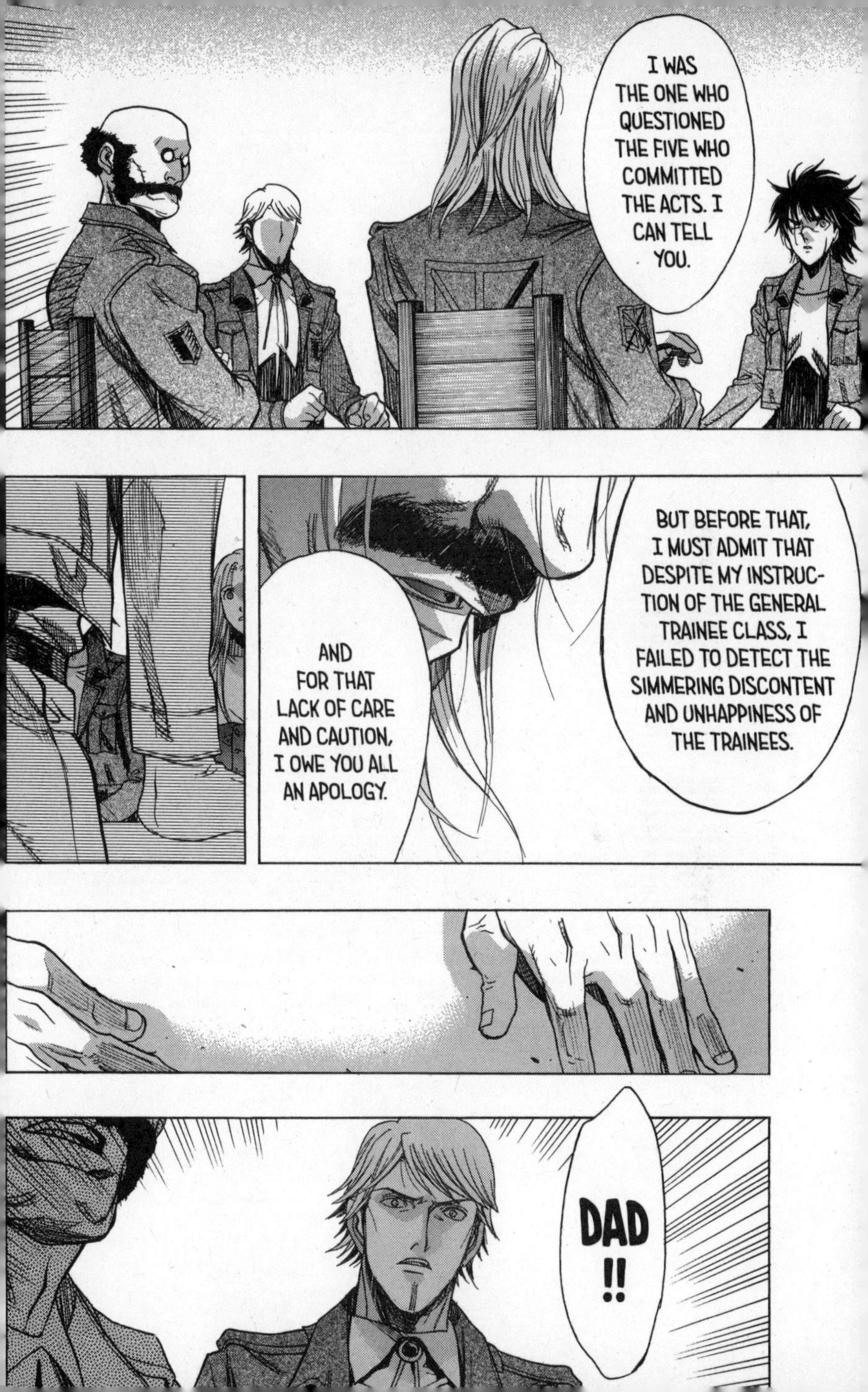
I WAS THE ONE WHO QUESTIONED THE FIVE WHO COMMITTED THE ACTS. I CAN TELL YOU.
BUT BEFORE THAT, I MUST ADMIT THAT DESPITE MY INSTRUCTION OF THE GENERAL TRAINEE CLASS, I FAILED TO DETECT THE SIMMERING DISCONTENT AND UNHAPPINESS OF THE TRAINEES.
AND FOR THAT LACK OF CARE AND CAUTION, I OWE YOU ALL AN APOLOGY.
DAD !!

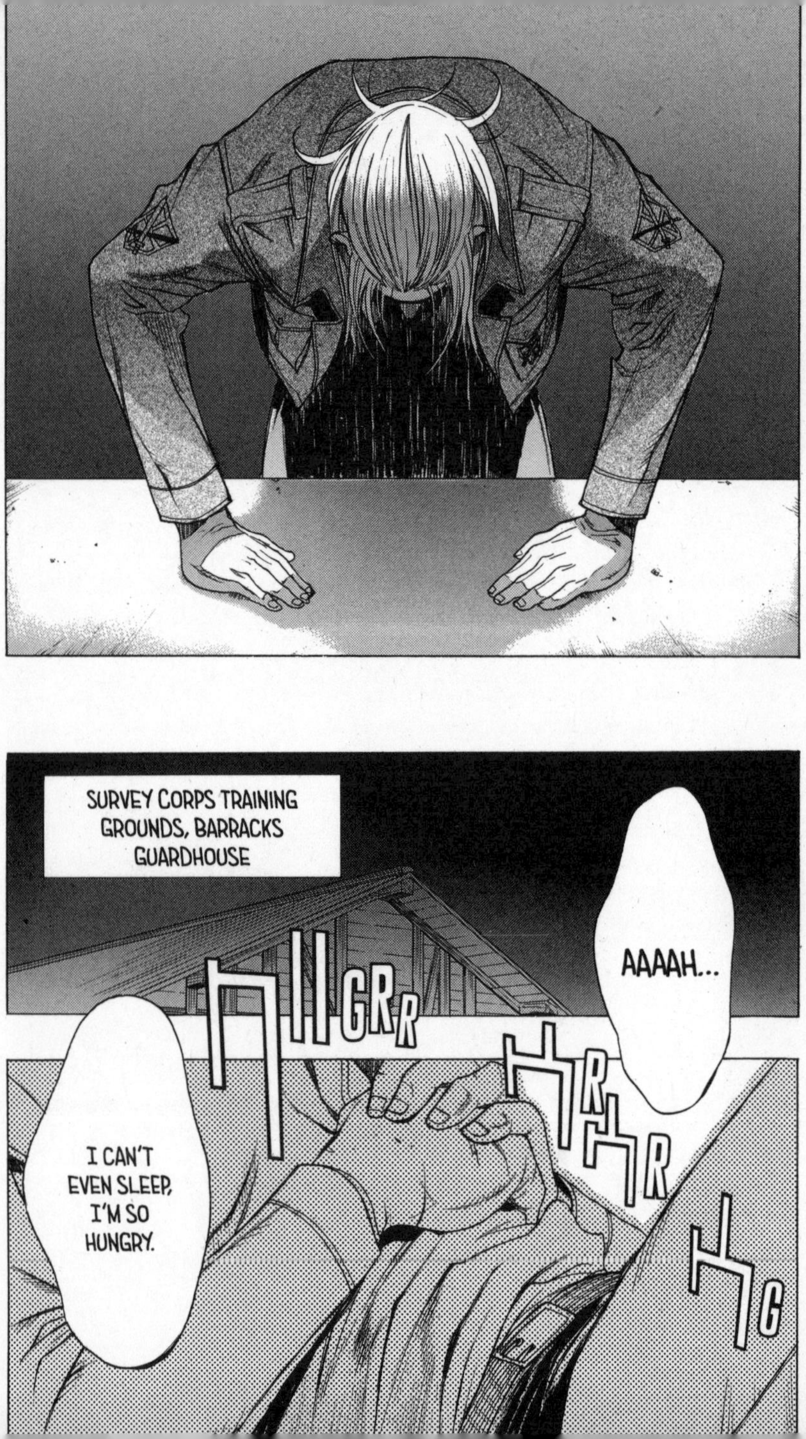
SURVEY CORPS TRAINING GROUNDS, BARRACKS GUARDHOUSE
AAAAH...
GRRR
GRR
G
I CAN'T EVEN SLEEP, I'M SO HUNGRY.

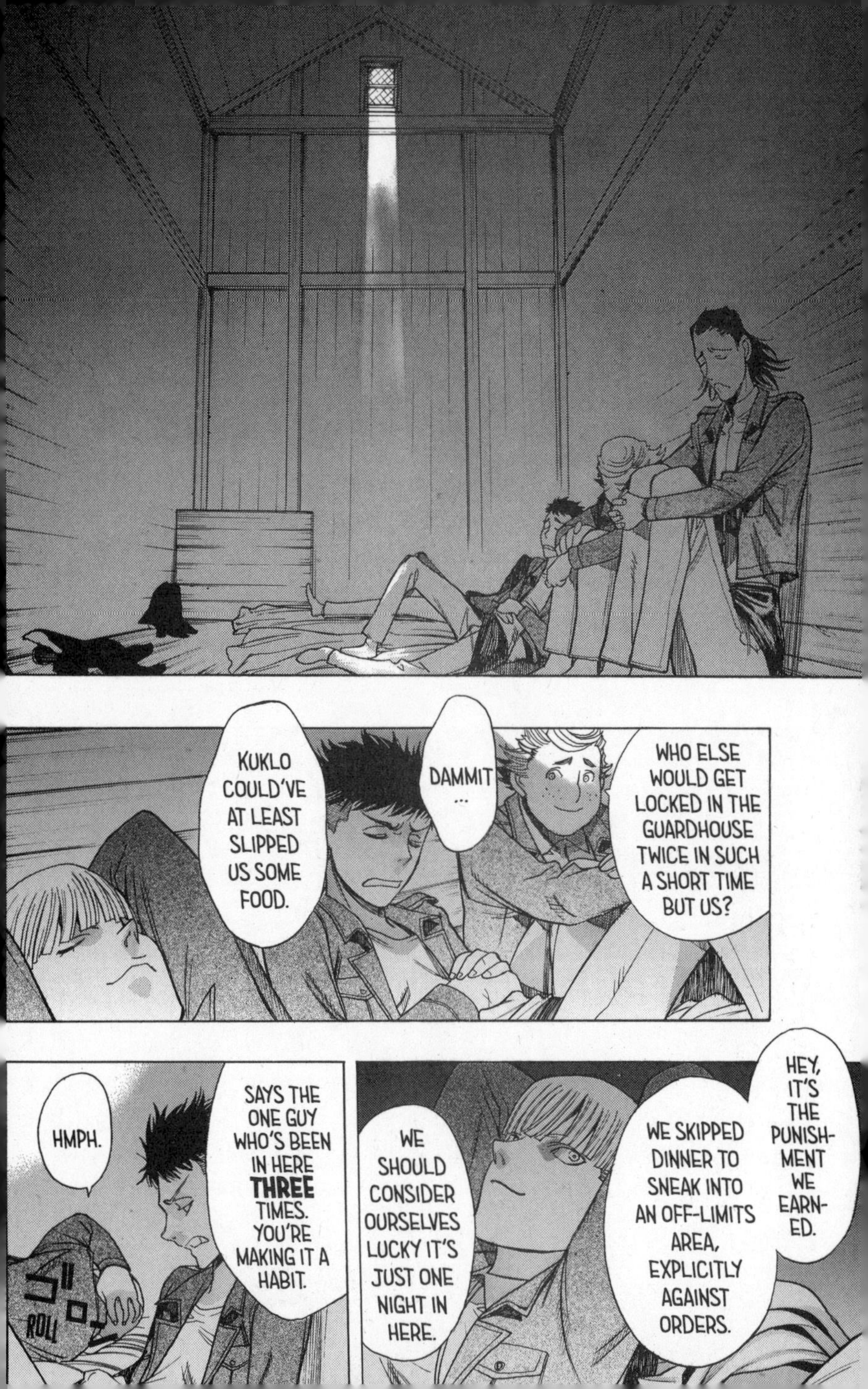
WHO ELSE WOULD GET LOCKED IN THE GUARDHOUSE TWICE IN SUCH A SHORT TIME BUT US?
DAMMIT ...
KUKLO COULD'VE AT LEAST SLIPPED US SOME FOOD.
HEY, IT'S THE PUNISHMENT WE EARNED.
WE SKIPPED DINNER TO SNEAK INTO AN OFF-LIMITS AREA, EXPLICITLY AGAINST ORDERS.
WE SHOULD CONSIDER OURSELVES LUCKY IT'S JUST ONE NIGHT IN HERE.
SAYS THE ONE GUY WHO'S BEEN IN HERE **THREE** TIMES. YOU'RE MAKING IT A HABIT.
HMPH.
ゴロ
ROLL

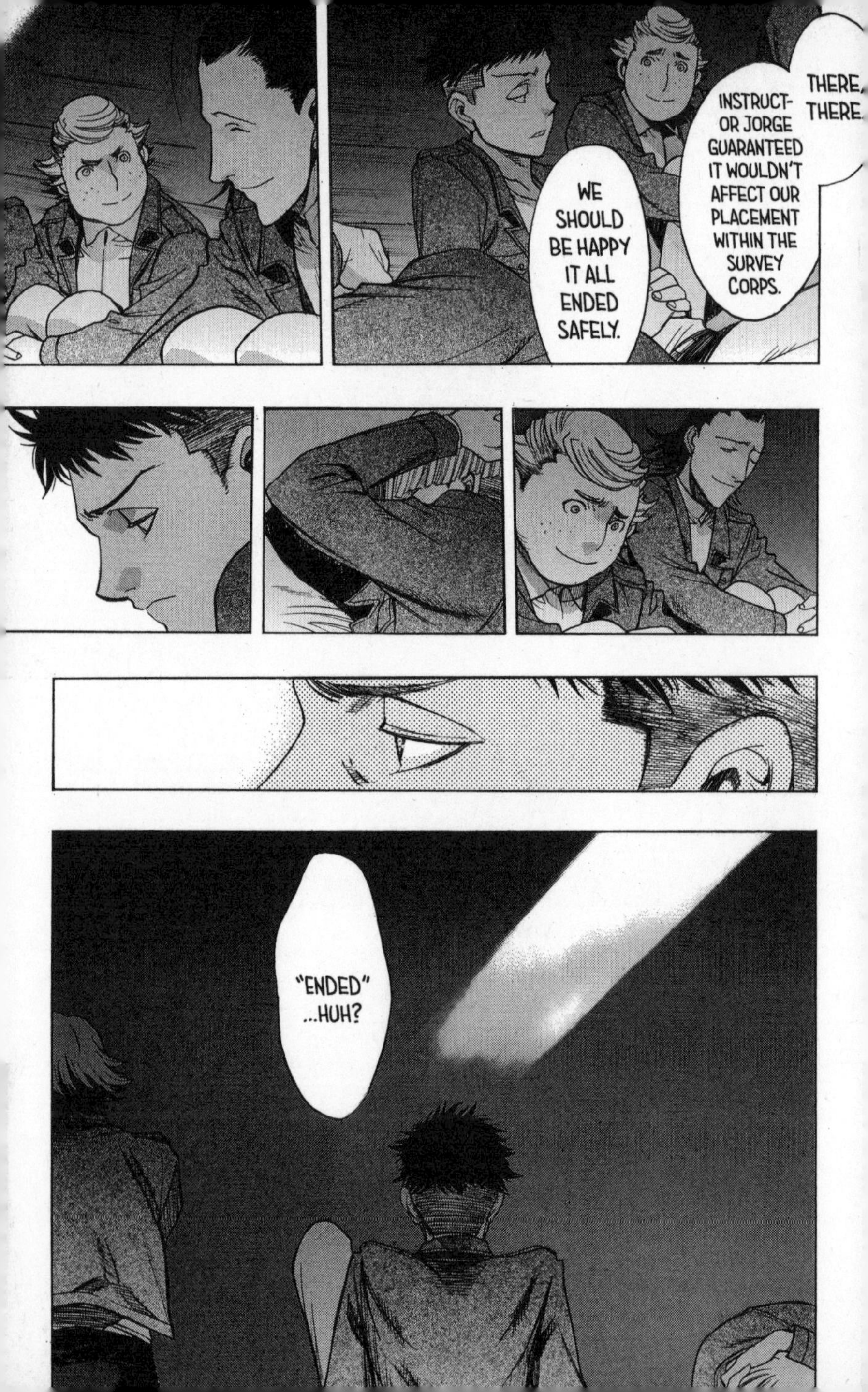
THERE, THERE.
INSTRUCT-OR JORGE GUARANTEED IT WOULDN'T AFFECT OUR PLACEMENT WITHIN THE SURVEY CORPS.
WE SHOULD BE HAPPY IT ALL ENDED SAFELY.
"ENDED" ...HUH?

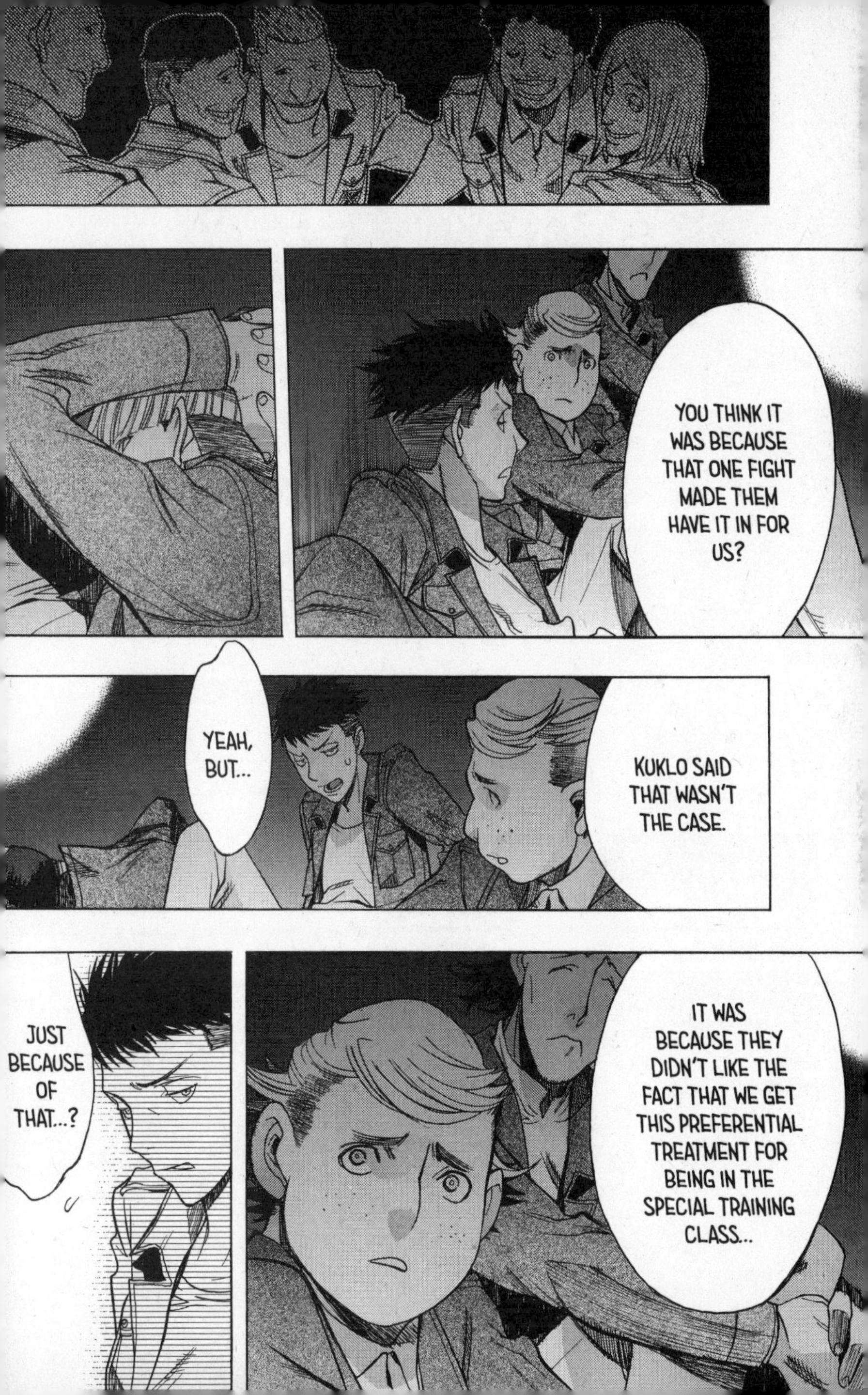
YOU THINK IT WAS BECAUSE THAT ONE FIGHT MADE THEM HAVE IT IN FOR US?
KUKLO SAID THAT WASN'T THE CASE.
YEAH, BUT...
IT WAS BECAUSE THEY DIDN'T LIKE THE FACT THAT WE GET THIS PREFERENTIAL TREATMENT FOR BEING IN THE SPECIAL TRAINING CLASS...
JUST BECAUSE OF THAT...?

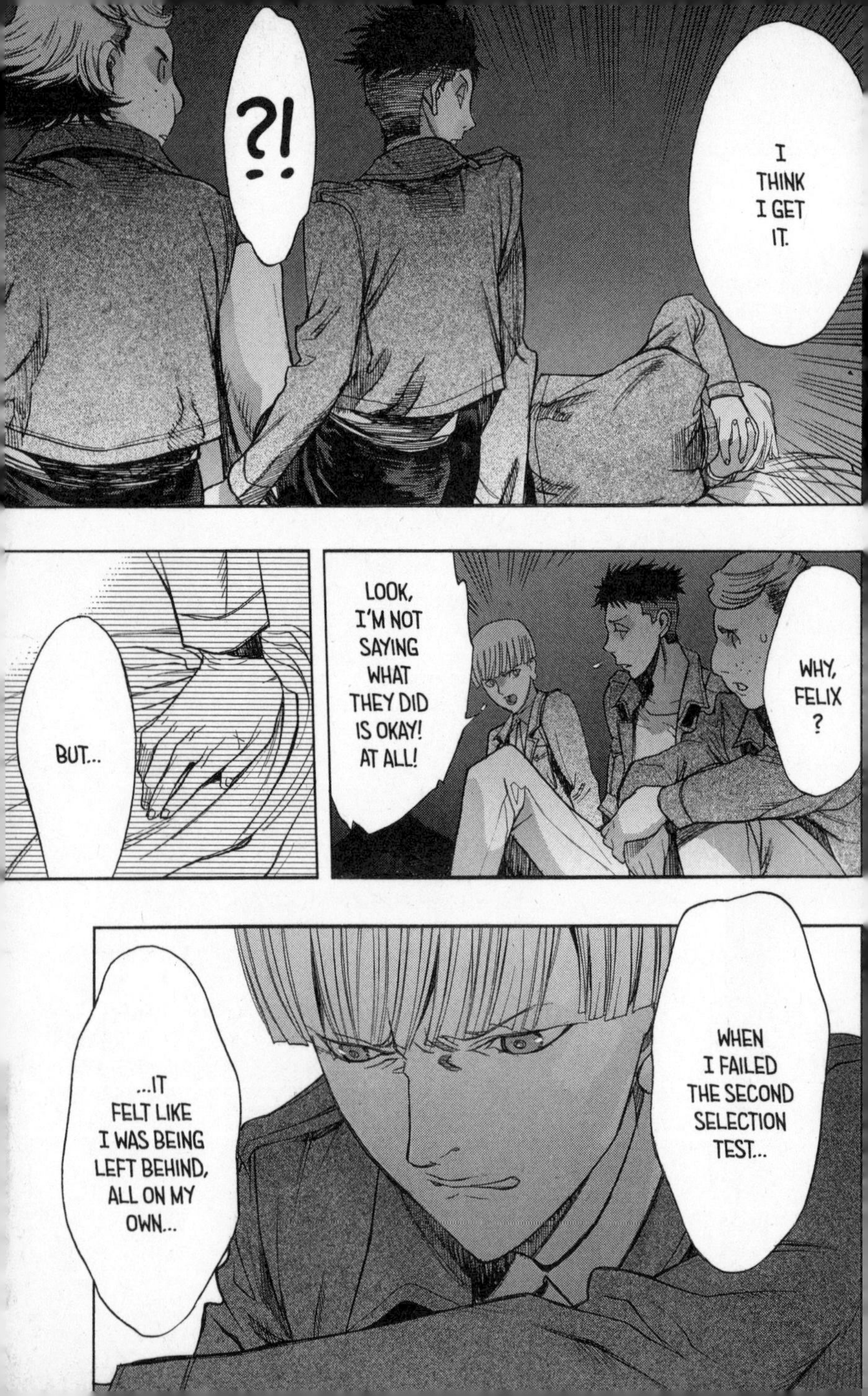
I THINK I GET IT.
?!
WHY, FELIX?
LOOK, I'M NOT SAYING WHAT THEY DID IS OKAY! AT ALL!
BUT...
WHEN I FAILED THE SECOND SELECTION TEST...
...IT FELT LIKE I WAS BEING LEFT BEHIND, ALL ON MY OWN...

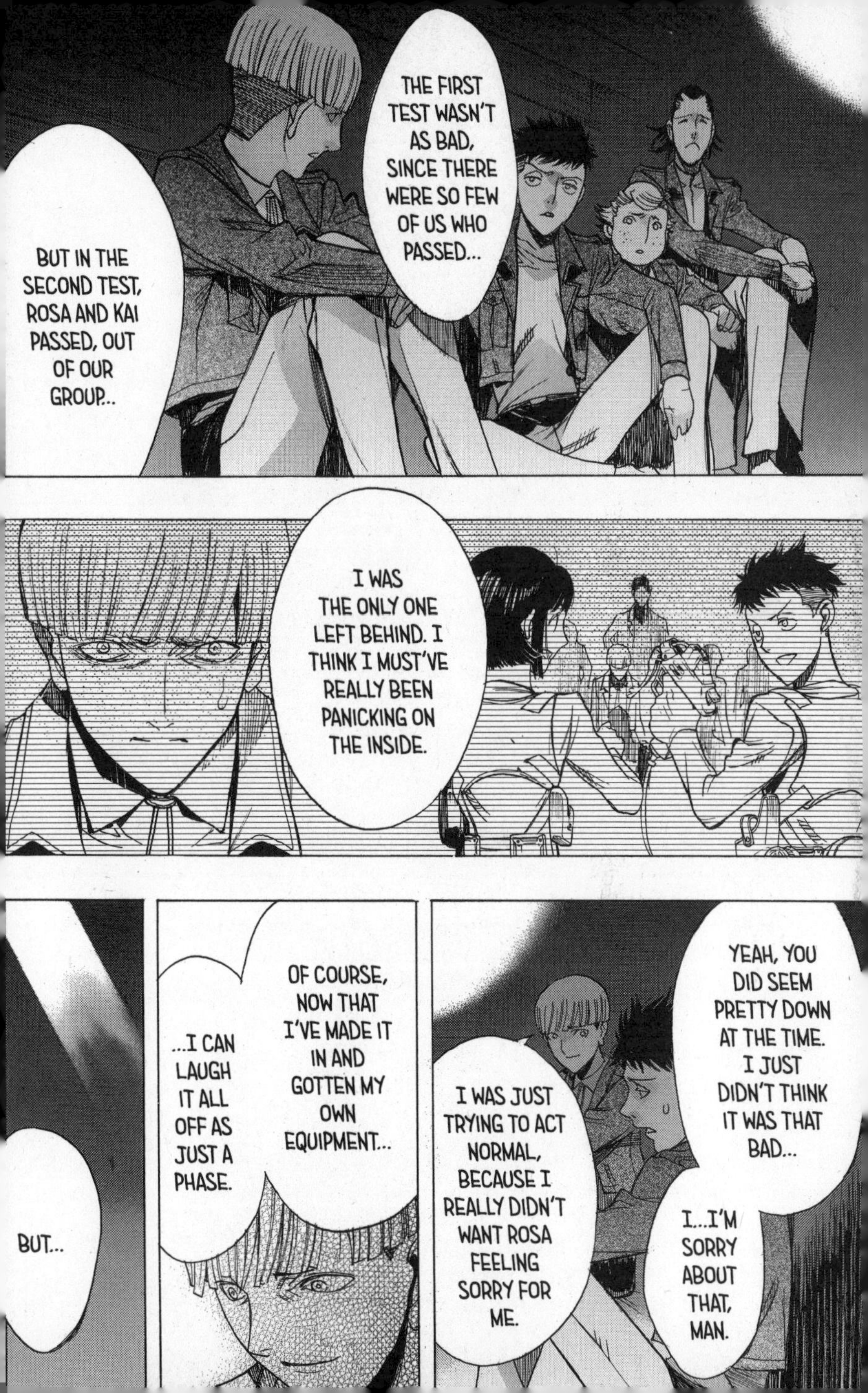
THE FIRST TEST WASN'T AS BAD, SINCE THERE WERE SO FEW OF US WHO PASSED...
BUT IN THE SECOND TEST, ROSA AND KAI PASSED, OUT OF OUR GROUP...
I WAS THE ONLY ONE LEFT BEHIND. I THINK I MUST'VE REALLY BEEN PANICKING ON THE INSIDE.
YEAH, YOU DID SEEM PRETTY DOWN AT THE TIME. I JUST DIDN'T THINK IT WAS THAT BAD...
I...I'M SORRY ABOUT THAT, MAN.
I WAS JUST TRYING TO ACT NORMAL, BECAUSE I REALLY DIDN'T WANT ROSA FEELING SORRY FOR ME.
OF COURSE, NOW THAT I'VE MADE IT IN AND GOTTEN MY OWN EQUIPMENT...
...I CAN LAUGH IT ALL OFF AS JUST A PHASE.
BUT...

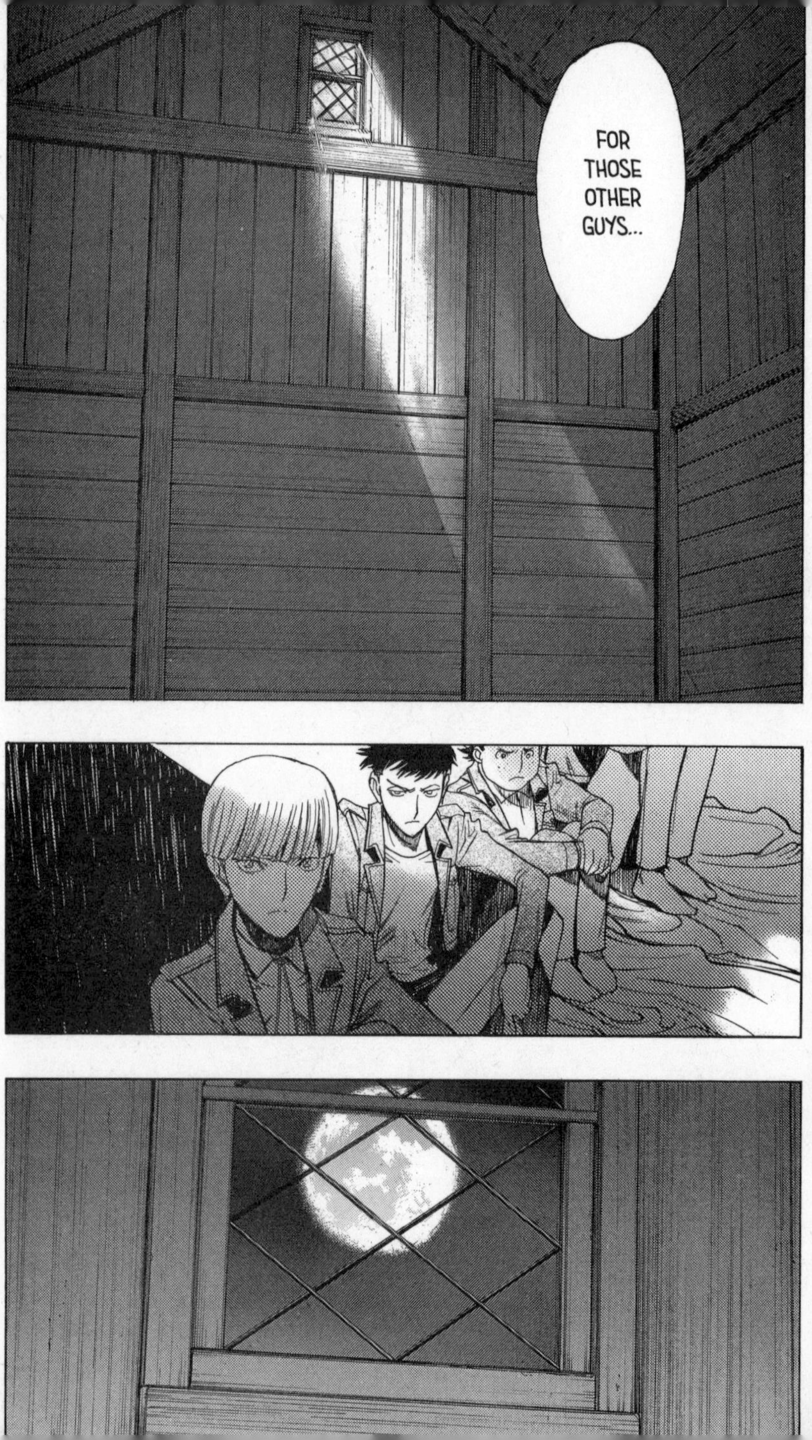
FOR THOSE OTHER GUYS...

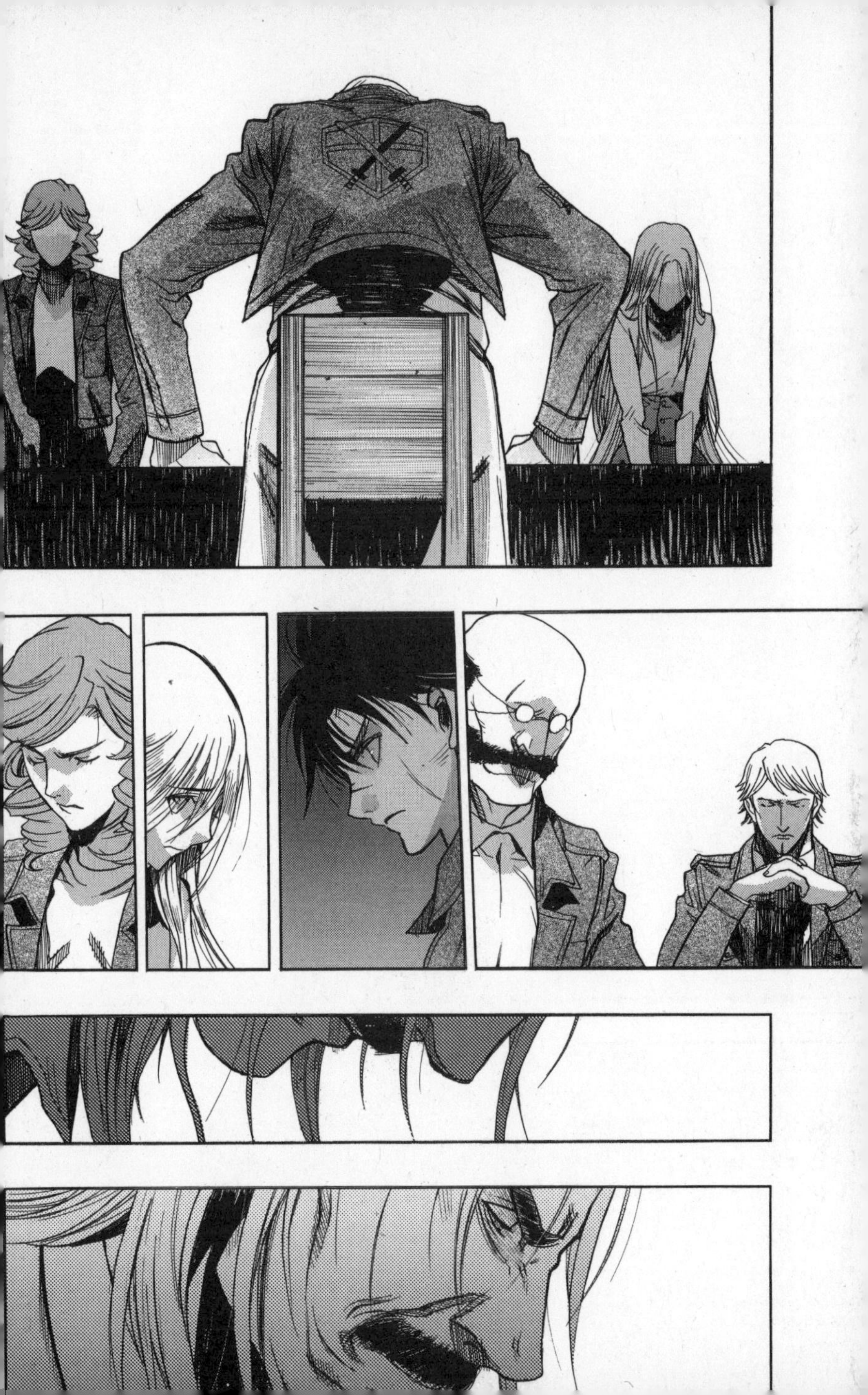

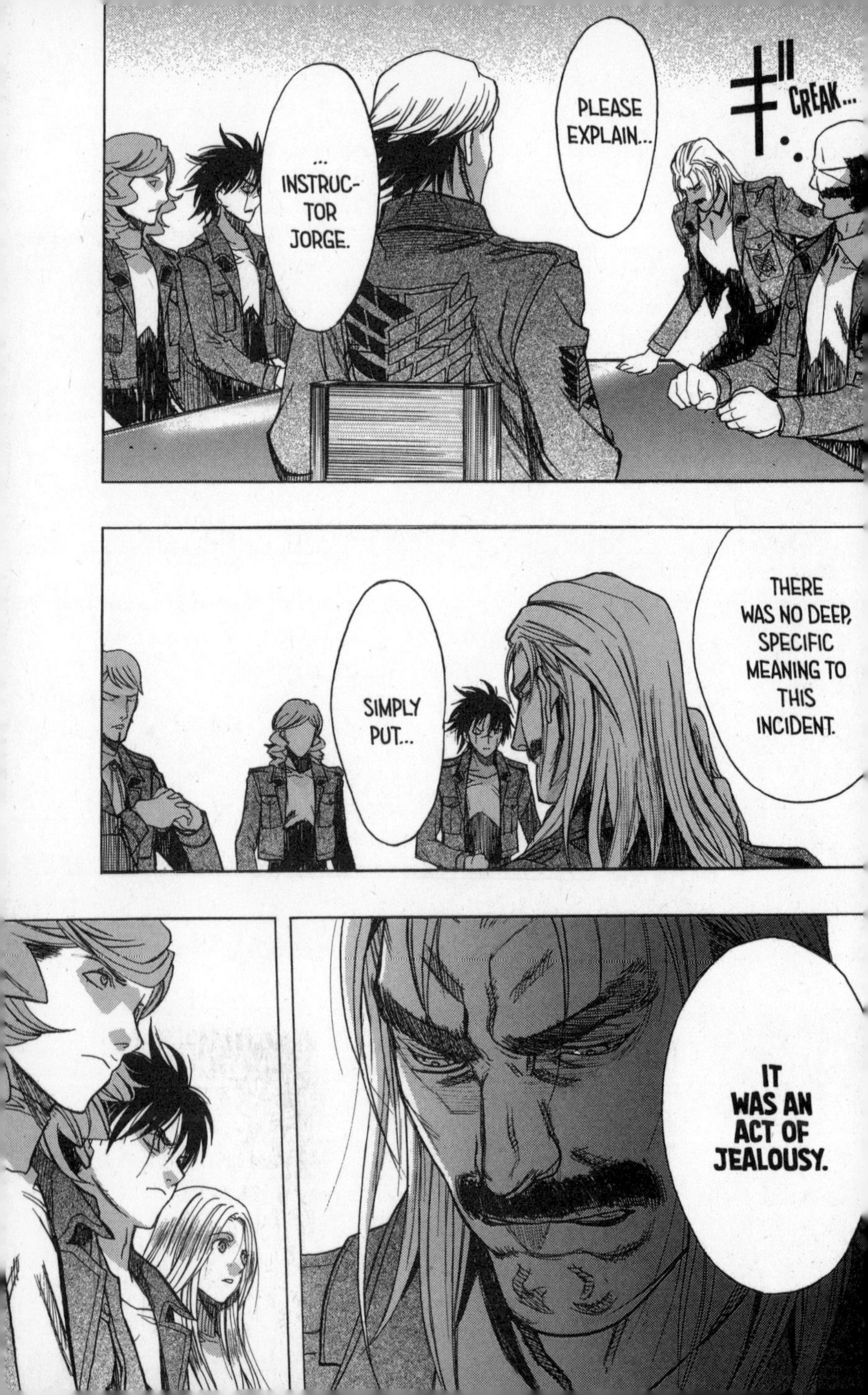
CREAK...
PLEASE EXPLAIN...
... INSTRUCTOR JORGE.
THERE WAS NO DEEP, SPECIFIC MEANING TO THIS INCIDENT.
SIMPLY PUT...
IT WAS AN ACT OF JEALOUSY.

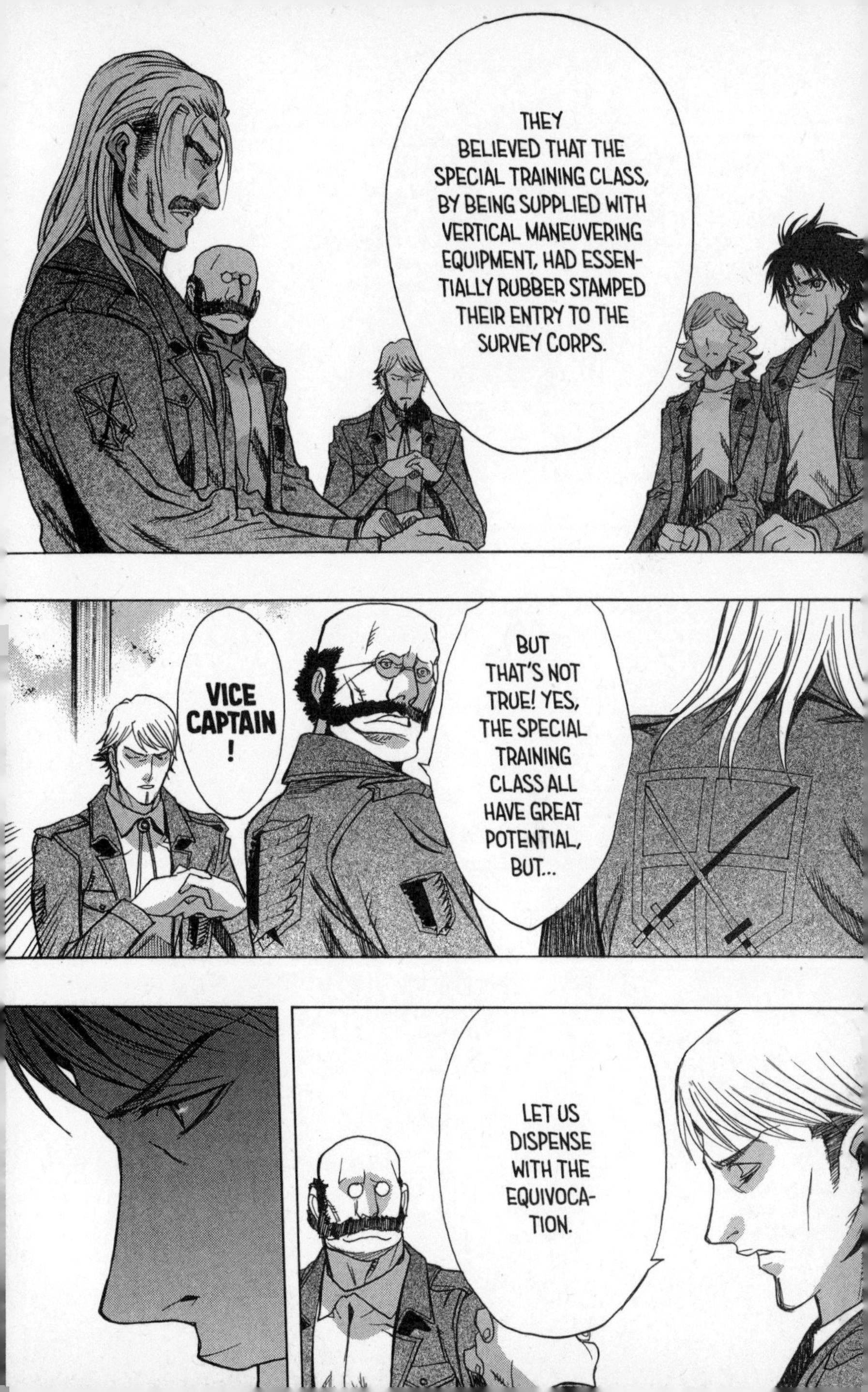
THEY BELIEVED THAT THE SPECIAL TRAINING CLASS, BY BEING SUPPLIED WITH VERTICAL MANEUVERING EQUIPMENT, HAD ESSEN-TIALLY RUBBER STAMPED THEIR ENTRY TO THE SURVEY CORPS.
BUT THAT'S NOT TRUE! YES, THE SPECIAL TRAINING CLASS ALL HAVE GREAT POTENTIAL, BUT...
VICE CAPTAIN!
LET US DISPENSE WITH THE EQUIVOCA-TION.

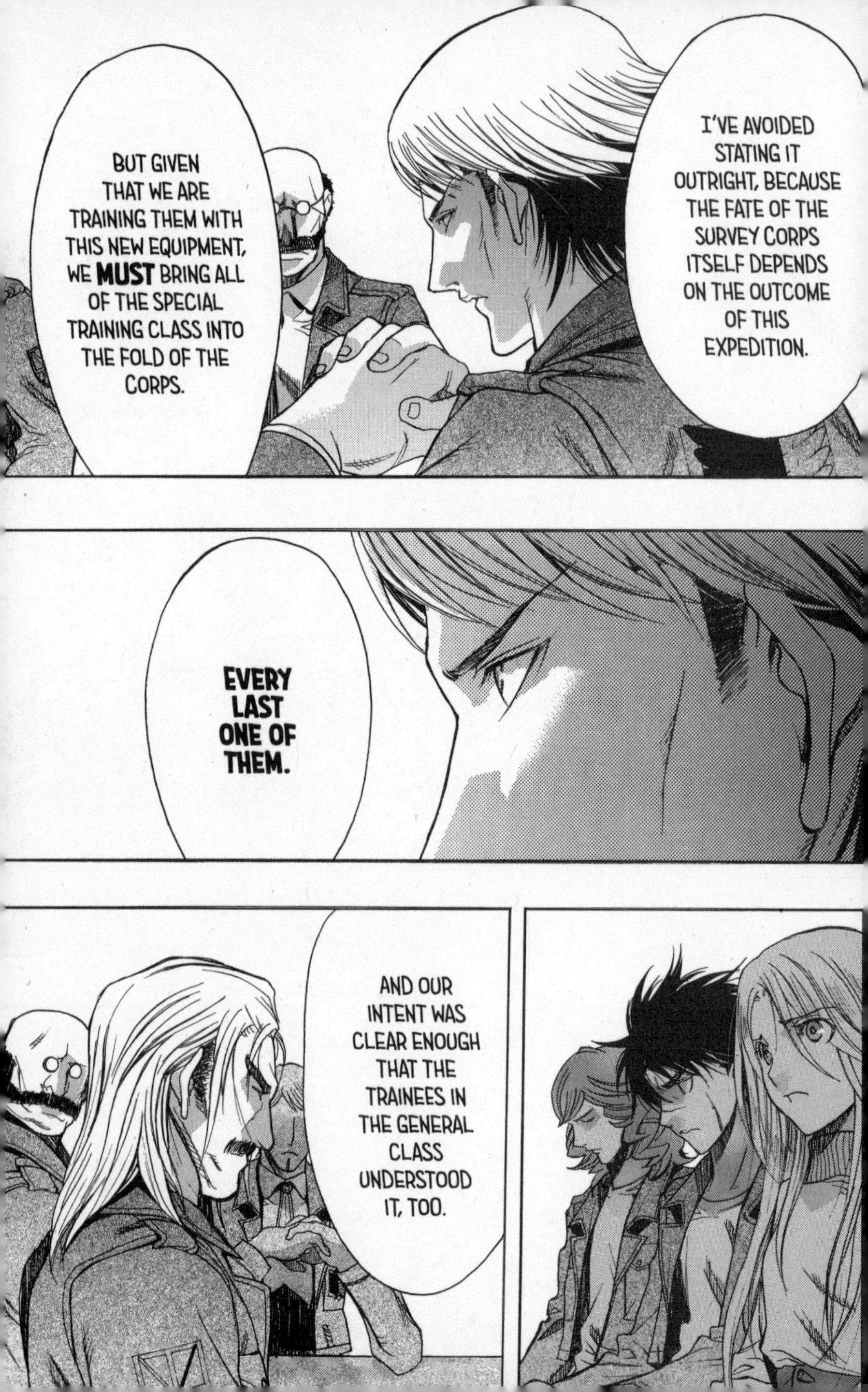
I'VE AVOIDED STATING IT OUTRIGHT, BECAUSE THE FATE OF THE SURVEY CORPS ITSELF DEPENDS ON THE OUTCOME OF THIS EXPEDITION.
BUT GIVEN THAT WE ARE TRAINING THEM WITH THIS NEW EQUIPMENT, WE **MUST** BRING ALL OF THE SPECIAL TRAINING CLASS INTO THE FOLD OF THE CORPS.
EVERY LAST ONE OF THEM.
AND OUR INTENT WAS CLEAR ENOUGH THAT THE TRAINEES IN THE GENERAL CLASS UNDERSTOOD IT, TOO.

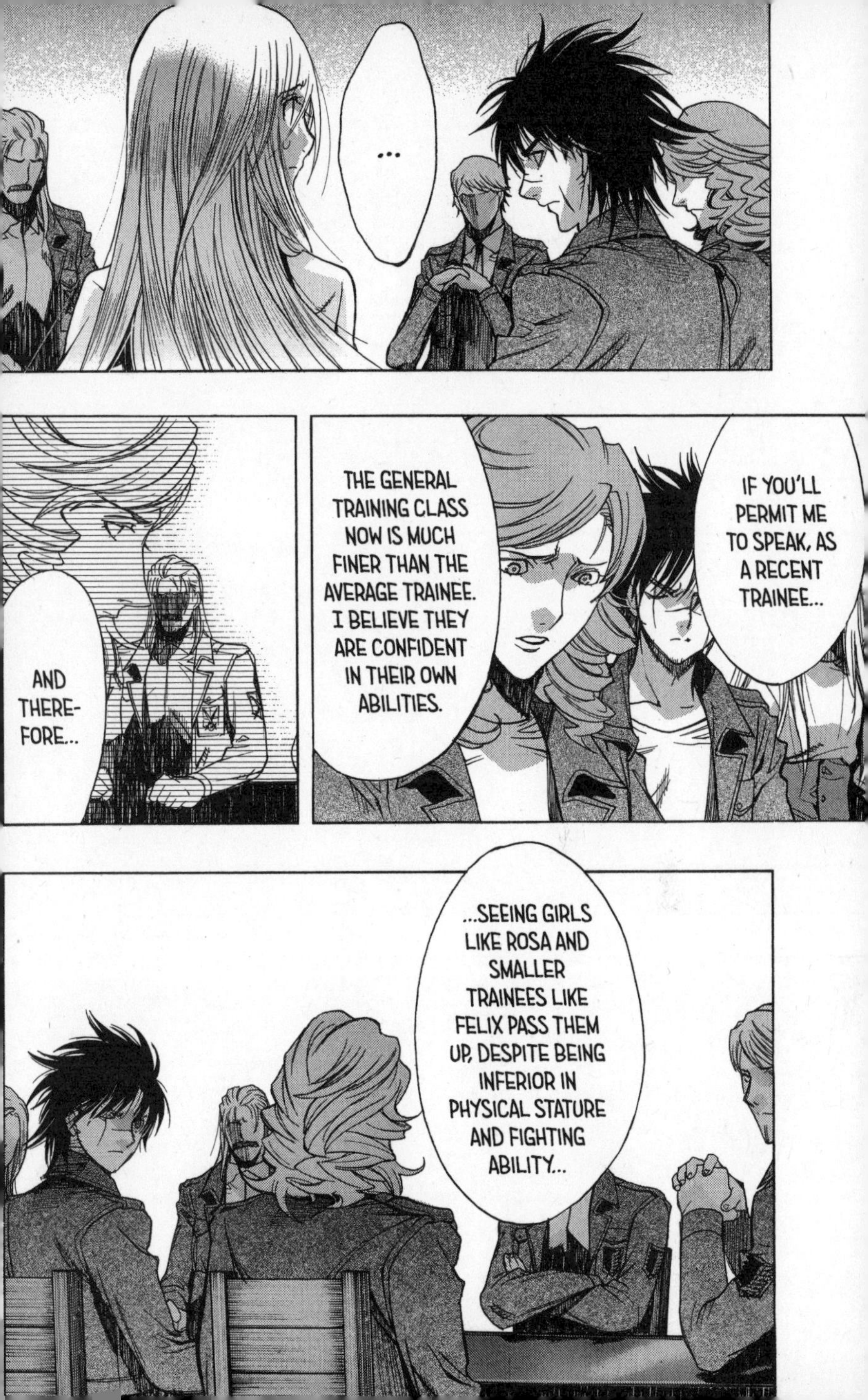
...
IF YOU'LL PERMIT ME TO SPEAK, AS A RECENT TRAINEE...
THE GENERAL TRAINING CLASS NOW IS MUCH FINER THAN THE AVERAGE TRAINEE. I BELIEVE THEY ARE CONFIDENT IN THEIR OWN ABILITIES.
AND THEREFORE...
...SEEING GIRLS LIKE ROSA AND SMALLER TRAINEES LIKE FELIX PASS THEM UP, DESPITE BEING INFERIOR IN PHYSICAL STATURE AND FIGHTING ABILITY...

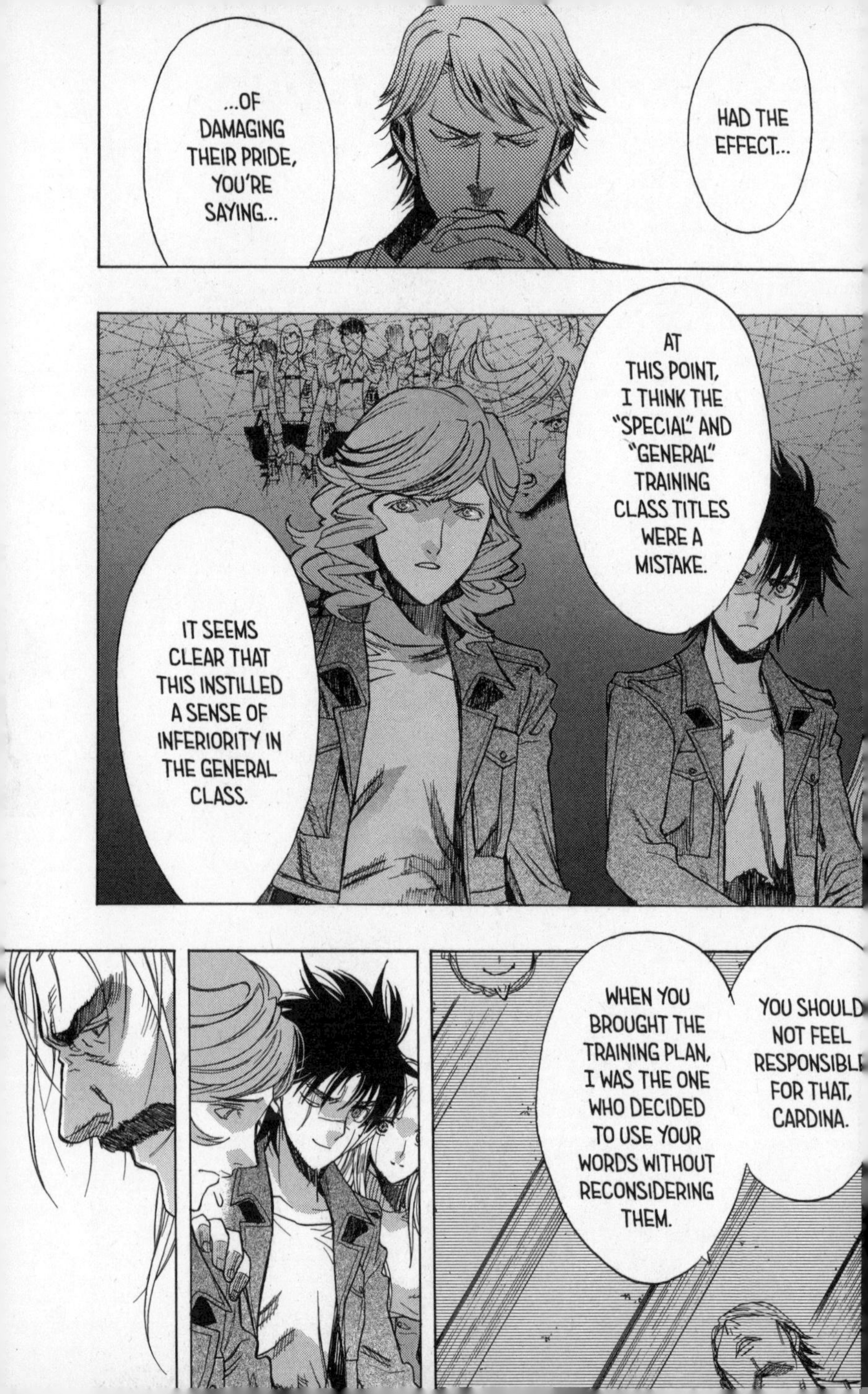
HAD THE EFFECT...
...OF DAMAGING THEIR PRIDE, YOU'RE SAYING...
AT THIS POINT, I THINK THE "SPECIAL" AND "GENERAL" TRAINING CLASS TITLES WERE A MISTAKE.
IT SEEMS CLEAR THAT THIS INSTILLED A SENSE OF INFERIORITY IN THE GENERAL CLASS.
YOU SHOULD NOT FEEL RESPONSIBLE FOR THAT, CARDINA.
WHEN YOU BROUGHT THE TRAINING PLAN, I WAS THE ONE WHO DECIDED TO USE YOUR WORDS WITHOUT RECONSIDERING THEM.

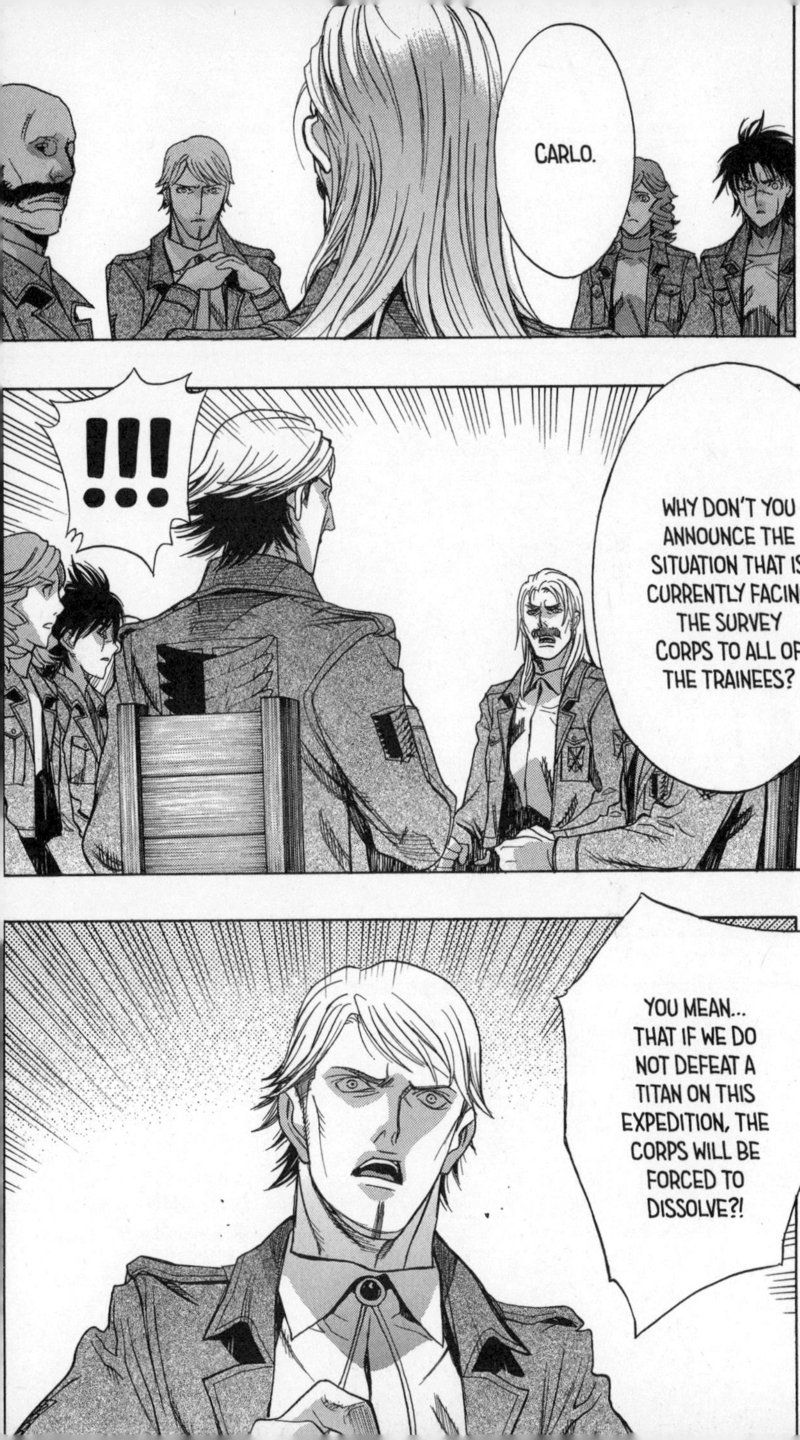
CARLO.
WHY DON'T YOU ANNOUNCE THE SITUATION THAT IS CURRENTLY FACING THE SURVEY CORPS TO ALL OF THE TRAINEES?
!!!
YOU MEAN... THAT IF WE DO NOT DEFEAT A TITAN ON THIS EXPEDITION, THE CORPS WILL BE FORCED TO DISSOLVE?!

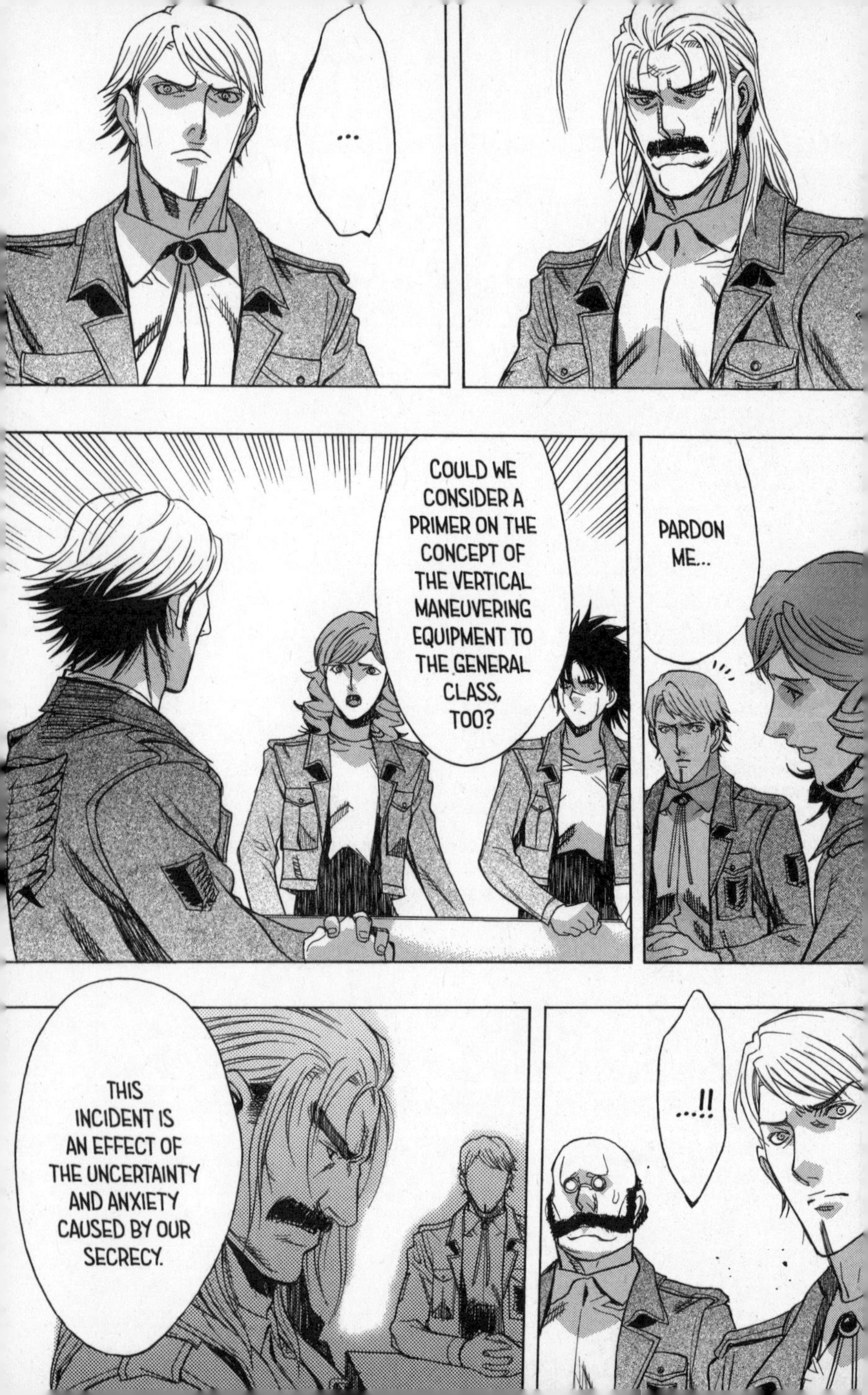
...
PARDON ME...
COULD WE CONSIDER A PRIMER ON THE CONCEPT OF THE VERTICAL MANEUVERING EQUIPMENT TO THE GENERAL CLASS, TOO?
...!!
THIS INCIDENT IS AN EFFECT OF THE UNCERTAINTY AND ANXIETY CAUSED BY OUR SECRECY.

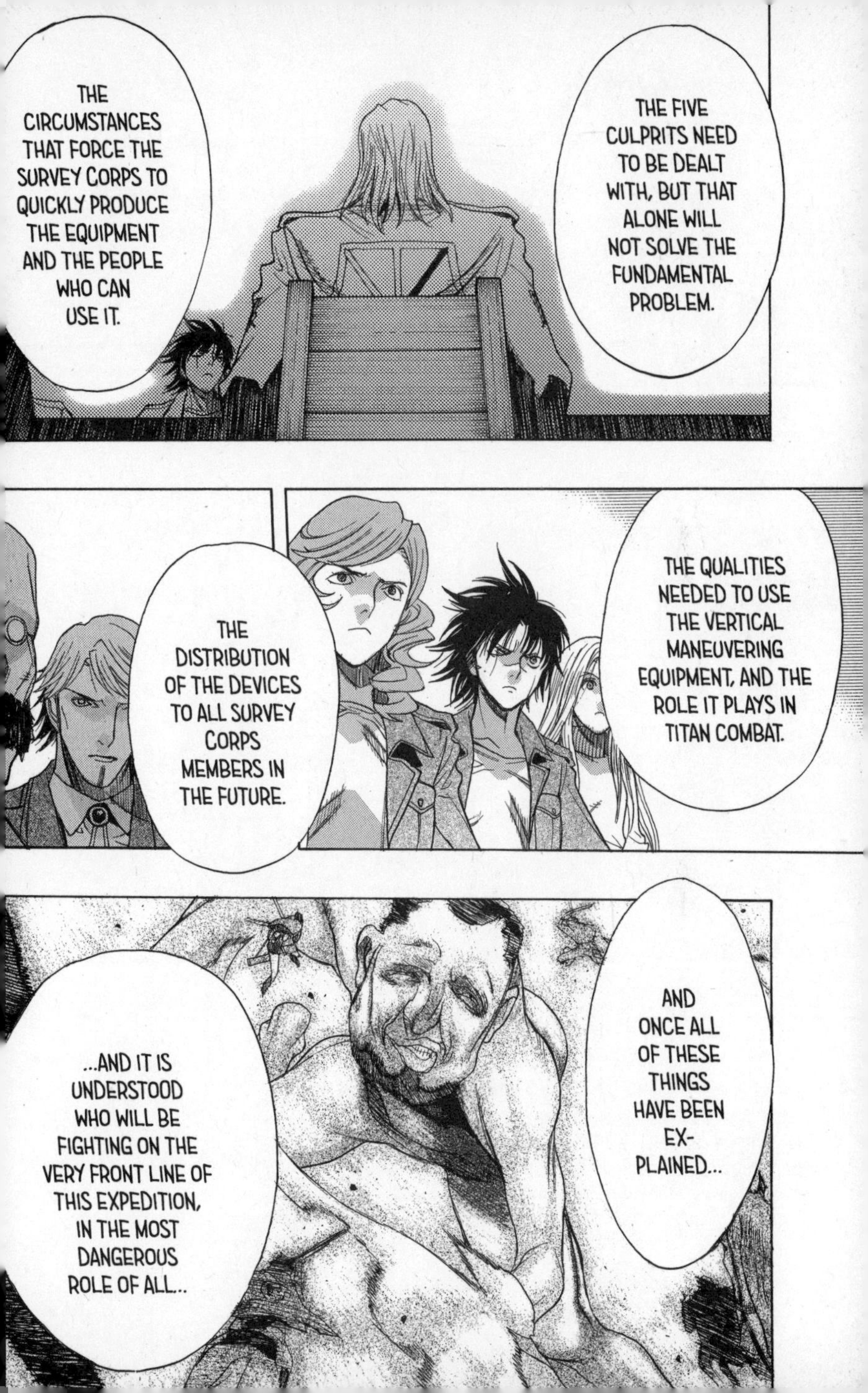
THE FIVE CULPRITS NEED TO BE DEALT WITH, BUT THAT ALONE WILL NOT SOLVE THE FUNDAMENTAL PROBLEM.
THE CIRCUMSTANCES THAT FORCE THE SURVEY CORPS TO QUICKLY PRODUCE THE EQUIPMENT AND THE PEOPLE WHO CAN USE IT.
THE QUALITIES NEEDED TO USE THE VERTICAL MANEUVERING EQUIPMENT, AND THE ROLE IT PLAYS IN TITAN COMBAT.
THE DISTRIBUTION OF THE DEVICES TO ALL SURVEY CORPS MEMBERS IN THE FUTURE.
AND ONCE ALL OF THESE THINGS HAVE BEEN EX-PLAINED...
...AND IT IS UNDERSTOOD WHO WILL BE FIGHTING ON THE VERY FRONT LINE OF THIS EXPEDITION, IN THE MOST DANGEROUS ROLE OF ALL...

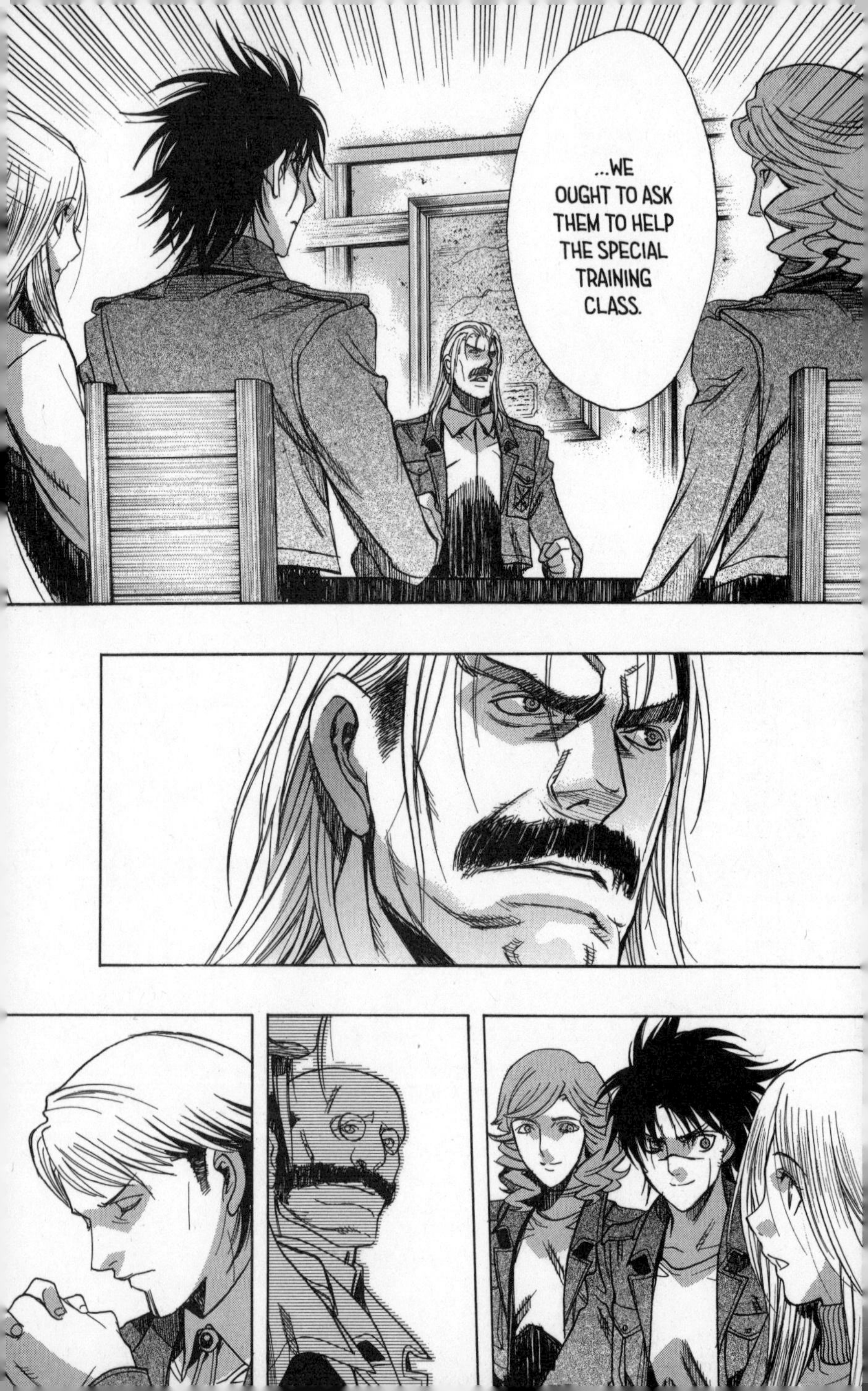
...WE OUGHT TO ASK THEM TO HELP THE SPECIAL TRAINING CLASS.

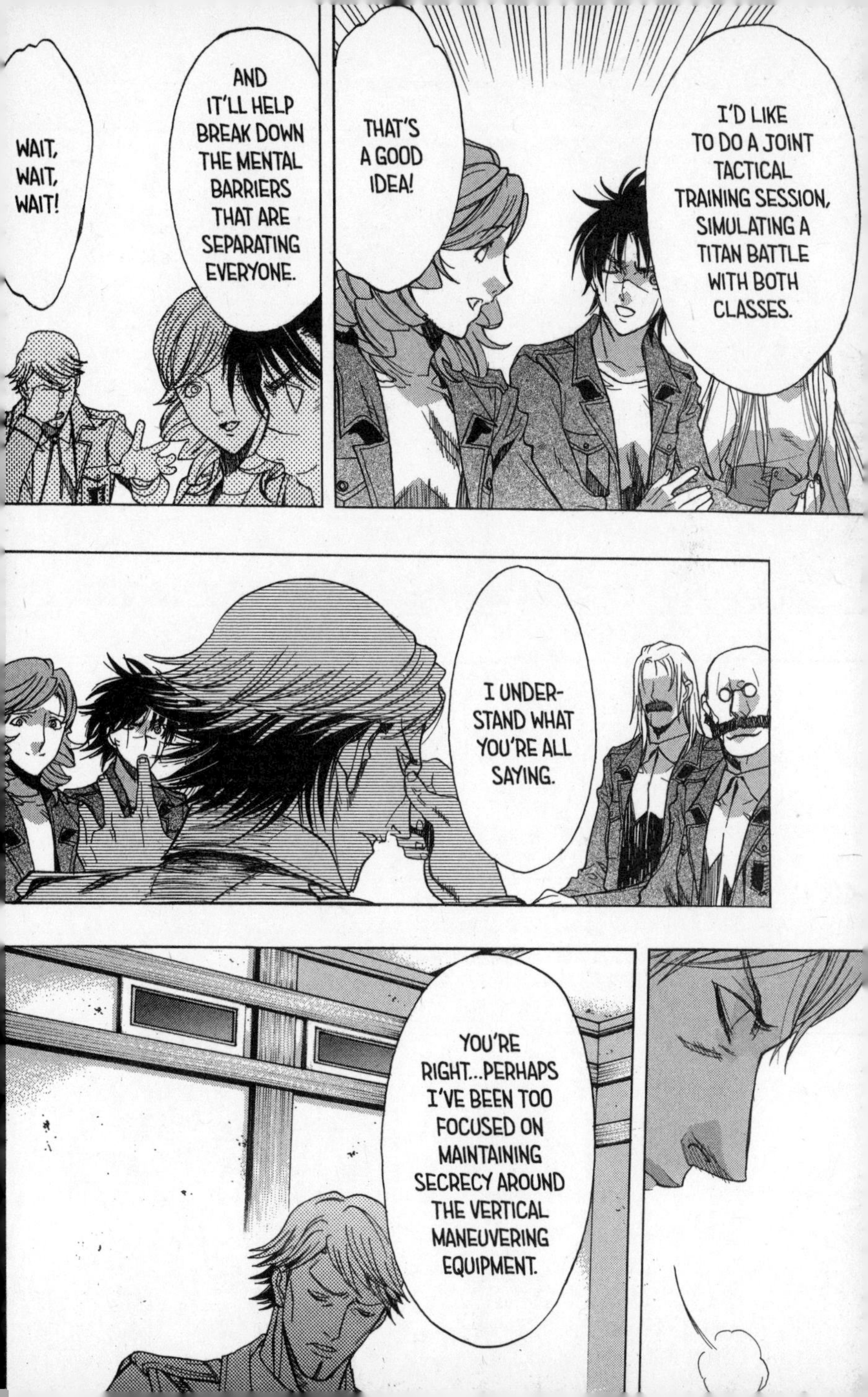
I'D LIKE TO DO A JOINT TACTICAL TRAINING SESSION, SIMULATING A TITAN BATTLE WITH BOTH CLASSES.
THAT'S A GOOD IDEA!
AND IT'LL HELP BREAK DOWN THE MENTAL BARRIERS THAT ARE SEPARATING EVERYONE.
WAIT, WAIT, WAIT!
I UNDER-STAND WHAT YOU'RE ALL SAYING.
YOU'RE RIGHT...PERHAPS I'VE BEEN TOO FOCUSED ON MAINTAINING SECRECY AROUND THE VERTICAL MANEUVERING EQUIPMENT.

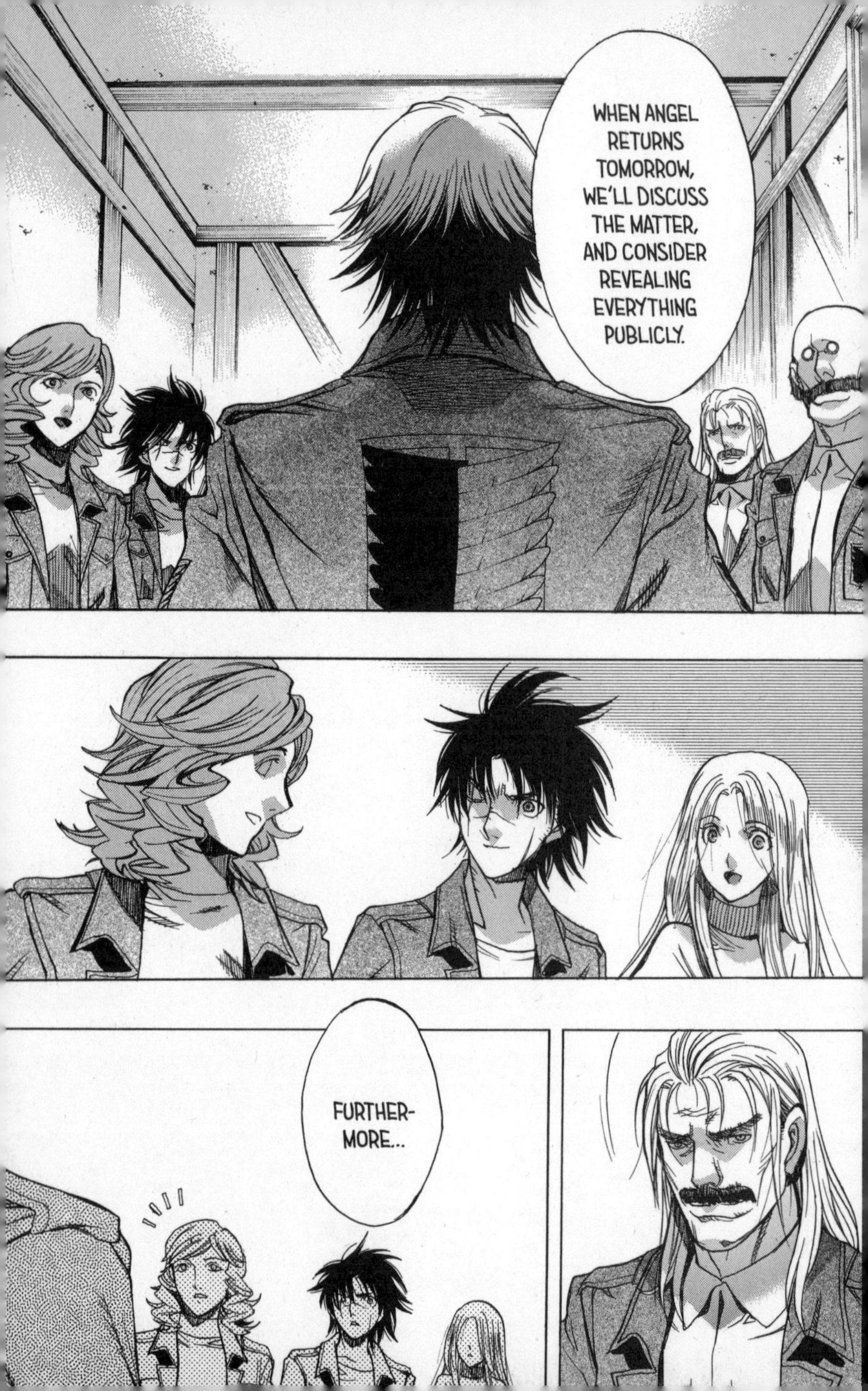
WHEN ANGEL RETURNS TOMORROW, WE'LL DISCUSS THE MATTER, AND CONSIDER REVEALING EVERYTHING PUBLICLY.
FURTHER-MORE...

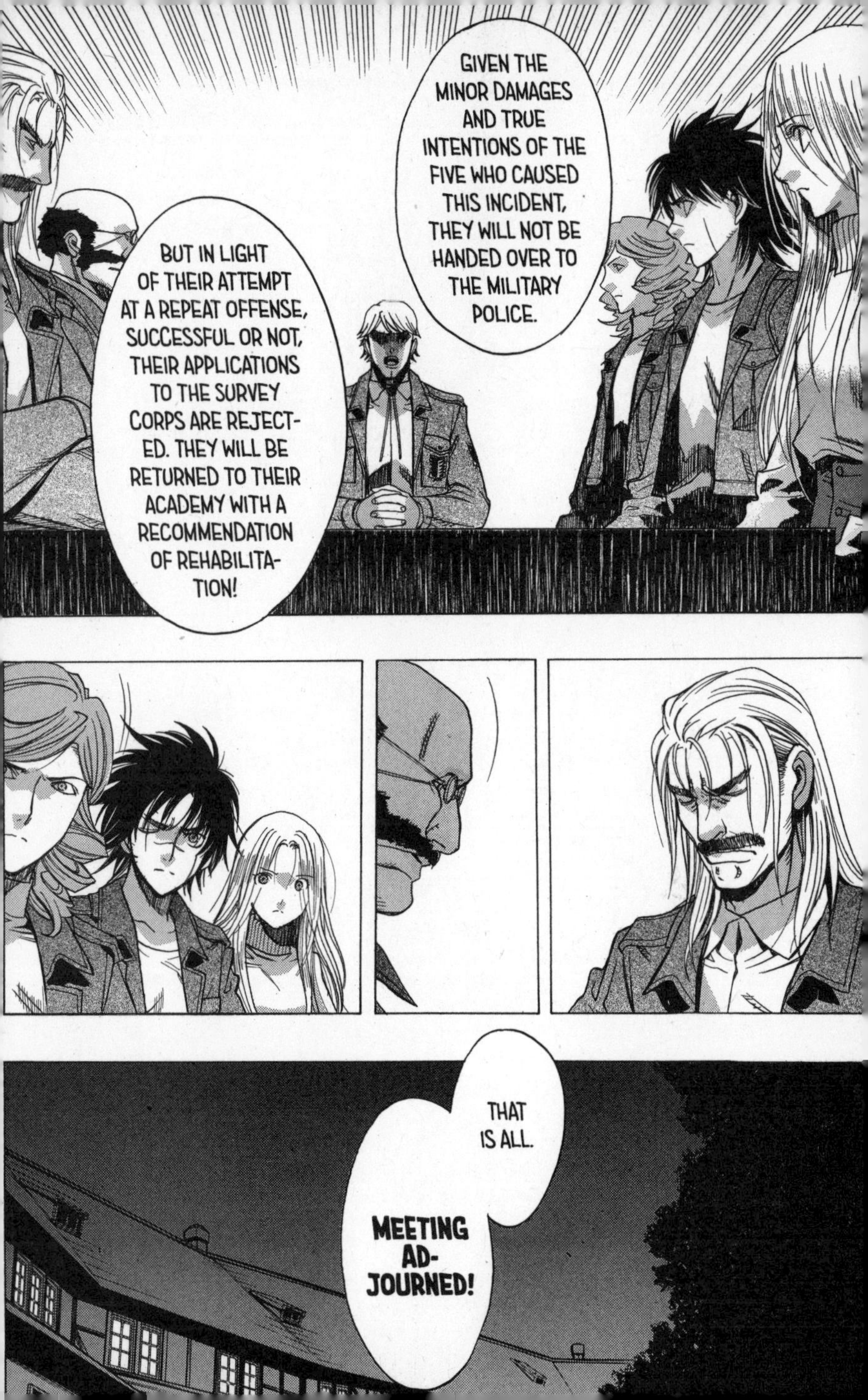
GIVEN THE MINOR DAMAGES AND TRUE INTENTIONS OF THE FIVE WHO CAUSED THIS INCIDENT, THEY WILL NOT BE HANDED OVER TO THE MILITARY POLICE.
BUT IN LIGHT OF THEIR ATTEMPT AT A REPEAT OFFENSE, SUCCESSFUL OR NOT, THEIR APPLICATIONS TO THE SURVEY CORPS ARE REJECT-ED. THEY WILL BE RETURNED TO THEIR ACADEMY WITH A RECOMMENDATION OF REHABILITA-TION!
THAT IS ALL.
MEETING AD-JOURNED!

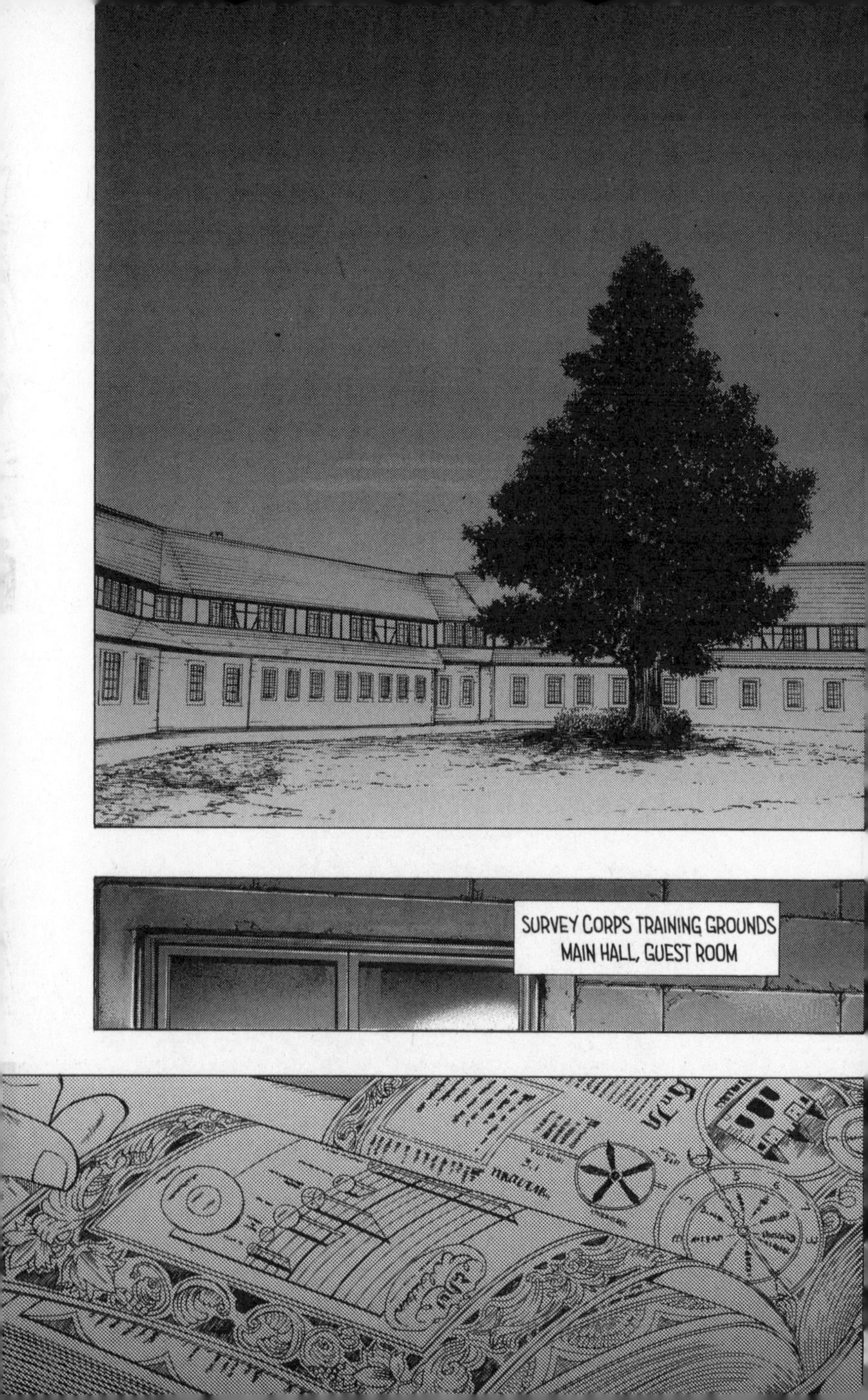
SURVEY CORPS TRAINING GROUNDS
MAIN HALL, GUEST ROOM

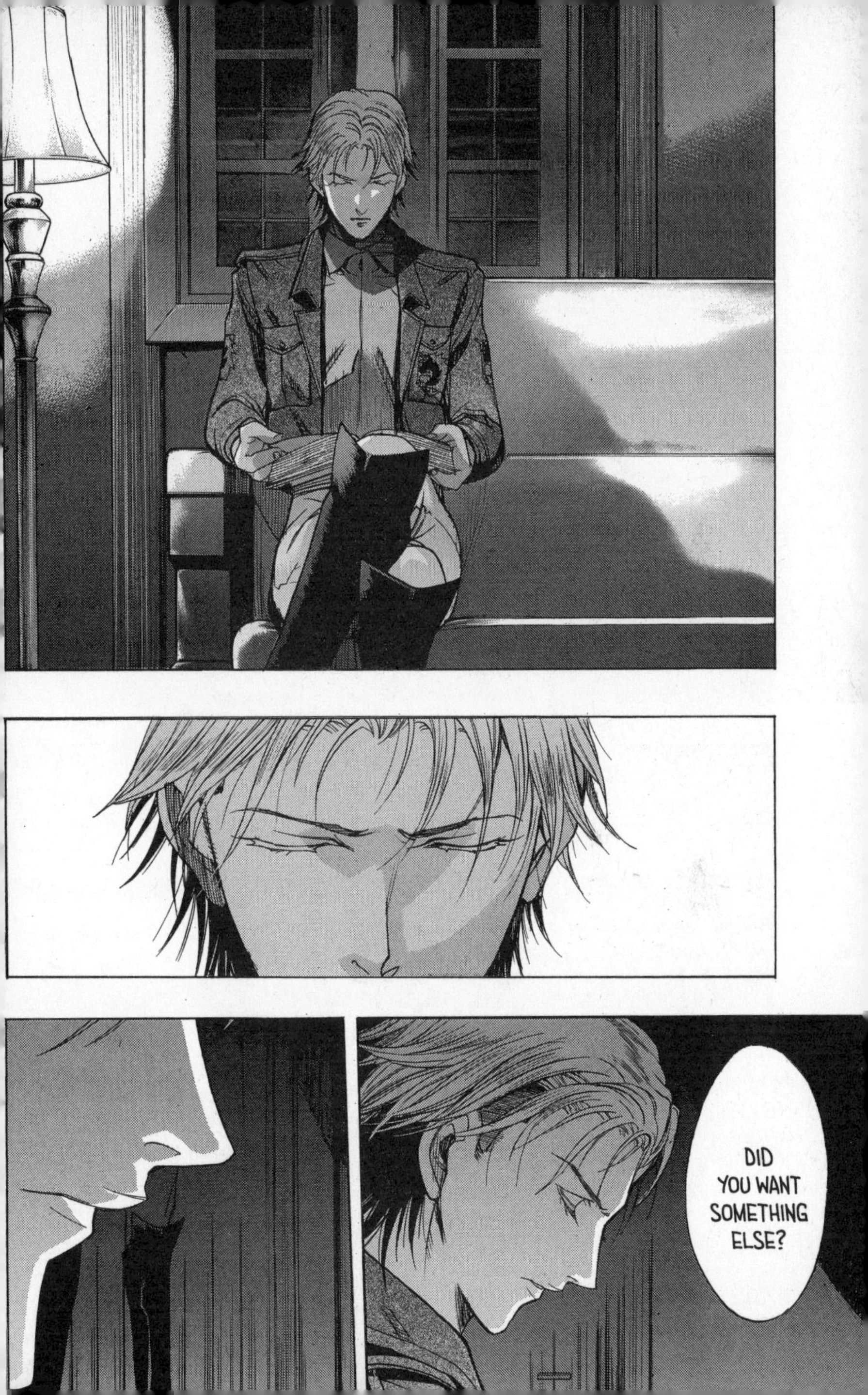
DID YOU WANT SOMETHING ELSE?

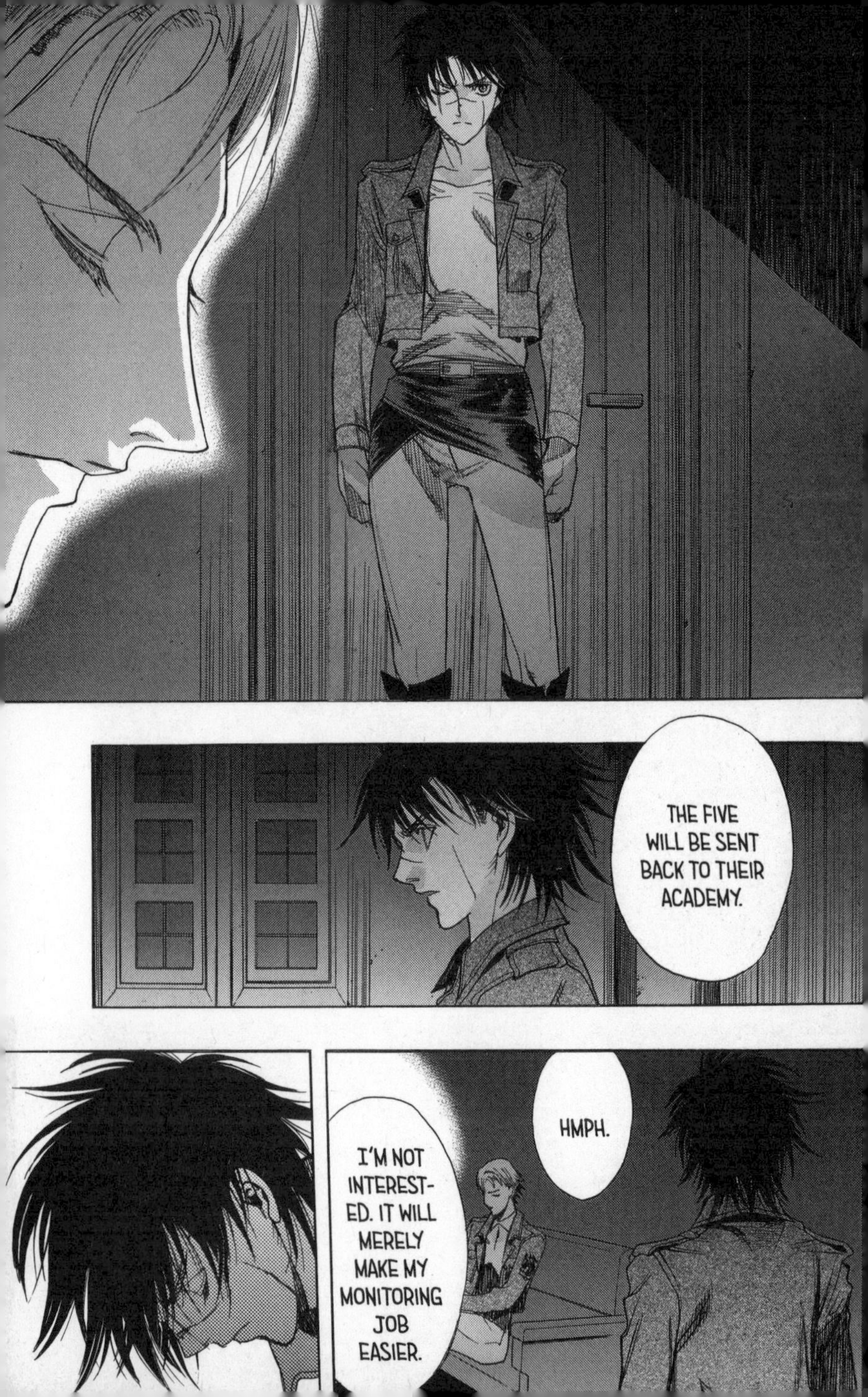
THE FIVE WILL BE SENT BACK TO THEIR ACADEMY.
HMPH.
I'M NOT INTEREST-ED. IT WILL MERELY MAKE MY MONITORING JOB EASIER.

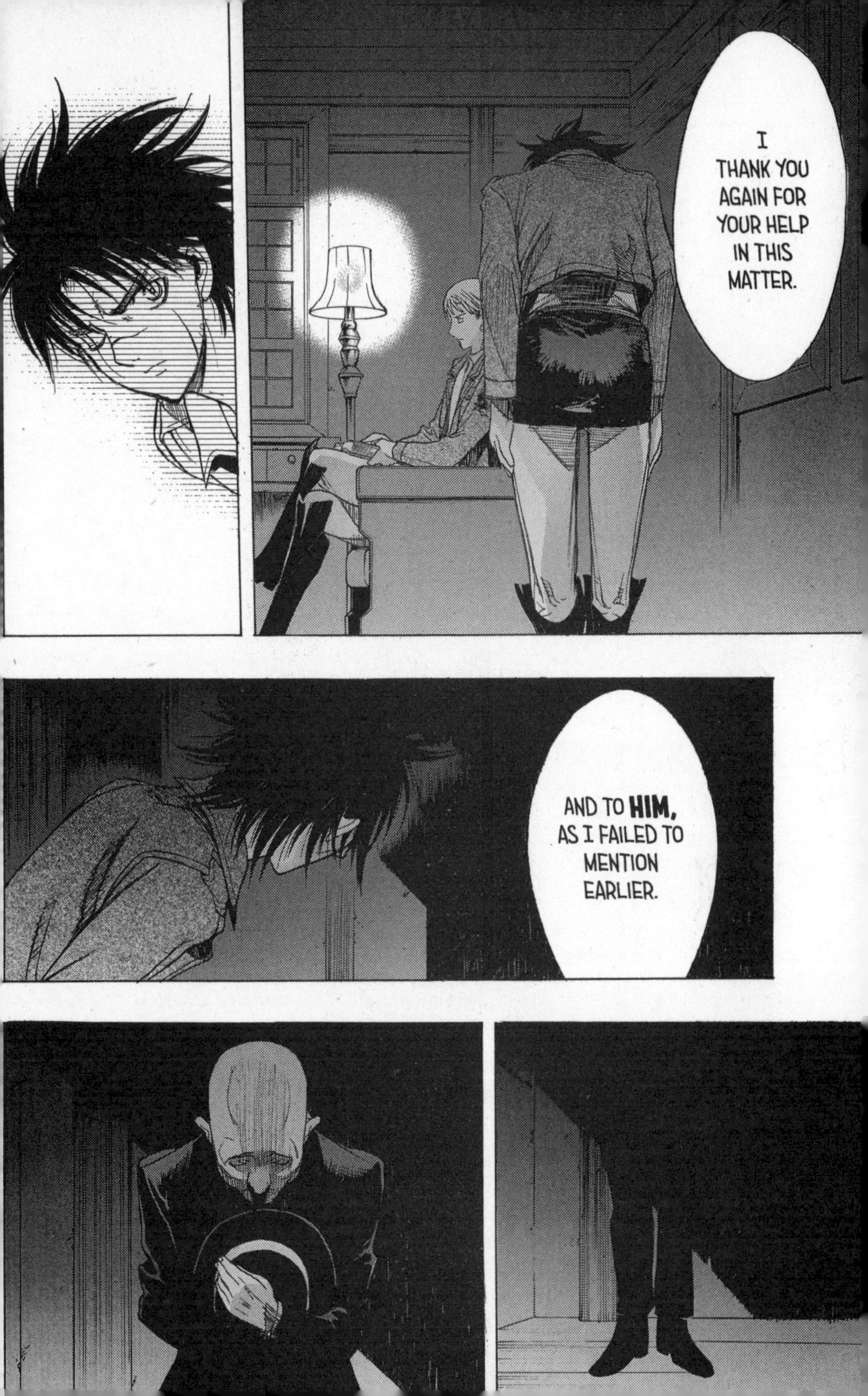
I THANK YOU AGAIN FOR YOUR HELP IN THIS MATTER.
AND TO **HIM,** AS I FAILED TO MENTION EARLIER.

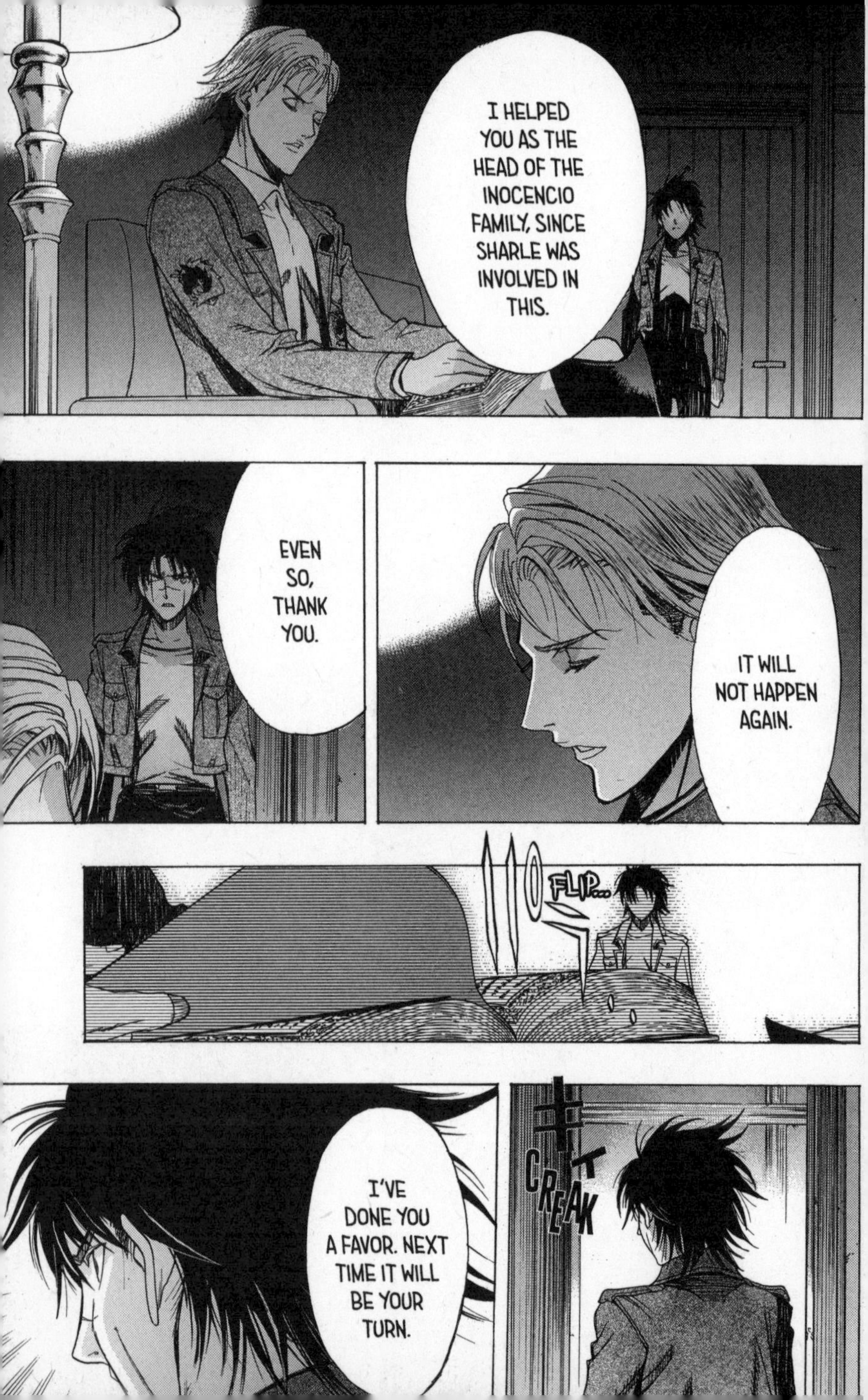
I HELPED YOU AS THE HEAD OF THE INOCENCIO FAMILY, SINCE SHARLE WAS INVOLVED IN THIS.
IT WILL NOT HAPPEN AGAIN.
EVEN SO, THANK YOU.
FLIP...
CREAK
I'VE DONE YOU A FAVOR. NEXT TIME IT WILL BE YOUR TURN.

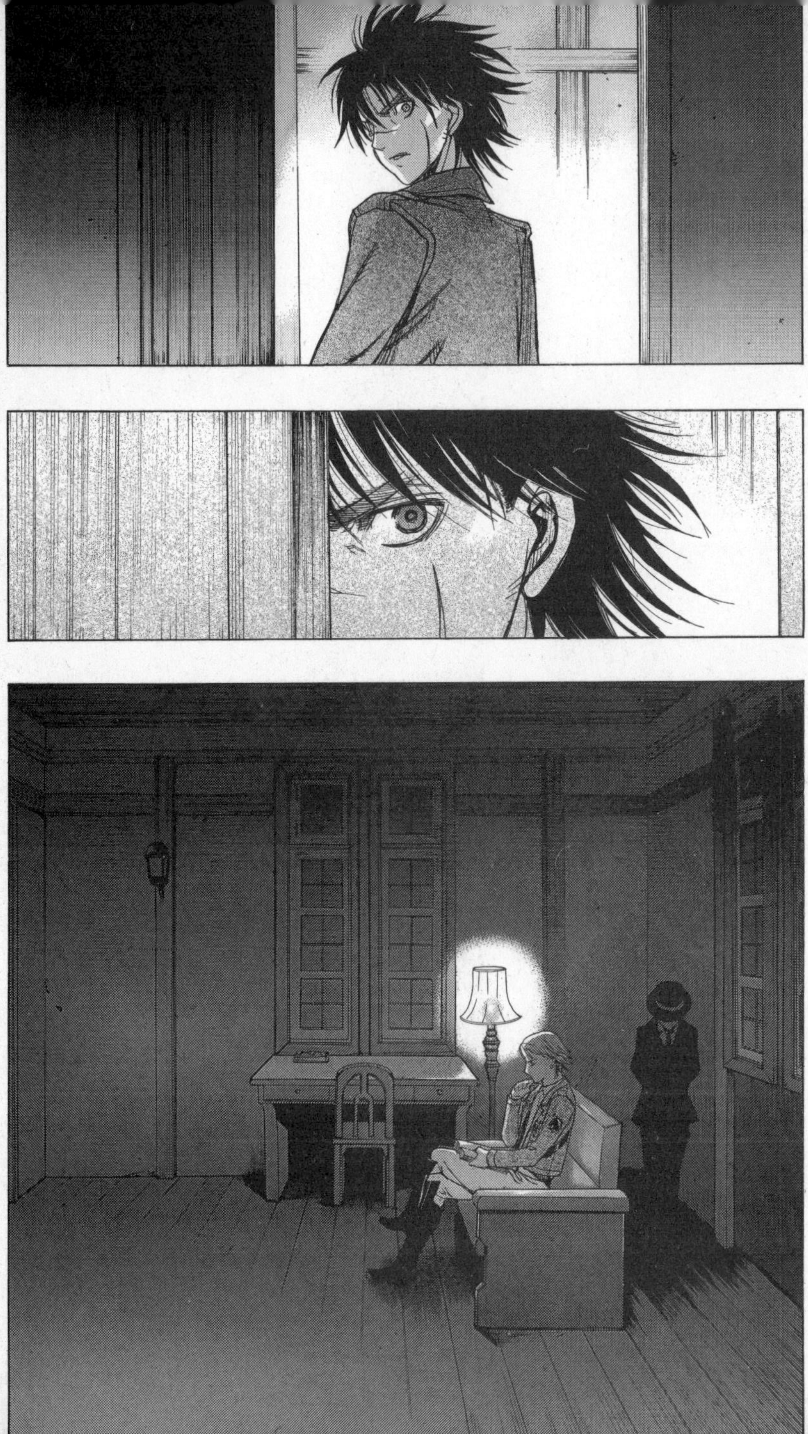

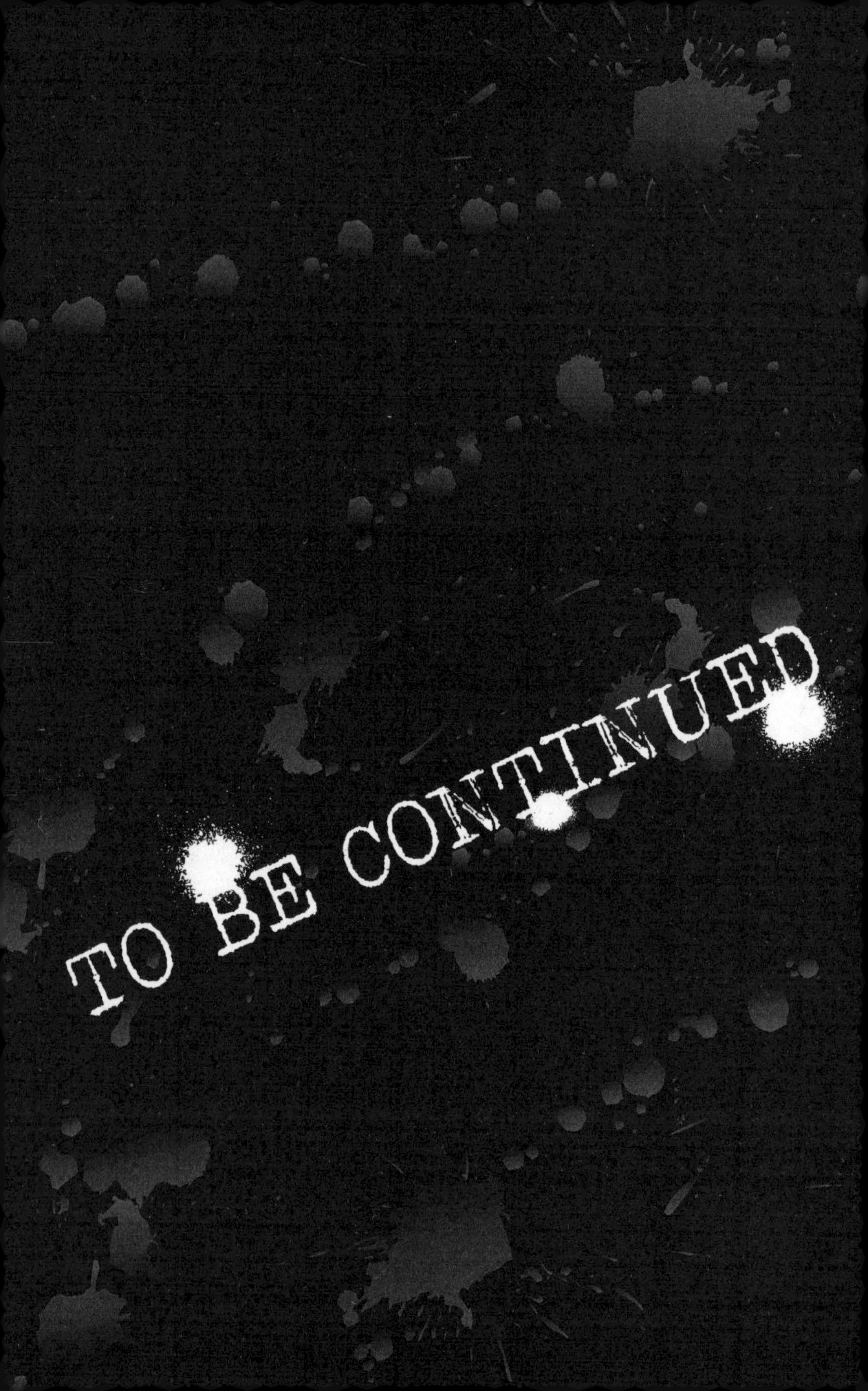
TO BE CONTINUED

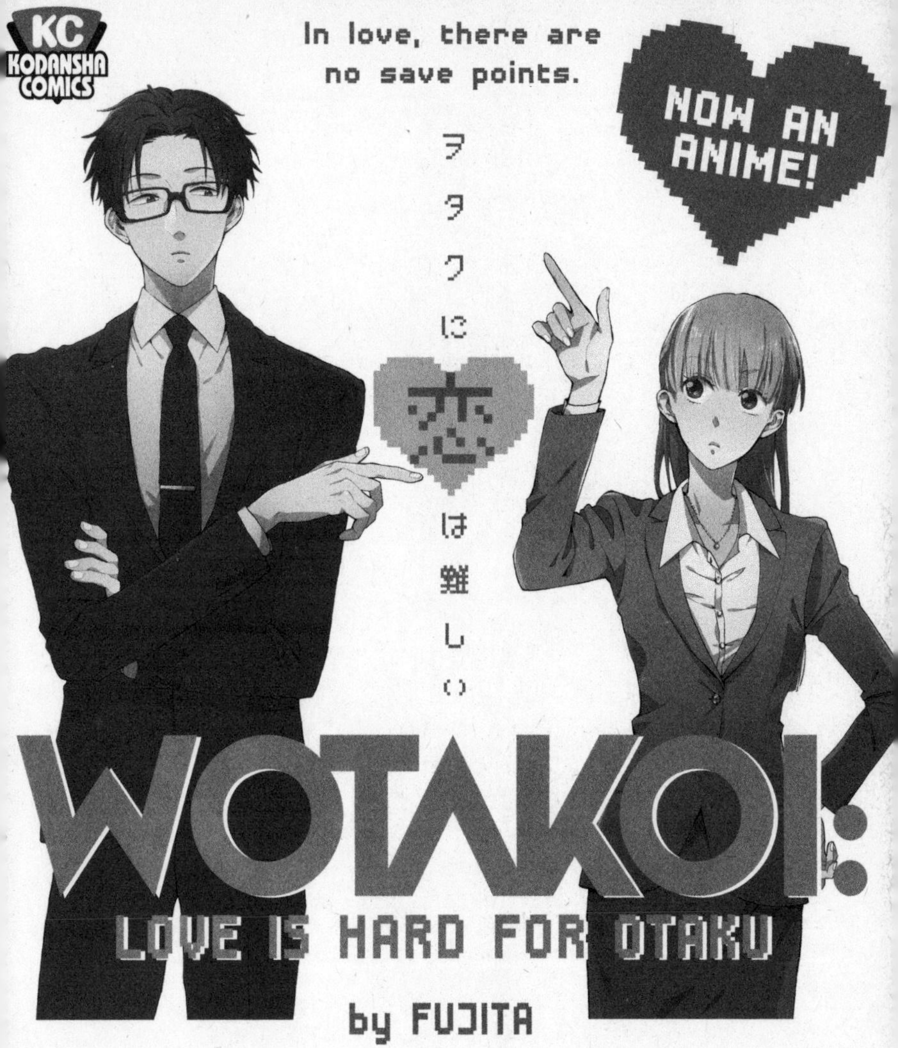
KC KODANSHA COMICS
In love, there are no save points.
NOW AN ANIME!
ヲタクに恋は難しい
WOTAKOI:
LOVE IS HARD FOR OTAKU
by FUJITA

Narumi has had it rough: Every boyfriend she's had dumped her once they found out she was an otaku, so she's gone to great lengths to hide it. At her new job, she bumps into Hirotaka, her childhood friend and fellow otaku. When Hirotaka almost gets her secret outed at work, she comes up with a plan to keep him quiet. But he comes up with a counter-proposal: Why doesn't she just date him instead?